A·N·N·U·A·L E·D·I·T·I·O·N·S

T5-CVB-910

Criminal Justice
Twenty-Fifth Edition

01/02

G19013

EDITORS

Joseph L. Victor
Mercy College, Dobbs Ferry

Joseph L. Victor is professor and chairman of the Department of Law, Criminal Justice, and Safety Administration at Mercy College. Professor Victor has extensive field experience in criminal justice agencies, counseling, and administering human service programs. He earned his B.A. and M.A. at Seton Hall University, and his Doctorate of Education at Fairleigh Dickinson University.

Joanne Naughton
Mercy College, Dobbs Ferry

Joanne Naughton is assistant professor of Criminal Justice at Mercy College. Professor Naughton is a former member of the New York City Police Department, where she encountered most aspects of police work as a police officer, detective, sergeant and lieutenant. She is also a former staff attorney with The Legal Aid Society. She received her B.A. and J.D. at Fordham University.

McGraw-Hill/Dushkin
530 Old Whitfield Street, Guilford, Connecticut 06437

Visit us on the Internet
http://www.dushkin.com

Credits

1. Crime and Justice in America
Unit photo—McGraw-Hill/Dushkin photo.
2. Victimology
Unit photo—McGraw-Hill/Dushkin photo.
3. The Police
Unit photo—Courtesy of Insurance Institute for Highway Safety.
4. The Judicial System
Unit photo—© 2001 by PhotoDisc, Inc.
5. Juvenile Justice
Unit photo—© 2001 by Cleo Freelance Photography.
6. Punishment and Corrections
Unit photo—© 2001 by Cleo Freelance Photography.

Copyright

Cataloging in Publication Data
Main entry under title: Annual Editions: Criminal Justice. 2001/2002.
    1. Criminal Justice, Administration of—United States—Periodicals. I. Victor, Joseph L., *comp*. II. Naughton, Joanne, *comp*. III. Title: Criminal justice.
HV 8138.A67   364.973.05   77–640116
ISBN 0–07–243368–X   ISSN 0272–3816

Twenty-Fifth Edition

Cover image © 2001 by PhotoDisc, Inc.

Printed in the United States of America   1234567890BAHBAH54321   Printed on Recycled Paper

To the Reader

In publishing ANNUAL EDITIONS we recognize the enormous role played by the magazines, newspapers, and journals of the public press in providing current, first-rate educational information in a broad spectrum of interest areas. Many of these articles are appropriate for students, researchers, and professionals seeking accurate, current material to help bridge the gap between principles and theories and the real world. These articles, however, become more useful for study when those of lasting value are carefully collected, organized, indexed, and reproduced in a low-cost format, which provides easy and permanent access when the material is needed. That is the role played by ANNUAL EDITIONS.

During the 1970s, criminal justice emerged as an appealing, vital, and unique academic discipline. It emphasizes the professional development of students who plan careers in the field and attracts those who want to know more about a complex social problem and how this country deals with it. Criminal justice incorporates a vast range of knowledge from a number of specialties, including law, history, and the behavioral and social sciences. Each specialty contributes to our fuller understanding of criminal behavior and of society's attitudes toward deviance.

In view of the fact that the criminal justice system is in a constant state of flux, and because the study of criminal justice covers such a broad spectrum, today's students must be aware of a variety of subjects and topics. Standard textbooks and traditional anthologies cannot keep pace with the changes as quickly as they occur. In fact, many such sources are already out of date the day they are published. *Annual Editions: Criminal Justice 01/02* strives to maintain currency in matters of concern by providing up-to-date commentaries, articles, reports, and statistics from the most recent literature in the criminal justice field.

This volume contains units concerning crime and justice in America, victimology, the police, the judicial system, juvenile justice, and punishment and corrections. The articles in these units were selected because they are informative as well as provocative. The selections are timely and useful in their treatment of ethics, punishment, juveniles, courts, and other related topics.

Included in this volume are a number of features designed to be useful to students, re-searchers, and professionals in the criminal justice field. These include the *table of contents abstracts*, which summarize each article and feature key concepts in bold italics; a *topic guide* for locating articles on specific subjects; a list of *World Wide Web* sites that can be used to further explore the topics as the sites are also cross-referenced by number in the topic guide; and a comprehensive section on *crime statistics*, a *glossary*, and an *index*. In addition, each unit is preceded by an *overview* that provides a background for informed reading of the articles, emphasizes critical issues, and presents challenge questions.

We would like to know what you think of the selections contained in this edition. Please fill out the postage-paid *article rating form* on the last page and let us know your opinions. We change or retain many of the articles based on the comments we receive from you, the reader. Help us to improve this anthology—annually.

Joseph L. Victor
Editor

Joanne Naughton
Editor

Contents

UNIT 1

Crime and Justice in America

Four selections focus on the overall
structure of the criminal justice
system in the United States. The
current scope of crime in America
is reviewed, and topics such as
criminal behavior, organized crime,
and policing practices are discussed.

The concepts in bold italics are developed in the article. For further expansion please refer to the Topic Guide, the Glossary, and the Index.

**UNIT 2**

Victimology

Five articles discuss the impact of crime on the victim. Topics include the rights of crime victims and the consequences of family violence.

The concepts in bold italics are developed in the article. For further expansion please refer to the Topic Guide, the Glossary, and the Index.

UNIT 3

The Police

Four selections examine the role
of the police officer. Some of the
topics include the stress of police
work, multicultural changes,
and ethical policing.

UNIT 4

The Judicial System

Six selections discuss the process by which the accused are moved through the judicial system. The courts, the jury process, and judicial ethics are reviewed.

The concepts in bold italics are developed in the article. For further expansion please refer to the Topic Guide, the Glossary, and the Index.

Juvenile Justice

Seven selections review the juvenile
justice system. The topics include
effective ways to respond to violent
juvenile crime and juvenile detention.

UNIT 5

The concepts in bold italics are developed in the article. For further expansion please refer to the Topic Guide, the Glossary, and the Index.

ix

UNIT 6

Punishment and Corrections

Six selections focus on the current state of America's penal system and the effects of sentencing, probation, and capital punishment on criminals.

The concepts in bold italics are developed in the article. For further expansion please refer to the Topic Guide, the Glossary, and the Index.

The concepts in bold italics are developed in the article. For further expansion please refer to the Topic Guide, the Glossary, and the Index.

Topic Guide

This topic guide suggests how the selections in this book relate to the subjects covered in your course.

The Web icon (☺) under the topic articles easily identifies the relevant Web sites, which are numbered and annotated on the next two pages. By linking the articles and the Web sites by topic, this ANNUAL EDITIONS reader becomes a powerful learning and research tool.

TOPIC AREA	TREATED IN	TOPIC AREA	TREATED IN
Battered Families	6. Childhood Victimization 9. Sweden's Response to Domestic Violence ☺ **11, 12, 13, 26, 27**	**Discretion**	15. Should Juries Nullify Laws They Consider Unjust or Excessively Punitive? ☺ **6, 19, 22**
Bias	15. Should Juries Nullify Laws They Consider Unjust or Excessively Punitive? 22. Racial Disparities Seen as Pervasive In Juvenile Justice ☺ **3, 4, 5, 6, 10, 27**	**DNA**	18. DNA: Fingerprint of the Future? 19. Creeping Expansion of DNA Data Banking ☺ **15, 17, 18**
Children	*See* Juvenile Justice	**Drugs**	2. Crime Bust 13. Why Harlem Drug Cops Don't Discuss Race 16. Get-Tough Policy That Failed ☺ **20, 25, 27**
Corrections	27. Reading, Writing, and Rehabilitation 28. Death Penalty on Trial 29. Ex-Cons on the Street 30. Past and Future of U.S. Prison Policy 31. Parole and Prisoner Reentry in the United States, Part I 32. Parole and Prisoner Reentry in the United States, Part II ☺ **28, 29, 30, 31, 32, 33, 34**	**Ethics**	10. Ethics and Criminal Justice 12. Policing the Police ☺ **14, 21, 28, 33**
		Eyewitnesses	17. Looking Askance at Eyewitness Testimony
		Family Violence	*See* Battered Families
Courts	14. How to Improve the Jury System 15. Should Juries Nullify Laws They Consider Unjust or Excessively Punitive? 16. Get-Tough Policy That Failed 17. Looking Askance at Eyewitness Testimony 18. DNA: Fingerprint of the Future? 19. Creeping Expansion of DNA Data Banking ☺ **19, 20, 21, 22, 24**	**Gender**	21. Young Women in the Juvenile Justice System ☺ **11, 34**
		Gun Control	2. Crime Bust 4. Well-Marked Roads to Homicidal Rage ☺ **17, 27**
Crime	1. Crunching Numbers 2. Crime Bust 3. Land of the Stupid 4. Well-Marked Roads to Homicidal Rage ☺ **1, 3, 5, 8, 9, 10, 15, 16, 23, 34**	**Jails**	27. Reading, Writing, and Rehabilitation ☺ **29, 32**
		Jury	14. How to Improve the Jury System 15. Should Juries Nullify Laws They Consider Unjust or Excessively Punitive? 17. Looking Askance at Eyewitness Testimony ☺ **1, 16, 19, 20, 21, 22, 24**
Crime Statistics	1. Crunching Numbers 2. Crime Bust ☺ **3, 10, 20, 32**	**Juvenile Court**	24. Juvenile Justice
Crime Victims	*See* Victimology	**Juvenile Justice**	20. Why the Young Kill 21. Young Women in the Juvenile Justice System 22. Racial Disparities Seen as Pervasive in Juvenile Justice 23. Youth Court of True Peers Judges Firmly 24. Juvenile Justice 25. Maximum Security Adolescent 26. Juvenile Probation on the Eve of the Next Millennium ☺ **1, 16, 17, 23, 24, 25, 26, 27**
Criminal Justice	1. Crunching Numbers 2. Crime Bust 3. Land of the Stupid 4. Well-Marked Roads to Homicidal Rage ☺ **3, 10, 14, 16, 18, 22, 24, 25**		
Death Penalty	28. The Death Penalty on Trial ☺ **30, 33**		
Delinquency	*See* Juvenile Justice		

● AE: Criminal Justice

The following World Wide Web sites have been carefully researched and selected to support the articles found in this reader. The sites are cross-referenced by number and the Web icon (●) in the topic guide. In addition, it is possible to link directly to these Web sites through our DUSHKIN ONLINE support site at *http://www.dushkin.com/online/*.

The following sites were available at the time of publication. Visit our Web site—we update DUSHKIN ONLINE regularly to reflect any changes.

General Sources

1. American Society of Criminology
http://www.bsos.umd.edu/asc/four.html
This is an excellent starting place for study of all aspects of criminology and criminal justice, with links to international criminal justice, juvenile justice, court information, police, governments, and so on.

2. Federal Bureau of Investigation
http://www.fbi.gov
The main page of the FBI Web site leads to lists of the most wanted criminals, uniform crime reports, FBI case reports, major investigations, and more.

3. National Archive of Criminal Justice Data
http://www.icpsr.umich.edu/NACJD/index.html
NACJD holds more than 500 data collections relating to criminal justice; this site provides browsing and downloading access to most of these data and documentation. NACJD's central mission is to facilitate and encourage research in the field of criminal justice.

4. Social Science Information Gateway
http://sosig.esrc.bris.ac.uk
This is an online catalog of thousands of Internet resources relevant to social science education and research. Every resource is selected and described by a librarian or subject specialist. Enter "criminal justice" under Search for an excellent annotated list of sources.

5. University of Pennsylvania Library: Criminology
http://www.library.upenn.edu/resources/subject/ social/criminology/criminology.html
An excellent list of criminology and criminal justice resources is provided here.

Crime and Justice in America

6. Campaign for Equity-Restorative Justice (CERJ)
http://www.cerj.org
This is the home page of CERJ, which sees monumental problems in justice systems and the need for reform. Examine this site and its links for information about the restorative justice movement.

7. Crime-Free America
http://www.crime-free.org
Crime-Free America is a grassroots, nonprofit group dedicated to ending the crime epidemic that it feels has gripped the United States over the last four decades. This site has links to the Bureau of Justice Statistics, forums, and crime watch profiles.

8. Crime Times
http://www.crime-times.org/titles.htm
This interesting site, listing research reviews and other information regarding biological causes of criminal, violent, and psychopathic behavior, consists of many articles that are

listed by title. It is provided by the Wacker Foundation, publisher of *Crime Times.*

9. Ray Jones
http://blue.temple.edu/~eastern/jones.html
In this article, subtitled "A Review of Empirical Research in Corporate Crime," Ray Jones explores what happens when business violates the law. An extensive interpretive section and a bibliography are provided.

10. Sourcebook of Criminal Justice Statistics Online
http://www.albany.edu/sourcebook/
Data about all aspects of criminal justice in the United States are available at this site, which includes more than 600 tables from dozens of sources. A search mechanism is available.

Victimology

11. Connecticut Sexual Assault Crisis Services, Inc.
http://www.connsacs.org
This site has links that provide information about women's responses to sexual assault and related issues. It includes extensive links to sexual violence–related Web pages.

12. National Crime Victim's Research and Treatment Center (NCVC)
http://www.musc.edu/cvc/
At this site, find out about the work of NCVC at the Medical University of South Carolina, and click on Related Resources for an excellent listing of additional Web sources.

13. Office for Victims of Crime (OVC)
http://www.ojp.usdoj.gov/ovc
Established by the 1984 Victims of Crime Act, the OVC oversees diverse programs that benefit the victims of crime. From this Web site, you can download a great deal of pertinent information.

The Police

14. ACLU Criminal Justice Home Page
http://aclu.org/issues/criminal/hmcj.html
This "Criminal Justice" page of the American Civil Liberties Union Web site highlights recent events in criminal justice, addresses police issues, lists important resources, and contains a search mechanism.

15. Violent Criminal Apprehension Program (VICAP)
http://www.fbi.gov/programs/vicap.htm
VICAP's mission is to facilitate cooperation, communication, and coordination among law enforcement agencies and provide support in their efforts to investigate, identify, track, apprehend, and prosecute violent serial offenders. Access VICAP's data information center resources here.

16. Introduction to American Justice
http://www.uaa.alaska.edu/just/just110/home.html
Prepared by Darryl Wood of the Justice Center at the University of Alaska at Anchorage, this site provides an excellent outline of the causes of crime, including major theories. An introduction to crime, law, and the criminal justice system, as well as data on police and policing, the court system, corrections, and more are available here.

17. Law Enforcement Guide to the World Wide Web
http://leolinks.com
This page is dedicated to excellence in law enforcement. It contains links to every possible related category: community policing, computer crime, forensics, gangs, and wanted persons are just a few.

18. National Institute of Justice (NIJ)
http://www.ojp.usdoj.gov/nij/lawedocs.htm
The NIJ sponsors projects and conveys research findings to practitioners in the field of criminal justice. Through this site, you can access the initiatives of the 1994 Violent Crime Control and Law Enforcement Act, apply for grants, monitor international criminal activity, learn the latest about policing techniques and issues, and more.

Judicial System

19. Center for Rational Correctional Policy
http://www.correctionalpolicy.com
This is an excellent site on courts and sentencing, with many additional links to a variety of criminal justice sources.

20. Justice Information Center (JIC)
http://www.ncjrs.org
Provided by the National Criminal Justice Reference Service, this JIC site connects to information about corrections, courts, crime prevention, criminal justice, statistics, drugs and crime, law enforcement, and victims.

21. National Center for Policy Analysis (NCPA)
http://www.public-policy.org/~ncpa/pd/law/index3.html
Through the NCPA's "Idea House," you can click onto links to an array of topics that are of major interest in the study of the American judicial system.

22. U.S. Department of Justice (DOJ)
http://www.usdoj.gov
The DOJ represents the American people in enforcing the law in the public interest. Open its main page to find information about the U.S. judicial system. This site provides links to federal government Web servers, topics of interest related to the justice system, documents and resources, and a topical index.

Juvenile Justice

23. Gang Land: The Jerry Capeci Page
http://www.ganglandnews.com
Although this site particularly addresses organized-crime gangs, its insights into gang lifestyle—including gang families and their influence—are useful for those interested in exploring issues related to juvenile justice.

24. Institute for Intergovernmental Research (IIR)
http://www.iir.com
The IIR is a research organization that specializes in law enforcement, juvenile justice, and criminal justice issues. Explore the projects, links, and search engines from this home page. Topics addressed include youth gangs and white collar crime.

25. National Criminal Justice Reference Service (NCJRS)
http://virlib.ncjrs.org/JuvenileJustice.asp
NCJRS, a federally sponsored information clearinghouse for people involved with research, policy, and practice related to criminal and juvenile justice and drug control, provides this site of links to full-text juvenile justice publications.

26. National Network for Family Resiliency
http://www.nnfr.org
This organization's main Web page will lead to a number of resource areas of interest in learning about resiliency, including General Family Resiliency, Violence Prevention, and Family Economics.

27. Partnership Against Violence Network
http://www.pavnet.org
The Partnership Against Violence Network is a virtual library of information about violence and youths at risk, representing data from seven different federal agencies—a one-stop searchable information resource.

Punishment and Corrections

28. American Probation and Parole Association (APPA)
http://www.appa-net.org
Open this APPA site to find information and resources related to probation and parole issues, position papers, the APPA code of ethics, and research and training programs and opportunities.

29. The Corrections Connection
http://www.corrections.com
This site is an online network for corrections professionals.

30. Critical Criminology Division of the ASC
http://sun.soci.niu.edu/~critcrim/
Here you will find basic criminology resources and related government resources, provided by the American Society of Criminology, as well as other useful links. The death penalty is also discussed.

31. David Willshire's Forensic Psychology & Psychiatry Links
http://www.ozemail.com.au/~dwillsh/
This site offers an enormous number of links to professional journals and associations. It is a valuable resource for study into possible connections between violence and mental disorders. Topics include serial killers, sex offenders, and trauma.

32. Oregon Department of Corrections
http://www.doc.state.or.us/links/welcome.htm
Open this site for resources in such areas as crime and law enforcement and for links to U.S. state corrections departments.

33. The Other Side of the Wall
http://www.prisonwall.org
This site contains resources on prisons and on the death penalty debate.

34. Stop Prisoner Rape, Inc.
http://www.spr.org/spr.html
Access this site to gain understanding into the social relationships that may develop in incarceration facilities.

We highly recommend that you review our Web site for expanded information and our other product lines. We are continually updating and adding links to our Web site in order to offer you the most usable and useful information that will support and expand the value of your Annual Editions. You can reach us at: *http://www.dushkin. com/annualeditions/*.

www.dushkin.com/online/

Unit Selections

1. **Crunching Numbers: Crime and Incarceration at the End of the Millennium,** Jan M. Chaiken
2. **The Crime Bust,** Gordon Witkin
3. **Land of the Stupid: When You Need a Used Russian Submarine, Call Tarzan,** Robert I. Friedman
4. **The Well-Marked Roads to Homicidal Rage,** Laurie Goodstein and William Glaberson

Key Points to Consider

❖ In your view, what is behind the dramatic drop in crime?

❖ What steps do you believe could be taken to prevent gun-related crimes?

❖ Are alcohol and drug arrests on your campus on the rise? Are you familiar with treatment modalities that have proven effective in helping chronic drug users to break away from addiction? Explain.

 **Links** **www.dushkin.com/online/**

6. **Campaign for Equity-Restorative Justice (CERJ)**
   http://www.cerj.org
7. **Crime-Free America**
   http://www.crime-free.org
8. **Crime Times**
   http://www.crime-times.org/titles.htm
9. **Ray Jones**
   http://blue.temple.edu/~eastern/jones.html
10. **Sourcebook of Criminal Justice Statistics Online**
    http://www.albany.edu/sourcebook/

These sites are annotated on pages 4 and 5.

Crime and Justice in America

Crime continues to be a major problem in the United States. Court dockets are full, our prisons are overcrowded, probation and parole caseloads are overwhelming, and our police are being urged to do more. The bulging prison population places a heavy strain on the economy of the country. Clearly crime is a complex problem that defies simple explanations or solutions. While the more familiar crimes of murder, rape, and assault are still with us, drugs are an ever-increasing scourge. The debate continues about how best to handle juvenile offenders, sex offenders, and those who commit acts of domestic violence. Crime committed using computers and the Internet is already an issue to be dealt with.

Annual Editions: Criminal Justice 01/02 focuses directly upon crime in America and the three traditional components of the criminal justice system: police, courts, and corrections. It also gives special attention to crime victims in the victimology unit and to juveniles in the juvenile justice unit. The articles presented in this section are intended to serve as a foundation for the materials presented in subsequent sections.

The unit begins with the essay "Crunching Numbers: Crime and Incarceration at the End of the Millennium" by Jan Chaiken, Director of BJS. Chaiken urges researchers to take advantage of this period of dramatically declining crime to learn as much as they can about the underlying causes of the drop in numbers. Then, in "The Crime Bust," Gordon Witkin explores several factors in an effort to explain the decline in crime rates. In "Land of the Stupid: When You Need Russian Submarine, Call Tarzan," Robert Friedman traces a Russian organized crime figure from his birthplace in Odessa to Miami, providing insight into this version of the now-familiar phenomenon of organized crime in America. The next article, "The Well-Marked Roads to Homicidal Rage," is part of a *New York Times* series on rampage killers. It discusses how relatives, colleagues, and officials overlook the warning signs projected by the killers.

Crunching Numbers: Crime and Incarceration at the End of the Millennium

by Jan M. Chaiken

This article is based on a presentation made by Dr. Chaiken on July 20, 1999, at the Office of Justice Programs' Annual Conference on Criminal Justice Research and Evaluation in Washington, D.C.

As we approach January 2000, the impulse to think about the future is nearly irresistible. At the Justice Department's Bureau of Justice Statistics (BJS), we compulsive statisticians know that the year 2000 is still part of the twentieth century, so we are more relaxed than most people about the arrival of a new millennium.

Our attitude toward the future may also be shaped by the fact that we statisticians are more oriented to the past: We know that the only *data* available are data from the past. This article, therefore, explores some of the complex trends in property crime, rape, and violence among intimates, all of which raise important questions for new research. It also highlights some of the implications of the high rates of incarceration, which are attracting researchers' attention.[1] Conclusions are left for the reader to draw.

Figure 1: Property Crime Rates, United States, 1973–98

Adjusted victimization rate per 1,000 households*

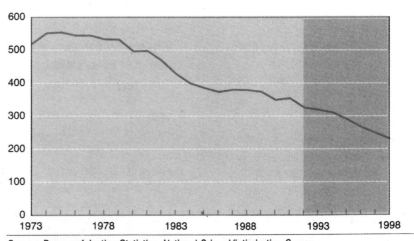

Source: Bureau of Justice Statistics, National Crime Victimization Survey

Note: The property crimes included are burglary, theft, and motor vehicle theft.

* The National Crime Victimization Survey redesign was implemented in 1993; the area with the lighter shading is before the redesign and the darker area after the redesign. The data before 1993 are adjusted to make them comparable with data collected since the redesign.

Decline in Property Crime— Does the U.S. Stand Alone?

As measured by the BJS National Crime Victimization Survey (NCVS), property crime has been declining in this country for at least 25 years[2] (see figure 1[3]). This type of crime, which includes larceny, burglary, theft in general, and motor vehicle theft, has fallen 58 percent since 1975. Burglary rates closely resemble property crime rates overall in their steep decline (see figure 2).

From *National Institute of Justice Journal*, January 2000, pp. 10-17. © 2000 by the National Institute of Justice. Reprinted by permission.

Figure 2: Burglary Rates, United States, 1973–98

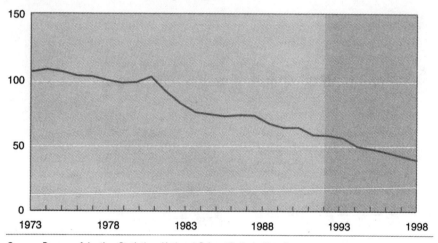

Adjusted victimization rate per 1,000 households *

Source: Bureau of Justice Statistics, National Crime Victimization Survey

* The National Crime Victimization Survey redesign was implemented in 1993; the area with the lighter shading is before the redesign and the darker area after the redesign. The data before 1993 are adjusted to make them comparable with data collected since the redesign.

This pattern has *not* been duplicated in other countries. In Canada, for example, although property crime has declined steadily since 1992, the decline is not nearly as steep as in the United States, and the longer term pattern in Canada is essentially flat— or has not changed.[4]

England and Wales use a victimization survey quite similar to the NCVS, which facilitates comparison of crime data with the United States. Not only has property crime been increasing in England and Wales, but the rates—once much lower than in the United States—now exceed ours.[5] For most of the period since 1981, burglary in England and Wales has been increasing, not declining, with a turnaround starting in 1992 or 1993 (see figure 3), a situation approximately the same as in Canada. In rates of motor vehicle theft, the patterns in the United States much more closely resemble those of England and Wales (see figure 4).

What is going on here? First, it is important to note that national trends are an aggregate of State and local trends, which may be moving in entirely different directions in some parts of the country than the overall numbers. So it is possible that in a particular State or community the

trends are quite a bit different from the national trend. But on a nation-wide basis, the differences among countries are palpable. In London, burglaries are a high-priority focus of the police and are frequent topics of news-paper articles and even announcements on public transit.

The downward shift in burglary and theft in the United States has attracted very little attention from researchers—especially compared to that given to trends in violent crime. To be sure, the reason for the downturn is difficult to understand if we accept the idea that it is not possible to find a valid explanation by pointing to something that happened in the United States but also happened in other countries.

What comes to mind as possible explanations? On the side of potential victims: More window and door alarms and more secure windows and doors; better illumination in yards and driveways and inside homes when no one is present; more private security and gated communities; less cash being carried because of greater use of credit cards and ATM cards for financial transactions. On the side of potential perpetrators: More drug dealers in prison; more criminals turning to robbery and lucrative Internet crime instead of burglary. And, of course, better research and evaluation!

Figure 3: Burglary Rates, United States and England/Wales, 1981–96

Victimization rate per 1,000 population

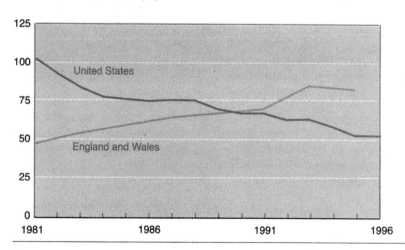

Source: Langan, Patrick A. and David P. Farrington, *Crime and Justice in the United States and in England and Wales, 1981-96*, Washington, DC: US Department of Justice, Bureau of Justice Statistics, October 1998 (NCJ 169284).

Note: U.S. surveys interview people age 12 or older; English surveys, age 16 or older. The U.S. surveys have been conducted annually since 1973. English surveys were conducted in 1981, 1983, 1987, 1991, 1993, and 1995. Burglary was defined in both countries' surveys as residential burglary.

Figure 4: Motor Vehicle Theft Rates, United States and England/Wales, 1981–96

Adjusted victimization rate per 1,000 households

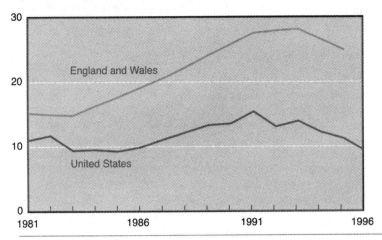

Source: Langan, Patrick A. and David P. Farrington, *Crime and Justice in the United States and in England and Wales, 1981–96*, Washington, DC: US Department of Justice, Bureau of Justice Statistics, October 1998 (NCJ 169284).

Note: U.S. surveys interview people age 12 or older; English surveys, age 16 or older. The U.S. surveys have been conducted annually since 1973. English surveys were conducted in 1981, 1983, 1987, 1991, 1993, and 1995.

When *U.S. News and World Report* examined these patterns, it favored this explanation for the drop in crime: People are more likely now than in the past to be home watching cable TV and videotapes, rather than being out on the town, so the nighttime burglar has fewer opportunities.[6]

Rape: Is It Really Declining?

People generally have two different reactions when they see the data on rape trends. Some say, when they see the decline reported by the NCVS (see figure 5), obviously our policies concerning violence against women are working—women are learning how to handle threatening situations or are aware of the alternatives for avoiding them.

Others disagree, believing that the downward trend is illusory, that it means only that women are becoming less willing to report rape and even more reluctant to mention it to the NCVS interviewers. The NCVS data are based on interviews, not police reports, and the respondents also are asked if they reported the crime to the police. We know that rape continues to be the crime reported least often, especially among women in their teens and early twenties, as well as college students.

BJS, the National Institute of Justice, and the Centers for Disease Control and Prevention (CDC) sponsor research to examine whether other methods of inquiring about sexual assault and rape yield better estimates of the true extent of victimization.[7] Whenever BJS compares the results of its NCVS surveys with those of the more explicit and reassuring methods used in surveys conducted by NIJ, CDC, and in other BJS research, it becomes clear that many of these crimes remain uncounted by the NCVS.

This is particularly true of rape by intimates, which women may mention to an interviewer in the context of fights with their partners or spouses but are less likely to mention in the NCVS context of crime. That may be either because they may not think it is a crime or because they may not want to contemplate the implications of their partner's behavior amounting to a violent crime.

BJS is working closely with NIJ, CDC, and the National Center for Health Statistics to better understand the incidence of domestic violence, including sexual assault, and to develop better ways to measure the extent of violence against women.[8] Particularly

Figure 5: Rape Rates, United States, 1973–98

Adjusted victimization rate per 1,000 people age 12 and older*

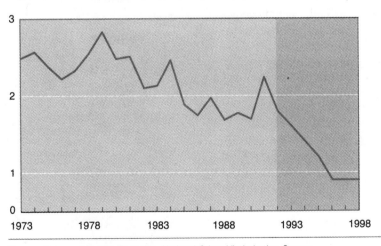

Source: Bureau of Justice Statistics, National Crime Victimization Survey

Note: Includes both attempted an completed rape.

* The National Crime Victimization Survey redesign was implemented in 1993; the area with the lighter shading is before the redesign and the darker area after the redesign. The data before 1993 are adjusted to make them comparable with data collected since the redesign.

because sexual assault, unlike property crime, may not actually be dwindling, it requires continued research and intervention—and improved measurement systems!

Declining Violence Among Intimates—The Gender Gap

The story of trends in violence among intimates is a remarkable one. The past decade has seen a real change in perceptions of the seriousness of violence against women, especially by a husband or partner. Legislation has been enacted at the State and Federal levels, the Violence Against Women Office was established in the U.S. Department of Justice, and funding has flowed to all the States for programs intended to reduce the occurrence of violence against women and assist victims. Although we are beginning to see numerous indications of the effectiveness of these programs in a broad sense, the trends in serious violence are not at all what might be expected given the recent strong emphasis on violence against women.

The overall decrease in serious, violent crime (by about 31 percent since 1994) has benefited men much more than women (see figure 6). For women, the victimization rate declined less than 15 percent in this period and overall is still slightly above the levels of the 1970's. When we examine particular population subgroups, we find some categories of women who are more likely than men to be victims of crime. Women college students, for example, are at greater risk of victimization than women of the same age who are not in college.[9] On the whole, the victimization of college women by crimes other than sexual assault is approximately the same as that for men, but women are in addition the primary victims of sexual assault. This is a form of gender equity that no one was hoping for.

When we examine homicide committed by intimates, we detect the possibility that a downward trend for

Figure 6: Violent Crime Rates, by Gender of Victim, United States, 1973–98

Adjusted victimization rate per 1,000 people age 12 and over*

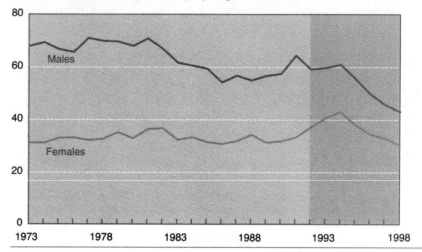

Sources: Bureau of Justice Statistics, National Crime Victimization Survey; and FBI Uniform Crime Reports

Note: The violent crimes included are rape, robbery, aggravated and simple assault, and homicide.

* The National Crime Victimization Survey redesign was implemented in 1993; the area with the lighter shading is before the redesign and the darker area after the redesign. The data before 1993 are adjusted to make them comparable with data collected since the redesign.

women victims began around 1994. However, the long-term downward shift in the number of men killed by their intimate partners is much steeper

(see figure 7). A reasonable interpretation of this disparity is that women who find themselves in situations so devastating that they might consider

Figure 7: Homicides by Intimates, by Gender United States, 1976–97

Number of homicide victims killed by an intimate

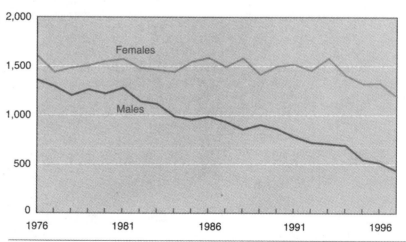

Source: FBI Uniform Crime Reports, Supplemental Homicide Reports, as presented in Bureau of Justice Statistics, *Homicide Trends in the United States*, at http://www.ojp.usdoj.gov/bjs/homicide/intimate.htm, and *Homicide Trends in the United States*, by James Alan Fox and Marianne Zawitz, Washington, DC: U.S. Department of Justice, Bureau of Justice Statistics, January 1999 (NCJ 173956).

Figure 8: Homicide of Male Intimates, by Weapon Type, United States, 1976–97

Number of male homicide victims killed by an intimate

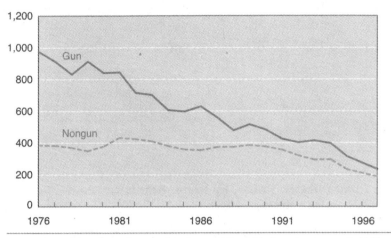

Source: FBI, Uniform Crime Reports, Supplemental Homicide Reports, as presented in Bureau of Justice Statistics, *Homicide Trends in the United States*, at http://www.ojp.usdoj.gov/bjs/homicide/intimate.htm, and *Homicide Trends in the United States*, by James Alan Fox and Marianne Zawitz, Washington, DC: U.S. Department of Justice, Bureau of Justice Statistics, January 1999 (NCJ 173956).

intimates has occurred, we see a long-term downtrend in the use of guns. Then, in the past few years, the use of other kinds of weapons also has declined (see figure 8). It should be noted that not all the men killed by intimates are killed by a woman: The data also include male intimates who kill men.

High Incarceration Rate—Problem or Solution?

Another major trend for researchers' consideration is the literally incredible increase in incarceration rates in the United States since 1975. Like the decrease in violent crime, this fact is fairly well known, although the details and the implications may not be. Not only has the incarceration rate more than quadrupled—after holding more or less steady for decades—but it has disproportionately affected minority racial and ethnic groups (see figure 9). This is so much the case in some communities that incarceration is becoming almost a normative life experience.

Such a high level of incarceration has grave implications for the body politic. For one thing, it fosters disrespect for legitimate authority among people who begin to feel that everyone they know is being put in prison. For another, because felons typically are not eligible to vote, they are likely to have no interest or role in elections and thus may be alienated from the political process. We are disenfranchising a group of people who currently are minorities, but—if current demographic trends continue—will become a majority of the population.

killing their partners increasingly have options such as shelters, protection orders, and police arrest policies that allow them, at the moment they feel compelled to kill, to resist that compulsion.[10] Men, on the other hand, continue to kill their intimate partners at about the same rate as a quarter of a century ago.

Looking in more detail at the circumstances in which this steep reduction in the number of men killed by

The latest figures, for 1996, show that on any given day, approximately 30 percent of black men ages 20 to 29 were under correctional supervision—either in jail or prison or on probation or parole in the community (see tables 1 and 2). Examining the numbers for State and Federal prisoners only (that is, omitting people who are on probation and parole), we find that 8.3 percent of black men ages 25

Figure 9: Incarceration Rates, United States, 1925–97

Number of inmates sentenced under State and Federal jurisdictions per 100,000 residents

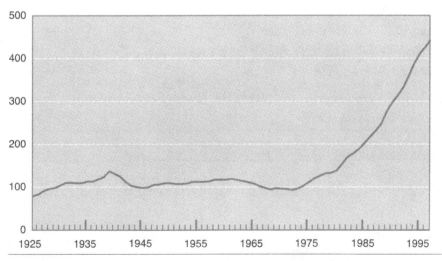

Sources: Data for 1925–84—*State and Federal Prisoners*, 1925–85 by S. Minor-Harper, Washington, D.C.: U.S. Department of Justice, Bureau of Justice Statistics, 1986 (NCJ 102494); data for 1985–95—*Correctional Populations in the United States*, 1995, Washington, D.C.: U.S. Department of Justice, Bureau of Justice Statistics, June 1997 (NCJ 163916); data for 1996–97—*Prisoners in 1997*, by Darrell K. Gilliard and Allen J. Beck, Washington, D.C.: U.S. Department of Justice, Bureau of Justice Statistics, August 1998 (NCJ 170014).

Table 1: Percentage of Men Under Correctional Supervision, by Race and Age, United States, 1996

White age	Percent of white men in age category	Black age	Percent of black men in age category
18–19	4.4	18–19	16.2
20–24	8.0	20–24	29.4
25–29	7.1	25–29	28.9
30–34	5.8	30–34	24.4
34–39	4.4	35–39	17.2
40 or older	1.3	40 or older	6.1

Source: Beck, Allen J., "Trends in U.S. Correctional Populations," in *The Dilemmas of Corrections: Contemporary Readings, Fourth Edition,* ed.by K.C. Haas and G.P. Alpert, Prospect Heights, IL: Waveland Press, 1999.

effective policies for crime reduction that unfairly affect any segment of the population should not be tolerated.

NCJ 180078

Notes

1. See, for example, Clear, Todd, and Dina R. Rose, *When Neighbors Go to Jail: Impact on Attitudes About Formal and Informal Social Control,* Research Preview, Washington, D.C., U.S. Department of Justice, National Institute of Justice, July 1999.
2. The National Crime Victimization Survey (NCVS) is the Nation's primary source of information about criminal victimization. Information is obtained annually from a nationally representative sample of roughly 43,000 households comprising more than 80,000 people who are asked about the frequency, characteristics, and consequences of their victimization by crime. The survey reports the extent of victimization from rape, sexual assault, robbery, assault, theft, household burglary, and motor vehicle theft for the population as a whole and for subpopulations such as women, the elderly, members of various racial groups, and city dwellers. NCVS data collection began in 1973; data from the redesigned survey were reported beginning in 1993.
3. This figure and the others accompanying this article are drawn from charts on the BJS Web site (http://www.ojp.usdoj.gov/bjs). The data presented in the figures are also on the Web site and are updated from time to time.
4. Tremblay, Sylvain, *Crime Statistics in Canada, 1998,* Ottawa, Ontario: Statistics Canada, Canadian Centre for Justice Statistics, 1999.
5. Langan, Patrick A., and David P. Farrington, *Crime and Justice in the United States and in England and Wales, 1981–96,* Washington, D.C.: U.S. Department of Justice, Bureau of Justice Statistics, October 1998 (NCJ 169284).
6. Witkin, Gordon, "The Crime Bust," *U.S. News and World Report,* May 25, 1998: 28–40.

to 29 were in prison at the end of 1996. This figure is more than three times higher than the 2.6 percent of Hispanic men who are in prison and more than 10 times higher than the rate for white men.

BJS has developed a statistical model that predicts the lifetime chances of going to prison if current patterns of imprisonment continue at the same levels. The model indicates that a young black man age 16 in 1996 had a 28.5 percent chance of spending time in prison during his life (see table 3). This figure does *not* include being arrested and spending a night or so in jail. It reflects actual prison sentences, which ordinarily are for at least a year and follow a conviction for a felony.

This does not seem to be the kind of trend that can be sustained very long, both because of its monetary costs and because of its corrosive effects on heavily affected communities. On the other side of the equation, however, there are those who believe that the dramatic decrease in violent crime that this country has experienced in the recent past can be attributed to the very fact that large numbers of people are behind bars. They see the investment as paying off in lower crime.

A Window of Opportunity

This unanticipated period of rapidly declining crime may be unique in our Nation's history. Indeed, there are those who warn that it surely must be a passing phenomenon. Whether or not that is the case, it would seem opportune for criminal justice researchers to seize the moment and learn as much as they can about the underlying causes of the decline. For the purpose of developing public policy, we are most interested in uncovering strong evidence about what has been done at the State, city, county, and Federal levels that helped make the decline happen. It also would be of interest to shed light on pockets where the overall national data are not borne out. Such efforts on the part of researchers may turn out to be vital in sustaining the decline of crime in the United States. At the same time, we know that even

Table 2: Incarceration Rates, by Race, Ethnicity, and Gender, United States, 1996

Number of sentenced prisoners per 100,000 residents of each group

All ages		Men Ages 25–29	
Men		Blacks	8,319
Blacks	3,098	Hispanics	2,609
Hispanics	1,278	Whites	829
Whites	370		
Women			
Blacks	188		
Hispanics	78		
Whites	23		

Source: Gilliard, Darrell K., and Allen J. Beck, *Prisoners in 1997,* Washington, D.C.: U.S. Department of Justice, Bureau of Justice Statistics, August, 1998 (NCJ 170014).

Table 3: Lifetime Likelihood of Going to Prison, United States, 1991

	Lifetime chance
All people	5.1%
White men	4.4
Black men	28.5

Source: Bonzcar, Thomas P., and Allen J. Beck, *Lifetime Likelihood of Going to State or Federal Prison,* Washington, D.C.: U.S. Department of Justice, Bureau of Justice Statistics, March 1997 (NCJ 160092).

ponent of the Office of Justice Programs, U.S. Department of Justice, and the Nation's primary source for criminal justice statistics. He was appointed BJS Director by President Clinton in 1994.

7. NIJ and CDC sponsored the research conducted for the National Violence Against Women Survey. Among the publications based on findings from that survey is *Prevalence, Incidence, and Consequences of Violence Against Women: Findings From the National Violence Against Women Survey,* by Patricia Tjaden and Nancy Thoennes, Research in Brief, Washington, D.C.: U.S. Department of Justice, National Institute of Justice and Centers for Disease Control and Prevention, November 1998 (NCJ 172837). NIJ and BJS sponsored research on the sexual victimization of college women, conducted by Bonnie S. Fisher, Francis T. Cullen, and Michael G. Turner. The final report of the study, "The Sexual Victimization of College Women: Findings From Two National Level Surveys," submitted December 1999 (NIJ grant 95-WT-NX-001 and BJS grant 97-MU-MU-001), will be made available by NIJ.

8. NIJ, CDC, and BJS addressed the issue of building data systems for monitoring and responding to violence against women in a jointly sponsored workshop. The proceedings and papers of the October 1998 workshop will be published by CDC.

9. Noted in Fisher, Cullen, and Turner, "The Sexual Victimization of College Women."

10. Dugan, Laura, Daniel S. Nagin, and Richard Rosenfeld, "Explaining the Decline in Intimate Partner Homicide' *Homicide Studies* 3, 3 (August 1999):187–214.

About the author

Jan M. Chaiken is Director of the Bureau of Justice Statistics (BJS), a component of the Office of Justice Programs, U.S. Department of Justice, and the Nation's primary source for criminal justice statistics. He was appointed BJS Director by President Clinton in 1994.

Acknowledgments

Dr. Chaiken would like to thank the staff of the BJS vicitimization statistics office, under the direction of Michael Rand; the staff of the corrections statistics office, under the direction of Allen Beck; and Patrick Langan and visiting fellow David Farrington for their assistance in preparing this presentation. He also wishes to thank Marianne Zawitz and visiting fellow James A. Fox for their work in preparing data from the BJS Web site's subsite on homicide trends. Marianne Zawitz also prepared the charts, reproduced here, that were part of the author's original presentation.

The CRIME Bust

What's behind the dramatic drop in crime? The prime suspect is not police, nor prisons, nor prevention

By Gordon Witkin

Less than a decade ago, violent crime seemed like one of those things people would just have to get used to. "It's possible you won't be able to solve this problem," New York Gov. Mario Cuomo said in 1989. "That's how horrible it is." From 1984 to 1993, the number of murders nationwide climbed 31 percent. During that period, 216,986 people were killed in the United States. When, in 1992, 7-year-old Dantrell Davis was killed in Chicago by a sniper while walking to elementary school holding his mother's hand, there was outrage but little surprise. By then, neighborhoods like his had acquired monikers—the "Graveyard," the "War Zone," or "Beirut." Violence, and—just as important—fear, spread almost everywhere. The situation aggravated race relations, destroyed businesses, accelerated flight from the cities, and trapped children indoors. Violent crime seemed to affect virtually everything, and it seemed intractable.

Then something extraordinary happened. Starting in 1994, violent crime began falling. The number of such crimes reported in 1996 was 13 percent below the 1992 level, and preliminary figures released this week by the FBI show an additional 5 percent drop in 1997. The trend line is even more steeply down for murder, which is considered the most reliable crime statistic because such a high percentage of killings are reported. From 1993 to 1996 the number of murders dropped by 20 percent—from 24,526 (a rate of 9.5 per 100,000 residents) to 19,645 (a rate of 7.4 per 100,000)—and the preliminary FBI numbers indicate an additional 9 percent murder reduction in 1997. The 590 murders in Los Angeles in 1997

were the fewest in 20 years. Boston had 43 murders in 1997, a 36-year low. In March, for the first time since the 1960s, Brooklyn went a full week without a single murder; a decade ago Brooklyn was suffering 13 to 15 killings weekly. It's hard to think of a social trend of greater significance.

Yet the national causes of the improvement remain mysterious. Not surprisingly, economists say it was the economy, demographers credit demography, cops say it was better police work, and politicians say it was their "get tough" policies. The news media have split the difference and concluded that it was a variety of causes.

But while the drop in crime can be linked to many factors, one really is more important than others. If we approach the question of who ambushed the crime rate as a detective might approach a murder case, it turns out that there is a prime suspect.

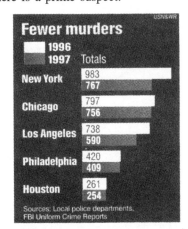

Fewer murders

	1996 / 1997 Totals
New York	983 / 767
Chicago	797 / 756
Los Angeles	738 / 590
Philadelphia	420 / 409
Houston	261 / 254

Sources: Local police departments, FBI Uniform Crime Reports

THE ECONOMY? Many social scientists have long believed in some sort of link between poverty and crime, so there's a simple logic to the idea that a

booming economy—a 4.3 percent unemployment rate at last count—must be driving crime rates lower. With more hope of finding legal jobs, young people are less likely to see crime as a necessary or desirable option.

But while possibly a factor, prosperity is probably not the key. Robbery and burglary fluctuate with economic conditions—but murders generally do not, according to Philip Cook, a Duke University public policy professor. For instance, crime rates rose sharply in the 1960s, a period of low unemployment. During the 1970s, Sun Belt cities had faster rates of economic growth than older cities—and higher crime rates too. New York City retains a stubbornly high unemployment rate of 9 percent, yet murders there have fallen 66 percent since 1990.

PREVENTION? There is clearly merit to the idea that investing in high-risk youngsters might help prevent violent crime, and experts say high-quality prevention initiatives can reduce violence rates by 20 percent to 25 percent. For instance, so-called early intervention programs that get at-risk kids into preschools at a young age and teach parenting skills to new mothers and fathers can have long-lasting positive effects. After-school programs involving music, sports, and drama can also be valuable, in light of research showing that the peak hours for juvenile violent crime are from 3 p.m. to 8 p.m.

But the good news pretty much ends there. Studies show that many prevention programs don't work, and others may or may not be effective, since so few have been evaluated. Among the ineffective approaches are some politically popular ideas like neighborhood block watches and citywide gun buyback programs. For the moment, the overall effects of prevention programs on crime are thought to be modest.

FEWER BATTERED WIVES? One of the most surprising components of the drop in violent crime is the steady 20-year slide in domestic murders. Killings involving intimate partners—spouses, ex-spouses, boyfriends, or girlfriends—fell from nearly 3,000 in 1976 to just over 1,800 in 1996, a decline of 40 percent. And though 3 of every 4 victims in 1996 were women, the largest portion of the decline by far was in the killing of men, especially black men killed by their female partners.

In part, there are fewer killings *by* spouses because there are fewer young people *with* spouses. In 1970, 55 percent of men ages 20 to 24 had never been married. By 1992, the proportion had increased to 80 percent. Experts say that women are also benefiting from more opportunities to escape bad relationships. Women are more financially independent, and organizations devoted to helping women in abusive relationships—hot lines, counseling centers, legal clinics, shelters—have grown dramatically after first emerging in the early 1970s.

But in 1996, there were only 447 fewer "domestics" than in 1993, accounting for just 9 percent of the murder reduction.

PRISONS? When crime started dropping, one of the first explanations experts considered was the shift of criminals from the streets to prisons. The number of people incarcerated in federal and state prisons and local jails has gone from 744,208 in 1985 to 1,725,842 as of last summer. Tough legislation in the 1980s increased the sentences for many crimes, especially drug offenses. From 1924 to 1974, America's incarceration rate was strikingly stable (about 110 per 100,000 population); since then the rate has almost quadrupled.

Some of the new criminals were arrested for "nonviolent" crimes (notably drug dealing). Still, criminologists generally believe that most new prisoners were incarcerated for violent crimes. One study showed that between 1979 and 1991, the number of offenders sent to state prisons for violent crimes doubled. Other studies—albeit controver-

sial—argue that each additional prisoner locked up means from 12 to 17 fewer crimes per year. Even liberal criminologist Franklin Zimring, while decrying the increase in drug incarcerations, concedes that "when you lock up an extra million people, it's got to have some effect on the crime rate." The more conservative social scientist James Q. Wilson is less grudging: "Putting people in prison is the single most important thing we've done."

But regional variations undermine the notion that imprisonment played the major role nationwide. New York City has displayed some of the most dramatic drops in crime, but the state prison population—70 percent of which is from the city—has increased only about 8 percent since 1993. Conversely, the law-and-order state Utah raised its incarceration rate by 19 percent from 1993 to 1996—but its violent-crime rate went *up*. Imprisonment, therefore, seems to be important but not the underlying cause of the crime drop.

POLICE? No factor has been cited more often to explain the crime drop than better policing. And at first glance, there is a strong case that an improvement in policing techniques is indeed the key. During much of the 1970s and 1980s, the police themselves had argued there was little they could do about crime, that rates were determined by demographics and social conditions. But nurtured by reform-minded groups like the Police Foundation and the Police Executive Research Forum, a more educated, innovative brand of cop has ascended to the chief's chair in the 1990s.

The influence of the new breed has been most dramatically displayed in New York. Commissioner William Bratton and his successor, Howard Safir, created a model of policing that is important for two reasons. The drop in murders in the Big Apple—from 1,946 in 1993 to 983 in 1996—accounted by itself for 20 percent of the drop nationwide. And other big-city departments have adopted some of New York's crime-fighting innovations.

Bratton put primary responsibility in the hands of his 76 precinct commanders and then held them personally accountable for reducing crime in their

neighborhoods. To facilitate this program, he used a process called "Compstat," for "compare statistics." The NYPD can now plot each reported crime on a color map that gives police a more sophisticated understanding of crime trends, patterns, and "hot spots." The maps serve as the basis for twice-weekly strategy meetings that involve grilling the commanders and brainstorming on crime-fighting tactics and deployments. The sessions have enabled the commissioners to weed out weak performers; Bratton replaced half his precinct commanders within a year. "The focus on actual results is perhaps the most significant cultural change in policing since the turn of the century," says University of Maryland criminologist Lawrence Sherman. Other cities have shifted resources toward the high-crime "hot spots." The New Orleans Police Department has built substations and deployed cops 24 hours a day in troubled public housing, which has helped bring the city's murder count down from 421 in 1994 to just 266 last year.

Many experts also attribute part of New York's success to Bratton's focus on nuisance crimes—street prostitution, public urination, or blaring boomboxes. Bratton consciously took to the heart the "broken windows" theory postulated by James Q. Wilson and criminologist George Kelling in a 1982 *Atlantic Monthly* article: that just as a broken window left untended is a sign that nobody cares and will inevitably lead to more broken windows, so too, small crimes like vandalism will lead to more serious crimes if left unpunished. Supporters believe that New York's attention to low-level crimes encouraged honest citizens to begin reclaiming their neighborhoods. New York cops also found that many of these lawbreakers were wanted on warrants, were carrying illegal weapons, or provided intelligence on other crimes.

After years of skepticism, researchers are also starting to believe that having *more* cops makes a difference. In 1960, there were three reports of violent crime for every police officer in Los Angeles. By 1990, there were 10 reported crimes for every cop. In the 1970s and 1980s, many big-city police departments actually shrank because of budget crunches. But now in Los Angeles, the ratio is

1990 **Tools of the trade.** Much of the increase in violent crime in the '80s and the early '90s was among young people using guns.

1998 Road block.... Cracking down on small automobile infractions has helped reduce major crimes.

back down to 6.9 crimes per cop, in part because the city has added 2,270 police since mid-1993; murder there has plummeted. Houston has added 1,400 cops since 1991, and the murder rate there has fallen by 58 percent. And the Clinton administration has helped to fund 70,000 new local police officers, though the political imperative of spreading them broadly has diluted the program's impact.

Almost all the experts now agree this smarter policing deserves a hefty chunk of credit for the drop in violent crime. But a closer look at regional variations again raises questions. The crime rate has also dropped precipitously in cities like Washington, D.C., where the police department has been, at best, troubled and, at worst, thoroughly dysfunctional. Conversely, a metropolitan area like Nashville, which has increased its police manpower by 16 percent since 1994, has nonetheless seen its annual murder totals climb from 73 to 112 in that time. Clearly, smarter policing was spectacularly decisive in some cities like New York, but it probably was not the key factor nationwide.

CRACK. To truly understand why crime went down, it's important to review the recent history of murder. After a brief post-World War II spike, crime resumed a decades-long drop. The murder rate reached a low of 4.5 per 100,000 people in 1957 and 1958. Why? The usual explanations apply: The economy was good, communities were stable, guns were scarce on the streets, and most marriages were intact.

Then, starting in the mid-1960s, crime began to rise. Conservatives like to attribute this to loose morals, but a far more likely explanation is simple demographics. Beginning in this period, the huge post-World War II baby boom generation moved into its crime-prone late teens and 20s. A child born in 1946 turned 19 in 1965. The baby boomers peaked at 35 percent of the population in 1980, and so did the murder rate, at 10.2 per 100,000.

At that point, the situation began to turn around. Those crime-prone baby boomers became more law-abiding adults. Between 1980 and 1985, the murder rate dropped by 23 percent. Demographically, the downward trend should have continued into the early 1990s, since the number of volatile 15-to-24-year-olds shrank from 42 million in 1980 to 38 million a decade later.

But around 1986, something scary and unexpected began to occur—the

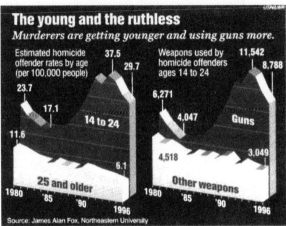

The young and the ruthless
Murderers are getting younger and using guns more.

Estimated homicide offender rates by age (per 100,000 people)
37.5
29.7
23.7
17.1
14 to 24
11.6
6.1
25 and older
1980 '85 '90 1996

Weapons used by homicide offenders ages 14 to 24
11,542
8,788
6,271
4,047
Guns
4,518
3,049
Other weapons
1980 '85 '90 1996

Source: James Alan Fox, Northeastern University

spread of crack cocaine. The recipe that used heat and baking soda to turn cocaine hydrochloride, or powder, into crack created a smokable, pre-packaged product with a unit price low enough to lure the masses. Cocaine powder required an investment of at least $75 to $100 for a gram, but a hit of crack was $5. Economically depressed inner-city neighborhoods provided fertile ground for the drug.

The result was an explosion of street-corner crack markets that proved dangerously unstable for a number of reasons. First, the crack "high" lasts as little as 10 minutes, so users often want more right away. That means a large number of transactions involving extremely agitated people. To buy more, they needed cash quickly, and they were often willing to rob people at gunpoint to get it. The lucrative environment of crack's formative years also created a dangerous number of disputes between buyers and sellers, or buyers and rip-off artists, and a feverish competition for retail turf.

Criminologists like Alfred Blumstein of Carnegie Mellon University also believe the crack markets kicked off an incendiary chain reaction involving kids and guns. The sheer number of transactions required crack-selling organizations to recruit large numbers of inner-city, minority teens—many of whom saw no other job opportunities—to act as street-level worker bees. These kids were carrying both drugs and cash, and they felt compelled to carry guns as well to protect themselves from robberies. This behavior spread beyond the drug trade, as those not involved began carrying guns to protect themselves from those who were. "Many also saw guns as conferring a measure of status and power," writes Blumstein. "Gun possession escalated into an arms race that diffused the weapons broadly throughout the community." And so the typical teenage dispute—over a girl, a ballgame, or "respect"—that years before might have resulted in a fistfight was now resulting in shooting. And dying.

The statistics from that era couldn't be clearer. The overall murder rate soared from 7.9 per 100,000 in 1985 to 9.8 per 100,000 in 1991, but the rate of murders by adults was stable, and so was the rate among young people using weapons other than firearms. In other words, virtually the entire violent-crime wave of the late 1980s and early 1990s could be blamed on young people with guns (see "The young and the ruthless" chart).

Then, starting in the early 1990s, the crack crisis began to wane in America's big cities. The proportion of youthful arrestees testing positive for cocaine in Detroit, for instance, dropped from 45 percent in 1987 to just 5 percent in 1996. In Manhattan, the proportion fell from 70 percent in 1987 to 21 percent in 1996. A variety of studies also suggest that today's crack market is increasingly dominated by an older, mostly male group of heavy users. That's good news, because this age group is less prone to violence, and many of these users have long-term, stable relationships with their suppliers.

Why have young people turned off crack? Many observers cite the "younger brother syndrome," in which teens are turned away from the drug because of an emaciated older sibling ravaged by addiction or confined to a wheelchair from a bullet fired in a crack deal gone bad. "A strong social norm against crack use began gathering momentum around 1989 or 1990. Youths have decided that crack is not cool," says Bruce Johnson of the National Development and Research Institutes in New York.

The level of violence associated with the crack markets themselves has also dropped as the result of a brutal settling-out process. Cops say the worst of the Wild West brawls over turf have been fought, and territories have been established. Many of the most reckless players from the late 1980s are dead or in prison, and those remaining have found peaceful ways to resolve disputes.

Police and imprisonment did play a narrowly focused role in stemming the crack problem. Many big-city departments—to some extent jarred into action by the unexpected crack epidemic—teamed with federal agencies to break up violent crack-selling gangs and wipe out street-corner retail markets; in New York, Commissioner Safir, for instance, has enlisted the feds in a large-scale offensive against drug trafficking in northern Manhattan. Local police pressure—along with the proliferation of beepers and cellular phones—has moved at least some of the crack markets indoors. One low-profile Brooklyn dealer told researcher Richard Curtis that prior to the police sweeps of the early 1990s, "Who'd bother to call me on my beeper? Wouldn't have to. You could buy it like a supermarket. [But when the police destroyed the supermarkets], they created my business." In terms of reducing violence, indoors is "a wonderful place for the market to be," says Mark Kleiman of the School of Public Policy and Social Research at the University of California-Los Angeles. "A guy standing on a street corner selling drugs has basically painted a target on his shirt. He'd better be ready to defend himself. A guy with a beeper and a client list doesn't have to shoot anyone."

Experts believe that the link between crack, guns, and crime can also be demonstrated in places where crime hasn't dropped—smaller cities in the heartland where crack has only recently arrived. Indianapolis, traditionally a low-crime city, "was very late in the cocaine epidemic," says Mayor Stephen Goldsmith, "but then the drug wars followed crack, and continue to drive the homicide rate

1988 Crack. The high lasted only 10 minutes, so crack users often wanted more right away. That meant transactions involving extremely agitated people.

to unacceptable levels" (see "The trends of two cities" charts). Crack vials and crime-scene tape have become part of the day-to-day routine in neighborhoods like the Meadows. The proportion of Indianapolis arrestees testing positive for cocaine jumped from 24 percent in 1992 to 50 percent in 1994, and it has dipped only slightly since. The city's murder count, which was only 57 as recently as 1987, rose to 118 last year.

But in most big cities, the story is increasingly one of relative peace. The passing of the crack epidemic—along with the associated reduction in fear—is helping to disrupt the crucial link between kids and guns, with a hefty assist from the cops' antigun enforcement efforts. In New York, "our street research tells us kids are less inclined to carry guns these days," says Jeffrey Fagan of Columbia University's Center for Violence Research and Prevention.

The result is that violence among young people—which had pushed crime rates up starting in the mid-1980s—is finally headed in the opposite direction. Juvenile murder arrests declined by 3 percent from 1993 to 1994, 14 percent from 1994 to 1995, and another 14 percent from 1995 to 1996.

Still, the numbers obscure a sobering reality driven home by horrors like the shootings in Jonesboro, Ark. Though the 1996 juvenile murder arrest rate was the lowest since 1989, it was still 50 percent higher than the rate in the early 1980s. "The youth homicide problem looks better, but only because the early 1990s were so bad," says criminologist James Alan Fox of Northeastern University. "So let's not fool ourselves into thinking everything's resolved. It's not."

This raises another question: Is there any way of keeping crime from

getting worse again? Law enforcement officials are well aware that baby boomers' children are now reaching the traditionally crime-prone years of 15 to 24. Between 1996 and 2005, the teenage population will have increased by 20 percent, to more than 30 million by 2006—the largest number of teens since

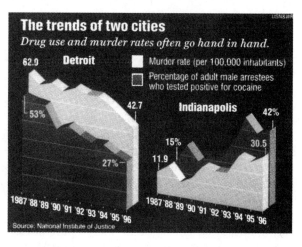

The trends of two cities
Drug use and murder rates often go hand in hand.

USN&WR

Detroit — 62.9
53% — 42.7
27%

☐ Murder rate (per 100,000 inhabitants)
☐ Percentage of adult male arrestees who tested positive for cocaine

Indianapolis
15% — 42%
11.9 — 30.5

1987 '88 '89 '90 '91 '92 '93 '94 '95 '96

Source: National Institute of Justice

1975. Some criminologists predict a *Mad Max* landscape of "superpredators," in which the number of teenage killers could once again top 4,000, as it did in the early 1990s.

Others argue that the fears are overblown: that the year-to-year rise is small and won't be that noticeable, that the growth in the number of teenagers will be offset by a continued fall in the crime rate for adults, and that the drop in teen violence for the past three years proves that it's hard to predict what teens will do. "Demographics do not have to be destiny," argues Attorney General Janet Reno. Perhaps not. In the past 15 years, public policy has indeed made a difference, by improving policing and incarcerating more criminals. But hindsight also teaches that sometimes things come along—like crack—that are unforeseeable and relatively impervious to political solutions. It's not clear whether policy makers or the public can develop the wisdom or political will to identify such incipient trends—a new popular drug, for example—and address them before they trigger another crime wave.

ANNALS OF CRIME

LAND OF THE STUPID

When you need a used Russian submarine, call Tarzan.

BY ROBERT I. FRIEDMAN

On a September day last year, at the tail end of Hurricane Floyd, I took a taxi ride to the Federal Detention Center in downtown Miami to interview a man known as Tarzan. His real name is Ludwig Fainberg, and until recently he was the ringleader of the Russian mob in South Florida. When I got to the prison, the guards took my passport, my keys, and a pack of chewing gum I had in my pocket. ("It'll cost us two thousand dollars to unjam a lock from that gum if an inmate gets hold of it," one of the guards said.) I was led to a large rectangular room where prisoners in gray jumpsuits silently waited for their lawyers and guests.

In a glass-walled cubicle at the back I spotted Tarzan, a pallid man in his early forties, glaring grimly as he slumped over a brown Formica table. He used to have wild, acid-rock hair, but now it had been shorn; he once took pride in a steroid-enhanced physique, but today he looked like a deflated tire. Tarzan slammed a thick document down on the table. It was his indictment, and it consisted of thirty counts, among them conspiring to distribute cocaine and heroin, buying stolen property, counterfeiting, and money laundering. "'United States versus Tarzan,'" he said, paraphrasing a bit. "I already spent a million dollars on lawyers. Who can fight the U.S. government?"

Since the collapse of Communism, the Mafiya, as it is known to outsiders (Russian gangsters affect disdain for the term), has become bigger, more brutal, and better armed; it is widely believed to be richer than any other criminal cartel—richer, even, than its counterpart in Colombia. The Russian mob buys and swaps drugs, money, handguns, assault carbines, submachine guns, anti-aircraft missiles, helicopters, plutonium, enriched uranium, and submarines. In 1996, James Moody, who was then the F.B.I.'s deputy assistant director in charge of organized crime, warned Congress that the Russian mob, which has thirty crime syndicates operating in more than seventeen North American cities, has "a very real chance" of becoming "the No.1 crime group in the United States." And, until recently, the No. 1 Russian crime figure in Miami was Ludwig Fainberg.

I began investigating the world of Russian organized crime in the late nineteen-eighties, venturing into strip clubs in New York and Miami, suburban homes in cities like Denver, and prison cells across the United States. Of all the mobsters I came into contact with, Tarzan was certainly the most garrulous. He first became conspicuous in Miami in the early nineties. A strip club he owned in a warehouse district near Hialeah Race Track—Porky's, inspired by the film of that name—attracted so many Russian mobsters, from Tashkent to Brighton Beach, that local policemen referred to it as Redfellas South. It was the place to go for recreational drugs, bootleg cigarettes, and stolen bottles of Stolichnaya—or, for bigger spenders, thousand-dollar-a-night Eurasian prostitutes and Colombian cocaine. At various times, Fainberg also owned not only a residence in Miami but a restaurant, several luxury cars, and a pleasure boat.

As we chatted in the prison cubicle, Tarzan spoke expansively about his disreputable past, but he also took pains to mention his eleemosynary activities, and described numerous fund-raisers that he had held for Jewish charities at a restaurant and night club he owned called Babushka. Fainberg, who is Jewish, insists that he never stole from Jewish organizations. "You've got to be kidding!" But, according to statements that he made to undercover agents for the Drug Enforcement Agency, the operating costs for these events tended to run high—eighty-five cents of every dollar. He certainly had the qualities of a mobster: he was greedy (he allegedly stole tip money from the strippers at his club); he was ruthless (he once forced a woman to eat gravel); and he was ambitious (he brokered a complicated negotiation involving the transfer of a Russian military submarine to Colombian narcotraffickers). In Russia, Fainberg told me, dishonesty is a trait that is bred in the bone. Deprivation has taught Russians to be cunning predators—it's the only way to survive, he said. "We lived by the eleventh commandment—don't get caught." Americans, by contrast, were trusting souls, he thought. Their rules were made to be broken. "America is the land of the stupid" he said. "The land of make-believe. If you ask me to describe America in one word, I would tell you this is Disneyland. And I'm surprised that Mickey Mouse is not yet the President."

Fainberg was born in 1958 in Odessa, a Black Sea port that was once the Marseilles of the Soviet Union. His parents soon divorced, and when he was three he moved with his mother, who had remarried, and his stepfather to Czernowitz, a small city in Ukraine. He sang in a boys' choir and participated in a boxing program set up by the Soviet military. More to the point, his stepfather, who worked for a Soviet factory that made rugs and fur hats, was a prosperous dealer on the burgeoning black market. He'd trade merchandise for choice cuts of meat, theatre tickets, and fresh vegetables. " My mother had nice clothes and jewelry," Fainberg said. "We took a vacation once a year to Odessa, a stunning city with a boardwalk and gorgeous beaches." It was a city, he said, "filled with mobsters and entertainers."

One day in 1972, when Fainberg was fourteen, his mother and stepfather announced that they were moving the family to Israel, where they hoped to increase their already considerable wealth. Ludwig, who had never known the family to identify with Judaism in any way, was confused. "Jew" was just something stamped on their passports, he thought, signifying their ethnic group. "I knew only that I was circumcised."

Before leaving, the Fainbergs converted their money into gold and diamonds, stashing some in shoes with hollow heels and hiding the rest in secret compartments in specially built tables and a piano, which they shipped to Israel. There they lived on a kibbutz. Fainberg, with his wild mane and his flair for daredevil stunts—he once jumped off a second-story roof—soon acquired his nickname. "One of the kids said, 'You look like Tarzan'—you know, build, hair, muscles."

At eighteen, Fainberg, who was now six feet one, was drafted into the Israeli Navy, and he applied to an élite Navy Commando unit. He washed out during basic training, and served the remaining three years of his service in the weapons-control room of a destroyer. In 1979, Fainberg moved to West Berlin, claiming to be a boxer defecting from the Soviet Union. Like many young Russian émigrés he says, he joined a mob crew. His specialty was credit-card fraud. Then he tried his hand at extortion. Working for a local racket—run, he later learned, by a notorious gangster named Efim (Fima) Laskin, who had sold weapons to the Red Brigades, in Italy—he was ordered to go to a certain restaurant and abduct a Russian named Leonid, who owed the gang money. Fainberg and his accomplices drove Leonid to a bank so that Leonid could get cash for them. But shortly after they arrived the hostage's friends—a group of rival mobsters—showed up and dealt Fainberg's men a severe beating. Fainberg, who happened to be in a store buying cigarettes at that moment, escaped, but the rival mob put out a contract on him. He fled to Cologne and went into hiding. A few years later, he landed in Brooklyn, at Brighton Beach.

From the middle to the late nineteen-seventies, the Soviet government was under intense diplomatic pressure from the West to let Jews emigrate freely. In response, the authorities searched the Gulag for Jewish criminals—some of them

quite recent converts to the faith—and shipped them to America. (During the Cold War, criminal-background information was unavailable to United States immigration officials, and their ability to screen criminals was severely limited.) More than forty thousand Russian Jews settled in Brighton Beach. Most were decent, hardworking citizens, but the criminals among them resumed their careers as thieves and swindlers. By the time Fainberg arrived, in 1984, Brighton Beach had already become the seat of the Organizatsiya, as the Russian Jewish mob was called. "It was the Wild West," Fainberg told me. "I took my gun everywhere."

Fainberg quickly discovered that there were two distinct communities in Brighton Beach. Affluent Russians lived in well-kept Art Deco apartment buildings near the ocean; poor Russians lived–sometimes ten to a room—in decaying clapboard houses amid crack dens on the area's many side streets. Even the local McDonald's had folded. Bordered on one side by the shore and on another by an enormous middle-class housing project, referred to by the émigrés as "the great wall of China," the Russians built a closed world. It was modelled on Odessa. On frigid winter mornings, beefy men in fur hats strolled the boardwalk, stopping at venders to buy piroshki. Movie houses showed first-run Russian-language films; the conversations in the cafés were in Russian and Ukrainian. Tarzan spent much of his time in mob haunts, flirting with the wives of big-time mafiosi and "getting into fistfights," as he recounts it. Soon after he arrived in Brooklyn, he married Maria Raichel, a princess of the Russian Mafiya and a beauty. (Maria's grandfather was said to have stabbed a man to death in Russia. Her first husband and his brother, known as Psyk—Russian for psycho—became high-level extortionists, but, because of their uncontrollable behavior, they eventually fell into violent conflict with other Russian gangsters, who ordered hits on them.)

Fainberg took up with a fellow-émigré named Yossif Roizis, known to his friends as Gregory, or Grisha. Their families had been friends in Ukraine and were neighbors in Israel. Roizis had spent three years in prison in Siberia for hitting a man who was recovering from an appendectomy—hitting him so hard that his fist penetrated the abdominal cavity and killed him. Now Roizis headed one of the most feared Russian gangs in Brighton Beach. He owned a wholesale furniture store with branches in Coney Island, Italy, and Russia, which the D.EA and a knowledgeable figure in the Genovese underworld say fronted for a heroin business involving Italian and Russian mobsters. Fainberg says that he helped Roizis's crew with torch jobs and extortion. He also went into business with the owners of a furniture store in nearby Bensonhurst. Roizis wanted Tarzan's partners, a brother and sister, to stock their store with his store's furniture. "I can't get them to do that, " Tarzan said. "Well, then it's time for them to disappear," Roizis replied. They did. ("I asked Roizis what happened to them," Fainberg said, "but he never told me anything.") Tarzan took over the business.

Inevitably, the Russian mobsters crossed paths with their Italian counterparts. One day, according to Fainberg, an old woman walked into the furniture store and asked to buy a twin-size mattress on credit. "You've got to be crazy," a clerk replied. Fainberg overheard the conversation and gave the woman the mattress and box spring as a gift. He even loaded it onto his truck and delivered it to her house. He said he felt sorry for her, and, besides, they had samples to spare. Two years later, a powerfully built Italian sauntered into a video store that Fainberg owned and asked for him. "I was scared shitless," Fainberg recalled. "He looked like Luca Brasi in 'Godfather.'" Introducing himself as Frank, the man said, "I'm the son of the old

woman you gave the mattress to. I owe you. Anything you want is yours."

Fainberg was awestruck. "You could feel his power," he said. "He was the kind of man who wouldn't take no for an answer.

Over the next several months, if the landlord attempted to raise the rent at the video store Tarzan would call Frank. When an Italian extortionist tried to shake Tarzan down, Frank's boys had the thug pistol-whipped. As we spoke, Tarzan repeatedly assured me that he didn't know the identity of his patron until, one day in 1987, he saw him identified in the *Times* as the late Frank Santora, a notable member of the Colombo organized-crime family. Santora had been shot twice at close range outside a dry-cleaning store on a quiet Brooklyn street.

After that, life became more dangerous for Fainberg and his friends. One of those singled out for merciless treatment was Alexander Slepinin, nicknamed the Colonel, a three-hundred-pound, six-foot-five black belt who claimed to have served with the Russian Special Forces in Afghanistan. Slepinin had tattoos of a panther and a dragon on his upper torso—signs that he had spent time in Soviet prisons. He was trained in a variety of martial arts, and kept a large collection of knives and machetes, which he used to dismember extortion victims in his bathtub before disposing of the body parts.

On a June morning in 1992, while Slepinin was sitting in his Cadillac on a residential street in the Sunset Park section of Brooklyn, he was ambushed by a group of Russians. According to eyewitnesses, the big man, wheezing heavily, begged his assailants for mercy. "We are not in the church," one of the hit men replied. Slepinin tried to squeeze out of the car through the passenger door, but he was shot three times in the back. The bullets were aimed to insure that his death would be agonizing. Thrashing and moaning, Slepinin continued to beg for his life. Two bullets to the back of the head

finally finished him off. "He was a big, huge motherfucker—a monster, a cold-blooded killer," one of the alleged assassins, an infamous Russian gangster named Monya Elson, told me during an interview at the Metropolitan Correctional Center in Manhattan. He was being held there on charges of heading a racketeering outfit called Monya's Brigade, which was responsible for three murders, including Slepinin. (The case is still pending.) Although Elson maintained that he was innocent, he also said, "The F.B.I. and everybody have to fucking give me an award."

Fainberg is more sentimental. "My mother loved the Colonel," he recalled gloomily. Even before Slepinin's death, Tarzan had decided that it was time once again to move to a safer neighborhood. He had not been getting along with his wife anyhow, he said, and in 1989 he left her, and Brighton Beach, and headed south.

Long before Fainberg got to Florida, in 1990, the Miami Beach Police Department had noticed that an inordinate number of newly arrived Russian taxi-drivers were involved in many of the same crimes that had made the Italian Mafia so powerful: extortion, narcotics gambling, and prostitution. Diana Fernandez, an assistant United States Attorney, says that, following the collapse of the Soviet Union, in 1991, "Miami was a boomtown for the Russian mob." The mobsters had become rich in the era of privatization, and they bought rows of luxury condominiums in North Miami Beach or spent millions for mansions on Fisher Island, one of the city's most fashionable residential areas. Several of the buyers were former high-ranking Russian military officers and ex-K.G.B. officials. They had found their perfect dacha: a base for money laundering which was also convenient to South American cocaine.

In Miami, Fainberg met William Seidle, a very successful car dealer.

A veteran D.E.A. agent told me that Seidle has been under investigation by numerous federal agencies for more than twenty years, although he has never been indicted. Seidle's friends respond to these allegations with bafflement. "Bill Seidle is a great guy," William Lehman, a former Democratic congressman, told me. Lehman, who represented North Dade County for twenty years and has known Seidle for fifty years, says that Seidle enjoyed Fainberg's "outrageousness" but that he himself ran a "kosher" business.

Seidle liked Fainberg from the moment they met. "Tarzan was a boisterous, bigmouthed yiddel," he told me in Miami, speaking with obvious affection. "He's a Jewboy, you know. Just a bigmouth kid, always bragging, boisterous—but very nice, very kind." Seidle saw in Fainberg a younger version of himself: a risk-taker. In Miami, Fainberg ran a furniture and moving company out of a warehouse owned by Seidle. A local charitable foundation gave Fainberg donated clothes, which he sold for profit. Before long, Seidle and Fainberg decided that there was a lot of money to be made in strip clubs. According to government informants, in 1991 Seidle staked Tarzan to the club that became Porky's, in return for a hidden share of the off-the-book profits. Tarzan was proud of his upward mobility in his adopted land: "From schmattes to the big tits!" he told me. "Can you imagine! What a country!" Seidle, for his part, denies receiving club profits, acknowledging only that he collected rent as the club's landlord.

At Porky's, Fainberg held court for visiting dons from the former Soviet Union. One of the most powerful was Anzor Kikalischvili, a Moscow-based businessman who had long been on a C.I.A list of prominent Soviet organized-crime figures and, in a conversation taped by the F.B.I., once boasted that he had more than six hundred "soldiers" in South Florida. In one conversation, Kikalischvili warned a Russian couple with whom he had

a partnership in a Miami deli that if they didn't pay him two hundred and fifty thousand dollars for his share he would skin them like animals. The couple fled the country, and Fainberg, who had introduced them to Kikalischvili, became a partner in the deli.

In addition to extortion, Fainberg had a habit of degrading women. "This is cultural," he explained to me, in an effort to defend himself. "In Russia, it was normal for men to beat women. In the stories Dostoyevsky, Chekhov, and Gorky wrote, to slap a woman is normal, it's part of life. And to do something like that in America, something that you grew up with—you're arrested, for domestic violence!" In an incident observed by the F.B.I. and the D.E.A. from surveillance cars across the street from Porky's, Fainberg chased a girlfriend out of the club and decked her. On another occasion, he allegedly beat a girlfriend's head against the door of his Mercedes until the car was covered with blood; and he regularly abused his common-law wife, a frail young woman named Faina Tannenbaum whom he had brought with him from New York. When the police arrived at their home in response to 911 calls, she would quiver in fear, and was sometimes found huddled inside a locked car with her daughter. Tannenbaum never pressed charges, however. In 1996, as she was driving to pick up her daughter at a day-care center, her car hit a tree and she was killed. Her blood-alcohol level was far over the legal limit, and the car was travelling at more than ninety miles per hour in a thirty m.p.h. zone.

Fainberg's ambitions went beyond strip clubs. According to F.B.I. wiretap affidavits and Fainberg's own admissions to undercover agents, he and Seidle had a "grow lab" for hemp in a warehouse near Hialeah, with giant halogen lights. (Seidle denies this.) Fainberg boasted to two government undercover agents that

he had a connection for "tons" of marijuana from Jamaica.

For Fainberg, marijuana was just a gateway drug. In the early nineties, the Mafiya had little contact with the Colombian drug cartels, but Fainberg helped forge a connection, brokering cocaine deals between the Colombians and the most powerful mob family in Russia's St. Petersburg. In one instance, according to the D.E.A., he conspired to smuggle more than a hundred kilograms of cocaine a month in crates of frozen shrimp which were flown from Guayaquil, Ecuador, to St. Petersburg. He also ran small amounts of cocaine directly out of Miami. (He denies this.) And wiretap affidavits allege that his couriers "bodied" cocaine by the kilo.

Fainberg's principal link to the Colombians was through two men, Juan Almeida and Fernando Birbragher. Almeida, who is the son of a Cuban-American real estate and construction mogul in Miami, had been a major cocaine dealer since the mid-nineteen-eighties, according to the D.E.A. Birbragher, a Colombian and a friend of Seidle's, had strong ties to the Medellín and the Cali cartels. He was indicted in 1982 on charges of laundering seventy-three million dollars for Colombian drug lords; he pleaded guilty in 1984 to a lesser charge of conspiring to defraud the United States government. One D.E.A. agent told me that Birbragher was a very close friend of the late Pablo Escobar, the notorious leader of the Medellín cartel. "Birbragher used to buy Escobar sports cars and do a lot of favors for him," the agent said. D.E.A. officials also strongly suspect that Birbragher laundered drug money for Manuel Noriega, the former Panamanian President, who was convicted in 1992 of drug trafficking, racketeering, and money laundering.

Fainberg worked closely with Almeida, who told him that they wouldn't have trouble with the law as long as they didn't sell drugs in America. According to F.B.I. sources, Fainberg's cocaine business did so well that he soon found himself fending off hostile takeover attempts from other Russian mobsters eager to do business with the Colombians.

By the mid-nineties, the Colombians had a thriving arrangement with the Russians—the Colombians supplied the cocaine and the Russians laundered the money. Now, according to D.E.A. officials, Fainberg and Almeida saw a way to expand this business. The Mafiya had access to military hardware from the former Soviet Union. Goods stored in deteriorating facilities and guarded by indifferent, bribable soldiers were easily available—everything from aircraft and armored personnel carriers to submarines.

In the fall of 1992, Fainberg travelled to Latvia, where, he told me, he knew people who could help him procure six heavy-lift Russian military helicopters. The choppers were intended for Pablo Escobar, who hoped to use them to transport chemicals to cocaine-refining laboratories in the jungle. (Fainberg told undercover agents that a "rich American Jew"—thought by the D.E.A. to be Seidle—was financing ten per cent of the cost of the trip, a charge Seidle heatedly denies.) Fainberg was accompanied by Almeida, Birbragher, and a group of Colombian and Cuban thugs. The trip was a failure, and Almeida and Birbragher blamed Fainberg. "He is an idiot," Almeida told me with disgust. "He didn't know anybody."

But in mid-1993 Fainberg succeeded. According to the D.E.A., he and Almeida bought as many as six MI-8 Russian military helicopters for something under a million dollars each. Fainberg later boasted to undercover agents that he had bought the helicopters to traffic cocaine for a group of "Colombian drug barons" headed by Escobar, and, after purchasing the helicopters, he stayed behind in Moscow to oversee the final details. At the request of the Colombians, Fainberg later said, the helicopters' seats were removed and

fuel bladders were added to extend their range. With everything set, Fainberg went to a final meeting with the sellers. He was taken into a conference room and left alone with two big Russian guys. "They were like heavy weight lifters," he told me. "They were incredible hulks. I was in deep shit." One of the men opened the window. Parked outside were a Range Rover, a Mitsubishi Montero, a Lexus, and a Mercedes. When the man whistled, the doors opened and out came men armed with automatic weapons. "Well, that's my people," the man said to Fainberg. "I was waiting for your people."

"At that point, I understood I'm not going to leave Russia," Fainberg recalled. "I'm going to be buried in the motherland." The weight lifters informed him that he had neglected to pay the local Mafiya for permission to buy the helicopters. Fortunately for Fainberg, "his people" —the Colombians—held a certain mystique for the Russians, and by alluding to his close connections with them he was able to buy time.

He telephoned Anzor Kikalischvili, the Russian don, who happened to be visiting Miami. Kikalischvili, who wanted Fainberg's help in obtaining a green card, said he'd make some calls and try to smooth things over, but meanwhile Fainberg would have to explain why he hadn't cut "the boys" in for a share. In another series of frantic phone calls, Fainberg described his predicament to Almeida. Almeida advised him to tell the Russians that the helicopters were for Pablo Escobar and that no one had told Escobar he was required to pay a bribe. Fainberg and Almeida hoped that the Russians might make an exception for Escobar, but the Russians were stubborn. If Escobar wanted the choppers, they replied, he would have to come to Moscow himself

Almeida says he decided that the only way to get the helicopters—and to save Fainberg—was to pose as Escobar. At Sheremetyevo Airport, in Moscow, Almeida, dressed like

the Colombian, was welcomed by a motorcade of thick-necked men driving black Mercedeses. (This is Almeida's account. Tarzan never mentioned an Escobar impersonation to me.) Almeida says he was escorted like a head of state to a five-star hotel in the center of the city and led into a dark room, where more thick-necked men sat around a long conference table. Almeida walked past them to the head of the table, where the don presided. There was a nervous silence. Suddenly, the Russian seized him in a bear hug and cried, "Pablo! Pablo Escobar! What took you so long? Let's do some real shit. Cocaine!"

To celebrate their new friendship, the Russians took Almeida and Fainberg out for a night on the town. They went to a dingy boxing ring called the Samurai Club, where chain-smoking mobsters and their girlfriends, wearing Italian designer clothes, had gathered to watch a match. Young men dressed in street clothes were led into the ring. Mafiya rules: only one could walk out alive. Blood spattered the crowd as spectators swilled vodka and placed bets on their favorite combatant. As implausible as this seems, Fainberg and Almeida have separately offered almost identical versions of the incident. The spectacle went on through the night. There was no air-conditioning in the club, and the stench of blood, Tarzan says, nearly made him vomit. The following day, he was permitted to fly out of Moscow. The helicopters, Fainberg told various federal undercover agents, were subsequently delivered to the Colombian drug barons.

Meanwhile, in the United States, the activities of the Russian mob were alarming a great many law-enforcement agencies. In 1994, Louis J. Freeh, the director of the F.B.I. said that the Russian Mafiya posed "a significant direct threat to the United States." In a few years, the Russians had supplanted the Cubans as one of the top crime groups in South Florida. Local, state, and federal officials set up a task force called Operation Odessa, and eventually developed ties with Canadian, Russian, and German police. Richard Gregorie, a bearded, professorial assistant U.S. Attorney who helped launch Operation Odessa, says of the Russians, "Their obvious sophistication far exceeds that of La Cosa Nostra at its infant stage."

Operation Odessa's agents had so far been unable to infiltrate Fainberg's close-knit world. That assignment fell to Fainberg's old Brighton Beach friend Grisha Roizis, who had by this time acquired the nickname the Cannibal. (A booking sergeant in Brooklyn had once called him "a fucking dirty Jew," and Roizis, although handcuffed, managed to bite off the tip of the sergeant's nose.) Roizis was by now indebted to the D.E.A. In 1992, he had been jailed in Romania on a U.S. warrant for heroin trafficking, and he became an informant in return for his release. He had no trouble getting close to Fainberg. "Gregory and I were like brothers," Fainberg told me. "He's the one who helped me when I arrived in Brighton Beach. He *loved* me!"

In October of 1994, Roizis, using seventy-two thousand dollars in cash supplied by the D.E.A., bought a managing partnership in Babushka, Fainberg's restaurant. Many people found the Cannibal's presence in the restaurant disturbing. A Brooklynite named Vladimir Ginzburg, who the F.B.I. believe was a key operative in Fainberg's cigarette-bootlegging operation, had repeatedly told Fainberg that his buddy was working for the federal government. "I warned Tarzan about the rumors," Ginzburg said. "Tarzan didn't listen. So I asked Tarzan why he trusted him. He said they were both from the same town. He knew his father. He had his friends checked out. And Roizis had a cruel criminal past. That counts for a lot. Tarzan didn't have a comparable past—and Tarzan wasn't so

smart. He had steroids for brains. He had a big-muscle peanut brain."

With Fainberg's confidence secured, Roizis got to his work. One day, a man named Alexander Yasevich walked into Babushka, posing as an arms-and-heroin dealer, and Roizis embraced him like a long-lost comrade. Fainberg dimly recognized Yasevich from Brooklyn; Yasevich had moved there from Odessa as a teen-ager. But, unbeknownst to Fainberg, Yasevich had joined the Marines, and then become an undercover agent for the D.EA.

Five days later, they met again, at Porky's. Fainberg was in a mood to boast, and told Yasevich of his criminal exploits. The two men began to hang out together. Yasevich was offered free sex at the hotel next door to Porky's, and ate in expensive Japanese restaurants. They consumed enormous amounts of exotic concoctions, such as raw quail eggs drenched in *sake* and ice-cold vodka. The drinking and kibbitzing paid off for Yasevich. He learned that Fainberg was in the midst of executing his most audacious caper yet: the purchase of a hundred-million-dollar Soviet-era diesel-powered submarine, for "the people associated with the late Pablo Escobar." (Escobar had been hunted down and killed by Colombian authorities in December of 1993.) As a gift, Yasevich gave Fainberg a "safe" cell phone, which, of course, was closely monitored by the D.E.A.

When Fainberg was first approached about the submarine, the prospect unnerved him. The Russian helicopters had nearly cost him his life. But this time he made sure to clear the deal through Anzor Kikalischvili, whom he met with in Helsinki and, later, in Moscow. Finally—through the most powerful crime boss in St. Petersburg, a man named Misha Brave—Tarzan, Almeida, and Nelson Yester, a Cuban-American on the lam from a federal cocaine indictment, met two corrupt, high-ranking Russian

military officers. Fainberg and Yester were taken to the front gate of Kronstadt, a sprawling naval base in the Baltic, where numerous abandoned diesel submarines bobbed on their sides, leaking oil, fluid, and battery acid into the harbor. Richard Palmer, who was a C.I.A. station chief in the former Soviet Union, told me that at such bases "anything is available—the Soviet fleet is rotting, and the sailors haven't been paid for months."

Initially, the Miamians wanted to buy a huge attack submarine for Escobar's East Coast drug trade. But a retired Russian submarine captain whom Fainberg nicknamed the Admiral suggested that they operate on the West Coast, where America's anti-submarine net was less active. According to the D.E.A., a Russian active-duty officer suggested that Fainberg and his associates buy a small, diesel-powered Piranha-class submarine. Made of titanium and much quieter than other models, the Piranhas are used to plant saboteurs, troops, and spies behind enemy lines. But the Colombians considered the Piranha too expensive, and they wanted a submarine with greater range.

They finally agreed on a three-hundred-foot-long Foxtrot-class attack submarine, a model manufactured between 1958 and 1984, with a range of several thousand miles. It could disappear for days at a time and resurface, when required, to deliver drugs. Drug lords calculated that it could carry up to forty tons of cocaine. The Admiral told Fainberg that he had slipped a similar submarine past the Americans during the Cuban missile crisis. The Colombians planned to base the sub, which would be demilitarized and retrofitted to resemble an oceanographic-research vessel, in Panama or somewhere else on the Pacific side of Central or South America. From there, it would transport the drugs underwater to a ship outside Santa Barbara's territorial waters. The ship would then deliver the cocaine to ports along the Pacific

Coast. A consortium of St. Petersburg mobsters and two active-duty admirals wanted twenty million dollars for the vessel. Fainberg bargained them down to $5.7 million. (A million of that would be his fee.) The money was to be passed through a dummy company in Switzerland in order to give an air of legitimacy to the oceanographic-research front. Fainberg planned to hire the retired captain for five hundred dollars a month and to secure a crew of seventeen to twenty-five men for a two-year contract; he even got permission to take photographs of the vessel to send to the Colombians. Tarzan told undercover agents that, at a party at a dacha, Misha Brave, the St. Petersburg crime boss, made a side deal with him to procure a "test shipment" of ten kilograms of cocaine from Miami for thirty thousand dollars a kilo. (Fainberg's cost per kilo was four thousand dollars.) To Tarzan, everything looked good.

On Tuesday, January 21, 1997, Fainberg was pulled over on a Miami street by a marked Metro-Dade Police Department vehicle. He was driving a white 1996 Jaguar convertible. As he spoke with the officers, two agents from the D.E.A., Brent Eaton and Detective Joseph McMahon, who had been trailing him in an unmarked car, approached. Eaton and McMahon introduced themselves and invited him to join them in their car. They told Fainberg that he was in trouble and would be arrested. They asked him to accompany them to a place where they and a few other officers could speak with him confidentially. Fainberg argued that he was a "nicer person" than they thought and said that he hadn't "done anything wrong."

At the interview site, a D.E.A. training room near Miami International Airport, Fainberg was offered a seat and a cup of coffee. McMahon told him that he was giving him a chance to work with the government

rather than be arrested. Fainberg replied that he could be very useful to the government but was not well acquainted with United States laws and preferred to consult with his attorney before making a decision. Eaton told Fainberg that although he certainly had a right to consult with his lawyer, a man named Kieran Fallon, it might not be a wise decision, since Fallon represented other targets of the investigation. "I thought you would tell me what you have and ask me questions," Fainberg said, according to a transcript of the interrogation. "I don't know what to say, because I don't know what you think I have done."

McMahon asked Fainberg if he had ever bought liquor for Porky's or for Babushka from any source other than a legitimate wholesaler or liquor store. "Never!" Fainberg declared.

The detective asked him about his relationship with Anzor Kikalischvili.

"Anzor! I know nothing about what he does in Russia," Fainberg said. "I met him at my club. He is a sex maniac, always looking for girls. I helped him once when he opened a bagel store in Aventura."

"Tell us about Juan Almeida's activities," McMahon said.

"I don't know what he is up to," Fainberg said. "He speaks Spanish most of the time."

"You mean you travel all over the world with Almeida and you don't know what he's up to?"

"Yes."

"You know that those helicopters you get go to Colombian drug traffickers," McMahon said.

"They go to legitimate people," Fainberg replied.

When the officers accused him of lying, Fainberg said, "Maybe I should go to jail, then find out what you have."

The agents had had enough. They placed him under arrest, handcuffed him, and drove him to the D.E.A. processing room, where he was fingerprinted, photographed, and allowed to call his attorney.

Almeida surrendered to the authorities several days later. (His accomplice Nelson Yester remains at large.) Not only had Fainberg bragged about their activities to various undercover agents but he had even introduced Almeida to Yasevich, the D.E.A. undercover agent. At the time, Almeida told Yasevich that he represented a client with unlimited funds who was interested in buying a Russian diesel submarine; he added, with a laugh, that the vessel was going to be used to transport stolen gold off the coast of the Philippines.

Almeida, a suave man with a salesman's charm, told me in Miami that the sub was intended for an underwater museum in South Florida. (Fainberg makes a similar claim.) After Almeida was arrested, his lawyer, Roy Black, said that the sub was intended to carry tourists around the Galápagos Islands. As for the Russian helicopters, Almeida claimed that the aircraft were actually contracted by Helitaxi, a Bogotá-based company, to do heavy lifting at oil rigs in South America.

The investigation produced five hundred and thirty wiretapped conversations, in English, Russian, Hebrew, Yiddish, and Spanish. (It took a team of twenty translators a year to transcribe and analyze the tapes.) On the tapes and in conversations with the undercover agents, Fainberg implicated himself and others in numerous crimes. Louis J. Terminello, Fainberg's civil lawyer, says the only thing that his client is guilty of is having a big mouth. "It's the high-school kid who wants the high-school girl to believe that he's got the biggest dick in the world."

After months of sullen denial, Fainberg decided to coöperate. "He's admitted to everything," a D.EA agent named Pamela Brown told me several months after his arrest. "He keeps saying, 'Well, this would have all been legal in Russia.' " But then, after negotiating at least six proffer agreements, the feds decided to let him stand trial. They could not corroborate much of his information, and he said that he would never testify unless he was released on bail. There was little likelihood of that happening. The feds had a good idea what Fainberg would do if he obtained bail: informants reported that he was working with several powerful Israeli drug dealers in Miami who were going to help him flee to Israel; it is difficult to extradite Israeli nationals.

Finally, Fainberg, who faced a possible life sentence, pleaded guilty to one count of federal racketeering, which included conspiring to sell cocaine, heroin, and the Russian submarine, and sundry other crimes. He testified against Almeida, who was convicted of conspiracy to smuggle and distribute. "Tarzan's big mouth ruined my life," Almeida says. According to well-placed government sources, Almeida, who is awaiting sentencing, made threats against the judge and the prosecution team.

As for the Cannibal, Grisha Roizis—the man who helped the feds the most—in July of 1998 he seemed to be without a care in the world as he stood erect, his Popeye-like arms bulging out of a lime-green polo shirt, calmly awaiting sentencing in Federal District Court. In return for services rendered to the government, the judge sentenced him to time served and waived further jail time.

Less than a year later, Roizis was in trouble again: he was arrested by the Italian police in Rimini for money laundering, extortion, kidnapping, and racketeering. Most of his victims were small-time Russian entrepreneurs in Italy. Some of his illicit gains were allegedly passed through the Bank of New York. Apparently, shortly after working for the D.E.A. Roizis had begun to run a thriving criminal empire on the Adriatic Coast.

The Russian mob in South Florida today is the hub of a sophisticated and ruthless operation. But Ludwig Fainberg is no longer a member. At the conclusion of my conversations with him in prison in September, he said ruefully, "America's built on Mafia! All over the world, when you ask 'What do you know about America?' they say, 'Mafia, "Godfather," Bugsy Siegel, Meyer Lansky!' I swear, I can't believe John Gotti got life in jail. How can you kill your own history?"

Then, in October, after living in America for fifteen years, Fainberg was deported to Israel, with fifteen hundred dollars in his pocket. He had served a mere thirty-three months. His light sentence was in return for his operation which reportedly included providing intelligence on several alleged Russian mob heavyweights. Even as he awaited deportation, Fainberg told me that, given what he knows about the sex industry, he'll soon be rich again. He was already cooking up a new scheme. "I'm going to Cuba. A few of my Russian friends already own resorts there." But his enthusiasm for the land he was leaving was undimmed. "I love this country!" Tarzan said. "It's so easy to steal here!"

The Well-Marked Roads to Homicidal Rage

By LAURIE GOODSTEIN and WILLIAM GLABERSON

Shots explode at a school in Oregon, a brokerage office in Atlanta, or a church in Fort Worth, and the nation is witness to another sudden, seemingly random violent rampage. Before the ambulances leave, the news crews arrive. The killers' neighbors, friends or families submit to interviews, and inevitably, they say something like this: "He just snapped."

But the killers do not just snap. An examination by The New York Times of 100 rampage murders found that most of the killers spiraled down a long slow slide, mentally and emotionally. Most of them left a road map of red flags, spending months plotting their attacks and accumulating weapons, talking openly of their plans for bloodshed. Many showed signs of serious mental health problems.

But in case after case, the Times review found, the warning signs were missed: by a tattered mental health care system; by families unable to face the evidence of serious mental turmoil in their children or siblings; by employers, teachers and principals who failed to take the threats seriously; by the police who, when alerted to the danger by frightened relatives, neighbors or friends, were incapable of intervening before the violence erupted.

James Davis, whose co-workers had nicknamed him Psycho, warned his colleagues at a tool warehouse in Asheville, N.C., "If they ever decide to fire me, I'll take two or three of them with me." His employers did fire him, and feared he would respond with violence, but despite his threats, they failed to protect his co-workers when Mr. Davis returned to take his revenge.

In 34 of the 100 cases, however, families or friends of the killers desperately did try to find help for a person they feared was a ticking time bomb, but were rebuffed by the police, school administrators or mental health workers.

Sylvia Seegrist caromed in and out of mental institutions 12 times in 10 years, while her parents searched for a residential program where she could stay in treatment. They knew she was dangerous. She had

stabbed a psychologist and tried to strangle her mother, and had hidden a gun in her apartment. But each time, she was released from the hospital when she seemed to improve.

"We were always fearful that maybe some tragedy would happen," said Ruth S. Seegrist, Sylvia's mother. "She threatened it: 'Someday before I kill myself, I'll bring some people down with me.'" Sylvia opened fire in a suburban Philadelphia shopping mall in 1985, killing three people and wounding seven.

In response to the recent spate of rampage-style mass shootings in schools, workplaces, stores and other public places, The New York Times re-examined 100 such violent incidents that occurred in the United States over the last 50 years. The Times gathered extensive information on all 100, and looked closely at more than 25 of the cases, a surprising number of which attracted little but local attention. The examination included reviews of court cases, news coverage and mental health records, and interviews with families and friends, psychologists and victims, in an effort to glean what the people closest to each tragedy had learned. In some cases, reporters questioned the killers themselves.

Based on this information, The Times found that in 63 of the 100 cases (which involved 102 killers), the killers made general threats of violence to others in advance. Fifty-five of the 100 cases involved killers who regularly expressed explosive anger or frustration, and 35 killers had a history of violent behavior and assaults. They were so noticeably unstable that even in their very separate circles they had been awarded similar nicknames: "Crazy Pat," "Crazy John," "Crazy Joe."

And in 40 cases, family members and others said they noticed a sudden change in behavior in the period before the rampage.

"The more you find out about each of these cases, the more it makes sense," said Prof. Dewey G. Cornell, a clinical psychologist at the University of Virginia and director of the Virginia Youth Violence Project, which

studies school safety and violence prevention. "This notion that someone just snaps is based on ignorance and denial," Professor Cornell said. "People don't just snap. Pressures build up."

Many psychologists caution that it is impossible to predict violent behavior, and that most people who threaten violence never follow through. Often, it is only in retrospect that each killer's life appears to be a coherent chilling narrative foretelling obvious danger. Looking back, it is easy to marvel, how could the people who knew the murderer have failed to see it coming? In particular, how could so many psychiatric workers, and even the police, have missed the warning signs?

In many cases, there was no single person in the potential killer's life to put together the lethal clues. Colleagues, friends, family members, mental health professionals, teachers and the police may have independently sensed something disturbing, but they did not communicate with one another. Frightened neighbors or co-workers decided it was safest to keep their distance. Friends laughed off homicidal talk. Parents did not know where to turn, or just hoped the irrational fury was merely a phase.

"It's like looking at the night sky," said Robert Granacher Jr., a psychiatrist in Lexington, Ky., who has examined the records of several rampage murderers. "If you only see one or two stars, you may not see the whole constellation. It's the same with these fragmentary bits of information; no one has the whole picture."

In the end, the review of these cases suggests that if people understood more about mental illness and connected the clues, many of these types of rampage killings could be prevented.

IN rural Giles County, Tenn., on Nov. 15, 1995—before school shootings regularly made headlines—a slight 17-year-old strode down the hall of Richland School with his black .22 Remington Viper.

His name was Jamie Rouse, and as always, he was dressed in black. He walked up to two female teachers who were chatting in the hall, and without a word shot each of them in the head. One teacher was gravely wounded, the other died. Then Jamie Rouse smiled and aimed for the school's football coach. But a student named Diane Collins happened to cross his path. A bullet tore through her throat. She was 16 when she died that day.

Jamie Rouse had sent distress signals for years to the adults in his life. More startling, the police say he had told as many as five teenage friends exactly how he planned to bring his rifle to school and begin killing. None of them had called anyone for help. In fact, the night before, word of the planned massacre was passed like macabre gossip along a chain of students, from Jamie, to his close friend Stephen Abbott, to a teenager that Mr. Abbott worked with at the gas station, Billy Rogers.

"He told me something was going to happen at school the next day, that I was going to lose a couple of friends," Mr. Rogers later testified. "Steve told me if there was a God he better make it snow tonight so we ain't got school tomorrow."

The rampage killers in the study, young and old, often talked for months in advance about their murderous plans. And in 54 of the 100 cases, killers like Jamie Rouse provided explicit descriptions of who, where or when they intended to kill.

Charles Whitman, the infamous sniper who shot 45 people, killing 14, from atop the tower on the campus of the University of Texas at Austin in 1966, had told a college psychiatrist four months before the attack that he had been "thinking about going up on the tower with a deer rifle and start shooting people."

Michael Carneal, a high school freshman in Paducah, Ky., told schoolmates that "it would be cool" to shoot into a student prayer group. He did as he had promised, killing three people and injuring five in 1997.

Andrew Wurst, 14, showed a group of friends a gun hidden in his father's dresser drawer and told them he planned to use nine shells to kill nine people he hated, and then kill himself. In 1998, he started shooting at his eighth-grade prom, killing a popular teacher and injuring three other people.

In case after case, friends, family members and others who heard the threats and did not take action later said they did not act because it seemed unfathomable that a human being would carry through with such threats. Others said they had heard the killer boast of violence so often that, like the villagers hardened to the boy who cried wolf, they just did not take it seriously.

In testimony, Stephen Ray, one of Jamie Rouse's closest friends, said that it had sounded ridiculous when Mr. Rouse "might have" said something about shooting someone the day before the killings, when Mr.

Rouse was fuming over a fender-bender with a schoolmate's car.

Mr. Ray, now 21 and a college student in Knoxville, trembled in an interview in his dormitory this winter when he said it was hard to tell at the time that Jamie Rouse's blustery threats were real. Even when Mr. Rouse showed up in the morning with a rifle and a box of bullets, Mr. Ray said, he did not believe Jamie would really do it.

"It wasn't a joke," Mr. Ray said in a tone of amazement. "It wasn't a high school prank. It was something real."

Tennessee prosecutors said they were frustrated that legal rules barred them from charging Mr. Ray with a crime because he did nothing active to foster the plan. They did prosecute the teenager who drove Mr. Rouse to school that morning.

Failing to act in the face of warning signs, the prosecutors said, was not a crime. In retrospect, there were many people guilty of that.

In ninth grade, Jamie had scratched an inverted cross on his forehead, a symbol other students had told him was a sign of Satan worship. Many people, including teachers, had noticed the mark, which lasted a few weeks, and talked about it among themselves.

At home during his junior year, Jamie held his brother Jeremy at gunpoint and threatened to kill him. As punishment, Jamie's parents took away his gun.

As his senior year began, he submitted his entry for the yearbook: "I, Satan, James Rouse, leave my bad memories here to my two brothers." By that time, according to testimony at his trial, Jamie Rouse was working nights, taking Max Alert to stay awake and Sominex to get to sleep, and listening to heavy metal music cranked very loud because it drowned out the voices in his head that he later told psychiatrists he had been hearing at the time.

The spring before the shootings Mr. Rouse got into a violent fight with two other boys at school. But when teachers broke it up, "Jamie just would not calm down," recalled Ronald W. Shirey Jr., the football coach that Jamie had missed shooting, in an interview in his living room a few miles from the school. "He was just totally out of control, and saying, 'I will kill you,'" Mr. Shirey said.

The school called the police after that fight. Mr. Rouse faced juvenile charges and was suspended for three days.

But time passed. His mother later said it had not occurred to her to get counseling for him. And when hunting season started, Jamie's parents gave him his rifle back.

Long after the crime, Mr. Shirey said, when government investigators sought to study ways to prevent school shootings, they asked him to circulate a survey among the teachers at Richland School, which has students from kindergarten through 12th grade,

to gather information about Jamie Rouse. No survey came back with more than a paragraph, he said.

"You can't find a teacher up there that was close to Jamie Rouse since elementary school," Mr. Shirey said. "Nobody knew enough about him to say anything."

The adults noticed Jamie Rouse but did not know him, and the teenagers who knew him did not tell.

SHE was dressed in the green Army fatigues and knit cap she wore all four seasons of the year as she drove into the parking lot of the Springfield Mall in suburban Philadelphia. She leaped out of her car firing a Ruger semiautomatic rifle, and continued spraying bullets as she ran through the mall, killing three people and injuring seven, all strangers. Among the dead was a 2-year-old boy whose family had been shopping for a church charity fashion show.

Sylvia Seegrist was 25 the day of her murder spree in 1985. Her crime was the culmination of 10 years of mounting psychosis, crippling delusions and violent assaults on people who tried to help her.

Her mother, in a recent interview in her apartment a few miles from the site of Ms. Seegrist's rampage, remembered the "feelings of hopelessness, helplessness, despair, of incredible sadness" as she and her husband watched their only daughter overtaken by schizophrenia.

They also feared her. "I'll take you out," Mrs. Seegrist recalls her daughter threatening.

The Times' study found that many of the rampage killers, including Sylvia Seegrist, suffered from severe psychosis, were known by people in their circles as being noticeably ill and needing help, and received insufficient or inconsistent treatment from a mental health system that seemed incapable of helping these especially intractable patients.

Only a small percentage of mentally ill people are violent, and many advocates bristle at any link between mental illness and violence out of concern that it will further stigmatize an already mistreated population.

However, the Times investigation of this particular style of violence—public rampage killings—turned up an extremely high association between violence and mental illness. Forty-seven of the killers had a history of mental health problems before they killed; 20 had been hospitalized for psychiatric problems; 42 had been seen by mental health professionals.

Psychiatric drugs had been prescribed at some point before the rampages to 24 of the killers, and 14 of those people were not taking their prescribed drugs when they killed. Diagnoses of mental illness are often difficult to pin down, so The Times tabulated behavior: 23 killers showed signs of serious depression before the killings, and 49 expressed paranoid ideas.

Some of the killers who survived their rampages have made it clear they preferred to be thought of as criminal rather than mentally ill. Back in 1966, Robert Benjamin Smith, an 18-year-old high school senior in Mesa, Ariz., said he believed he was God when he herded five women and two children into the back room of a beauty school, forced them to lie down in a circle and methodically shot each person in the head, killing five of them.

In a letter Mr. Smith sent to a Times reporter from prison in January, he brushed off questions about illness and wrote, "Lessons? The sole thing I have learned worth the telling is the ironclad necessity of retaining control over one's essential bodily fluids." He blamed "sexual self-stimulation" for his crime and noted that he had tried to amputate his penis while in prison using the pull-tab from a can of diet soda.

"The more ill they are, the less sensibility there is" in the violent attack itself, said Anthony G. Hempel, chief forensic psychiatrist at the Vernon campus of North Texas State Hospital. Dr. Hempel, who has studied mass murderers, said that in contrast to the killers who "go postal," gunning for their bosses, "when someone goes and kills strangers or they kill children, the odds of them being mentally ill are higher."

Sylvia Seegrist was first hospitalized at 16, and schizophrenia was diagnosed. Each of the dozen times she was discharged, psychiatrists deemed that she no longer posed a threat to herself or others.

No one said she was getting better, though. At the local health club Ms. Seegrist was seen taking steam baths in her camouflage clothing. At the library, she spouted a tangle of theories about nuclear weapons, energy shortages and famine. Between her daughter's hospitalizations, Mrs. Seegrist found a gun in Sylvia's apartment, she said. Ms. Seegrist told her mother she planned to use it to kill her parents and then herself.

Mrs. Seegrist said the family could not afford private rehabilitation programs, and their insurance covered only short-term hospitalization.

Sylvia Seegrist, now 39, is serving a life sentence at a prison in Pennsylvania. She declined an interview, instead writing two letters to The Times, a weave of lucid fragments and unintelligible passages about benzene and Styrofoam. On the back of an envelope, she writes that her killings were a form of public service.

She also seems to assert that she had to kill to ensure she would be imprisoned instead of being sent yet again to a state mental hospital.

"Sure had all kinds of theories in my head," she wrote, "expressed them at political meetings, just doll, understand, please 10 yrs. of beat-up, orphan in state hospitals that are 300 % worse than even Sing-Sing prison. All the throwaways retarded smearing feces

on themselves, when I read research materials at Ivy league colleges, and watched nothing but CNN and C-Span at home."

She said she had no choice. "It had to be 'a serious crime' or I'd get the state hospital i.e. Nazi camp."

ROXIE M. WALLACE knew something was wrong when her grown son Jeffrey visited her, and padlocked his room. He sometimes slept with a knife by his bed. He was growing increasingly paranoid, she realized. He would talk incessantly about evil forces. Most disturbing, she said in interviews and letters, her son sometimes growled "like a small dog or a wolf."

Mr. Wallace offers a glimpse into how difficult it can be to shake someone out of a delusional universe, even when friends and relatives notice and want to do something about it. Mr. Wallace, like other rampage killers, was convinced he was defending himself against an intricate conspiracy. Of the 100 cases in the study, 49 involved killers who had shown extreme, irrational suspicion and mistrust. In their paranoia, they think they must defend themselves against threats that other people do not see.

Even now, incarcerated in an isolated Florida prison, Mr. Wallace, 38, insists that he had no choice but to open fire in 1997 at a Key West bar where he once worked, killing one person and injuring three others.

In a long prison interview, Mr. Wallace was unable to deviate from his convoluted theory that the bar was the center of an organized-crime drug and prostitution ring with ties—he was sure—to Satanism, President Clinton and Garrison Keillor, host of the public radio program "Prairie Home Companion."

Mr. Wallace's lawyers argued unsuccessfully that he was insane, but Mr. Wallace insists his actions were perfectly rational.

"The best example I can give," Mr. Wallace said, "is you're in your house and somebody breaks in and you have to defend yourself and you end up killing somebody. It's terrible but what else can you do?"

From her home in Tennessee, Mrs. Wallace said she had tried for years to maneuver her son toward help when he did not want it. "I was afraid he was either going to kill himself or he was going to 'fight back' to save himself like a caged animal," she said.

Many rampage killers are extremely difficult to treat, say psychiatrists who have interviewed them. They may deny their illness and resist medication and treatment, and are often shrewd about masking symptoms to avoid being hospitalized involuntarily.

Even those who do receive psychiatric treatment do not always get the help they need.

Joseph Brooks Jr. was a policeman's son from Detroit and one of the few black students to win entrance to both a prestigious local preparatory school and the Massachu-

setts Institute of Technology. Friends in the fraternity house where Mr. Brooks lived recall no hint of anger or illness, only that Mr. Brooks was absurdly meticulous about his chores, and studied so compulsively that they nicknamed him Books. But in his third year at M.I.T., he tried to commit suicide, was hospitalized for obsessive-compulsive disorder, and later received a diagnosis of paranoid schizophrenia.

Back in Detroit, living alone, Mr. Brooks, 28, sought treatment with Dr. Reuven Bar-Levav, a well-known local psychiatrist who ran group therapy sessions in Southfield attended by a close-knit clientele of upper-middle-class patients coping with depression or anxiety disorders—nothing as severe as paranoid schizophrenia. Mr. Brooks joined the group sessions, but refused to take the medication he had been prescribed, telling friends that the drugs made him tremble, gain weight and lose concentration.

Ronald Rissman, a fellow patient in the therapy group Mr. Brooks joined, said in an interview, "It was obvious he was not in touch with reality. He would laugh inappropriately. Within a matter of two or three group sessions, it became apparent to most of the senior patients that he did not belong there, that he should have been institutionalized."

Mr. Rissman said he and several other patients and therapists in the group practice repeatedly went to Dr. Bar-Levav with their concerns about Mr. Brooks. And in one group session—with Mr. Brooks in the room—a patient named Mary Gregg told the group she was afraid of Mr. Brooks, Mr. Rissman recalled.

After about eight group sessions, Dr. Bar-Levav finally terminated Mr. Brooks's treatment and referred him to other therapists.

Eight months later, on June 11 last year, Mr. Brooks returned to the psychiatrist's office and killed Dr. Bar-Levav. Mr. Brooks then pivoted and fired into the therapy group he had once attended, killing Mrs. Gregg and wounding four others, including Mr. Rissman, who leapt up to close the door. Mr. Brooks then turned the gun on himself.

Dr. Bar-Levav had been given some warning: while in treatment, Mr. Brooks had handed a gun over to another therapist in the practice and confessed he had come close to killing his girlfriend's mother and committing suicide. And just before the killings, Mr. Brooks sent Dr. Bar-Levav a 52-page manuscript critiquing the therapy he had received from him. The critique contained obsessive, paranoid passages about a "German American woman" humiliating him in his therapy group, and hints of menace. The local police emphasized in interviews with The Times that Dr. Bar-Levav should have alerted them.

"We would have taken that weapon away from him," said Joseph Thomas, the chief of police in Southfield, Mich. But even had the police confiscated the gun, the killing would

Rampage Killers in 100 Cases

Figures are the number of cases in which the killers had these characteristics.

Mental Health Problems Were Prominent

 47 History of mental health problems

 42 Previously seen by mental health professional

 24 Psychiatric drugs prescribed

 14 Off prescribed psychiatric drugs at time of crime

 23 Symptoms of depression

 20 Previous psychiatric hospitalization

 26 Suicide attempt or fixation

 49 Paranoid talk

There Were Frequent Warning Signs

 63 Made general or specific threat

 40 Behavior changed before killing

 35 History of violent behavior

 25 Displayed weapons in public

But Cultural Influences Seemed Small

 11 Liked violent TV

 6 Played violent video games

 4 Interest in occult or Satanism

To compile this data, The New York Times reviewed newspaper reports, court records and psychiatric reports, and interviewed the police, prosecutors, defense attorneys, victims, families, friends, and when possible, the killers themselves.

The New York Times

not have been prevented. Mr. Brooks easily obtained a second permit and a second gun—an expensive limited-edition combat-style handgun, which he used to kill Dr. Bar-Levav.

The psychiatrist's daughter, Dr. Leora Bar-Levav, a therapist herself who worked with her father and is now carrying on his practice, rejected with a pained wince the suggestion of negligence. In a conversation in the practice's new offices in Southfield, she said the problem was instead a permissive society and a narcissistic patient who had rejected treatment.

"You can lead a horse to water, but you can't make him drink it," she said. "Denial is very potent."

A MAN storms a warehouse where he was recently fired, leaving a trail of shell casings, three dead workers and four more wounded. The news story the next day begins, "A disgruntled former employee went on a shooting rampage."

In the turmoil that follows a rampage shooting by a killer like James Davis in Asheville, N.C., there is usually a scramble to pinpoint the cause. And in a world of rapid news cycles, the answers come quickly.

Mr. Davis was the "disgruntled employee." In news coverage last year, Dung Trinh was described as so bereaved at the death of his mother that in September he shot at nurses in a hospital in Anaheim, Calif., where she had once been treated. Sometimes the reason is reported to be a broken marriage, a spurned romance or fi-

nancial misfortune. Mark O. Barton, a rampage killer in Atlanta, was reported to have singled out day traders because he had suffered huge losses in the market.

These are the kinds of events that often result in the observation, "He just snapped."

But the incident that is often simplistically cited as the cause—a firing, a divorce, an eviction—is on closer examination just the final provocation to a troubled, angry person who has already left numerous warning markers, often available for many to see.

When he opened fire in the day-trading office, Mr. Barton already had problems deeper than his recent stock losses. Eight hours earlier, he had killed his second wife and his children, and he was still the prime suspect in the deaths six years earlier of his first wife and her mother.

Colin Ferguson, who opened fire on rush-hour commuters on the Long Island Rail Road, had displayed such menacing behavior that he received an eviction notice, which further fueled his fury.

Most of the workplace shooters had been fired or disciplined precisely because they were already threatening violence, behaving bizarrely or getting in fights. Of the 81 adult murderers The Times looked at, 49 were unemployed.

Mr. Davis was no mild-mannered worker who just mysteriously snapped, according to court records and interviews.

He repeatedly picked fights at the tool warehouse where he worked in Asheville, and had often told colleagues that if he were ever fired, he would return to kill his bosses.

He had seen combat in Vietnam and been hospitalized with schizophrenia after the war. He lived alone, and co-workers knew he owned a .44 Magnum with a scope and had practiced firing it in his basement.

"You can have it because I probably wouldn't need it much longer."

James Floyd Davis on giving his niece a video game a few days before his workplace rampage

---

One Wednesday in May 1995, he got into another fight at work, his last.

That weekend, his family noticed him acting strangely. For example, Mr. Davis, an unemotional recluse, told his sister he loved her. And though James had never given anything to anybody, his brother, William, later said, James had wanted to give his niece a chess set and video game the weekend before. His siblings tried to persuade him to go to a hospital for psychiatric help, but he refused.

That Monday, James Davis was fired. His bosses were so anxious about his reaction that they agreed to break the news in a room where they could use a table to deflect an attack. Some employees planned escape routes when they heard of Mr. Davis's firing.

Just after midnight on Wednesday, William Davis called the police from his house 100 miles away to tell them that James had left home in a nervous frenzy and left all his personal belongings with their mother.

"I don't see why you got to wait till he kills himself or somebody," William Davis told the police, according to a transcript of his telephone call. "If you send a patrol car out to that plant, he's probably sitting there. Or notify them." William Davis told the police, "I don't know for sure, but I know and believe by the warning signs he gave me he's going to die." The Asheville police did drive by James Davis's house, but said that when they saw there was no vehicle in the driveway, there was nothing else they could do.

William Davis testified that he got in his car around 2 a.m. and drove to what he thought was his brother's workplace. But because he had not lived in Asheville for many years, he went to the wrong plant. The gate was shut, so he drove back to his mother's house to sleep.

James Davis never came home. That morning, on Wednesday, May 17, he stormed the Union Butterfield plant. Two of the victims were the bosses who fired him.

"I live for the rest of my life knowing that if someone had listened to me, no one would have died," William Davis said in an interview. "I could have stopped it if someone would have listened."

Last spring, with Mr. Davis already on death row, a jury considered a civil suit claiming that his employers had failed to protect the other employees from a man they knew to be violent. A lawyer for the company argued there was no way anyone could foresee such an attack.

A lawyer for the victims said, "This case is a human tragedy because this could have been prevented."

The jury agreed, awarding the families of two of the victims $7.9 million. An appeal has been filed.

EVEN the cases that drew wide attention offer fresh insights when re-examined in the context of the Times review.

One spring day, Kipland P. Kinkel, a freckle-faced boy with a history of behavior problems in school, disrupted his ninth-grade literature class by abruptly yelling out loud, "God damn this voice inside my head!"

His teacher took immediate action. He wrote up a disciplinary note. "In the future," it asked, "what could you do differently to prevent this problem?"

Kip dutifully filled out the answer: "Not to say 'Damn.' "

"I am a horrible son. I wish I had been aborted. I destroy everything I touch. I can't eat. I can't sleep. I didn't deserve them. They were wonderful people. It's not their fault or the fault of any person, organization, or television show. My head just doesn't work right. God damn these VOICES inside my head."

From the note Kip Kinkel left on the coffee table in his house after killing his parents

The note was signed by the teacher. Kip took it home to his mother, and she signed it too.

Nobody paid attention to the part about the voice inside Kip's head.

One month later, on May 20, 1998, Kip was suspended from school for buying a stolen gun and stashing it in his locker. That afternoon, back at home in a wooded neighborhood called Shangri La, Kip Kinkel, 15, shot his father and then his mother.

The next morning he drove to his school in Springfield, Ore., and shot 24 people in the cafeteria, killing two students.

Sometimes even concerned parents, like the Kinkels, or other caring adults, find the specter of serious mental or emotional problems in a child so disturbing that they lapse into denial, the study found over and over.

The youngsters themselves often unwittingly assist in the denial by being reluctant to tell someone about hearing voices or having bizarre thoughts, in fear of being labeled mentally ill. Complicating the picture is the fact that in adolescents like Kip, the symp-

toms are most likely just emerging, psychiatric experts say.

Kip Kinkel's parents, while perhaps unwilling to face the serious implications of his outburst in class, had not been blind to his problems, according to interviews and court records. They were both schoolteachers, and such behavior would have been hard to ignore. Starting at age 6, when Kip hit a boy twice his age with a piece of metal bar, he was susceptible to uncontrollable rages.

As a teenager, like many of the killers in the study, he showed an inordinate fascination with weapons. He collected knives, secretly built explosives and boasted to friends that he wanted to be the next Unabomber. He detonated explosives at a local quarry and was caught by the police throwing rocks at cars off a highway overpass, a prank that some psychologists say is an early indication of a potential for violent tendencies.

His mother took him to a therapist. Kip showed symptoms, the therapist noted, of "major depressive disorder," and was prescribed Prozac.

But William Kinkel, Kip's father, did not approve of therapy, and never attended the sessions, Mark Sabitt, Kip's defense lawyer, said in an interview. Mr. Sabitt said that Mr. Kinkel was "a very proud individual and aware of his image in the community. He was very skeptical of counseling in general and closed to the notion of someone in his family needing treatment, or even worse, being mentally ill. It just didn't fit with the image he had of his kids and what he hoped they would be."

After nine therapy sessions and three months of summer vacation on Prozac, Kip's behavior improved, so his parents discontinued the therapy and the medication. Kip's father bought him the Glock semiautomatic pistol his son had been pestering him for.

At Kip's sentencing hearing, the defense presented a family tree showing severe mental illness, including schizophrenia, affecting three generations on both maternal and paternal sides.

When Kip's victims addressed the judge, some said he was faking insanity. Others said that even if insane, he should be held responsible for ripping apart their lives.

"I don't care if you're sick, if you're insane, if you're crazy," said Jacob Ryker, one of the students who finally tackled Kip, despite gunshot wounds in his own chest and arm. "I don't care. I think prison, a lifetime in prison is too good for you. If a dog was to go insane and if a dog got rabid and it bit someone, you destroy it. So I stand here and I ask, why haven't you been destroyed? I question myself for not pulling the trigger."

AN agitated Sgt. William Kreutzer Jr. telephoned a friend in his squad at Fort Bragg, N.C. He said the shooting would begin the next morning at daybreak, just when 1,300 soldiers were on a field stretching before their morning run.

"He said he was going to 'mow them down,'" said his friend, Specialist Burl F. Mays.

True, Sergeant Kreutzer was an odd loner who talked about killing so often that the men in his company had nicknamed him Crazy Kreutzer and Silence of the Lambs. But when Specialist Mays arrived early the next morning and saw Sergent Kreutzer was not in, he feared that this time it was no idle threat. He told his superiors just before 5 a.m. and was asked to check Sergeant Kreutzer's room.

He found that the bed had not been slept in. On the desk he found a draft of Sergeant Kreutzer's will.

Specialist Mays later testified that when he then tried to alarm superiors, the first sergeant dismissed his concerns, saying something like, "Kreutzer is a pussy, he wouldn't do anything like this."

The case of Sergeant Kreutzer, told in court records and interviews, illustrates an altogether different common case: the depressed and angry misfit provoked by the people around him.

Park Elliott Dietz, a psychiatrist and expert on mass killers, said people who become mass murderers are often "handled in a provocative, ineffective way." Their outrageous fantasies of violence draw public condemnation or ridicule. Humiliation, Dr. Dietz said, often precedes rampage killing.

Sergeant Kreutzer, a gawky perfectionist, had long been the object of ridicule in his squad at Fort Bragg. When his unit was sent to the Sinai, other soldiers tied his shoelaces together while he slept. They filled his boots with sand. Sergeant Kreutzer, 26, had always wanted to be a soldier, but he lagged behind on company runs and sometimes misplaced equipment. He cried when criticized. When he repeatedly threatened to kill other soldiers, they took it as a joke.

Fifteen months before his final ambush, when Sergeant Kreutzer had an outburst in which he threatened to kill soldiers, and it became common knowledge, his superiors sent him to a military social worker.

"He told me that he had specific plans to kill the people in his squad," the counselor, Darren Fong, told military investigators, the court-martial documents show. But when he was returned to full duty, Sergeant Kreutzer was not referred to Army psychiatrists. He was barred from access to weapons for two weeks.

The morning of Oct. 27, 1995, Sergeant Kreutzer hid in the woods and fired onto a field of American soldiers who thought they were at peace. He wounded 18 of them, and killed Maj. Stephen Mark Badger, an intelligence officer and a father and stepfather of eight children.

Sergeant Kreutzer kept firing until he was tackled from behind by two comrades.

Minutes later, he spoke to a military police officer, Bruce W. Hamrick.

"He said he kept warning people that he was going to kill somebody," Mr. Hamrick testified, "but that nobody would listen."

Reporting for this series was by Fox Butterfield, Ford Fessenden, William Glaberson and Laurie Goodstein, with research assistance from Anthony Zirilli and other members of the news research staff of The New York Times.

Unit Selections

5. **A Healing Approach to Crime,** Tag Evers
6. **Childhood Victimization: Early Adversity, Later Psychopathology,** Cathy Spatz Widom
7. **Man and His Son's Slayer Unite to Ask Why,** William Glaberson
8. **Every Day I Have to Forgive Again,** Marie Ragghianti
9. **Sweden's Response to Domestic Violence,** Lars Nylén and Gun Heimer

Key Points to Consider

❖ Interest in restorative justice has grown considerably in the United States since the early 1990s. Explain the restorative justice theory.

❖ In your view, what would it take to transcend negative consequences of childhood victimization?

❖ What is needed in order to switch from calling oneself a victim of crime to a "survivor of crime"?

 **Links** **www.dushkin.com/online/**

11. **Connecticut Sexual Assault Crisis Services, Inc.**
    http://www.connsacs.org
12. **National Crime Victim's Research and Treatment Center (NCVC)**
    http://www.musc.edu/cvc/
13. **Office for Victims of Crime (OVC)**
    http://www.ojp.usdoj.gov/ovc

These sites are annotated on pages 4 and 5.

For many years, crime victims were not considered an important topic for criminological study. Now, however, criminologists consider that focusing on victims and victimization is essential to understand the phenomenon of crime. The popularity of this area of study can be attributed to the early work of Hans von Hentig and the later work of Stephen Schafer. These writers were the first to assert that crime victims play an integral role in the criminal event, that their actions may actually precipitate crime, and that unless the victim's role is considered, the study of crime is not complete.

In recent years, a growing number of criminologists have devoted increasing attention to the victim's role in the criminal justice process. Generally, areas of particular interest include calculating costs of crime to victims, taking surveys of victims to measure the nature and extent of criminal behavior, establishing probabilities of victimization risks, studying victim precipitation of crime and culpability, and designing services expressly for victims of crime. As more criminologists focus their attention on the victim's role in the criminal process, victimology will take on even greater importance.

This unit provides sharp focus on several key issues. In the lead article, "A Healing Approach to Crime," Tag Evers examines a program that arranges face-to-face encounters between crime victims and perpetrators. Long-term consequences of childhood victimization and the processes linking it to poor outcomes in later life are uncovered in the essay that follows, "Childhood Victimization: Early Adversity, Later Psychopathology." Rampage murder is the theme of the next article "Man and His Son's Slayer Unite to Ask Why." By exchanging letters with his son's killer, a man strives to make sense of what occurred. "Every Day I Have to Forgive Again" presents the stories of victims struggling to come to terms with their feelings about aggressors they have every reason to hate. The unit closes with a look at the comprehensive approach that Sweden takes to fight its domestic violence problem in "Sweden's Response to Domestic Violence" by Lars Nylén and Gun Heimer.

Victimology

A HEALING APPROACH TO Crime

BY TAG EVERS

Tim Coursen and his wife, Amy Miller, are light sleepers. Late one night two summers ago, the Madison, Wisconsin, couple woke up to strange noises in their house. While Miller stayed upstairs with their five-year-old daughter, Coursen went downstairs to investigate. Coursen interrupted a burglary in progress. Enraged, he confronted two intruders and chased them. As they fled, one of the would-be thieves threatened Coursen with a utility knife.

The invasion of their home had a profoundly disruptive effect on the Coursen-Miller family. Gone was a sense of safety and refuge. The couple's daughter began having nightmares, sometimes several in one night. Coursen fretted over his aggressive response to the intruders. Sleep became elusive, every creak in the old wooden house another possible break-in.

No one was hurt, but Coursen, Miller, and their daughter had become crime victims just the same. "Our perception of our home, our personal sanctuary, was dramatically changed," says Coursen.

Soon after the break-in, police apprehended the perpetrators: Jason Walker, eighteen at the time of the incident, and Charles Brigham, seventeen. The two were charged and convicted. That is how the story might have ended, had not Coursen and Miller learned from a relative in Minnesota about the University of Wisconsin-Madison Law School's Restorative Justice Project. They called Bruce Kittle, director of the project, and requested a "victim-offender mediation"—a

Tag Evers is a writer based in Madison, Wisconsin.

face-to-face meeting with the men who invaded their home.

The Restorative Justice Project in Wisconsin is one of 300 such programs in the United States, according to the Center for Restorative Justice and Mediation at the University of Minnesota. There are more than 700 victim-offender mediation programs operating in Europe, Australia, and New Zealand.

In restorative justice theory, crime is defined as a violation of human relationships, a harmful act committed against a victim and a community. In contrast to the criminal justice system, which treats crime principally as an offense against the state, the primary concern in the restorative justice framework is the harm caused by the criminal act. Making things right, rather than simply punishing the offenders, is the goal.

Coursen and Miller met with Jason Walker at their house, in a session mediated by Kittle. Before the encounter, Kittle met separately with the victims and the offender. He warned Coursen and Miller not to expect much from Walker. The young man had been recalcitrant and "closed off," cooperative only to the extent that his participation had been mandated as part of his probation agreement, Kittle said.

That changed during the meeting. "Something great happened," says Coursen. "I felt like I made real contact with Jason."

Coursen told Walker about the evening of the attempted break-in, his reaction, and the pain and paranoia that followed. Walker told his side of the story: what he and Brigham were thinking that night, how they were out looking for "stuff," and how they hadn't considered the impact of their actions.

During the session, Coursen and Miller's daughter became frightened and crawled on her belly out of the living room. Her parents took her to the security of a neighbor's home. Her behavior dramatically underscored the traumatic effects of the crime. Still, Coursen viewed the session as a success.

"The meeting was by far the most meaningful part of the whole process for our family," he wrote later for a neighborhood newspaper, "because it allowed us to tell him directly about the negative impact his actions had on us. It provided an opportunity for him to acknowledge to us his regret for what he had done to our family and the community, allowing for the possibility of reconciliation and forgiveness to occur."

Walker, Coursen, and Miller signed a restitution agreement stipulating that Walker perform community service at a homeless shelter, a commitment he made independent of his other probationary requirements. The young man also volunteered to help the Coursen-Miller family with home repairs.

Months later, the couple repeated the process with Brigham. They requested that Brigham volunteer at the local community center since the crime had increased the level of fear in their neighborhood. Coursen says Brigham seemed indifferent to the process, but he believes the mediation may yet yield fruit. "Even if he doesn't realize the significance now, maybe some part of it will dawn on him later," says Coursen.

Like many victims, Coursen felt left out of the criminal justice process. Though persistent in his efforts to be kept informed of the case, he says he felt as though he were a "disposable element," churned through a system that cared little about him as a crime victim. He says that meeting with Walker and Brigham, on the other hand, helped his family recover.

The criminal justice system is offender-driven, says Kittle. "It is not uncommon for offenders to perceive themselves as victims, as screwed-over by the system itself," he says. "The tendency is to rationalize behavior, to blame others. The criminal justice system does little to help offenders take responsibility for what they've done."

Victim-offender mediation was pioneered in Ontario, Canada, in the mid-1970s by Mennonites. It spread to Elkhart, Indiana, in 1978 in a program founded by Howard Zehr. He says the new approach marks a much-needed shift in the way we think about crime.

"When crime is an offense against the state, when we define crime solely as the breaking of laws, then it is up to the state to invoke a coercive penal response," says Zehr, who now teaches sociology and restorative justice at Eastern Mennonite University in Harrisonburg, Virginia. "When we focus on the harms of wrongdoing, when we ask what needs to be done to repair these harms, we suddenly realize these questions can't be answered without a three-dimensional approach, involving victim, offender, and community in the resolution of conflict."

Interest in restorative justice has grown considerably in the United States since the early 1990s. The American Bar Association endorsed the practice of victim-offender mediation in 1994. In 1996, the U.S. Department of Justice convened the first national conference on restorative justice.

Rehabilitating prisoners is supposedly the foundation of the U.S. "corrections" system. But that ideal seems laughable as politicians ratchet up the tough-on-crime rhetoric with every election cycle.

Nationwide, more than a million and a half people are now behind bars, many of them packed into overcrowded facilities. Spending on corrections is the fastest-growing component of most state budgets. In several states, including California, total expenditures on corrections exceed spending on higher education.

> '**T**here is a reason why people commit crimes again and again. A big part of that has to do with lack of empathy on the part of the offender for victims.'

Prisons have become, in effect, colleges for crime, often turning out meaner and craftier criminals. Society's response has been to build more prisons, issue longer sentences, spend more on punishment and less on programs to prevent crime in the first place.

Advocates of restorative justice want to change all that. They insist their approach is not a "soft" alternative to the "tough" system of criminal justice.

Taking personal responsibility for one's actions is hard, says Walter Dickey, director of the University of Wisconsin-Madison Law School's Frank J. Remington Center, which is home to the Restorative Justice Project.

"There is a reason why people commit crimes again and again," says Dickey, who used to run Wisconsin's Department of Corrections. "A big part of that has to do with lack of empathy on the part of the offender for victims. The more understanding offenders have of the real costs of their actions, the less crime we'll have in the streets. Get people to own up to what they've done, and you will have less crime."

The offender is not the enemy, claims Kittle. "Offenders are people who admittedly committed crimes, sometimes terrible crimes," he says. "They are people who need to be punished appropriately. But they are also people who need help. We cannot turn our backs on these people if we ever hope to actually reduce the amount of crime occurring in our communities."

While concerned about offenders taking responsibility and straightening out their lives, advocates of restorative justice remain principally committed to victims and the harms they have suffered.

"All roads begin and end with the victim," says Dave Doerfler, director of the Victim Offender Mediation/Dialogue program operated under the auspices of the Victim Services Division of the Texas Department of Criminal Justice. "If we can meet the needs of victims, the needs of offenders will be met as well."

Doerfler claims his program is entirely victim-centered. Some victim-offender mediation programs contact the offender first, and if the offender is willing to admit responsibility and engage in the process of mediation, the victim is contacted to see if he or she is willing to participate. The Texas program is different in that victims must initiate the process, otherwise, no mediation will occur.

The program has a waiting list of nearly 300 crime victims who want to meet their offenders, Doerfler says. About half are the loved ones of murder victims, and another 25 percent are survivors of attempted murder, muggings, or sexual assaults.

"The majority of cases grow out of what victims have discovered within themselves—this need to meet with the one who caused them so much pain, a need that was not provided for by their experience in the criminal justice system," says Doerfler. Preparation for these violent cases takes twelve to twenty-four months. Victims practice role-playing, therapeutic writing, and other exercises in what Doerfler calls "structured grieving."

"The experience of a crime victim is one of having control taken away from you," Doerfler says. "Extensive preparation leading up to the mediated dialogue—and the dialogue itself—allows victim pain to be acknowledged and ventilated in a healthy way, in a way that has a profound impact on both the victim and the offender."

Restorative justice has drawn criticism from victim advocates who are working in the area of sexual and domestic abuse.

"Any time pseudo-legal or extra-legal means of dealing with such crimes takes place, there is the possibility of revictimization," says Denise Gamache, associate director of the criminal office of the Battered Women's Justice Project in Minneapolis. She is also troubled because she thinks restorative justice might roll back some of the progress that advocates for battered women have made. "Victim advocates have worked for the better part of two decades to get the criminal justice system to take family violence seriously, so we are suspicious when crimes against women appear to be shoved out of the system."

These advocates point out that victim-offender mediation originated as a method for handling nonviolent property crimes, often with juveniles. They question the idea that the model can be extended to violent crimes, particularly sexual abuse, rape, and domestic violence.

"Acquaintance or partner dynamics are different," says Donna Dunn, sexual-assault program director for the Minnesota Center for Crime Victim Services. "The assumption 'if it works for property crimes, it will work elsewhere' sets off red flags."

In cases of domestic violence, the destructive patterns of manipulation that led to violence in the first place put the victim at risk in subsequent interactions, critics claim.

Mark Umbreit, director of the Center of Restorative Justice and Mediation at the University of Minnesota, concedes that Dunn and her colleagues have a point. He notes that "98 percent of victim-offender mediations nationwide are property offenses and minor assaults." While there is a growing trend to use the model for crimes of serious violence, Umbreit thinks sexual and domestic-abuse cases require special care.

"Sexual-assault cases must be victim-initiated," says Umbreit. "As for domestic abuse, I'd rather recommend mediation for an attempted murder case than for a case involving domestic violence."

Kay Pranis, director of the Restorative Justice Initiative for the Minnesota Department of Corrections, also believes mediation is generally inappropriate for cases of domestic abuse. But Pranis, who once served as board chair for a battered women's advocacy group in Minnesota, nonetheless observes that the criminal justice system is not particularly effective in dealing with domestic violence.

"A lot of victims don't report abuse," Pranis says. "The system is designed to punish, to inflict harm. The victim wants the abuse to stop, but doesn't

necessarily want this person removed from her life."

The problem of domestic abuse is one of secrecy and denial, adds Pranis. "We need to explore options that will break the code of silence that shields offenders."

Michelle Van de Casteele was so traumatized by childhood abuse that she had a tubal ligation at the age of thirty, to make sure she would never become an abusive parent. She endured beatings from her father and five older brothers. One of her older brothers, Robert Michael Van de Casteele, abused her sexually.

A few years ago, Michelle learned that Robert Michael was sentenced to prison for second degree sexual assault of a minor. The victim was not a family member. Michelle's family had lied to her, claiming that Robert Michael was in prison for drunk driving, not sexual assault. She discovered the truth just as she was beginning to deal with the wounds caused by the incest.

In late summer of 1996, with her brother's release date coming up in less than two years, Michelle found herself paralyzed by fear and thoughts of suicide. She was certain Robert Michael would try to reestablish contact upon his release. She contacted the Wisconsin Parole Board and expressed her fears, hoping to influence the terms of his parole. But her brother had not been incarcerated for abusing or assaulting her. Because the statute of limitations on that crime had already expired, technically, Michelle was not a crime victim. She wrote letters that were added to his file, but the system could do little to help her.

Michelle persisted nonetheless. Over a period of six months, she tracked down every lead in the hope that something could be done to prevent Robert Michael from reentering her life. She also wanted to meet with her brother to communicate her desire for no further contact. Finally, she was referred to Kittle's Restorative Justice Project.

Michelle met with Kittle, who immediately put her in touch with a therapist trained in sexual abuse. Kittle agreed to pursue a mediated dialogue between Michelle and her brother, once the therapist thought she was ready.

Next, Kittle met with Robert Michael, who agreed to talk with his sister, though he initially denied he was responsible for her pain. Michelle, undeterred, prepared herself to tell her

brother face-to-face about the damage he had done.

Nearly a year later, after getting the green light from the therapist, Kittle arranged a conference between the two siblings. During the session, which took place last March at Fox Lake Correctional Institute, Michelle told her story, expressed her anger at Robert Michael, and described how the abuse had affected her life.

Robert Michael broke down and admitted his guilt. He also provided Michelle with key details illuminating the pattern and duration of the abuse, details which Michelle had suppressed.

The two reached an agreement prohibiting Robert Michael from contacting his sister, stipulating that he undergo sex-offender treatment as well as alcohol and drug treatment, and arranging for financial restitution to pay for Michelle's therapy.

"I walked out happy as hell," says Michelle. "Like a huge load had been lifted from my shoulders." She has no interest in forgiving her brother and is relieved his parole could be revoked if he tried to threaten her newly articulated safety.

"She stared her demons down," says Kittle. "That's what these conferences are about."

Not every victim is likely to have such a successful outcome, advocates point out. The possibility exists that some who use the increasingly popular term "restorative justice" may be doing more harm than good.

Last spring, victim advocates, including Gamache and Dunn, met with Zehr and other practitioners of restorative justice in Washington, D.C. The two groups discussed their different concerns and found some common ground.

Zehr believes the meeting was helpful. "Restorative justice is at a crossroads," he says. "It's an exciting time and a dangerous time. Dangerous because the movement is growing so fast that some are calling their work 'restorative' when, in fact, it isn't." As the movement grows, its leaders are trying to build coalitions with competing movements, such as victim advocacy.

The adversarial nature of the criminal justice system and the realities of politics pose huge barriers to restorative justice. Nonetheless, Dickey, who has seen various corrections efforts come and go, is optimistic about this one.

"The program sells itself," he says. "Restorative justice and victim-offender mediation may not change everything about the current system, but the truth of it will win out."

Childhood Victimization:
EARLY Adversity
LATER Psychopathology

by Cathy Spatz Widom

Childhood physical abuse, sexual abuse, and neglect have both immediate and long-term effects. Different types of abuse have a range of consequences for a child's later physical and psychological well-being, cognitive development, and behavior. But there is another side to the issue: Because these crimes often occur against a background of more chronic adversity, in families with multiple problems, it may not be reasonable to assume that before being victimized the child enjoyed "well-being." Parental alcoholism, drug problems, and other inadequate social and family functioning are among the factors affecting the child's response to victimization. Gender differences add to the complexity. Disentangling all these factors is difficult, as researchers have found.

Clearly, more needs to be learned about the long-term consequences of childhood victimization and the processes linking it to outcomes later in life. This article discusses what is known from earlier studies and also presents the findings of more recent research.[1]

Consequences and What Gives Rise to Them

Child maltreatment has physical, psychological, cognitive, and behavioral consequences. Physical consequences range from minor injuries to brain damage and even death. Psycho-logical consequences range from chronic low self-esteem, anxiety, and depression to substance abuse and other self-destructive behavior and suicide attempts. Cognitive effects include attention problems, learning disorders, and poor school performance. Behavioral consequences range from poor peer relations to physical aggression and antisocial behavior to violent behavior. These consequences are influenced by such factors as gender differences and the context in which victimization occurs.

Gender differences. Differences between men and women in manifesting the effects of childhood victimization have received only limited attention from scholars. Some researchers, exploring how men and women differ in showing distress, have suggested there is some conformity to traditional notions of male and female behavior.[2] Some have noted that differences between men and women in manifesting the consequences of abuse may parallel gender differences in the way psychopathology is expressed. Thus, aggression (in males) and depression (in females) may express the same underlying distress, perhaps reflecting gender-specific strategies for maintaining self-esteem in the face of perceived rejection.[3]

Differences in the way boys and girls react to abuse have been reported in a few studies. In one, boys were found to have more externalizing and girls to have more internalizing symptoms.[4] An examination of depression and conduct disorders in sexually abused children revealed that girls were more likely than boys to develop depressive disorders and less likely to develop conduct disorders.[5]

Family and community—the context. The long-term impact of childhood trauma may depend on the larger—family or community—context.[6] In a study of children kidnaped and held underground, preexisting family pathology was identified as a factor in the victim's long-term adjustment. Four years after the incident, the children from troubled families were more maladjusted than those from healthier families.[7] The findings of other research were not as clear; rather, subsequent maladjustment was linked more to whether victimized children received appropriate play materials and maternal involvement than to whether they were abused.[8] Parental alcoholism is another contextual factor linked to child abuse[9] and to alcoholism later in life in the offspring.[10]

In the same way, practices of the community and the justice and social service systems may have long-term effects. Researchers have called attention to the ways in which children who are members of racial and ethnic minorities encounter discrimination, which diminishes their self-esteem

From *National Institute of Justice Journal,* January 2000, pp. 3-9. © 2000 by the National Institute of Justice. Reprinted by permission.

How the Study Is Being Conducted

The study is based on a "prospective cohorts design," so-called because it follows a group of people (a cohort) for an extended period, enabling researchers to examine sequences of development over time. In the case of this study, the design helps sort out the effects of childhood victimization from other, potentially confounding effects traceable to different causes. The subjects were told they were part of a study of the characteristics of people who had grown up in the area in the late 1960's and early 1970's.

The cases of children who were abused and/or neglected were drawn from county juvenile and adult criminal court records in a metropolitan area of the Midwest between 1967 and 1971. The children were young—age 11 or younger—at the time of the incident.

The comparison group. To create a control group against which to compare the abused and neglected children, a group of children who had not been reported as victimized but who were similar in other respects to the study subjects were identified. To match children younger than school age at the time of the incident, county birth records were used. To match school-age children, records of more than 100 elementary schools were used.

Sample size and characteristics. The original sample consisted of 1,575 people, of whom 908 were study subjects and 667 were controls. Of these, 1,916 were interviewed for the study. Just under half the interviewees were female, about two-thirds were white, and the mean age at the time of the interview was 28.7. There were no differences between the abused/neglected group and the controls in gender, race/ethnicity, or age.

Some caveats. Because the study findings were based on court cases, they most likely represent the most extreme incidents of childhood abuse and neglect. What is more, they were processed before enactment of child abuse laws, when many cases went unreported and thus never came to the attention of the authorities. The findings are therefore not generalizable to unreported or unsubstantiated cases of abuse and neglect.

Because cases brought before the courts disproportionately represent people at the lower end of the socioeconomic spectrum, the study's subjects and controls were drawn from that stratum. For this reason, it would be inappropriate to generalize to cases involving people from other socioeconomic strata.

and exacerbates the effects of victimization.[11] Elsewhere, researchers have suggested that victimized children are more likely to develop problem behavior in adolescence partly because of juvenile justice system practices that disproportionately label them as juvenile offenders and adjudicate them as such.[12]

Studying the Long-Term Effects in Depth

In a systematic study of the long-term consequences of early childhood abuse and neglect, the author is examining the experiences of more than 900 people who were victimized in childhood. Begun in 1986, the study first focused on the extent to which,

as the victims grew into adulthood, they became involved in delinquency and crime, including violent crime.[13] The current focus is on how their intellectual, behavioral, social, and psychological development was affected. This second phase began in 1989, more than 20 years after the victimization. (See "How the Study Is Being Conducted.")

Intellectual performance. When tested at about age 29, the study subjects and the comparison group both scored at the lower levels of the IQ scale, with the majority in both groups below the standard mean of 100 (see figure 1). Those who were abused or neglected, however, scored significantly lower than the comparison group, and these lower levels per-

sisted irrespective of age, sex, race, and criminal history.

Overall, both groups averaged 11.5 years of schooling, but the abused and neglected group completed significantly fewer years. Thus, the childhood victims were less likely to have completed high school: Fewer than half, in contrast to two-thirds of the people in the control group.

Behavioral and social development. The occupations of both groups ranged from laborer through professional. In the sample overall, the median job level was that of semiskilled worker, with fewer than 7 percent in the two groups holding managerial or professional jobs (see figure 2). The abused and neglected individuals had not done as well as the control group: Significantly more of them held menial and semiskilled jobs. Conversely, a larger proportion of people in the control group held higher level jobs, ranging from skilled worker through professional.

Unemployment and underemployment disproportionately affected the abused and neglected group (see figure 3). In both groups, more than one-fifth had been unemployed in the 5-year period before they were interviewed for the study. Not surprisingly, people in the control group were more likely than the victims to be employed. For underemployment, the story is similar: Significantly more victims of childhood abuse and neglect were underemployed in the 5 years before the interview than were controls.

The quality of interpersonal relations also is affected by childhood victimization, and here again there are no surprises (see figure 4). Using marital stability as the measure of success, child abuse and neglect victims did not do as well as control group members. Almost 20 percent of the controls reported a stable marriage, compared to only 13 percent of the abuse and neglect group. Frequent divorce and separation were also more common among abused and neglected people.

As reported in previous research, childhood victimization also increases the risk of criminal behavior later in life—as measured by arrests for delinquency and adult criminality, including violent crime.[14] The current study confirms these findings. The odds of arrest for a juvenile offense were 1.9 times higher among abused and neglected individuals than among controls; for crimes committed as an adult, the odds were 1.6 times higher (see table 1). Childhood abuse or neglect increases the risk of being arrested for violent crime, whether in the juvenile or adult years, as well as for crime in general. It is perhaps most important to note, however, that a substantial proportion of the abused and neglected children did not become delinquents or criminals.

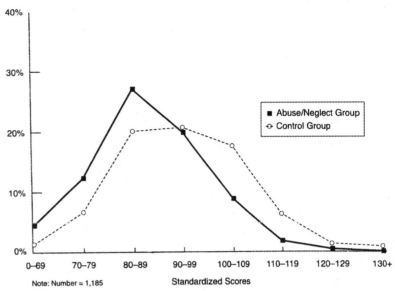

Figure 1: IQ Scores—Abused/Neglected Group and Control Group

Note: Number = 1,185

Standardized Scores

IQ scores are based on the Quick Test. See Ammons, R.B., and Ammons, C.H., "The Quick Test (QT). Provisional Manual," *Psychological Reports* 11 (1962): 11–162 (monograph supplement 7-V!I).

Psychological and emotional fallout. Suicide attempts, diagnosis of antisocial personality disorder, and alcohol abuse and/or dependence were some of the measures of psychopathology. The abused and neglected individuals were significantly more likely than the controls to have attempted suicide and to have met the criteria for antisocial personality disorder (see table 2), findings irrespective of age, sex, race, and criminal history. High rates of alcohol abuse were found in both groups (more than 50 percent in

each), although the abuse/neglect victims were not at greater risk than the controls, a finding that departs from other research but that methodological differences might explain.[15]

As other research has shown, gender can affect the development of psychopathology in abused and neglected children later in life. The current study revealed some of these gender-based differences. Females abused and neglected in childhood were more likely than controls to attempt suicide, to abuse alcohol or be dependent on

it, or to suffer from an antisocial personality disorder. Like females, male victims were found at greater risk than controls of attempting suicide and developing an antisocial personality disorder, but they were not at greater risk of developing alcohol problems (see table 3).

The findings of males' higher risk for antisocial personality disorder and females' higher risk for alcohol problems parallel previous research revealing conformity to gender roles. However, the finding that females are, like males, at risk for antisocial personality disorder (as well as criminal behavior)[16] may call for reconsidering the assumptions of externalizing and internalizing as the respective pathways of male and female response.

The context of victimization. The findings confirmed earlier research identifying context as a factor influencing the long-term outcome for victims. This became evident in analyzing the relationships among childhood victimization, having a parent who had been arrested, and the likelihood of the offspring's developing antisocial personality disorder. The analysis revealed that among people who had a parent with a history

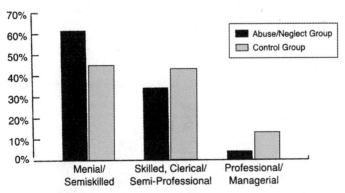

Figure 2: Occupational Status—Abused/Neglected Group and Control Group

Note: Number = 1,167

Occupational status was coded according to the Hollingshead Occupational Coding Index. See Hollingshead, A.B., "Four Factor Index of Social Class," New Haven, CT: Yale University Working Paper, 1975.

Figure 3: Employment History— Abused/Neglected Group and Control Group

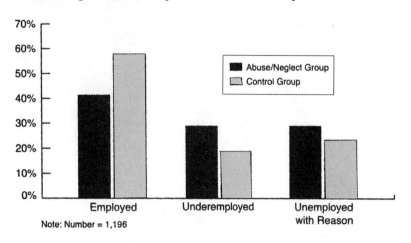

Note: Number = 1,196

Employment history findings are based on a measure used in Robins, L.N., and D.A. Regier, eds., *Psychiatric Disorders in America: The Epidemiological Catchment Area Surveys*, New York: Free Press, 1991:103.

of arrest, abuse or neglect in childhood did not increase the likelihood of their developing an antisocial personality disorder (see table 4).

However, where there was no parental criminality, being abused and/or neglected did increase the risk for this disorder. This complicates attempts to understand the consequences of childhood victimization and also suggests multiple factors in the development of antisocial personality disorder.

A different picture and set of relationships were found for alcohol abuse. When parental alcohol/drug abuse, childhood victimization, and subsequent alcohol problems in offspring were analyzed, the parents' substance abuse problem emerged as the critical factor in the development of the same problem in the children, and this held true whether or not the child had been victimized (see table 5). The study also showed that, as a group, the children who were abused or neglected were no more likely than controls to develop alcohol problems, whether or not the parent had the same problem.

The strong influence of parental characteristics on the offspring, regardless of victimization, warrants more careful consideration, but is consistent with earlier literature on the genetic transmission of alcoholism.

Multiple Mechanisms

The study generated more—and more systematic—evidence that the consequences of childhood victimization extend well beyond childhood and adolescence, persisting into young adulthood. Such victimization affects many functions later in life, and what was revealed in this study most likely represents only the tip of the iceberg, which further research could bring to light. On the other hand, some expected outcomes (such as increased risk for alcohol problems in abused and neglected children) did not materialize, raising questions for further study.

Disentangling the pathways. One of the difficulties in assessing risk of negative consequences is sorting out the children's multiple problems and those of their parents. As previous research has shown, adverse effects interact, so that the combined effects of two types of problems may be greater than their sum.[17] Whether this interaction effect applies to childhood victimization is not known, although it is likely.

This study has not yet tried to distinguish among the many mechanisms by which childhood victimization affects development and psychopathology. When it comes to the influence of contextual factors, children may simply be modeling their parents' behavior. But it also is possible that abuse or neglect may produce immediate effects that then irremediably affect subsequent development, which in turn may affect still later outcomes.

Direct and indirect pathways. Some pathways may be direct—persisting into adulthood. Abused and neglected children may show aggressiveness and behavior problems in childhood, delinquency in adolescence, and antisocial and criminal behavior in adulthood. It also is likely that this path leads to abusive behavior in the home, manifested in spouse or child abuse. In other instances there may be a delayed reaction, occurring years later.

Figure 4: Marital History— Abused/Neglected Group and Control Group

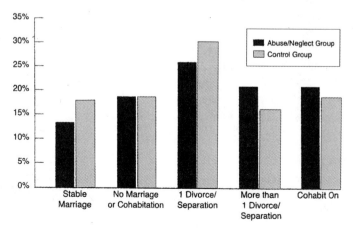

Table 1: Childhood Victimization and Later Criminality

	Abuse/Neglect Group (676)	Control Group (520)
	%	%
Arrest as juvenile	31.2***	19.0
Arrest as adult	48.4***	36.2
Arrest as juvenile or adult for any crime	56.5***	42.5
Arrest as juvenile or adult for any violent crime	21.0*	15.6

*p≤ .05   **p≤ .01   ***p≤ .001

Note: Numbers in parentheses are numbers of cases.

Table 2: Childhood Victimization and Later Psychopathology

	Abuse/Neglect Group (676)	Control Group (520)
	%	%
Suicide Attempt	18.8***	7.7
Antisocial personality disorder	18.4***	11.2
Alcohol abuse/dependence	54.5***	51.0

*p≤ .05   **p≤ .01   ***p≤ .001

Note: Numbers in parentheses are numbers of cases.

Diagnoses of antisocial personality disorder and alcohol abuse/dependence were determined by using the National Institute of Mental Health DIS-III-R diagnostic interview.

Table 3: Childhood Victimization and Later Psychopathology, by Gender

	Abuse/Neglect Group	Control Group
	%	%
Females	(338)	(224)
Suicide attempt	24.3***	8.6
Antisocial personality disorder	9.8*	4.9
Alcohol abuse/dependence	43.8**	32.8
Males	(338)	(276)
Suicide attempt	13.4**	6.9
Antisocial personality disorder	27.0**	16.7
Alcohol abuse/dependence	64.4	67.0

*p≤ .05   **p≤ .01   ***p≤ .001

Note: Numbers in parenthesis are numbers of cases.

Diagnoses of antisocial personality disorder and alcohol abuse/dependence were determined by using the National Institute of Mental Health DIS-III-R diagnostic interview.

Abuse or neglect may encourage certain dysfunctional ways of coping. An example is impulsive behavior that in turn gives rise to deficiencies in problem solving or in school performance, less than adequate functioning on the job, or antisocial personality disorder. Adaptations that might serve well at one stage of development may no longer do so at a later stage, placing the person at risk for further unfavorable situations or subsequent victimization that may trigger psychopathology.

Some early, adverse experiences may be indirect, creating byproducts. They may change the environment or the family situation, which in turn may predispose a person to problem behavior. They also may expose the child to further harmful experiences. In this way, the consequences may be due not so much to the abuse or neglect, but to the chain of events it triggers.

No doubt there are many other mechanisms by which abuse and neglect affect a child. Hopefully, future models that explain long-term consequences will examine some of them, because finding a single mechanism that explains all cases of abuse and neglect is highly unlikely.

Notes

1. This article summarizes the author's "Childhood Victimization: Early Adversity and Subsequent Psychopathology," in *Adversity, Stress, and Psychopathology*, ed. B. P. Dohrenwend, New York: Oxford University Press, 1998: 81–95.
2. Downey, G., et al., "Maltreatment and Childhood Depression," in *Handbook of Depression in Children*, ed. W. M. Reynolds and H. F. Johnson, New York: Plenum, 1994; Dohrenwend, B. P., and B. S. Dohrenwend, "Sex Differences in Psychiatric Disorders," *American Journal of Sociology* 81 (1976): 1447–54; Horwitz, A. V., and H. R. White, "Gender Role Orientations and Styles of Pathology Among Adolescents," *Journal of Health and Social Behavior* 28 (1987): 158–170; and Widom, C. S., "Sex Roles, Criminality, and Psychopathology," in *Sex Roles and Psychopathology*, ed. C. S. Widom, New York: Plenum 1984: 87–213.
3. Downey et al., "Maltreatment and Childhood Depression."
4. Friedrich, W. H., A. J. Urquiza, and R. L. Beilke, "Behavior Problems in Sexually Abused Young Children," *Journal of Pediatric Psychology* 11 (1986): 47–57.

Table 4: Antisocial Personality Disorder in Offspring—Relation to Parental Criminality

	Abuse/Neglect Group	Control Group	Row Significance
	%	%	
Either parent arrested	21.9 (365)	18.8 (170)	n.s.
Neither parent arrested	14.2 (365)	7.4 (350)	***
Column significance	*	***	

*p≤ .05   **p≤ .01   ***p≤ .001 n.s. = not statistically significant.

Note: Numbers in parentheses are numbers of cases.

Diagnoses of antisocial personality disorder and alcohol abuse/dependence were determined by using the National Institute of Mental Health DIS-III-R diagnostic interview.

Table 5: Alcohol Abuse/Dependence in Offspring—Relation to Parental Alcohol/Drug Problems

	Abuse/Neglect Group	Control Group	Row Significance
	%	%	
Either parent alcohol/ drug problem	63.2 (389)	56.6 (196)	n.s.
Neither parent alcohol/ drug problem	42.6 (284)	47.5 (324)	n.s.
Column significance	***	*	

*p≤ .05   **p≤ .01   ***p≤ .001 n.s. = not statistically significant.

Note: Numbers in parentheses are numbers of cases.

Diagnoses of antisocial personality disorder and alcohol abuse/dependence were determined by using the National Institute of Mental Health DIS-III-R diagnostic interview.

5. Livingston, R., "Sexually and Physically Abused Children," *Journal of the American Academy of Child and Adolescent Psychiatry* 26 (1987): 413–415.
6. Briere, J., and M. Runtz, "Symptomatology Associated With Childhood Sexual Victimization in a Nonclinical Adult Sample," *Child Abuse and Neglect* 12 (1988): 51–60; Harris, T., G. W. Brown, and A. Bifulco, "Loss of Parent in Childhood and Adult Psychiatric Disorder: A Tentative Overall Model," *Development and Psychopathology* 2 (1990): 311–328; Terr, L. A., "Chowchilla Revisited: The Effects of Psychiatric Trauma Four Years After a School-Bus Kidnaping," *American Journal of Psychiatry* 140 (1983): 1543–1550.
7. Terr, "Chowchilla Revisited."
8. Gibbin, P. T., R. H. Starr, and S. W. Agronow, "Affective Behavior of Abused and Controlled Children: Comparison of Parent-Child Interactions and the Influence of Home Environment Variables," *Journal of Genetic Psychology* 144 (1984): 69–82.
9. Famularo, R., et al., "Alcoholism and Severe Child Maltreatment," *American Journal of Orthopsychiatry* 56 (1986): 481–485; Reider, E. E., et al., "Alcohol Involvement and Violence Toward Children Among High-Risk Families," Paper presented at the annual meeting of the American Psychological Association, New Orleans, Louisiana, August 11–15, 1989.
10. Goodwin, D. W., et al., "Alcohol Problems in Adoptees Raised Apart From Alcoholic Biological Parents," *Archives of General Psychiatry* 28 (1973): 238–243; Goodwin, D. W., et al., "Alcoholism and Depression in Adopted-Out Daughters of Alcoholics," *Archives of General Psychiatry* 34 (1977): 751–755; Cloninger, C. R., et al., "Psychopathology in Adopted-Out Children of Alcoholics: The Stockholm Adoption Study," in *Recent Developments in Alcoholism,* Vol. 3, M. Galanter, ed., New York: Plenum, 1985.
11. Wyatt, G. E., "Sexual Abuse of Ethnic Minority Children: Identifying Dimensions of Victimization," *Professional Psychology: Research and Practice* 21 (1990): 338–343.
12. Smith, C. P., D. J. Berkman, and W. M. Fraser, *A Preliminary National Assessment of Child Abuse and Neglect and the Juvenile Justice System: The Shadows of Distress,* Washington, D.C.: U.S. Department of Justice: Office of Juvenile Justice and Delinquency Prevention, 1980.
13. Widom, C. S., "The Cycle of Violence," *Science* 244 (1989): 160–166.
14. These findings, based on the study of 1,196 of the original 1,575 subjects (the 908 abuse/neglect victims plus the 667 in the control group), should not be confused with findings from studies published previously (Widom, "Cycle of Violence, and Maxfield, M. G., and C. S. Widom, "The Cycle of Violence: Revisited Six Years Later," *Archives of Pediatrics and Adolescent Medicine* 150 [1996]: 390–395), which report on the entire original sample of 1,575.
15. See Widom, C. S., T. Ireland, and P. J. Glynn, "Alcohol Abuse in Abused and Neglected Children Followed-Up: Are They at Increased Risk?" *Journal of Studies on Alcohol* 56 (1995): 207–217.
16. These findings are not shown here. See Maxfield and Widom, "The Cycle of Violence: Revisited."
17. Rutter, M., "Protective Factors in Children's Response to Stress and Disadvantage," in *Primary Prevention of Psychopathology: Social Competence in Children,* Vol. 3, ed. M. V. Kent and J. E. Rolf, Hanover, NH: New England Press, 1979: 49–74.

about the author

Cathy Spatz Widom is a professor of criminal justice and psychology at the State University of New York at Albany. She is widely recognized for her work on the cycle of violence.

The author wishes to thank Patricia J. Glynn and Suzanne Luu for their help in the preparation of this article.

The research described in this article was supported by grants from the U.S. Department of Justice, National Institute of Justice (86-IJ-CS-0033, 89-IJ-CX-0007, and 94-IJ-CX-0031), and the U.S. Department of Health and Human Services, National Institute on Alcohol Abuse and Alcoholism (AA09238) and National Institute of Mental Health (MH49467).

Man and His Son's Slayer Unite to Ask Why

By WILLIAM GLABERSON

GLOUCESTER, Mass.—The envelope was hand-addressed. When Gregory Gibson glimpsed it one afternoon in November, mixed in with the junk mail and the bills, he knew right away what it was. The return address was a post office box in Norfolk, Mass., near Boston where, Mr. Gibson knew all too well, there is a state prison.

His son's killer was getting in touch.

So much came back that afternoon when the letter arrived at the Gibsons' clapboard house in Gloucester, a two-hour drive from the prison.

"I read the letter," Mr. Gibson said, "and, of course, all of a sudden, my head is spinning and I am right back in this whole welter of emotions."

It had been seven years since that winter night when his son Galen, an 18-year-old student at Simon's Rock College in western Massachusetts, had been gunned down by a fellow student named Wayne Lo. The consuming grief had abated; Mr. Gibson and his wife of 26 years had survived something most parents say is too painful even to consider.

Mr. Gibson's full beard and long brown ponytail were dulled now by the beginnings of gray. But, at 54, the gray might have come anyway—even if Galen, the oldest of the three Gibson children, had not been shot to death for no reason in one of those inexplicable rampages by another student with a semiautomatic.

There had been headlines for a few days after the December 1992 shootings at Simon's Rock, a school in Great Barrington designed for high-school-age students who are ready to begin college work. But the attention had long since faded by the afternoon Mr. Gibson carried the letter from a murderer into his book-lined home office and sat down at the desk.

In his mind's eye, Mr. Gibson said in a series of interviews, he had seen Mr. Lo many times over seven years, not only in his prison cell but also back on that awful night: an 18-year-old sophomore with a buzz cut and a scowl, crossing the quiet campus with that big Chinese-made SKS semiautomatic rifle.

He pushes the rifle through the door of a security shack and, from a foot away, fires two shots into the abdomen of a security guard, Teresa Beavers, severely wounding her. A young professor, Ñacuñán L. Sáez, happens to drive into the campus. Wayne Lo kills him in an instant with a bullet through the jaw.

Galen is studying in the library. Some students rush in, saying there has been an accident. Galen rushes out to see if he can help. Wayne Lo puts a bullet through his chest and one through his side and then keeps shooting, hitting some students, missing others.

In the end, two people were dead, four people were injured. And if the rifle had not jammed, Wayne Lo conceded recently in the first interviews he has given, there would have been more bodies.

At home in Gloucester, Mr. Gibson keeps cartons stuffed with documents from his son's short life and from the court proceedings that followed his death. There is, for example, a color photograph, taken by the police, introduced at the trial where Mr. Lo was convicted of murder in 1994. The picture shows exactly what Wayne Lo did. Galen's slender body is laid out, still in his tangled college-boy clothes. His eyes are slightly opened. His blood-drained skin is nearly the same metallic blue-gray as the stainless steel table.

When Mr. Gibson opened the envelope that day in November, he found two pages of Wayne Lo's carefully printed handwriting inside. "Dear Mr. Gibson," the letter began, "I really don't know how to start or what I should say." What Mr. Gibson went on to read, he would conclude, seemed to be a killer's effort to join him in the same search as people everywhere to understand how the unfathomable tragedy of random killing sometimes comes to innocent places.

Across the country, other families whose loved ones have been killed or wounded by rampage killers also try to find a place in their lives for the shattering events. Some join victims' rights groups. Others form gun control organizations. There are those who want to be alone with their experience, and there are those who say they have turned a corner and no longer want to look back.

Gregory Gibson had once been filled, he says, with vengeful hate. He also had a long period of paralyzing grief, "wondering if I would ever do anything again."

But by the time he found himself reading that letter from Mr. Lo, Mr. Gibson had long been on a path not usually taken by people who have endured what he has. For years, he has methodically forced himself to confront in extraordinary detail the crime that caused his family's heartbreak.

It is a search for meaning that he could not, and still cannot, fully explain.

"It's the story," he said to a visitor one night in the family's kitchen, still casually decorated with pictures of all three Gibson children. "All we've got now is absence and sickness. Somehow, if I follow this story long enough, it will be positive in the world rather than negative."

The Victim's Father

A Killing Sets Off A Search for Answers

It is impossible to know how people choose their paths through grief. But by the time Galen was killed, Gregory Gibson was already weaving together cerebral and practical approaches to life. He was a Swarthmore College graduate and a Navy veteran who, as a young man, had wanted to be a writer. After he concluded that his first novel was unpublishable, though, he set aside his writerly aspirations and went into the antiquarian-book business. It kept him in the world of ideas, he said, and kept bread on table as he and his wife, Anne Marie Crotty, reared their two boys, Galen and Brooks, who is now 22, and a girl, Celia, now 16.

After the crime, the Gibsons sued Simon's Rock, claiming the college's inattention to warning signs about Mr. Lo the day of the shooting was a factor in the murders. Simon's Rock, which is part of Bard College, denied any negligence but eventually settled the case for an undisclosed sum.

Still, for Mr. Gibson, the shortcomings of Simon's Rock were only part of the story he was working so hard to construct. He set out to learn as much as he could about every aspect of the narrative—characters, scenes, circumstances—that ended in Galen's murder. Mr. Gibson's search became absorbing, his son Brooks said; for a while, he worried that his father might be in too deep.

"He was really obsessed with the whole thing," Brooks said. "It would be all he would be talking about."

Mr. Gibson visited other victims of the shooting, sometimes leaving home for a few days to meet with a college student who might have seen something or with a gun owner with an expertise in the weapon Mr. Lo used. He talked to Mr. Lo's friends, and had Mr. Lo's parents to his home. He interviewed Galen's friends, lawyers in Mr. Lo's case, experts on violence, employees of Simon's Rock, authorities on firearms—even the gun dealer who sold his son's killer the semiautomatic.

Each member of the Gibson family dealt with what had happened differently. Galen's mother said that after Mr. Lo's trial she already knew more than she wanted to know about the crime. Of her husband, she said, "I think he hopes for some kind of answer, which I'm not sure he'll ever get." She was not interested in reading Mr. Lo's letter.

In an e-mail message forwarded by her father, Celia said she would prefer not to talk to a reporter. She cares about Galen and her father, she said, but "during this time of my life I have been thinking about lots of other things."

Brooks said he was not sure his father's search would ever end. "My dad," he said, "is an intellectual guy who is trying to figure out for the rest of his life why his son is dead."

In many conversations with a reporter beginning in January, Mr. Gibson said that, at first, the energy for his investigation came from fury that he focused largely on the administration of Simon's Rock. Just before Mr. Lo bought the used semiautomatic rifle for $129 at a gun shop in nearby Pittsfield, he had ordered, over the telephone, 200 rounds of ammunition from Classic Arms, a North Carolina arms supplier and brusquely demanded the package be sent to him, via next-day air, at the college. "I have to have it by tomorrow," an agitated Mr. Lo barked at the order clerk, according to police reports.

At the time, Massachusetts law provided that when an out-of-state resident wanted to buy a rifle in the state, the gun laws in the person's home state governed. The law in Montana, where Mr. Lo's parents lived, permitted 18-year-olds to buy rifles with no waiting period so Mr. Lo had.

Mr. Lo had slipped the rifle onto campus in a guitar case. But court testimony later showed that when the ammunition arrived in a long box, some Simon's Rock dormitory advisers had been alarmed when they saw a package in the mail room with its "Classic Arms" return address. But the college's dean, Bernard F. Rodgers Jr., decided after an administrative meeting that Wayne could take the package to his room. "I thought there was an issue here of privacy rights," Dean Rodgers testified in 1994.

After Mr. Lo had taken the package to his room and hidden the ammunition, Dean Rodgers asked Mr. Lo what had been in the package. Wayne lied, saying it had contained gun parts for his father. His father did not own a gun, but no one from Simon's Rock called to check the story.

Simon's Rock declined to make its administrators available for interviews for this article, but answered some questions in writing. The college regrets the deaths and suffering, according to the statement. But the college added: "If mistakes were made prior to the evening of December 14, 1992, which, in hindsight, might have derailed or at least revealed Wayne Lo's murderous plans, such mistakes must be viewed in the context of the setting and of the times (when school shootings were still relatively unheard of)."

Much of Mr. Gibson's quest to have Simon's Rock admit some responsibility in Galen's death, along with his search for how Mr. Lo could have so easily bought a semiautomatic rifle, can be found in a book he has written, his first to be published: "Gone Boy, A Walkabout: A father's search for truth in his son's murder" (Kodansha International, 1999).

The book is an elegant account of the missteps and deceptions that clear the way for random killing. But Mr. Gibson had not interviewed one central character: Wayne Lo. One of the book's most haunting images is of Mr. Gibson sitting in his car in the visitor's parking lot of the prison, the Massachusetts Correctional Institution-Norfolk, just staring off at the high, impenetrable walls. Someday, he mused in the book's final pages, he would like to confront the person who had caused all the pain.

The Killer

Time in Prison Leads To a Life Reconsidered

Wayne Lo, who is now 25, has been on a kind of journey, too. After the crime and for the first years of his imprisonment, he said not long ago, he believed that God had chosen him to commit carnage. Now, he calls that his period of denial.

"At the time I thought I did the right thing," he said recently. "But as I look back at it over time, more and more it doesn't make sense to me. And more and more I ask myself, Why? Why did I do it? I mean, Why?"

In more than five hours of interviews and 10 follow-up letters he described an evolution of consciousness that was something akin to a lifting of clouds. It happened gradually and, from what he said, it appeared that much remains obscured. In prison, Mr. Lo said, he has received no psychological counseling or medication. Nor does he feel the need for any.

The story Mr. Lo long told himself came down to this: In December 1992, he received a divine message to go to the gun store, order the ammunition with his mother's credit card, then lie and deceive and kill. He was so convinced that he was justified in his acts that he raged at his lawyers during his trial because they insisted on asserting that he was insane. Instead, he argued, his lawyers should have investigated his victims to uncover why a heavenly power had selected them to be shot.

Sitting back and talking one afternoon in a small, concrete-block room with a glass wall facing the main visiting area at the prison, he said the command to kill was a feeling. "It's not visual. It's not auditory," he said. "It's just, you realize it."

Amiable, with smooth, slightly dimpled cheeks and a sparkling intelligence, Wayne Lo often spoke with disarming frankness. He was also manipulative, controlling and so eager to portray himself in a positive light that

it was sometimes impossible to believe he thought he was telling the truth.

Still, his description of his own internal journey remained consistent. And, apart from tending his image with a public that has largely forgotten him, he seemed to have little to gain from describing a growing awareness of the consequences of his actions.

A jury rejected his lawyers' insanity defense, as often happens with abhorrent crimes that are meticulously planned. He was sentenced to life behind bars and, in 1998, Massachusetts' highest court rejected his appeal. "He'll die in prison," his lawyer, Carlo A. Obligato, said.

The new ideas began to occur to Mr. Lo last summer or earlier—he is not sure. He began to think, maybe it was not God who had told him to kill. And if it was not, could it be that what he had done was wrong?

By October, Mr. Lo said, he was experiencing such intense feelings of remorse that when, say, he caught himself alone in his cell laughing at a television sitcom, he would feel ashamed because Galen Gibson and Ñacuñán Sáez could no longer experience any emotions at all.

"What I really want at this point," Mr. Lo said, "is to go back in time and for this to not happen, not so I don't have to suffer, but those people—that this didn't have to happen to them.

"If I could go back and you would still put me in jail for the rest of my life but these people can live and these people don't have to get injured, I would do that, I would take that. But what's happened has happened."

In seven years in prison, Wayne Lo has had plenty of time to reconsider his life before the night at Simon's Rock when lives were changed. When he spoke about those early years, however, the limits of his growing clarity seemed clear.

He repeatedly insisted, for example, that he was "a very happy person" before the message to kill came, as he believes it did, out of nowhere. He professed confusion at prosecutors' descriptions of him as an angry youth. He said he did not know why some people at Simon's Rock told the police after the shooting that he would sometimes talk about wanting to kill large numbers of people or, perhaps, himself. Some students told the police that Mr. Lo was prone to anti-black, anti-gay and anti-Jewish tirades.

Mr. Lo did say he sometimes felt like an outsider, at Simon's Rock and, earlier, at home. He is the son of a colonel in the Taiwan air force who retired and moved with his wife and two boys to Billings, Mont., where they opened a Chinese restaurant in 1987. The moves, Mr. Lo said, created stresses. He was Taiwanese in Billings, a Montanan in Massachusetts.

Expectations for him in both places were high. The family had made the difficult move for the sake of Wayne and his brother Ryan, who is now a 20-year-old college student.

"Our whole hope is our two boys," Mr. Lo's father, Jawei Lo, said as his wife, Lin Lin, cried softly during a long interview in their living room and over lunch at their restaurant last month.

For seven years until this fall, the Los said, Wayne seemed vacant during annual visits. He would occasionally rock rhythmically when asked about his crime, his father said. Then in the fall he seemed to awaken, for the first time discussing what he had done.

"If he can feel regret, feel guilt," Mr. Lo said, "we all think that is the right direction."

This fall, Wayne asked his mother to have a copy of Mr. Gibson's book sent to him. In the interview, she said Mr. Gibson had shown them that there were constructive ways both families could struggle together to cope with their losses.

"He is supposed to hate Wayne because Wayne killed his son," she said. "But he wants to do something different than just hate."

In prison, Wayne Lo said that reading Mr. Gibson's book was an emotional experience, especially when he learned about the Gibsons' warm family and how it had been wounded by what he did. "The book really did a lot to open me up," he said.

In a letter to a former Simon's Rock teacher who had visited him, Sharon Flitterman-King, Mr. Lo wondered whether he should write to Mr. Gibson. She wrote Mr. Gibson and asked whether he would be willing to receive such correspondence. He said he would, if Wayne was willing to accept responsibility for what he had done.

Soon, Wayne was composing that first letter in his crisp handwriting. "I just finished reading your book," he wrote. "It was a good book, though I don't think you need to hear that from me, because you didn't need to write it, I mean, if it wasn't for my horrible act. There is so much I want to say, but it is hard to put all of it on paper."

The Letters

An Unlikely Team Sharing Information

On Dec. 1, two weeks shy of seven years since that murderous night in the Berkshires, Mr. Gibson wrote back: "Dear Wayne, Thank you for your letter. As you can imagine, I have been thinking about it a great deal."

More than a dozen letters have since been exchanged. The two men have yet to talk face to face. But separately over the months of their correspondence each has talked at length with a reporter about the other, the crime and their hopes for their fledgling relationship.

"He's going to help me resolve my feelings about the person who murdered my son, and maybe I can help him, too," Mr. Gibson said one day in February. "It helps him redeem his humanity and it helps me feel I put something into the situation other than hatred and rage. If we do pull it off, it is like some kind of alchemy."

Mr. Lo has concluded that he likes Mr. Gibson. But he does not expect Mr. Gibson to return the warmth.

"How could somebody ever?" he said. "I don't want him to like me. If he likes me, it would almost be that he would be disrespecting the memory of his son."

On some points, there was agreement. Mr. Gibson said he had been surprised to discover that he felt compassion and empathy for Mr. Lo. But, answering a question, he said: "Could I ever like the kid who killed my son? I don't think so."

To preserve some privacy, Mr. Gibson provided only a few excerpts of the letters; Mr. Lo said he would leave that decision to Mr. Gibson. But the interviews and letters to a reporter seemed to duplicate much of what the two men had been saying to each other.

Mr. Lo carefully described the evolution of his thoughts. As he had come to realize God would not have chosen him to inflict so much pain, he said, he had struggled to understand what made him into a killer.

He remains convinced, he said, that it was something outside of himself that gave him a message to do what he did. Perhaps, he said in answer to a question, it was a supernatural or satanic force.

Mr. Lo said he would still prefer not to consider the possibility that he was mentally ill. "Personally I am, I guess you could say, a proud person," he said. "I would like to think that I have control of myself, that I am not impaired in any way."

It is just human nature to have such hopes, Mr. Gibson said. "He's got dignity," he said of Mr. Lo. "He doesn't want to be regarded as an insane monster."

Mr. Lo was stubborn about several themes. He repeatedly insisted, for example, that people had lied when they portrayed him as a hateful bigot before the crime, fascinated by violence and hard-core music. It was true, he acknowledged, that seven weeks before the shooting he had become notorious on campus for a class paper he wrote proposing the extermination of all H.I.V.-positive citizens.

But he insisted that had merely been an effort to get a good grade with a strong argument, not a proposal he really believed. He was a lover of ballads and the Rush Limbaugh television show, he said, not just heavy metal music. It had merely been a coincidence, he insisted, that the night of the killings he had worn a sweatshirt with the name of a hard-core band. A photograph of him in the shirt after his arrest drew national attention because the band's name seemed to be his explanation: "Sick of It All."

Mr. Gibson said he was sorting out the new information he was learning. But he was forgiving of Mr. Lo's more obvious misstatements, saying that Mr. Lo's recollections of what he felt in the chaos around the crime may simply be mistaken.

At times, when he considered the more awful revelations from Mr. Lo, Mr. Gibson sounded depressed. Once that mood seemed to hit after Mr. Gibson learned that

Mr. Lo had said that the ease with which he had bought the gun, ordered the ammunition and fooled Simon's Rock officials had convinced him that his mission was guided by a divine force. "It all worked so seamlessly," Mr. Lo said. "I know it sounds terrible to say that."

At times, when he considered the unlikelihood of his bond with Mr. Gibson, Mr. Lo sounded hopeful. Maybe his other victims and their families, too, might want to hear his explanations and his remorse.

That appears unlikely. When told about Mr. Gibson's correspondence, Mrs. Beavers, the wounded security guard, said she thought this might be some new manipulation by Mr. Lo to make himself feel better. Baruc S. Sáez, Ñacuñán's brother, said he was not interested in anything Mr. Lo might say: "Me and my whole family have tried to forget Wayne Lo and view my brother's death like an accident."

So the story, for now, has narrowed to two people.

One, Mr. Gibson, who is not a churchgoer but says he believes in God, said he and Mr. Lo are contending together with the spiritual consequences of that December night. Someday, he might try to visit his son's killer in prison, he said.

The other, Mr. Lo, said he was willing to do whatever necessary to provide the answers his victims might need, no matter how difficult. "It is uncomfortable," he said, "in the sense that it just reaffirms every day and night: 'It's not a nightmare. I can't wake up from it: This is you, Wayne. You did it.' "

The partnership is difficult for any outsider to understand. Matthew L. David, another student shot that night, said it had been harder to recover psychologically than physically. He wished Mr. Gibson well, but said he had worked for seven years to put the experience behind him.

"Ultimately, 'why?' is not important any more," Mr. David said. "I don't know if I am ever going to know why. What I know is there were consequences to what happened." He had not read Mr. Gibson's book.

In prison, Mr. Lo said Mr. Gibson should get the answers he sought and then "he should just forget me."

At his kitchen table in Gloucester, Mr. Gibson said the work of the killer and the victim's father was not likely to be so simple as a quick exchange of letters and an atonement.

"I figure," Mr. Gibson said, "we've both got the rest of our lives to talk about this."

'Every Day I Have To Forgive Again'

They were hurt. Badly. So badly it changed their lives permanently. Yet the individuals whose stories are told here struggle to come to terms with their feelings about the people they've had every reason to hate.

BY MARIE RAGGHIANTI

A 29-YEAR-OLD POLICE OFFICER WHOSE WIFE IS pregnant with their first child is shot on the streets of New York City. For days his life hangs in the balance, his struggle to live transfixing New Yorkers. At last, it appears he will pull through—but he will be a quadriplegic.

A young woman in Texas is raped, beaten with a hammer, stabbed and left for dead. She manages to survive, but the crime leaves her devastated. "I felt unlovable, untouchable, a throwaway person," she said.

In Cleveland, a 7-year-old boy's mother is murdered. His father is arrested for the crime. In a sensational trial, his father is convicted and sent to prison. Ten years later,

after a retrial, his father goes free. But by then the boy's childhood is gone. The family has been shattered.

Today, Steven McDonald, the former police officer, occupies a wheelchair and is attached to a ventilator. He travels the country telling his story, speaking about the forgiveness he has found for his assailant. Ellen Halbert, who said the attack she experienced was so degrading that she was never going to talk about it, now devotes her life to aiding crime victims—*and* those convicted of crimes. And Sam Reese Sheppard, whose father, Dr. Sam Sheppard. was convicted and then acquitted of murder in two sensational trials, publicly prays for those who have wronged him and his family.

Is Anything Unforgivable?

FORGIVENESS IS A BASIC tenet of Christianity and other religions, and it has been emphasized by some therapists in the past decade as a requirement for recovery. But should we *always* try to forgive?

Harboring hatred can be damaging. As Sam Reese Sheppard commented: "It can be a cancerous emotion." And forgiveness often can bring healing, as Sheppard, Steven McDonald and Ellen Halbert attest.

Still, while we may admire those who can find forgiveness in their hearts, forgiveness may not always be the answer. Andrew Vachss, a writer and attorney who represents abused children, has noted: "A particularly pernicious myth for victims of abuse is that 'healing requires forgiveness' of the abuser." This only leads to further victimization, he added. "The abuser has no 'right' to forgive-

ness—such blessings can only be earned."

And there are some things that cannot be—and should not ever be—forgiven. As Elie Wiesel, the Nobel Laureate and Holocaust survivor, said in a prayer at the 50th anniversary of the liberation of Auschwitz: "God of forgiveness, do not forgive those murderers of Jewish children here."

—*The Editors*

Ellen Halbert took up the cause of victim's rights after being viciously attacked. Then she began visiting prisons. "I thought I'd feel a lot of anger," she says. "I ended up seeing that there are many victims in the system. I was overwhelmed by the wasted lives."

"I shout a lot. I've had some very heated conversations with God. But God played the greatest part in forgiving the young man who shot me."
—*Steven McDonald*

Three ordinary people whose experiences might easily have led to enduring rage, bitterness and feelings of vindictiveness or revenge instead have embraced forgiveness. Why were they— despite all that had happened to them— able to transform their experiences? What made them able to forgive? I resolved to find out.

"Every day I have to forgive again." I visited Steven McDonald, 43, at his home in Malverne, N.Y. Still youthful in appearance. he emanates friendliness and serenity and speaks candidly about the pain he has survived. "My family prayed that I would live," he said. "Their prayers were heard. Of course, they prayed that I would survive whole, not quadriplegic, but here I am."

McDonald recalled the night when he awoke in a hospital bed, unable to move, speak or even breathe. It was the beginning of a long journey back. "I have to tell you, when I have medical difficulties—and I've had quite a few—I shout a lot," he said. "I've had some very heated conversations with God."

He said he knew that the young man who shot him grew up in a difficult environment—that, to him, McDonald represented the enemy. "But God played the greatest part in forgiving the young man who shot me," he said.

McDonald corresponded with his assailant, Shavod Jones, for years afterward, during Jones' incarceration. He believes that Shavod might have become a success story. (He was killed in a motorcycle accident shortly after his parole in 1995.) When McDonald speaks to audiences, he tells them he has forgiven Shavod "unconditionally."

Yet McDonald makes it clear that he is still trying to come to terms with what happened to him. "The world we live in makes it difficult to feel love and forgiveness, not hatred and bitterness," he said. "I'm human. I still struggle every day. Even now I'm struggling with life. Every day I have to forgive again—and again. Every time I speak about [what happened]. I have to forgive anew.

"It's overwhelming how much pain you see." I spoke with Ellen Halbert on a visit to Texas. She clearly recalled how she felt after her attack in 1986. "At first I didn't tell the police I had been raped," she said. "I was never going to talk about it. It was so degrading." Then she discovered that what she was going through was what virtually all victims of rape experience. Eventually, she became an advocate of victims' rights. Today, at 57, she

is the director of the victims/witness division in the Travis County District Attorney's office in Austin. Tex.

In 1991 Halbert began touring prisons. "I had [by then] worked with many victims," she said. "I had heard their suffering and their pain. I thought I would feel a lot of anger." The experience surprised her, however. "Prison is a terrible place. I ended up seeing that there are many other victims in the system. There are the victims of crime." Her voice trailed off. "But in the prisons I saw so many more victims, especially women. I was overwhelmed by the wasted lives. I began to learn their life stories. I heard things that boggled my mind— what parents had done to their children."

Then, she said, she found herself seeing her attacker in a new way. "I think about him sometimes," Halbert noted, "about what will happen when he gets out [He's serving 20 years to life in prison.] I think about when he was growing up. Wasn't there anybody to reach out to him?' "

"I was born into a loving family," she added, "but the prisons are full of people who weren't. It's overwhelming how much pain you see."

"Rage doesn't go away." "It took me 20 years to cry for my mother," Sam Reese Sheppard told me. "When I could finally grieve for her, it was a turning point." Sheppard's world was shattered by his mother's murder, his father's arrest and the media frenzy surrounding the trial. He recalled the confusion and guilt he felt at age 7, when his mother died: his fears that his father might be sent to the electric chair, his nightmare that he would be sent there too.

"I've had my rage," Sheppard admitted. "I still do, at times. Forgiveness is a daily process. I have to work at it." However, he added, "I've learned that hatred is a cancerous emotion." Today, at 52, Sheppard lives in Oakland, Calif., where he is a dental hygienist. He also is

A Father Finds Hope in Tragedy

WHEN AZIM KHAMISA'S SON, TARIQ, 20, WAS SHOT and killed by 14-year-old Tony Hicks in San Diego in 1995, Khamisa could have let hatred and bitterness take over his life. Instead, he reached out to the family of the young man who had ended his son's life—and, along with the grandfather and guardian of his son's killer, founded the Tariq Khamisa Foundation. (His story was featured in PARADE on March 2, 1997.)

The foundation—guided by the notion that concern for children transcends race, religion, culture, ethnicity and economic status—presents programs designed to stop guns and violence and to promote forgiveness in San Diego elementary schools. For more information, write to The Tariq Khamisa Foundation, 2550 Fifth Ave., Suite 65, Dept. P, San Diego, Calif. 92103, call 1-888-435-7853 or send e-mail to *info@tkf.org*.

active in a citizens' group that opposes the death penalty. A practicing Buddhist, he believes that "nonviolence, reconciliation and peacemaking are probably the highest attributes we can aspire to."

His belief was put to the test in 1990, when he received several letters from Richard Eberling, the man who, some evidence suggests, was his mother's killer. Sheppard arranged to visit Eberling (now dead) in prison, where he was serving a sentence for another crime. Why did he want to come face-to-face with the man who might have been responsible for what happened to him? "I knew [the killer] must have suffered too as a child," Sheppard said. "These things don't come out of thin air."

Sheppard's suspicions were confirmed during his visit. "It was excruciating, but I had only pity for him," Sheppard said. "He was born out of wedlock, abandoned as an infant. He was virtually untouched by human hands in the early months of his life. There was no maternal bond. We know how serious this is."

Sheppard admitted that he struggles to maintain his perspective. "I doubt that true closure is possible," he said. "It's a long process, a daily one. But to live in anguish, pain and anger is a horrible way to live."

"There are bad people who were once good, and they may be good again," he added. "It's death to say that people can't change. People do change."

Marie Ragghianti has long been involved with the criminal-justice system: in the 1970s as head of Tennessee's Board of Pardons and Paroles, where her exposure of corruption led to a best-selling book and the movie "Marie"; and now as Vice Chair of the U.S. Parole Commission. (Note: This article does not reflect the views of the U.S. Parole Commission or the U.S. Department of Justice.)

Sweden's Response to Domestic Violence

By LARS NYLÉN, LL.M., and GUN HEIMER, M.D., Ph.D.

"Violence at home is a significant reason for disability and death among women, both in the industrialized world and in developing countries."[1]
—*Rebecca and Russel Dobash*

In 1993, the United Nations approved a declaration calling for the elimination of violence against women in all of its forms, from violence within marriage and sexual harassment in the workplace to female genial mutilation and forced prostitution. These issues were discussed further at the U.N. Fourth World Conference on Women held in Beijing in 1995. At about the same time, the European Council issued a declaration with strategies to fight violence against women in a democratic Europe. Additionally, through the World Health Organization, the United Nations began to view this violence as a female health issue.[2]

With the final report of the committee on Violence Against Women in June 1995, the issue of violence against women also started to attract significant attention in Sweden.[3] As in most Western countries, Sweden's response to violence and threats against women has varied considerably in the last decade. Swedish society has begun to view domestic violence against women not as the silent, hushed-up problem of the past but as a serious situation affecting the health of women.

In the past, to prosecute a domestic violence case, prosecutors needed explicit accusations from victims. In addition, Swedish legislation mandated that the courts view each criminal act as an isolated matter. Courts rarely could consider the aggravating circumstances or the number of repeat occurrences perpetrated by an offender. Moreover, the Swedish legislature previously viewed reconciliation between the involved parties as preferable to judicial intervention.

Now, domestic violence is a general indictable crime. On July 1, 1998, the government introduced a new offense into the Swedish Penal Code. One part of the new offense, *gross violation of a woman's integrity,* covers repeated acts committed by men against women with whom they have a close relationship. Its companion offense, *gross violation of integrity,* protects children and other close relatives. The new offense means that if a man commits certain criminal acts (e.g., assault, unlawful threat or coercion, sexual or other molestation, or sexual exploitation) against a woman to whom he is or has been married or with whom he is or has been cohabiting and seriously damages her self-confidence, the courts can sentence him for gross violation of the woman's integrity in addition to sentencing him on each traditional crime, such as aggravated assault. In this way, the new legislation allows the courts to take into account the entire situation of the abused woman and increase the offender's punishment to fit the severity and frequency of the acts.[4]

In September 1998, the Uppsala District Court issued one of the first sentences based on the new offense. On four occasions during a 6-week period in the summer of 1998, a man had battered his cohabitant, once bruising her entire face and, on another occasion, beating her severely and knocking out a tooth. The court sentenced the man to 10 months in prison.

Understanding the Crime

With the change in Sweden's attitude about violence against women, police officers began to examine the crime and its impact on society. Swedish police consider violence against women as the most extreme example of the imbalance or disparity between the sexes and a phenomenon that cannot be explained in the same ways as other crimes. In support of this belief, a process known as normalization[5] illustrates the difference between how men and women may rationalize domestic violence and may help explain why this type of violence continues to plague modern society. For men, the normalization process is a goal-oriented strategy designed to control women and prove their own masculinity. For women, the normalization process represents a defense mechanism, a way of rationalizing, adopting, accepting, and surviving the man's behavior. She makes excuses for him (e.g., it was her fault, he did not mean to do it, he is worried about something) and blurs the limits of what constitutes acceptable and unacceptable behavior. Eventually, she may accept the violence as a part of her life and gradually become more isolated. This process has much in common with survival strategies where the victim identifies with the aggressor, for example, the Stockholm Syndrome, which experts have observed in concentration camp settings and in hostage situations.

Reprinted courtesy of the *FBI Law Enforcement Bulletin,* November 1999, pp. 19-24.

For many, home represents a safe haven, but for some women, home is a dangerous place. According to the statistics collected by women's shelters in Sweden, a woman is battered every 20 minutes, and every year, 25 to 30 women in Sweden are battered to death by their husbands.[6] In a Canadian study of 12,000 women, 51 percent had encountered violence, and 25 percent had experienced physical or sexual violence by a current or former partner.[7] English studies have shown that when a woman, her friends, or her neighbors finally contact the police, the woman probably has been battered more than 30 times.[8]

Some studies have demonstrated that among pregnant women, battery occurs more often than diabetes and high blood pressure. Moreover, Canadian studies have shown that, in certain cases, pregnancy initiated the violence. These researchers found that for a controlling and possessive man, his partner's pregnancy could represent a threat to his special control over her and to his having her undivided attention and love. Often, the most violent men are those who subject their partners to violence during pregnancy.[9]

Gathering the evidence

The change in Sweden's attitude concerning domestic violence against women also has impacted the way police obtain evidence in such cases. To fulfill the demands of a proactive, preventive approach, the Swedish police have had to study the dynamics of domestic violence, which make evidence gathering especially difficult.

For example, domestic violence victims often experience one or more of the following concerns:

- fear of retaliation by the perpetrator or relatives;
- desire to protect next of kin from the perpetrator's aggressiveness;

" . . . Sweden's response to violence and threats against women has varied considerably in the last decade."

- risk of loss of economic and emotional security;
- fear of loss of residency and expulsion;
- pressure from relatives to not bring charges against the perpetrator;

- risk of losing cultural, religious, ethnic, or other support; and
- risk of facing further humiliation and doubt in the course of the judicial process.

As a result, victims act in what they believe to be the best way for them and their children to stay safe, both in the present and the future. They may blame themselves or give statements that exonerate the offender. At the same time, suspects may offer persuasive arguments in attempt to disavow their actions.

Officers must prepare themselves for these circumstances and may need to gather evidence in other ways. For example, thorough medical examinations can help overcome the difficulties inherent in these cases, and officers should cooperate with such specialists as gynecologists, pediatricians, psychiatrists, and medical examiners in order to get a complete and accurate picture of the facts of the case. Well-formulated evidence based on expert examination often proves crucial during the preliminary investigation and at the trial.[10]

In 1994, to further assist victims of domestic violence, Sweden founded the National Centre for Battered and Raped Women at the Department of Obstetrics and Gynecology at the Uppsala University Hospital. Patients receive around-the-clock emergency medical attention, as well as social services, police support, and legal assistance.

This comprehensive approach proves critical for women who come to health and medical care services because of battery or sexual abuse. Many not only have been mentally and physically abused but judicially and socially harmed, as well. Moreover, their perpetrators are often relatives. Also, because all of the offenses they have suffered include different degrees of mental violence, most of the women feel frightened that they will not be understood or believed. Therefore, they are very sensitive to other people's attitudes and to the way they are treated. These women seldom seek medical treatment, but when they do, they often may conceal the real reasons for visiting a doctor and try to explain away their visible injuries. Experts also have found that the amount and type of help a woman needs varies depending on her general life situation, on how long she has endured the violence, and whether she has any children. Therefore, police officers, social workers, and health care providers need to understand that they have the responsibility to give these women adequate medical, psychological, and social attention, which they can accomplish by:

- *discovering* the extent and length of abuse;
- *documenting* the physical evidence;

- *treating* the victim's physical, emotional, and mental injuries;
- *nurturing* the victim's self-image;
- *empowering* the victim to seek judicial action;
- *rehabilitating* the victim's sense of self-worth; and
- *cooperating* among themselves to develop a comprehensive, seamless approach to help the victim deal with the effects of domestic violence.

The Warning Bell

In 1996, as part of the preventive and proactive approach to domestic violence cases, the police in Uppsala, Sweden, developed a database modeled on one from the Merseyside Police in Liverpool, Great Britain. This database, the Warning Bell, allows police to quickly access information in connection with a domestic violence incident. The Warning Bell provides responding police officers with information about the crime victims, prior incidents, possible suspects, and any previous enforcement or protective measures taken. With the advent of the database, police officers no longer need to rely on one another's randomly ac-

"Often, the most violent men are those who subject their partners to violence during pregnancy."

quired personal knowledge from previous interventions. Instead, officers can use information from the database to support an investigation, especially when victims waver about participating in the judicial process. The courts also can use this information to implement the new Swedish Penal Code offense (*gross violation of a woman's integrity*) when the case goes to trial. Moreover, through a more detailed report of every intervention, social service authorities can better assess the results of their procedures.

At the same time that they developed the database, the Uppsala police conducted a study of the observations made and measures taken by the police officers responding to domestic violence incidents. The study revealed that the victim contacted the police the most (62 percent of the time), while someone other than the victim (e.g., neighbors, relatives, or witnesses) contacted them 26 percent of the time. The alleged male offender or an anonymous caller each contacted the police 3 percent of the time, while in 5 percent of the cases, the identity of the caller was not classified.

The study further showed that in 50 percent of the cases, a police patrol unit arrived at the location within 15 minutes, and in 78 percent of the cases, within 30 minutes. Slightly more than 52 percent of the cases occurred in the evening, or at night, usually between 6 p.m. and 3 a.m. In all cases, the suspected perpetrator was the victim's current or former husband or boyfriend. Seventy-eight percent of the cases occurred at the woman's residence or what had been the joint home of the involved parties. The analysis of interventions also confirmed what the police generally had known—that domestic violence takes place on all days of the week but occurs more often on Friday and Saturday evenings or nights.

Often, a general opinion exists among police officers that domestic violence correlates with alcohol intoxication. In light of this belief, the responding police officers in the Uppsala study reported their judgment of whether the involved parties seemed intoxicated. In 48 percent of the cases, police officers determined that the women *were not* under the influence of alcohol. Conversely, in only 19 percent of the cases, the police judged that the men *were not* under the influence of alcohol. The police also surmised that 17 percent of the women and 34 percent of the men were obviously or strongly intoxicated at the time of the intervention. While alcohol use was associated with some of these domestic violence cases, long-standing research has shown that alcohol use in itself does not cause domestic violence.[11]

Finally, the Uppsala study showed the police interventions led to a reported crime in 74 percent of the cases. In over 11 percent of the cases, the interventions resulted in formal contact with social services. Reconciliation between the involved parties as the sole means of arbitration occurred in only 13 percent of the cases. These findings reveal that the police and the victims themselves have begun to employ more proactive measures to combat domestic violence.

Meeting the Judicial System

Bringing a domestic violence case to trial often proves difficult. What causes women to resist the judicial process? First, the treatment from the police and the handling of the preliminary investigation influence the victim's desire and ability to assist, especially if, at the same time, she is affected by the normalization process. Also, in many areas of the judicial system, an old-fashioned, patriarchal opinion of women still exists; for instance, that husbands can punish their wives. Moreover, the woman may perceive that the investigation could shift the guilt from the perpetrator to her. This is especially true if a report to the police would mean far-reaching negative social consequences for the man if convicted. Additionally, women often view the police investigation and the subsequent trial as a public repetition of the traumatic experience of the criminal offense, something many naturally try to avoid.

However, the court needs detailed information to correctly understand and judge the case. Therefore, authorities should consider appointing an advocate to brief the victim about the trial's procedures and to support her throughout the process. Also, many victims doubt the authorities' ability to protect them during and after a judicial process. In Sweden, commonly used protection methods include police protection (bodyguards in special cases), alarm kits, or changes of identity and location. Still, domestic violence victims often do not feel sufficiently safe to fully cooperate in the judicial process. Further, victims may underestimate the difficulties associated with these types of formal protective measures and the adjustments that are necessary for the measures to work. Therefore, simpler measures may more effectively protect victims and allay their fears. Swedish authorities presently are studying the possibilities of electronically monitoring men who have violated restraining orders.

Conclusion

In Sweden, recent studies show that the problem of violence against women is significant and requires renewed attention not only from the law enforcement profession but also society in general. While this problem cuts across all boundaries, its countermeasures require a multifaceted and active approach in every community. Society's attitudes and outlooks must change; law enforcement must create new procedures; the judicial system must acquire knowledge and authority to intervene and take appropriate legal action; and medical and social services must look at victims in a holistic and comprehensive manner.

From such a joint knowledge base, Swedish society has begun to build a working, all-inclusive solution to domestic violence—a crime that adversely affects the health, productivity, and lifestyles of women around the world. The Swedish experience clearly shows that close operational cooperation among health and medical services, law enforcement and judicial authorities, and social and volunteer agencies, with confidence and respect for the primary roles of the different organizations, stands as the surest, practical way to eliminate such a devastating threat to women.

Endnotes

1. Rebecca and Russel Dobash, Violence Research Centre, Department of Social Policy and Social Work, Great Britain.
2. U.N. Declaration on the Elimination of Violence Against Women, 48/104, December 1993; and WHO precongress meeting on Violence Against Women: In Search of Solutions, July 1997.
3. "A Centre for Women Who Have Been Raped or Abused," The Committee on Violence Against Women, interim report Swedish Official Report Series (SOU) (1994): 56; and "Violence Against Women," final report SOU (1995): 60.
4. Swedish Government Bill, *Violence Against Women*, (1997/98): 55.
5. Eva Lundgren, "Normalization Process of Violence, Two Parties—Two Strategies." *Violence Against Women*, JÄMFO Report 14, Stockholm, Sweden (1989).
6. "Women Shelter Knowledge," National Institute of Public Health, Stockholm, Sweden (1994): 10.
7. Holly Johnson, "Violence Against Women Survey," *Statistics Canada*, 1993.
8. Gloria Laycock, Home Office Police Research Group, London, Great Britain.
9. H. Johnson and V. F. Sacco, "Researching Violence Against Women," *Canadian Journal of Criminology* (July 1995): 281–304.
10. "Women Subjected to Sexualized Violence," National Centre for Battered and Raped Women, Uppsala University Hospital, Sweden, 1996, contains instructions for medical personnel conducting examinations of women who have been subjected to domestic violence; and "Legal Certificates at Investigations of Violent and Sexual Crimes," National Board of Health and Welfare, Stockholm, Sweden, 1997: 5 (M) contains instructions for preparing forensic medical certificates in such cases.
11. B. Critchlow, "The Powers of John Barleycorn: Beliefs About the Effects of Alcohol on Social Behavior," *American Psychology* 41 (1986): 751–64.

Unit 3

Unit Selections

Key Points to Consider

❖ Is there "community policing" in your community? If not, why not? If so, is it working? Explain.

❖ Should the police be involved in community problems not directly concerned with crime? Explain your response.

❖ How would you define "racial profiling"?

 **Links**   **www.dushkin.com/online/**

These sites are annotated on pages 4 and 5.

The Police

Police officers are the guardians of our freedoms under the Constitution and the law, and as such they have an awesome task. They are asked to prevent crime, protect citizens, arrest wrongdoers, preserve the peace, aid the sick, control juveniles, control traffic, and provide emergency services on a moment's notice. They are also asked to be ready to lay down their lives, if necessary.

In recent years the job of the police officer has become even more complex and dangerous, illegal drug use and trafficking is at epidemic levels, racial tensions are explosive, and violent crime continues to increase at alarming rates.

The role of the police in America is a difficult one, and as the police deal with a growing, diverse population, their job becomes even more difficult.

Thus the need for a more professional, well-trained police officer is obvious.

The lead article in this section, "Ethics and Criminal Justice: Some Observations on Police Misconduct," discusses police misconduct in terms of ethical violations. This is followed by "On-the-Job Stress in Policing—Reducing It, Preventing It," which looks at some sources of job-related stress and the effects it can have on officers. In "Policing the Police," Kenneth Jost deals with such issues as excessive use of force, the Supreme Court Miranda ruling (and the attempt to overturn it by congressional legislation), as well as racial profiling. "Why Harlem Drug Cops Don't Discuss Race" profiles a racially mixed narcotics team in New York City.

Ethics and Criminal Justice: Some Observations on Police Misconduct

by Bryan Byers
Ball State University

One need not look far to see evidence of the societal importance placed on ethics in criminal justice. Ethics has been a hot topic in the 1990s and promises to be equally important as we venture into the new millennium. Often, the issue of ethics in criminal justice is considered synonymous with police ethics. However, ethics touches all of the main branches of criminal justice practice as well as the academic realm. Due to the high profile nature of policing in our society, however, ethics is commonly connected with policing. Therefore, particular focus is given to this dimension in the following discussion. Within this essay the topic of ethics is addressed by first examining a general understanding of this concept. Second, a brief discussion of our societal concern over ethics and criminal justice practice is examined. Third, the discussion centers on selected scholarship in criminal justice ethics. Finally, some concluding remarks are offered.

ETHICS AND ETHICAL ISSUES: A PRIMER

According to the Merriam-Webster Dictionary, "ethics" is defined as (1) "a discipline dealing with good and evil and with moral duty" or (2) "moral principles or practice." The first definition suggests that ethics is a discipline or area of study. This certainly has been the case when we examine the academic field of Philosophy. Criminal justice is, admittedly, a hybrid discipline drawing from many academic fields—one be-

ing Philosophy. Interestingly, a good portion of the published academic scholarship in criminal justice ethics is philosophical in nature and can be found in the journal *Criminal Justice Ethics*. The other part of the definition suggests that ethics is a combination of cognition ('moral principles') and behavior ('practice'). Therefore, we might conclude that ethics is the study of the principle and practice of good, evil, and moral duty.

As we consider the nature of criminal justice, and in particular policing, within contemporary society, the behavior of law enforcement officers is continually the target of ethical evaluation. The field of law enforcement has been under scrutiny during various historical epochs for behavior that has been called into question on ethical grounds. Whether it be search and seizure "fishing expeditions" prior to *Mapp v. Ohio,* the fallout from the Knapp Commission report (*a la Serpico*) or the latest instance of police misconduct to flood the media, essentially the concern is over conduct or behavior. Cognitive processes and the socialization that reinforces unprofessional and unethical conduct influence the onset and proliferation of undesirable behavior. Thus, while one must be concerned with psychological and sociological forces that help to produce police unprofessionalism and unethical behavior, we should not lose sight of the role choice has in police misconduct.

One would be hard pressed to produce credible evidence to suggest that policing has not become more professional over the past sev-

eral decades. It seems equally unreasonable to suggest that the entire field of policing is corrupt and permeated with graft. However, and as most readers will know, such an explanation has been offered. The venerable "rotten barrel theory"[1] of police corruption suggests such permeation within a police department. As most readers know, the rotten barrel theory of police corruption suggests that unethical, and illegal behavior, not only occurs at the individual officer level but is pervasive enough within a police department that unethical conduct may be traced to top administrative officials.

Another interpretation of police corruption is the "rotten apple theory."[2] This approach does not suggest that corruption and unethical conduct is so pervasive that it spreads to the highest ranks and throughout the organization. This approach, rather, suggests that there are a few "rotten apples" in a police department and inappropriate behavior is isolated to a few individuals. Police administrators have been keen on this explanation in the wake of police corruption because it avoids suggestion of wholesale departmental corruption, allows for a tidy response (e.g., fire the offending officer), and does not necessarily have to result in a tarnished image of an entire department.

An additional form of police misconduct has also been identified. In addition to the rotten apple and the rotten barrel, there may also be a "rotten group theory" of police corruption. According to a 1998 report

From *Academy of Criminal Justice Science (ACJS) Today,* September/October 2000, pp. 1, 4-7. Reprinted with permission of the Academy of Criminal Justice Sciences.

by the General Accounting Office on police corruption in the United States, "The most commonly identified pattern of drug-related police corruption involved small groups of officers who protected and assisted each other in criminal activities, rather than the traditional patterns of non-drug-related police corruption that involved just a few isolated individuals or systemic corruption pervading an entire police department or precinct."[3]

Whether unethical behavior is systematic, small group, or individual, one cannot deny the importance placed on the intellectual process that allows for such conduct to take place. One might still be left wondering what it is about policing that produces opportunities to engage in unethical behavior. That is, what is it about the policing profession that affords officers the opportunity to engage in unethical conduct? The answer might be found in the concepts of "authority" and "power." Police wield a tremendous amount of power and authority within society. The powers to arrest, question and detain are entrusted with the police. The authority given to the police to protect our belongings and persons is unmatched by any other profession. Unethical or illegal behavior results when a law enforcement officer makes a conscious decision to abuse authority or wield power that is not appropriate to the situation. What is fundamental to unethical behavior by police is the conscious decision to abuse authority or power and circumstances, peer pressure, socialization, loyalty, and individual psychology are secondary in their ability to explain the behavior.

It might be best to interpret the role played by factors such as circumstances, peer pressure, socialization, loyalty, and individual psychology as a means of excusing or justifying the unethical or illegal act committed by an officer. That is, while the individual officer makes a decision to violate the public's trust and engage in unethical behavior,

one might suggest that the officer's loyalty to his peers was a justification for the conduct. Let us examine this dynamic by way of an ethical dilemma. Assume that Officer X has just pulled over a drunk driver and realizes that the suspect is a fellow officer and friend. In fact, the driver has helped Officer X out of a few "tight spots" over the years. Instead of placing the colleague through a field sobriety test, Officer X helps his buddy park the car and then drives him home with the understanding from his friend that he will "sleep it off." What was the ethical dilemma? The choice between doing what was appropriate (the field sobriety test and subsequent arrest if appropriate) and being loyal to his friend. This situation, at the very least, describes a scenario ripe for abuse of discretion. Since discretion is a power that police have, it can be abused. Thus, many might examine this situation and suggest that the officer abused his discretionary authority. The officer made a decision to abuse his power but did so out of loyalty to the friend that is promoted through socialization behind the "blue curtain."

CONCERN OVER ETHICS: CAN WE CALL IT A TREND?

Media reports of police misconduct pepper us whenever there is an incident of alleged misbehavior or corruption. It might be the nightly newscaster reporting on the Rodney King incident at the start of the 1990s. It could be the recent case of the Philadelphia Police Department officers viewed on tape kicking a downed felony crime suspect at the birth of the twenty-first century. Whatever the instance, the topic of ethics and ethical behavior within the criminal justice profession grabs headlines. The media likes to report on such "ethical misadventures" because it sells. Some of the public, and powerful leaders, use such instances to legitimize their negative attitudes toward police. The police

loathe the "bad press" in the wake of their self-perception of "doing good" for the community.

The media might be the only winner in the wake of police misconduct. However, the public loses and so do the fields of policing and criminal justice, in general. Even the academic field of criminal justice loses because policing is so closely linked in the public mind to it. I am reminded of this reality when recalling my flight back from the 1991 Academy of Criminal Justice Sciences meeting in Nashville. As plane passengers do, I began a conversation with the person seated next to me. We engaged in the typical small talk of "where are you from" and "where are you going." When my fellow passenger heard that I was returning from a "criminal justice" meeting, his response was immediate and unequivocal. He said, "why are cops such jerks?" The conversation occurred in the wake of the Rodney King incident and he was referring to the behavior of the L.A. police officers captured on tape. Admittedly taken aback, I was speechless. Part of the reason was personal given my experiences in the field as a practitioner and those of close family members and friends. The other part of my speechlessness was professional and social scientific in nature given how astounding it was to me to find a person willing to generalize so broadly from one highly celebrated incident. This seemingly innocuous exchange had an indelible impression on me. It made me think about the impact the field of criminal justice might have in the topic of ethics.

There is little doubt that real world events and their impact on the collective conscience influence the academic field. In fact, one could reasonably argue that societal events drive research agendas and define, to some degree, what is popular to investigate criminologically and what is not. Ethics may be no exception. For instance, the Rodney King incident, one might argue, had a tremendous impact not only on the practical dimensions of policing and police-community relations but also on the academic field of criminal justice. For instance, the book jacket for *Above the Law: Police and the Excessive Use of Force* by Jerome Skolnick and James Fyfe has a frame from the Rodney King video just below the title. The impact goes beyond one book, however.

Using 1991 as a pivotal year, given that the Rodney King beating occurred then, the author decided to conduct a computer search for articles on ethics in criminal justice. The findings, albeit not scientific, are interesting nonetheless. Using Periodical Abstracts, an on-line search method at my institution and offered through the university library, a search was conducted for "criminal justice" + "ethics" comparing the years 1986–1990 to 1991–1999. What I wanted to find out is this: were there more publications in criminal justice ethics prior to Rodney King or after? Since the incident occurred relatively early in 1991, that year was placed in the "post-Rodney King" group of years. From 1986 (the first year the index covers) through 1990, there were 28 "hits" or publications on criminal justice ethics. From 1991 through 1999 there were 152 publications. Admittedly, the "post" period encompassed nine years and the "pre" period only contained five years. However, it is still rather telling that such a difference exists.

Only time will tell if the aforementioned suggests a trend for the discipline. However, there is certainly every indication that criminal justice scholarship and practice will continue with an emphasis on ethics. A key reason why ethics promises to have a strong future presence has less to do with the lasting impact of Rodney King and more to do with constant reminders that ethical misadventures keep occurring. For example, during the past ten years, the cities of New Orleans, Chicago, New York, Miami, and Los Angeles, to name a few, have all reeled in the aftermath of ethical transgressions among their sworn law enforcement officers.

ETHICS AND CRIMINAL JUSTICE PRACTICE

In addition to the Rodney King case, there have been many other instances in which law enforcement officers have been found in ethically compromising or illegal positions. Every major city police force in the United States has experienced some form of unethical or illegal behavior within its ranks. Some of the situations in recent history have involved drugs and drug units. A few examples are listed below:

- A 1998 report by the General Accounting Office cites examples of publicly disclosed drug-related police corruption in the following cities: Atlanta, Chicago, Cleveland, Detroit, Los Angeles, Miami, New Orleans, New York, Philadelphia, Savannah, and Washington, DC. [4]
- On average, half of all police officers convicted as a result of FBI-led corruption cases between 1993 and 1997 were convicted for drug-related offenses.[5]
- A 1998 report by the General Accounting Office notes, ". . .several studies and investigations of drug-related police corruption found on-duty police officers engaged in serious criminal activities, such as (1) conducting unconstitutional searches and seizures; (2) stealing money and/or drugs from drug dealers; (3) selling stolen drugs; (4) protecting drug operations; (5) providing false testimony; and (6) submitting false crime reports."[6]
- A 1998 report by the General Accounting Office notes, "Although profit was found to be a motive common to traditional and drug-related police corruption, New York City's Mollen Commission identified power and vigilante justice as two ad-ditional motives for drug-related police corruption."[7]
- As an example of police corruption, the GAO cites Philadelphia, where "Since 1995, 10 police officers from Philadelphia's 39th District have been charged with planting drugs on suspects, shaking down drug dealers for hundreds of thousands of dollars, and breaking into homes to steal drugs and cash."[8]
- In New Orleans, 11 police officers were convicted of accepting nearly $100,000 from undercover agents to protect a cocaine supply warehouse containing 286 pounds of cocaine. The undercover portion of the investigation was terminated when a witness was killed under orders from a New Orleans police officer. [9]

Part of the fallout from a major finding of unethical or illegal behavior within a police department is a call to "clean up" the agency. As a result, departments in the aftermath of such an embarrassing situation might become more open to citizen review panels, pledge to re-examine their internal affairs division, require officers to participate in "ethics training," or reinforce the importance of "ethics codes."

The concept of citizen review panels has been in existence for several decades; the first panel may have been formed in Philadelphia around 1958. Citizen review panels, sometimes also called civilian review boards, are in place in some jurisdictions for the purpose of assisting with the investigation of citizen complaints that police officers within the jurisdiction engaged in the unfair treatment of civilians. Review panels can help to build or repair strained police-community relations. However, officers sometimes respond to such efforts with a defensive posture and resentment over "civilians trying to tell them how to do their job."

A department might also pledge to examine its own internal affairs division, the policy and procedure for investigating complaints and cases against officers, and typical responses to officers who have violated departmental policy and/or who have violated the law. It is important to note from the onset that a police department internal affairs division runs the risk of being considered "suspect" from officers and a community's citizenry alike. Officers can view internal affair or "I.A." as the "enemy" and a division that is bent on punishing officers who are risking their lives on the streets every day. From the community, there might be the perception that the police department cannot possibly take on the task of investigating itself. At the very least, this cannot be done "ethically." Thus, I.A. can find itself in a no win situation. Whether a division in a large department or an officer charged with this responsibility in a smaller department, the I.A. role is critical. However, internal remedies are effective only if they are meted out in a fair and just fashion. I.A. recommendations that are carried out by police administration must bolster the respect of line officers. If perceptions exist that an officer has been treated unfairly, the department will lose any deterrent effect I.A. recommendations might produce.

Yet another response is the concept of "ethics training" for police officers and recruits. The notion of "ethics *training*" (with an emphasis on 'training') is an interesting one given that the concept of 'training' assumes that what a person is being "trained in" can be taught. In this case, the term 'ethics training' suggests, either correctly or incorrectly, that ethics can somehow be taught to people. I prefer the term "Ethics Awareness Training" in lieu of the aforementioned. Why? The reason is rather elementary. Is it possible to teach someone to be ethical as "ethics training" might suggest? This seems far-fetched, at best. If a department has an officer who has a propensity toward unethical behavior, and this person was not weeded out during the hiring process, the

best one might hope for is a heightened awareness and sensitivity for ethical issues and dilemmas. Emphasizing codes of ethics, common today in most disciplines and professions[10], is another avenue for police departments in the wake of ethical scandal. However, if a code of ethics[11] is printed in the departmental policy and procedure manual, never to be referred to again, it will have very little impact. A code of ethics for any department or organization must be a "living document" that is referenced often and held in high esteem. The code should be a document that officers have pride in and believe to be relevant to their lives as law enforcement officers. Otherwise, the code will have little, if any, impact on officer decision making and conduct.

THE SCHOLARS WEIGH IN

As mentioned above, a large portion of the academic scholarship in criminal justice ethics is philosophical in nature. However, a few academicians have attempted to examine ethics in criminal justice empirically and quantitatively. When discussing scholarship in criminal justice ethics, a few names immediately come to mind including James Fyfe, Herman Goldstein, Victor Keppeler, Carl Klockars, Joycelyn Pollock, Lawrence Sherman, Jerome Skolnick and Sam Souryal. This is certainly not an exhaustive list, and we cannot possibly survey all of the literature in this field here. However, I would like to spend a few moments discussing two major studies funded by NIJ. The studies are *The Measurement of Police Integrity by Klockars*, Iv-kovitch, Harver, and Haberfeld[12] and *Police Attitudes Toward Abuse of Authority: Findings from a National Study* by Weisburd and Greenspan.[13] Both studies were published in May of 2000. While the two studies do not represent the entire literature on police ethics, both studies are national in scope, recent and empirical.

The Klockars et al. study used 3,235 police officer respondents from

30 police agencies within the United States. The respondents were given 11 vignettes describing various types of possible police misconduct. In response to each vignette, officers were asked to answer six questions intended to measure " . . . the normative inclination of police to resist temptations to abuse the rights and privileges of their occupation." While the results indicate vast differences from agency to agency regarding the "environment of integrity," one finding is consistent with the protections afforded members of the police subculture. The survey revealed that most officers would not report a fellow officer who was engaged in "less serious" types of misconduct (e.g., running a security business on the side, receiving free meals and gifts, or even leaving a minor traffic accident while under the influence). What this suggests, even though the survey revealed little tolerance for what was defined as "serious" police misconduct, is that there is a culture of acceptance within police ranks for some forms of misconduct. While such conduct is typically referred to as "grass eating" (less serious forms of police misconduct) as opposed to "meat eating" (more serious forms of police misconduct), many members of society would find the behavior unacceptable. James W. Birch in *Reflections on Police Corruption*[14] makes an interesting observation regarding such behavior. He states that the public creates an environment for "grass eating" that makes it difficult to not accept the "discount" or the free meal. It would appear that there may be a different definition of what constitutes "misconduct" depending on whether a person is a member of the police subculture or an outsider looking in.

The second NIJ study, by Weisburd and Greenspan, entitled *"Police Attitudes Toward Abuse of Authority: Findings From a National Study"* is the result of the Police Foundation's national telephone survey of over 900 officers from various agencies across the country and addresses police attitudes concerning excessive force. The results indicate that the majority of respondents believed it was not acceptable to use more force than was legally permissible to effect control over a person who had assaulted an officer. However, respondents reported that "... it is not unusual for officers to ignore improper conduct by their fellow officers." Other findings suggest that the majority of officers/respondents believed that serious instances of abuse were rare and that their department maintained a 'tough stand' on police abuse of citizenry. What about possible solutions to the problem of police abuse? Officers report two fruitful avenues for addressing police abuse. First, it was reported police administrators could have an impact on the occurrence of police abuse by "taking a stand" against abuse and through better supervision. Second, officers believed that training in ethics, interpersonal skills and cultural diversity would be effective in preventing abuse. What about turning fellow officers in for abuse? This was perceived as risky. While the majority of officers maintained that the "code of silence" was not essential to good policing, the majority also maintained that whistle blowing was not worth the consequences within the police subculture.

TOWARD A CONCLUSION

It is difficult to conclude this discussion because there is so much more to say about the topic of ethics in criminal justice. However, I will attempt to make a few concluding observations to make closure on this discussion. First, ethics is an important area within criminal justice practice and scholarship since criminal justice practitioners, especially the police, are continually under scrutiny. Therefore, the discipline has an obligation to remain interested in this topic and to promote the study of ethics. Second, scholars can be of assistance to practitioners by studying the sociological and psychological forces that impact ethical and unethical behavior. There is much the academy can offer criminal justice agencies in the form of research within organizations and training pertinent to ethics. Third, unethical behavior is the result of a conscious decision-making process to abuse one's authority while in a position of public trust. However, one must still take into account social forces that help to perpetuate, excuse, and justify unethical behavior. Fourth, there has been a proliferation of ethics scholarship in criminal justice since the Rodney King case but there is a need for more research of an empirical nature much like the two studies profiled in this essay. While qualitative and philosophical literature is important to our understanding of ethics in criminal justice there is a need for additional research of a quantitative nature. With more study of ethics and ethical dilemmas faced by police, we might better understand the dynamics that propel officers into the dark side of policing and the factors that serve to justify misbehavor.

ENDNOTES

1. Police Deviance and Ethics. http://faculty.ncwc.edu/toconnor/205/205lec11.htm.
2. Knapp Commission Report. (1973). New York: George Braziller.
3. Government Accounting Office., Report to the Honorable Charles B. Rangel, House of Representatives, Law Enforcement: Information on Drug-Related Police Corruption. Washington, DC: USGPO (1998 May), p. 3.
4. Ibid. p. 36–37.
5. Ibid. p. 35.
6. Ibid. p. 8.
7. Ibid. p. 3.
8. Ibid. p. 37.
9. Ibid. p. 36.
10. The Academy of Criminal Justice Sciences (ACJS) recently adopted a code of ethics modeled after the American Sociological Association's (ASA) code.
11. The International Association of Chiefs of Police (IACP) has a model code of ethics and also publishes a training key on ethics and policing.
12. Klockars, C.B., S.K. Ivkovich, W.E. Harver, and M.R. Haberfeld. (2000, May). "The Measurement of Police Integrity." National Institute of Justice, Research in Brief. U.S. Government Printing Office: Washington, DC.
13. Weisburd, D. and R. Greenspan. (2000, May). "Police Attitudes Toward Abuse of Authority: Findings from a National Study." National Institute of Justice, Research in Brief. U.S. Government Printing Office: Washington, DC.
14. Birch, James W. (1983). "Reflections on Police Corruption" Criminal Justice Ethics, Volume 2.

On-the-Job Stress in Policing—

Reducing It, Preventing It

Police officers and members of their families consider their job to be one of the most stressful. It is hard to disagree with that assessment, as officers themselves report high rates of divorce, alcoholism, suicide, and other emotional and health problems.[1] No job is immune from stress, but for the law enforcement officer, the strains and tensions experienced at work are unique, often extreme, and sometimes unavoidable.

Fortunately, many law enforcement agencies, recognizing the high toll exacted by stress on officers and their families, are tackling it with an array of creative prevention and reduction strategies. Through the CLEFS (Corrections and Law Enforcement Family Support) program of the National Institute of Justice, several of these agencies are receiving support.

This article summarizes an NIJ report that documented the causes and effects of job-related stress affecting law enforcement officers and their families. Much of the information was drawn from interviews, conducted as part of the study, with officers themselves and their family members.[2] Also included in this arti-

cle are highlights of some stress prevention and reduction programs reported in the study and of some of the CLEFS projects.

Sources of Stress

Exposure to violence, suffering, and death is inherent to the profession of law enforcement officer. There are other sources of stress as well. Officers who deal with offenders on a daily basis may view some sentences as too lenient; they may perceive the public's opinion of police performance to be unfavorable; they often are required to work mandatory, rotating shifts; and they may not have enough time to spend with their families. Police officers also face unusual, often highly disturbing, situations, such as dealing with a child homicide victim or the survivors of vehicle crashes.

The nature of the organizations in which officers work may also be a source of stress. Police departments historically have been structured along military lines and as a result often have been rigidly hierarchical and highly bureaucratic, with management styles that can be inflexible. Al-

though in many instances police culture is changing, in many others the leadership remains predominately white and male, opportunities for advancement are limited, and despite the ubiquity of the personal computer, a large amount of paperwork still is required.

Is Stress Getting Worse?

Officers may increasingly view stress as a normal part of their job, but they also see themselves as being under considerably more pressure than they or their colleagues were 10 or 20 years ago. They see new sources of stress in the high level of violent crime and in what they perceive as greater public scrutiny and adverse publicity. They also feel that police camaraderie has declined; they fear contracting air- and blood-borne diseases such as TB and HIV/AIDS; and they see themselves as having to deal with such relatively new issues as cultural diversity and the imperative of "political correctness."

Even widely accepted changes in law enforcement can lead to more stress for some officers. Although

From *National Institute of Justice Journal*, January 2000, pp. 18-24. © 2000 by the National institute of Justice.
Reprinted by permission.

How One Agency Pinpointed Stress

When the Baltimore Police Department decided to seek out the sources of stress in the agency, they turned for assistance to public health researchers at nearby Johns Hopkins University. With the Fraternal Order of Police as the third partner, the Department created Project SHIELDS to take on this task as well as to develop response strategies.

The sources of stress were identified by means of a survey, conducted by the researchers, among line officers and spouses/life partners. Some of the results were surprising. For example, fully two-thirds of the officers said they considered media reports of alleged police wrongdoing to be stressful to them. The same proportion said that what they view as lack of administrative support for officers in trouble was a major source of stress. Almost one-fourth reported low energy or chronic back pain, which they believed was related to job stress.

After the Hopkins researchers complete their analysis of the survey data, they and the project's advisory board (officers and family members) will help the Department develop a response. Total quality management (TQM) teams will be established to focus on selected issue drawn from the research findings. Consisting of officers from all ranks, the TQM teams will develop strategies to address aspects of organizational stress identified in the survey as particularly problematic.*

*Unpublished progress report of "Law Enforcement Work Stress and Family Support (Project SHIELDS)," Johns Hopkins University School of Hygiene and Public Health, Baltimore, submitted to the National Institute of Justice, U.S. Department of Justice, by Robyn Gershon, Principal Investigator, March 31, 1999.

community policing may mean more job satisfaction, greater overall department efficiency, and higher morale, the transition to it can cause apprehension on the part of the officers who on a day-to-day basis must operationalize this fundamental shift in the philosophy of policing. Performance expectations are new and perhaps not fully understood by all officers. Whether or not stress is increasing, identifying the causes is a first step toward reducing and preventing it. (See "How One Agency Pinpointed Stress.")

Counting the Ways: The Effects of Stress

The physical and emotional effects of stress are numerous and often severe. Any one of them can impair job performance. The consequences of job-related stress commonly reported by police officers are:

- Cynicism and suspiciousness.
- Emotional detachment from various aspects of daily life.
- Reduced efficiency.

- Absenteeism and early retirement.
- Excessive aggressiveness (which may trigger an increase in citizen complaints).
- Alcoholism and other substance abuse problems.
- Marital or other family problems (for example, extramarital affairs, divorce, or domestic violence).
- Post-traumatic stress disorder.
- Heart attacks, ulcers, weight gain, and other health problems.
- Suicide.

According to many counselors who work with police officers, difficulties with intimate relationships are the most common problem they treat.

Families Feel Stress, Too

If the effects on officers are severe, they can be similarly serious for officers' family members. In one survey of the spouses of police officers, a very large percentage said they experienced unusually high levels of stress because of their spouse's job.[3]

Stress felt by spouses is a concern in and of itself and also because a

stressful home environment can adversely affect the officer's job performance. Even conditions, situations, or incidents that may not trouble the officers themselves—or that they may even enjoy, such as shift work or undercover work—can mean severe problems for their families. Sources of stress commonly cited by officers' spouses include:

- Shift work and overtime.
- Concern over the spouse's cynicism, need to feel in control in the home, or inability or unwillingness to express feelings.
- Fear that the spouse will be hurt or killed in the line of duty.
- Officers' and others' excessively high expectations of their children.
- Avoidance, teasing, or harassment of the officer's children by other children because of the parent's job.
- Presence of a gun in the home.
- The officer's 24-hour role as a law enforcer.
- Perception that the officer prefers to spend time with coworkers rather than with his of her family.
- Too much or too little discussion of the job.
- Family members' perception of the officer as paranoid or excessively vigilant and overprotective of them.
- Problems in helping the officer cope with work-related problems
- "Critical incidents," or the officer's injury or death on the job.[4]

Because stress affects family members, they are often the first to recognize the officer's need for help, and they can play a crucial role by encouraging him or her to seek assistance before the problem becomes worse. This is the concept behind the Spousal Academy, a component of the comprehensive officer and family support program offered by the Collier County (Florida) Sheriff's Office.

The Academy offers training to spouses and other domestic partners of deputies and recruits who are enrolled in the Office's training academy. The 10-hour program involves an introduction to the nature of law enforcement work and an opportunity to discuss expectations about the effect the spouses' occupation will have on family life. Participants learn about the structure of the Sheriff's Office, about such human resource issues as employee benefits (health insurance, for example), and about stress management and conflict resolution. Two related programs in the development stage are peer support groups for spouses and life partners and for deputies' adolescent children.[5]

Soliciting feedback from participants is part of the program. Several noted the program's effectiveness in conveying the reality of what an officer does on the job. In the words of one spouse, "I now realize some of what my husband goes through." One of the comments heard most frequently concerns the value of simply meeting and interacting with other spouses. As one participant characterized the spouse's role, "Sometimes, this can be a lonely job."[6]

Countering Domestic Violence

There is some belief that a relatively large proportion of law enforcement officers may be involved in domestic violence, in part because of the stressful nature of the job.[7] Many law enforcement agencies have begun to turn their attention to the issue and devise ways to respond.

One agency, the Los Angeles (County) Sheriff's Department (LASD), has adopted a zero-tolerance policy toward domestic violence, with a full range of disciplinary actions that could include dismissal from the force. To reduce the number of domestic violence incidents among the LASD's 8,000 sworn officers, the Department bolstered the policy with a training program for all supervisory personnel; a vigorous information dissemination campaign (which included development of an educational video to be shown to all staff); and counseling services for individuals, couples, and families. The Department has trained more than 1,200 supervisors to spot signs of stress and domestic violence.[8]

Why Start or Expand a Stress Program?

Why should law enforcement agencies spend time and money on a law enforcement stress program and perhaps set aside space for it? The answer has to do with the implications of stress for the department. Essentially, stress reduces the quality of departmental performance.

Stress Affects Agency Performance

The cumulative negative effects of stress on officers and their families typically affect the agency through impaired officer performance and the related problems of tardiness, absenteeism, and low morale. The consequence for the department is lower productivity. Stress-related performance inadequacies also may generate labor-management friction and lead to civil suits. There may be adverse public reaction as a result of stress-related incidents, such as an officer's suicide or a case of police brutality. Even problems that are confined to only a few individuals or that occur rarely can have major repercussions. For instance, a single incident in which a handful of officers abuse alcohol or other drugs can lower public confidence in the entire agency.[9]

Though establishing and operating a stress reduction program requires a financial outlay, it can mean cost savings in the long term. That is because stress affects the bottom line. Agencies can find it enormously costly when employee turnover increases as a result of stress-related early retirement or long-term disability. Robert Peppler, Assistant Sheriff of the San Bernardino (California) Sheriff's Department noted the cost to his agency: "We have a tremendous investment in cops," he said, "and if they leave after one traumatic incident, we have lost a tremendous amount. A dollar in psychological services now can save us hundreds of thousands down the road."[10]

Why Not an EAP?

Many agencies have access to city- or countywide employee assistance programs (EAP's). Law enforcement staff and their families may be eligible for services from additional providers. These may include police chaplains, wellness programs, support groups, and local private service providers. This prompts the question: Why shouldn't an agency rely on other existing programs rather than develop its own stress reduction program?

The fact that a service is available does not necessarily mean it is meeting—or can meet—the distinctive needs of police officers. Mental health practitioners, police administrators, and others, when asked about city or county EAP's, said police officers do not use them because these programs do not provide enough confidentiality, because EAP staff usually do not understand law enforcement, and because the officers feared the stigma that might be attached to using an EAP.

What Stress Reduction Programs Look Like

Approaches to reduce or prevent stress can take many forms, among them:

- Services provided by a private mental health practice or an individual therapist working with one or more law enforcement agencies.
- Peer support and referrals from specially trained police officers.
- Psychological services set up in the agency through the union, chaplaincy, or employee assistance program.
- A combination of these arrangements.

Almost all programs are geared primarily to line officers, because they constitute the largest group in any law enforcement agency, they deal with the public on a day-to-day basis, they are widely believed to experience high levels of stress, and they may have limited means to pay for extended counseling. Most programs

A Little Help From Your Friends—Peer Support in New York City

Sometimes it takes a tragedy or critical incident to prompt a law enforcement agency or related organization to develop or expand a stress reduction program for police officers.

That was the case in New York City, where 26 police officers committed suicide in the 2-year period from 1994 through 1995. The unusually high number was the result of such factors as perceived pressure from the media and allegations of corruption. The crisis spurred the Patrolmen's Benevolent Association, supported by the city council, to establish a peer support program by officers for officers. The Members Assistance Program (MAP) trained 150 officer volunteers to aid fellow officers and an additional 26 to aid their families. The peer support officers staff a 24-hour hotline, serve as a point of first contact and screening for officers who report stress-related difficulties, and encourage individuals who need more intensive help to seek it.

MAP also trained 60 mental health practitioners in law enforcement stress, and these practitioners began taking referrals from the peer support officers. Between 1996, the year the program started, and 1998, the hotline received some 1,500 calls, resulting in more than 650 referrals.*

*"NYC Patrolmen's Benevolent Association Members Assistance Program. Program for the Reduction of Stress for New York City Police Officers and Their Families," final report submitted to the National Institute of Justice, U.S. Department of Justice, grant 96-FS-VX-007, December 1998.

mal time to reach them may be 6 to 8 months into the job, after they have experienced on-the-job stress. Some agencies offer inservice training not only for line officers but also for midlevel managers and command staff, prospective retirees, and nonsworn personnel.

Because, as noted above, the structure and management of the agency can be a significant source of stress, mental health professionals should consider working with departmental management and unions to play and implement organizational change. This can be done in a number of ways, all of which fall within the domain of management:

- Training command staff in effective supervision.
- Training field training officers to constructively supervise rookies.
- Eliminating rotating shift work.
- Improving the match between officers' capabilities and the demands of specific assignments.

also provide at least minimal services (that is, referral to other treatment providers) to nonsworn personnel and former employees, as well as to officers' and other employees' family members and close friends.

Services typically include assessment and referral to mental health or other practitioners; critical incident debriefing; intervention for other types of crises; short-term counseling for both individuals and families; and long-term counseling and other services, including treatment for substance abuse.

Most mental health practitioners emphasize the importance of involving family members, when possible, in all these services. To varying extents, all programs include referrals to outside sources of assistance. For some programs that operate with limited resources, referral to outside services is the primary component. That is often the case with programs staffed largely by peers. (See "A Little Help From Your Friends—Peer Support in New York City.")

Preventing Stress

The most common method for preventing stress is to train officers to recognize its signs and sources and to develop individual coping strategies. Training helps encourage officers and nonsworn personnel to use stress reduction techniques and services and dispels the stigma frequently attached to seeking assistance.

One period during which officers could be taught about stress is when they are at the academy, according to most of the police officers, program administrators, and independent mental health practitioners who were asked about this issue. They felt that the initial training period was a possibility because recruits are a captive audience and because the information may remain with them throughout their entire police career. There is some thinking that "inoculation" during recruit training is not the best approach, because most recruits are not experienced enough to recognize that stress comes with the job. The opti-

What NIJ Is Doing

The issue of job-related stress for law enforcement officers and their families has received attention at the highest levels of government. In the 1994 Omnibus Crime Act, the President and Congress recognized the severity of the problem and mandated a Federal Government response. The National Institute of Justice was assigned the task of sponsoring research, establishing pilot programs, and conducting program evaluations that support State and local efforts.

Research and Development

Since the start of the Corrections and Law Enforcement Family Support program, NIJ has sponsored research and program development in some 30 agencies and related organizations (labor unions and employee professional organizations, for example). These projects include the development of innovation treatment and training programs as well as research into the nature and causes of stress.

In one study now under way, NIJ is exploring the nature and extent of job-related stress for police in a single geographic region. And to improve access to service, NIJ provided support to the Metro Nashville Police Department in creating an online resource of information for the families of law enforcement officers, particularly those in underserved communities. Available on the Internet, the resource is a new type of service delivery system.[11] The Web site contains, among other things, materials developed by psychologists for preparing workshops on stress, message boards, a chat room, links to related Web sites, recommended readings, and postings from police psychologists and consultants.

From LEFS to CLEFS

Originally geared solely to law enforcement, the NIJ program has expanded to include corrections officers. In some cases, corrections officers experience more intense stress-generating incidents than do law enforcement officers. They may, for example, encounter violent behavior by inmates more often and over longer periods of time.

NIJ support for research and development is given to corrections agencies as well as law enforcement agencies. A study of pro-grams to reduce and prevent stress among corrections staff is under development.

Acknowledgements

Peter Finn, coauthor of the report on which this summary is based, contributed to the preparation of this article. Mr. Finn is an Associate with Abt Associates Inc., a public-policy and business research and consulting firm headquartered in Cambridge, Massachusetts. He also serves as a special police officer with the Belmont, Massachusetts, Police Department. Vincent Talucci, manager of the CLEFS portfolio of grants of NIJ, and Jenifer Wood, a former manager of CLEFS grants, also contributed.

Notes

1. Burke, R. J., "Career Stages, Satisfaction, and Well-Being Among Police Officers," *Psychological Reports* 65 (1989): 3–12; and Delprino, R. P., K. O'Quin, and C. Kennedy, "Identification of Work and Family Services for Law Enforcement Personnel," final report submitted to the National Institute of Justice, 1997 (NIJ grant 95-IJ-CX-0113).
2. The NIJ report is *Developing a Law Enforcement Stress Program for Officers and Their Families,* by Peter Finn and Julie Esselman Tomz, Issues and Practices, Washington, D.C.: U.S. Department of Justice, National Institute of Justice, March 1997 (NCJ 163175).
3. The survey was conducted as part of a study by Leanor Boulin-Johnson, professor of African-American Studies and Family Studies at Arizona State University. See "On the Front Lines: Police Stress and Family Well-Being," testimony of Leanor Boulin-Johnson before the Select Committee on Children, Youth, and Families, U.S. House of Representatives, 102nd Congress, 1st Session, May 20, 1991, Washington, D.C.: U.S. Government Printing Office, 1991: 32.
4. Borum, R., and C. Philpot, "Therapy With Law Enforcement Couples: Clinical Management of the 'High-Risk Lifestyle,'" *American Journal of Family Therapy* 21 (1993): 122–135.
5. Ferguson, Edward T., and Acey L. Edgemon, "Collier County Sheriff's Office Law Enforcement Family Support Initiative," draft executive summary, report submitted to the National Institute of Justice, U.S. Department of Justice, April 1, 1999.
6. Unpublished program evaluations by participants in Spousal Academy, Collier County (Florida) Sheriff's Office, no date.
7. "On the Front Lines: Police Stress and Family Well-Being," testimony of B. J. Anderson before the Select Committee on Children, Youth, and Families, U.S. House of Representatives, 102nd Congress, 1st Session, May 20, 1991, Washington, D.C.: U.S. Government Printing Office, 1991: 61–63.
8. Unpublished progress report of the Family Violence Prevention and Recovery Project (FVPRP), Los Angeles County Sheriff's Department, submitted to the National Institute of Justice, U.S. Department of Justice, by Audrey L. Honig, Principal Investigator, FVPRP, and Steven E. Sultan, Project Coordinator, FVPRP, for period September 1, 1998, through March 3, 1999.
9. Springer, K., "When the Helper Needs Help: Stress and the Law Enforcement Employee," *EAP Association Exchange* 25 (1995): 6–11.
10. Finn and Tomz, *Developing a Law Enforcement Stress Program for Officers and Their Families:* 3.
11. The site address is http://policefamilies.com.

Policing the Police

BY KENNETH JOST

THE ISSUES

Rafael Perez had wanted to be a policeman since childhood. After four years in the Marines, he joined the Los Angeles Police Department in 1989. He did well and was assigned to a special anti-gang squad in the Rampart Division, just west of downtown.

The densely populated Rampart area is home to many Asian and Hispanic immigrants and to some of the city's most feared street gangs. When Perez started in the elite squad, Rampart had one of the highest murder rates among the city's 18 police divisions. Today, violent crime has declined there—perhaps a credit to the LAPD's aggressive anti-gang and anti-drug efforts.

The Rampart Division, however, is taking no bows for its work these days. Instead, Rampart has become the name of a stunning scandal of police misconduct ranging from manufacturing evidence and committing perjury to stealing drugs and shooting unarmed suspects. The spreading scandal threatens hundreds, perhaps thousands, of criminal convictions and deals a body blow to the LAPD's efforts to regain public confidence after a troubled decade marked by the Rodney King beating and the O. J. Simpson murder trial.

Perez was once in the middle of the corruption but is now the source of the scandal's most damning disclosures. Facing trial in September on charges of stealing 6 pounds of cocaine from a police evidence room, Perez negotiated a plea bargain by promising to tell all he knew about misconduct in the Rampart Division.

"There's a lot of crooked stuff going on in the LAPD," Perez told authorities, according to transcripts of the interviews obtained by the *Los Angeles Times*.[1]

The Rampart scandal emerged as law enforcement agencies around the country were coming under renewed scrutiny on a variety of issues. The New York City Police Department was still reeling from the brutal sodomizing of a Haitian immigrant in 1997 when four white officers last year shot and killed an unarmed West African immigrant, Amadou Diallo, in the vestibule of his Bronx apartment building. Their trial, moved to Albany because of massive local publicity about the case, ended last month with the officers' acquittal on all counts—a verdict that served only to renew the debate over police tactics and racial attitudes.

Meanwhile, civil-rights and civil-liberties organizations were mounting attacks on "racial profiling," the practice of making traffic or other investigative stops on the basis of an individual's race or ethnicity. Two states, Maryland and New Jersey, have signed federal court consent decrees agreeing to end the practice after lawyers from the American Civil Liberties Union (ACLU) gathered evidence showing racial patterns in highway stops by state police. Other suits are pending. Critics also want to require police to collect racial data on traffic stops in other states to determine the extent of the practice—which law enforcement officials insist is not widespread.

The public focus on police practices comes at a time of declining crime rates and generally increasing police professionalism. A recent survey of both rank-and-file police personnel and officers suggests that the vast majority of police recognize legal constraints on their conduct, try to stay within the law and disapprove of colleagues who do not.

Still, policing the police—either through internal management or external review—remains a difficult job. "Cops and teachers exercise the most unsupervised discretion of any government employees in living up

 From *Congressional Quarterly*, March 17, 2000, pp. 211-230. © 2000 by Congressional Quarterly, Inc. Reprinted by permission.

Black Motorists on I-95 Still Targeted

The state of Maryland settled a racial-profiling suit in January 1995 by agreeing to halt the practice and to furnish racial data on traffic stops to the American Civil Liberties Union of Maryland to monitor the agreement. Despite the settlement, the data showed that a disproportionate number of motorists stopped since then along the I-95 corridor in Maryland—more than two-thirds—were people of color.

Detentions and Searches
January 1995–June 1999

	Number of Stops	Percent
African-Americans	1,205	60.7%
Hispanics	117	5.9
Whites	641	32.3
Other	23	1.2
Total non-white	1,322	67.8
Total searches	1,986	

Note: Total does not add to 100 percent due to rounding.

Source: American Civil Liberties Union of Maryland

to the public trust or not," says Edwin Delattre, dean of Boston University's School of Education and author of a book on police ethics. "If you look at a cop on the street, there's nobody immediately looking over the cop's shoulder."

"The gap between the best and worse police departments is bigger than ever," says Samuel Walker, a professor of criminal justice at the University of Nebraska in Omaha and author of a history of U.S. law enforcement. "In places like San Diego and Charlotte, there is good discipline. They care about their citizens. That's simply not true in New York and Los Angeles."

Police officials tend to simultaneously minimize the extent of abusive practices while insisting they are taking steps to prevent them. Abuse-of-force cases are "insignificant arithmetically," says James Powers, chief of the Fredericksburg, Va., police department and an adviser to an International Association of Chiefs of Police (IACP) study on the use of force. "But perception-wise, it's very significant. One misuse of force to us is catastrophic. And for a long, long

time, we've been taking every step we know to restrict or prohibit the improper use of force."

"There is no excuse for stopping someone because they're black or Hispanic or because they're a black person in a white neighborhood," says Earl Sweeney, director of the New Hampshire Police Standards and Training Council and chair of the IACP's highway safety committee. But Sweeney says racial-profiling abuses "have been perpetrated by a minority of individuals, in some cases well-motivated but poorly trained. We really think the answer is in policy, training and supervision."

Many of the most volatile police controversies—such as the two recent New York City cases—are racially charged. Public mistrust of police remains high in many minority communities.

"Given the large numbers of African-Americans today in prison or under the jurisdiction of the criminal justice system, there are questions in the black community whether this has resulted from discriminatory practices on the part of the police,"

says Hubert Williams, president of the Police Foundation, a Washington-based research organization.

In Los Angeles, however, many of the officers implicated so far, including Perez, are Hispanics who were targeting Hispanic offenders and suspects.

"This is not a black-white or white-brown incident," says Elizabeth Schroeder, associate director of the ACLU of Southern California. "You've got minority cops who are beating up minorities."

The efforts to control police conduct from the outside began in earnest in the 1960s, when the U.S. Supreme Court, under Chief Justice Earl Warren, handed down a series of decisions aimed at protecting the rights of suspects and criminal defendants. The best known of those rulings—the so-called *Miranda* decision in 1966—required police to advise suspects after their arrest of their right to remain silent and to have a lawyer present during any questioning.

At around the same time, efforts were being made to increase the number of minority officers on urban police forces. In addition, police critics sought to establish civilian review boards to receive and in some cases adjudicate complaints regarding police conduct.

Today, those changes are widely, but not universally, accepted. In particular, the *Miranda* rule has become an ingrained police practice—and universally known through three decades of police stories on television and film. But law enforcement groups are lining up behind an effort to relax the *Miranda* decision by breathing life into a 1968 law that sought to partly lift its enforcement in federal courts.

The Justice Department has generally refused to invoke the law—known as Section 3501—because of doubts about its constitutionality. But the Supreme Court will consider a case next month in which a federal appeals court invoked the law to turn back a defendant's challenge to a confession that he claimed police obtained before giving him his *Miranda* warnings.

"We do not want to be in a situation where officers know that they can torture a suspect to get a confession" says Gene Voegtlin, legislative counsel for the IACP, which filed a brief urging the court to uphold Section 3501. "But we believe you need to have some flexibility so that society is not punished for small oversights by having confessions thrown out and convictions lost."

But Williams says there is no need to relax or overturn *Miranda*. "Why would we—at a time when the crime rate is spiraling down, when we're trying to focus on community policing—why open up the door for inappropriate practices by some officers that in the past have vastly colored the reputation of the whole force?" Williams asks.

As the justices prepare to hear the *Miranda* case, here are some of the questions being debated by police and their critics:

Should the Miranda *rule regarding police interrogation be relaxed?*

Charles Dickerson was not physically mishandled or psychologically coerced when an FBI agent and an Alexandria, Va., police detective questioned him about a 1997 bank robbery. But a federal judge found that Dickerson—contrary to the FBI agent's testimony—had not been "Mirandized" before he gave a statement linking himself to the getaway vehicle used in the holdup. On that basis, the judge blocked the government from using Dickerson's statement in his scheduled trial.

Three years later, Dickerson has yet to be tried. Instead, his case goes before the U.S. Supreme Court next month in a crucial test of the federal law aimed at partially overturning *Miranda*—Section 3501. Critics of *Miranda* hope the court will use the case to relax the application of a decision that they say has hurt law enforcement by making confessions harder to get and allowing some defendants to avoid conviction be-

cause of technical mistakes unrelated to any improper conduct by police.

"When you have technical errors or inadvertent oversights—good-faith mistakes—you end up punishing society by excluding evidence that could be used to keep dangerous people off the streets," says Voegtlin of the police chiefs' association.

Supporters of the *Miranda* decision deny that the ruling has greatly hampered law enforcement, but also insist that the mandatory warnings are essential to protect suspects' rights in police interrogation.

"It's ridiculous to think that a lay person understands their rights under the Fifth Amendment," says Lisa Kemler, co-author of a brief in the case on behalf of the National Association of Criminal Defense Lawyers. "The police setting is inherently coercive. All of the things that the [Supreme Court] talked about in the *Miranda* decision are still true today."

The effects of the *Miranda* decision have been debated ever since the Supreme Court handed down its decision on June 13, 1966. In recent years, an academic critic of the decision, University of Utah law professor Paul G. Cassell, has sought to prove the ruling's adverse effects on law enforcement in voluminous scholarly articles as well as in court briefs.

The Supreme Court case, however, does not directly concern the pros and cons of the *Miranda* ruling. Instead, the case tests Congress' power to pass a law to change a decision that the Supreme Court itself indicated might be subject to legislative revision.

Section 3501 of the federal Criminal Code provides that any "voluntary" confession can be introduced in federal courts. The law lists the giving of warnings as two out of five factors for a court to consider in determining whether a statement was voluntary.

The defenders of Section 3501 note that the court itself said that the procedures laid out in the *Miranda*

decision might not be the only way to protect suspects' rights.

"*Miranda* itself is not a constitutional mandate," says Kent Scheidegger, legal director of the California-based Criminal Justice Legal Foundation. "The court created some rules for the implementation of constitutional rights that are not themselves constitutionally required, and those rules are subject to revision by Congress."

Critics of the law, however, insist that Congress had no power to overturn a decision defining constitutional rights. "If Congress can overrule *Miranda* by legislation, then it can overrule anything," says Yale Kamisar, a University of Michigan law professor and longtime defender of the ruling.

"The *Miranda* opinion says that these warnings aren't the only solution as long as you come up with an alternative that is equally effective," Kamisar adds. "The proponents of the statute never mention the [court's] statement that you'd have to come up with an alternative that is equally effective."

Cassell, who will present the arguments in defense of the law before the Supreme Court next month, says that police will "absolutely" continue to give the warnings even if the statute is upheld. "The warnings aren't the problems," Cassell says. "The problems are the vast procedural apparatus that's been erected around the warnings."

In fact, some pro-law enforcement observers say *Miranda* has actually benefited police. "*Miranda* is probably the best thing that's ever happened to police, even though they may not know it," says Craig Bradley, a law professor at Indiana University in Bloomington and former federal prosecutor and Justice Department official.

The ruling "gives police something very easy to comply with," Bradley continues. And compliance with the warnings typically limits further inquiry into police conduct.

"In *Miranda*, the court condemned a number of techniques"

such as psychological pressure and deceptive tactics, Bradley says. "After *Miranda,* no one looks into that any more. There's very little examination of police tactics short of outright brutality."

Voegtlin agrees on some of the benefits of the ruling. "The *Miranda* decision gave law enforcement some valuable guidelines," he says. "It put policies and procedures into place to protect officers as well as suspects. Once it was certified that the warnings were given, there wasn't a question of the voluntariness of the confession."

Still, the police chiefs' group is joining other law enforcement organizations in urging the court to uphold the law limiting *Miranda* impact. "For someone to go free because of a technical oversight is wrong," Voegtlin says, "and that's what we're trying to remedy."

Are stronger measures needed to prevent use of excessive force by police officers?

Public confidence in New York City's finest was still recovering from the brutal sodomizing of Haitian immigrant Abner Louima in 1997 when it was shaken again a year ago by the Amadou Diallo shooting. But NYPD officials say that the controversy over Diallo's death and the prosecution of four white police officers for the shooting obscures an encouraging trend: a decline in police shootings and civilians killed or wounded by police fire.

In all, New York City police shot and killed 11 civilians in 1999. That figure is sharply down from the previous year's total of 19. Moreover, the number has been declining steadily since 1990, when 41 civilians were killed. The number of wounded also fell to 31 last year from 43 in 1998, and the number of incidents dropped to 155 from 249 in the same period.

"Generally, when it comes to the use of firearms, we are the most restrained large city police department in the United States," New York City

Police Commissioner Howard Safir told a *New York Times* columnist last month.[2]

Police organizations nationwide are also trying to reassure the public about improper use of force by officers. A study released by the IACP in January showed that police used force fewer than 3.5 times per 10,000 calls for service, and suspects were injured in fewer than 3 percent of the instances when force was used.

"The incidence of use of force is minuscule compared to the number of citizen contacts, and the incidence of use of improper force is also minuscule in relation to that number," Fredericksburg Police Chief Powers said.[3]

Outside critics and observers, however, see no cause for complacency. "Excessive force has long been and continues to be a serious problem with enormous racial overtones in New York City," says Norman Siegel, executive director of the New York Civil Liberties Union. "And it will probably continue as long as mayors and police commissioners continue to deny the painful problem of police brutality, until civilian review boards become more effective, until police departments such as New York City's become more racially representative of the people they police and until they get better training."

"Whenever police abuse their authority, it's a social problem that needs to be controlled," says Geoffrey Alpert, a professor at the University of South Carolina's College of Criminal Justice in Columbia and an adviser to police departments on use of force. "It's a very powerful tool that they're given, and to abuse it flies in the face of why we give it to them."

Civil-rights and civil-liberties organizations often emphasize external mechanisms to try to control use of excessive force by police, such as civilian review boards, civil damage suits and criminal prosecutions. The effectiveness of civilian-review mechanisms is a subject of sharp dispute between civil-rights advocates

and police unions and public officials in many cities. In New York, for example, Mayor Rudolph Giuliani is strongly opposed to the city's civilian review board, although the City Council voted overwhelmingly several years ago to keep it in existence.

"A number of them are very successful and have documented records of achievements," says the University of Nebraska's Walker, author of a forthcoming book on police accountability. "A number of them are abject failures. It's a question of determining which ones work, and why."

"Civilian review can be useful if it's a cooperative venture that doesn't just have to do with problems," Delattre says. "If the only time they're engaged is over some type of crisis, or if it has inordinate power, you're not going to have anything except a higher wall of resistance and silence [from police]."

Legal actions also have mixed results on officer conduct, experts say. Alpert says civil damage suits don't radically affect police behavior. "A lot of that information stays in the legal offices and never filters back to the police department," he says.

As for criminal prosecutions of questionable police behavior— which are relatively few in number in any event—Alpert says officers on patrol often respond by becoming more reluctant to initiate investigations of suspicious circumstances. "For a lot of these shootings that are relatively close calls, they're likely to say 'the system is just punishing us for doing our jobs' and become more careful in not going out on a limb," he says.

Police officials are more likely to emphasize improved recruitment and training as ways to prevent excessive use of force. "We now give psychological tests and do extensive interviews before hiring," says Fredericksburg Police Chief Powers. "We take every step we can to make sure that officers are not predisposed to that. And we do extensive training and talk about what is the proper use of force."

Categorical rules on use of force also may reduce civilian injuries, according to Carl Klockars, a professor of criminal justice at the University of Delaware in Newark. Departments that specifically prohibit high-speed chases or the use of warning shots, for example, appear to have few civilians killed or injured by police conduct, Klockars says.

"Excessive force has been with us forever, and it's still with us," says the Police Foundation's Williams. "It has not abated significantly at all. But you've got to understand the environment police are working in. It's a very tough job, and in many instances they're just trying to do the best they can do."

Should the use of "racial profiling" be prohibited?

Christopher Darden and Johnnie Cochran squared off against each other in a Los Angeles courtroom as prosecutor and defense lawyer in the O. J. Simpson murder case. But the two African-American attorneys had something in common before the trail. Both had been victims of what they regarded as racially motivated traffic stops by police while working for the Los Angeles district attorney's office.[4]

Darden and Cochran are just two of the many African-Americans from all walks of life who have stepped forward during recent years to complain about being stopped for the not-so-fictitious offense of DWB—"driving while black." Minority groups representing blacks as well as Hispanics complain that police use racial or ethnic stereotypes in traffic enforcement or other investigative stops.

"This is not a new thing, by any means," says David Harris, a law professor at the University of Toledo who has studied the issue for the ACLU. "What is new is that we have begun over the last few years to see the collection of some of the data to substantiate what blacks and other minorities have been saying for a long time."

Some police officials acknowledge the practice while also expressing strong disapproval. "Whether racial profiling is existent in the United States—I'm sure that it probably is," says Jack Grant, manager of the Division of State and Provincial Police at the police chiefs' association. "We discourage it. Responsible police administrators do everything they can to prevent it. It cannot be tolerated as a practice in police work."

Many police officials and law enforcement supporters, however, also insist that race can sometimes be a legitimate factor for officers to consider in police investigations. "Racial profiling is wrong," says Cornelius Behan, retired police chief in Baltimore County, Md., "but it gets confused with sensible police procedures. It's wise to try to develop a profile of who the offenders are, and sometimes a legitimate profile would have race in it."

"The distinction is between profiling and discriminatory profiling," Delattre says. "Anybody who says you can enforce the law and protect public safety without profiling is trying to sell you a pipe dream. What you need are clear statements of policy about how to justify responsible profiling from profiling that's based on bigotry and that has the effect that bigotry has."

Racial and ethnic minorities have long been accustomed to being regarded with suspicion when they frequent "white" neighborhoods, whether on foot or in vehicles. The "driving while black" issue has become more visible in recent years because of stepped-up traffic enforcement aimed in large part at detecting drug offenses. "These pretext stops are about drugs," Harris says. "That's what the federal government has trained local law enforcement to use them for."

Harris and other critics of racial profiling say police who target blacks or other minorities in drug-interdiction efforts are operating on a false assumption that use of drugs is highest among African-Americans. "Police are focused on the drug

market in the inner city, and that's in African-American communities and other minority communities," the Police Foundation's Williams explains. "They look at the people they're arresting, and that's where they get their profile. So it always winds up with a heavy representation of African-Americans and Hispanics."

Critics also question the value of using traffic stops for drug enforcement, noting that the vast majority of people stopped in drug-related patrolling end up not being charged with any drug offenses. John Crew, director of the ACLU of Northern California's Police Practices Project, says data gathered for a class-action suit against the California Highway Patrol indicate that the CHP stopped about 33,000 motorists in 1997 in drug-related investigations but had a "hit rate" of less than 2 percent. "If you use a tactic that fails 98 percent of the time," Crew says, "normally that's not something that you would view as successful."

But Sweeney, who oversees training for all of New Hampshire's state and local police, defends the use of traffic enforcement for other anti-crime purposes. "Aggressive enforcement of the traffic laws keeps crime down," Sweeney says. "You have a tendency to detect people who are violating the laws."

"People who have been arrested tell you that they stay away from communities and areas where there is intensive enforcement of traffic laws," Sweeney continues. "If they're carrying drugs, carrying burglary tools, they're likely to be stopped while driving along that stretch of the highway."

While condemning racial profiling, police officials generally contend the problem is relatively isolated. Critics insist the practice is more widespread. To try to substantiate their beliefs, the ACLU and other critics favor legislation—passed in two states and pending in Congress and at least 18 other states—to require state and local law enforcement agencies to gather data on the race of persons stopped for traffic violations. Police groups generally oppose such proposals as unnecessary and expensive.

But Crew also notes that many police leaders have become more attuned to the problem, in part because of the effect that the perception of racial profiling has on public confidence in law enforcement.

"It's interesting to hear law enforcement groups talk about this not just as a civil-rights issue, not just a justice issue, but as an effective-policing issue," Crew says. "If they're going to be effective, they can't afford to have a large segment of the American population, people of color, disaffected from police."

BACKGROUND

A Checkered Past

The creation of the first full-time police departments in the United States in Philadelphia and Boston in the 1830s came not long after Sir Robert Peel established what is regarded as the first modern force, the London Metropolitan Police, in 1829. The London police quickly gained a reputation for professionalism, but urban police departments in the United States were beset by continuing scandals through the 19th century. Police departments were guilty of "pervasive brutality and corruption," according to historian Walker, and "did little to prevent crime or provide public services."[5]

A police-reform movement developed in the early 20th century. The reformers sought to rid police departments of political influence and cronyism and turn them into efficient, nonpartisan agencies committed to public service. They wanted police departments to be run by trained experts with job tenure to insulate them from political interference. They also wanted to improve

the recruitment and training of officers and to centralize a command structure for better accountability. Some progress was made on all of those goals. Still, a federal crime commission—reported in 1931 that physical brutality was "extensively practiced" by police departments around the country.[6]

The Supreme Court first stepped in to police the interrogation process in 1936 in a flagrant case in which three black tenant farmers "confessed" to the murder of a white farmer after being brutally tortured by local sheriff's deputies in Mississippi. An involuntary confession was unreliable, the court reasoned, and its use in court would violate the 14th Amendment's prohibition against depriving anyone of life or liberty without due process of law. In a second confession case six years later, the court shifted its focus by declaring that the Due Process Clause prohibited the use of any evidence—whether true or false—that police obtained through techniques that "shocked the conscience" of the community or violated fundamental standards of fairness.[7]

The high court ruled on more than 30 confession cases between 1936 and 1964, deciding whether a confession was voluntary by looking at the totality of the circumstances in each case.[8] In some cases, the court established that certain interrogation methods—including physical force, threats of harm or punishment, lengthy or incommunicado questioning, solitary confinement, denial of food or sleep and promises of leniency—were presumptively coercive and therefore constitutionally impermissible. But the court did not attempt to set out a specific checklist of procedures for police to assure that a suspect's statement would be deemed voluntary and therefore admissible in court.

Police professionalism "continued to make steady advances" during this period, according to historian Walker.[9] A "new generation" of police chiefs provided better leadership, while officers became more productive because of techno-

logical advances, such as patrol cars with sophisticated communications systems.

At the same time, racial flareups foreshadowed the crisis in police-community relations that fully developed in the 1960s. Racial disturbances in Detroit and New York City's Harlem in 1943 produced accusations of discriminatory enforcement against the cities' African-American populations, while the "Zoot Suit" riots in Los Angeles exposed tensions between blacks, Hispanics and the city's overwhelmingly white police force.

Some police chiefs and national organizations responded with programs to improve race relations. But, as Walker notes, recruitment of black police officers lagged, and the "pioneering efforts" in improving police-community relations did not keep pace with the rapidly changing context of race relations in the decades after World War II.

By the mid-1960s, the Supreme Court had a liberal majority that was determined to continue the civil-rights revolution it had launched with the landmark school-desegregation rulings of the 1950s. The court also was determined to bring about a due-process revolution in the administration of criminal justice across the country. In 1961 the court ruled that illegally obtained evidence could not be used in state trials; two years later it ruled that the states had to provide lawyers for indigent criminal defendants in felony trials if they could not afford to pay for one themselves.[10]

Then in 1964 the court held in *Escobedo v. Illinois* that a suspect has a right under the Sixth Amendment to consult with his lawyer during police interrogation once an investigation had moved from a general inquiry to focus specifically on him. The implications of the decision were unclear; one reading suggested that it applied only to suspects like Escobedo who already had an attorney.

But two years later the court made clear it had a broader interest

Chronology

Before 1900

Corruption and brutality are pervasive in U.S. police forces.

1900–1960

Police reform movements advance; Supreme Court begins to review confession cases.

1936

First Supreme Court decision to bar confession as involuntary.

1960s

Warren Court seeks to control police conduct.

1961

Supreme Court rules illegally seized evidence cannot be used in state court trials.

1966 .

Supreme Court in *Miranda v. Arizona* requires police to advise suspects of rights.

1968

Kerner Commission warns of deep mistrust of police by African-Americans; Congress passes law aimed at overturning *Miranda* in federal courts.

1970s

*Burger Court restricts **Miranda**, but does not overturn it.*

1971

Confession obtained in violation of *Miranda* can be used to impeach defendant's testimony at trial, Supreme Court rules.

1980s

Conservative era in law enforcement.

1986

Justice Department unit proposes effort to overturn *Miranda*, but plan is not pursued.

1990s

Police brutality and racial profiling emerge as major issues.

1991

Black motorist Rodney King is kicked and beaten by white Los Angeles police officers; they are acquitted in state trial in 1992, but two are convicted a year later of civil-rights violations.

1993

Black lawyer Robert Wilkins files anti-racial profiling suit after being stopped by Maryland state troopers; state settles suit in 1995 by agreeing to end racial profiling and provide racial data on traffic stops to ACLU.

1996

Supreme Court upholds pretextual traffic stops for drug enforcement.

1997

Black immigrant Abner Louima is sodomized by white New York police officers; Justin Volpe pleads guilty in 1999 and draws 30-year prison term.

February 1999

Black immigrant Amadou Diallo is fatally shot by four white NYPD officers; murder trial moved to Albany because of publicity in New York City.

April 1999

New Jersey attorney general issues report acknowledging racial profiling by state police; state settles Justice Department suit in December by agreeing to end practice.

September 1999

Rafael Perez implicates himself and other LAPD anti-gang officers in city's Rampart Division in widespread abuse, including planting evidence and shooting suspects.

December 1999

Supreme Court agrees to review appeals court ruling upholding 1968 law aimed at overturning *Miranda* in federal courts.

2000s

Racial profiling, police brutality continue as high-profile issues.

January 2000

Democratic presidential candidates Al Gore and Bill Bradley oppose racial profiling; GOP front-runner George W. Bush is ambiguous.

Feb. 25, 2000

NYPD officers are acquitted in Diallo shooting; former LAPD officer Perez gets five years in prison for stealing cocaine from police evidence room.

March 1, 2000

LAPD report blames Rampart scandal on lax supervision and "culture of mediocrity."

April 19, 2000

Supreme Court set to hear arguments on anti-*Miranda* law.

Controversial *Miranda* Ruling Still Stands

The U.S. Supreme Court's 1966 *Miranda* decision requiring police to advise suspects of their constitutional rights against self-incrimination before interrogation has been narrowed over the years by subsequent high court decisions, but not overturned.

CASE	VOTE	RULING
Miranda v. Arizona (1966)	5–4	Police must advise suspect before interrogation of right to remain silent, right to a lawyer, right to have lawyer appointed, and give warning that any statement can be used against him; police cannot use any statement obtained without such warnings.
Orozco v. Texas (1969)	6–2	Police must give *Miranda* warnings whenever a suspect is effectively in custody—in this case, in his home.
Harris v. New York (1971)	6–3	Statement obtained in violation of *Miranda* can be used to cross-examine defendant or impeach testimony at trial.
Michigan v. Tucker (1974)	8–1	Police can use statement in violation of *Miranda* as a lead for obtaining other evidence; Rehnquist opinion emphasizes *Miranda* not constitutionally required.
Michigan v. Mosley (1975)	7–2	Police did not violate *Miranda* by questioning suspect who invoked his right to silence about a second offense after they gave a second warning.
United States v. Mandujano (1976)	8–0	No *Miranda* warning needed for grand jury witness.
Brewer v. Williams (1977)	5–4	Police officer's speech pleading for "Christian burial" of child murder victim was "tantamount to interrogation" and violated suspect's *Miranda* rights.
Fare v. Michael C. (1979)	5–4	Probation officer need not give *Miranda* warnings before questioning juvenile suspect.
Rhode Island v. Innis (1980)	6–3	Police appeal to suspect's conscience did not amount to interrogation in violation of *Miranda*.
Edwards v. Arizona (1981)	9–0	Police must stop interrogation after suspect asks for lawyer.
Minnesota v. Murphy (1984)	5–4	No *Miranda* warning needed before interview with probation officer.
New York v. Quarles (1984)	5–4	Police did not violate *Miranda* by asking suspect, "Where's the gun?" before giving warnings; suspect's answer could be used as evidence at trial ("public safety exception").
Withrow v. Williams (1993)	5–4	*Miranda* violation can be basis for challenging state court conviction in federal habeas corpus proceeding.

in police interrogations by scheduling argument in four consolidated cases in which defendants challenged their convictions by claiming that police had obtained confessions from them in violation of their constitutional rights.

Miranda's Rights

Ernest Miranda confessed to the kidnap-rape of a Phoenix, Ariz., teenager in 1963 after an interrogation session with no overt indications of coercion. Police found Miranda, a 23-year-old laborer, after tracking the license plate of a truck driven by the assailant. Detectives went to his home, asked him to accompany them to the police station and there began questioning him about the crime. A line-up was inconclusive, but police told Miranda he had been identified. At that point, he admitted that he had raped the girl.[11]

The Supreme Court heard arguments in Miranda's effort to reverse his state court conviction and in three other confession cases on March 2 and 3, 1966. When he an-

nounced the decision in the cases on June 13, Chief Justice Warren acknowledged that Miranda's statement might not be deemed involuntary "in traditional terms." But Warren, a former district attorney in California, said that "incommunicado interrogation" and such recognized police techniques of undermining a suspect's will through flattery, isolation or trickery were inherently compulsive and violated the Fifth Amendment's "cherished" principle against self-incrimination.

To protect that right, Warren continued, police must advise a

Law OKs 'Voluntary' Confessions

Section 3501 of the federal Criminal Code (Title 18) attempts to partly overturn the *Miranda* decision as used in federal courts. The law provides that a confession "shall be admissible in evidence" in any federal prosecution "if it is voluntarily given." The law lists five situations—some of which track the four warnings required under *Miranda*—that a judge should consider in determining whether a confession was voluntary:

- The time between the defendant's arrest and arraignment in court.*

- Whether the defendant knew the nature of the offense with which he was being charged when he confessed.**

- Whether the defendant "was advised or knew that he was not required to make any statement and that any such statement could be used against him."

- Whether the defendant "had been advised prior to questioning of his right to the assistance of counsel."

- Whether the defendant "was without the assistance of counsel when questioned."

This recognizes that the longer a suspect is held without charges the greater the possibility that mistreatment prompted the confession.

**This recognizes the possibility that police sometimes threaten to hold suspects incommunicado until they confess.*

---

suspect of the right to remain silent, the right to an attorney and the right to have an attorney appointed if he cannot afford one, and must warn that any statement given after waiving those rights could be used in court against him. Warren acknowledged that the Constitution might not require this particular set of safeguards. But unless equally effective safeguards were established, police had to give those warnings for a suspect's statement to be admissible later in court.

The 5–4 decision stopped short of the most restrictive position urged in arguments: an absolute requirement to have an attorney present during any police interrogation. The dissenting justices nonetheless forcefully criticized the ruling. They argued for retaining what Justice Byron White called the "more pliable" method of testing confessions on the totality of the circumstances. And each of the four dissenters warned of a likely adverse effect on law enforcement. "We do know that some crimes cannot be solved without confessions," Justice John Marshall Harlan wrote, "and that the Court is taking a real risk with society's welfare in imposing its new regime on the country."

Those warnings were quickly picked up and amplified by police, prosecutors and politicians. The

court, critics said, had "handcuffed" the police. Congress responded in 1968 with a provision in the Omnibus Crime Control and Safe Streets Act seeking to overturn *Miranda* in federal courts and return to a voluntariness test. The main sponsor, Sen. John McClellan, D-Ark., had proposed a constitutional amendment shortly after the decision was announced, but turned to the easier legislative route instead.

Also in 1968, Republican presidential nominee Richard M. Nixon made the Supreme Court's criminal-procedure decisions a major focus on his campaign and promised to appoint law-and-order justices to the court if elected. The next year, as president, Nixon chose Warren E. Burger, a conservative judge from the federal appeals court in Washington, D.C., to succeed Warren as chief justice.

During Burger's 17 years as chief justice, both supporters and critics of *Miranda* found cause for disappointment. Initially, the court somewhat expanded the ruling—for example, to cover custodial interrogation outside a police station. In 1971, however, Burger and the four *Miranda* dissenters joined in a 6–3 decision carving out a major exception that allowed prosecutors to use a statement obtained in violation of the decision to cross-examine a defendant

at trial. Other exceptions and restrictions followed.

Still, the Burger Court stopped short of overturning *Miranda*. And police attitudes toward *Miranda* changed from hostility to acceptance. By the late 1980s, an American Bar Association survey found that "a very strong majority" of police, prosecutors and judges believed *Miranda* "does not present serious problems for law enforcement."[12]

Critics of the Warren Court's criminal-procedure rulings saw a better chance for undoing some of the decisions after President Ronald Reagan chose William H. Rehnquist to succeed Burger as chief justice in 1986. Within the Justice Department, the Office of Legal Policy proposed a direct challenge to *Miranda*, but Solicitor General Charles Fried largely rebuffed the idea.

"Most experienced federal prosecutors in and out of my office were opposed to the project, as was I," Fried wrote in his memoir.[13] Cassell points to cases in which federal prosecutors did try to use Section 3501, and their efforts were supported by the department on appeal.

Still, Justice Antonin Scalia, writing in a 1994 case, complained about the government's "repeated refusal" to invoke the provision in confession cases.[14] And a year earlier, the

Rehnquist Court signaled a sort of acceptance of by reaffirming—on a 5–4 vote with Rehnquist in dissent—that federal courts can set aside state court convictions if police violated a suspect's *Miranda* rights during questioning.[15]

Use of Force

Police came under intense, renewed criticism in the 1990s despite the easing of the controversy over interrogation practices. The issue was police use of force—a problem that flared up most dramatically in the beating of black motorist King in Los Angeles in 1991 and the sodomizing of Haitian immigrant Louima in New York City in 1997.[16] The incidents provoked new accusations of racism against both police departments from minority and civil rights groups and new concerns among police executives and government officials about how to control use of excessive force by police.

Police shootings of black civilians had touched off several of the racial disturbances that had erupted in the nation's big cities three decades earlier. The 1968 report by a presidential panel appointed to study the cause of the riots—the so-called Kerner Commission—found "deep hostility between police and ghetto communities" to have been a "primary cause" of the disorders.

Historian Walker also blames the lack of controls on the use of force by police. "Even the best departments had no meaningful rules on deadly force," Walker writes, "offering their officers many hours of training on how to shoot but not on when to use their weapons."[17]

Much progress was made over the next 25 years, according to Walker. Civilian review boards—favored by groups seeking to hold police accountable—gradually achieved a measure of acceptance after having been stoutly resisted by police unions, local politicians and some segments of the public. By the 1990s,

Race Colors Attitudes About Police Conduct

Most Americans—including a majority of blacks and a substantial majority of whites—have a favorable opinion of their local police. African-Americans are nearly four times as likely as whites to feel they are treated unfairly by local police, according to a recent Gallup Poll. Among blacks, younger men were nearly twice as likely as younger women to feel unfairly treated. Here are some questions from the poll:

Do you have a favorable or unfavorable opinion of your local police?

	Favorable	Unfavorable	Don't know
Blacks	58%	36%	6%
Whites	85%	13%	2%

Do you feel you're treated fairly by the local police in your area?

	Fairly	Not Fairly	Not Applicable/Did not answer
Blacks	66%	27%	7%
Whites	91%	7%	2%

Do you feel you're treated fairly by the local police in your area?

Black men Ages:	Treated Fairly	Not Treated Fairly
18–34	43%	53%
35–49	71%	23%
50+	68%	22%

Black women Ages:	Treated Fairly	Not Treated Fairly
18–34	67%	26%
35–49	75%	19%
50+	71%	18%

Source: The Gallup Organization. The survey is based on 2,006 phone interviews with a random sample of adults in the continental U.S. from Sept. 24, 1999, to Nov. 16, 1999.

Walker reports, more than three-fourths of the police departments in the nation's biggest cities had some form of external or civilian review of complaints.

In addition, local police departments began adopting rules to guide officers in the use of force. The rules appeared to bring results. New York City Police Commissioner Patrick Murphy instituted a rule in 1972 allowing officers to shoot only in "the defense of life" and requiring reports and reviews of any weapons discharge. Officer-involved shootings declined 30 percent over the next three years, according to research by James Fyfe, a professor of criminal justice at Temple University in Philadelphia and an expert on use-of-force issues.[18]

The beating of King by four white Los Angeles police officers after a high-speed car chase on March 3, 1991, put the issue of police brutality back on the national agenda. An 81-second videotape shot by a resident of a nearby apartment—broadcast countless times around the world over the next two years—showed the officers repeatedly kicking King and hitting him 56 times with their batons as he lay on the ground.

The episode produced a national outcry, but criminal prosecutions of the officers ended with mixed results. A predominantly white jury in a neighboring county acquitted the officers of state charges in April 1992; two officers were convicted of violating King's civil rights in a federal court trial in April 1993, but they were given relatively light sentences of 30 months each.

Meanwhile, though, a special commission appointed by Los Angeles Mayor Tom Bradley concluded that the incident was merely one example of what it described as "a tolerance within the LAPD of attitudes condoning violence against the public."[19]

Six years after the King beating, police brutality again became a national issue with an episode in New York that had none of the ambiguity or arguable justifications of the Los Angeles incident. New York police officers arrested Louima on Aug. 9, 1997, following an altercation outside a Brooklyn nightclub. Officer Justin Volpe later acknowledged that he struck Louima while taking him to the patrol car. Once at the station house, Volpe took Louima into a restroom and plunged a broken broomstick handle into the Haitian's rectum. Volpe pleaded guilty to six federal charges in May 1999 and was later sentenced to 30 years in prison; a second officer, Charles Schwarz, was convicted of beating Louima and holding him down during the sodomizing.*

The incident produced universal revulsion, even among sympathetic police observers. "This was clearly a case of sadism and racism," says Boston University's Delattre. Nonetheless, New York Mayor Giuliani, a strong police supporter, saw a positive sign in the willingness of Volpe's fellow officers to aid investigators in uncovering the incident and to testify against him. The trial, Giuliani said, "destroys the myth of the blue wall of silence" among police officers.

For his part, though, Walker says the King and Louima cases represented a setback for public perceptions of police accountability.

"All of the positive developments have been obscured by these horrific examples in New York and Los Angeles, which make it appear to the average citizen that nothing has

changed, and maybe things have gotten worse," Walker says.

'Driving While Black'

Racial profiling became the new flashpoint of police-community relations during the 1990s. African-Americans from many walks of life testified to their experiences of having been stopped and questioned by police seemingly for no reason other than their race.

By the end of the decade, the leading law enforcement groups were joining civil-rights and civil-liberties groups in saying that race alone should never be the basis for a traffic stop or other police investigation. But police were also continuing to defend the use of race as one factor in criminal profiling, particularly in anti-drug enforcement.

Police explained their use of race in deciding what drivers or pedestrians to stop for investigation by pointing to the statistics showing that African-Americans are more likely than whites to be arrested or convicted of many of the most common crimes, especially drug offenses and so-called street crimes. Courts up to and including the U.S. Supreme Court sanctioned the practice.

In one representative case, the Arizona Supreme Court in 1975 upheld a police officer's decision to question a Mexican male because he was sitting in a parked car in a predominantly white neighborhood. The use of race, the court said, was "a practical aspect of good law enforcement."[20]

Two decades later, the Supreme Court in 1996 gave police a blank check to use traffic violations as a pretext for stopping motorists for suspected drug violations. The ruling in *Whren v. United States* turned aside the plea by two black defendants that they had been stopped because of their race.

By the 1990s, though, racial profiling was being challenged not only by convicted defendants but also by

the innocent victims of the practice—people who were stopped, questioned, perhaps searched and then allowed to go on their way when police found no evidence of crime. The first major victory for critics of the practice came in a case brought by Robert Wilkins, a public defender in Washington, D.C., who was stopped by Maryland state police in May 1992 while driving with his family back to Washington. When Wilkins refused to consent to a search of his car troopers called for a trained narcotics dog to try to detect drugs, but no drugs were found.

Wilkins, represented by the ACLU of Maryland and two private Washington lawyers, filed a federal civil rights damage suit in May 1993 contending that the use of a racial profile violated his constitutional rights. The state agreed to settle the suit in January 1995. The state said it would adopt an official policy prohibiting racial profiling and, significantly, maintain detailed records of motorist stops to be provided to the ACLU to monitor any patterns of discrimination. Wilkins and his family were also awarded $50,000 plus attorney fees.

Critics of racial profiling won another settlement late last year after New Jersey officials acknowledged that some state troopers had singled out black and Hispanic motorists for anti-drug enforcement. The long-simmering issue recently erupted in the state when the head of the state police, Carl Williams, was quoted as saying it was "most likely a minority group" that was involved with marijuana or cocaine. The state's Republican governor, Christine Todd Whitman, fired Williams on Feb. 28.

Less than two months later, Whitman appeared with the state's attorney general at a news conference on April 20 to release a two-month study that confirmed a stark racial pattern in traffic stops by troopers at some stations. At year's end, the state signed an agreement with the U.S. Justice Department mandating

---

*Schwarz was fired from the force; he and two other current officers—Thomas Bruder and Thomas Wiese—were convicted in federal court in Brooklyn on March 6, 2000, of conspiracy to obstruct justice for attempting to cover up the incident; attorneys for the three defendants said they would appeal. Schwarz faces up to a life sentence in the first case; the three face up to five years in the second case.

an overhaul of the state police to end racial profiling and agreeing to the appointment of a federal monitor to oversee implementation of the accord.

The shift of opinion on the issue could be seen in comments by candidates in the 2000 presidential campaign. The two leading Democrats—Vice President Al Gore and former New Jersey Sen. Bill Bradley—both spoke out against racial profiling in a Jan.17 debate in Iowa. Bradley drew blood on the issue by challenging Gore to "walk down that hallway" in the White House and get President Clinton to sign an executive order barring racial profiling by federal law enforcement agents. Gore aides later noted that Clinton has ordered federal agencies to collect data on the practice.

For his part, the Republican front-runner, Texas Gov. George W. Bush, also criticized racial profiling in a Jan. 10 campaign debate in Michigan. "No one wants racial profiling to take place in any state," Bush said. But Bush also said, "It's not the federal government's role to run state police departments." The ACLU criticized what it called Bush's "vague" statements and challenged him to issue an executive order in Texas barring the practice.

Notes

1. Scott Glover and Matt Lait, "L.A. Police Group Often Broke Law, Transcripts Say," *Los Angeles Times*, February 10, 2000, p. A1. For other articles, see the *Times'* Web site: www.latimes.com/rampart.
2. Clyde Haberman, "Despite Diallo, Data Show Gun Restraint," *The New York Times*, Feb. 4, 2000, p. B1.
3. International Association of Chiefs of Police, "Police Use of Force in America," October 1999.
4. See Christopher A. Darden, *In Contempt* (1996), p. 110; "Cochran & Grace," "Johnnie Cochran: Driving While Black," Court TV, March 23, 1997, cited in David A. Harris, "The Stories, the Statistics, and the Law: Why 'Driving While Black' Matters," *Minnesota Law Review*, Vol. 84 (1999), pp. 265@ndash@;266.
5. Samuel Walker, *Popular Justice: A History of American Criminal Justice* (1980), p. 61. Other historical background is also drawn from this first edition and from a revised and updated edition published in 1998.
6. National Commission on Law Observance and Enforcement, *Lawless in Law Enforcement* (1931), p. 103, cited in Walker, *op. cit.*, p. 174.
7. The case of *Brown v. Mississippi* (1936) and *Lisenba V. California* (1941).
8. Background drawn from Yale Kamisar *et al.*, *Modern Criminal Procedure: Cases, Comments, and Questions* (8th ed. 1994), as summarized in Richard A. Leo, "The Impact of Miranda Revisited," *Journal of Criminal Law and Criminology*, Vol. 86, No. 3 (1996), pp. 624–625.
9. Walker, *op. cit.*, pp. 194–199.
10. The cases of *Mapp v. Ohio* (1961) and *Gideon v. Wainwright* (1963).
11. Account of interrogation taken from Paul G. Cassell, "The Statute That Time Forgot: 18 U.S.C. Section 3501 and the Overhauling of Miranda," *Iowa Law Review*, Vol. 85 (1999), pp. 183–191. The teenaged victim said she thought Miranda could be the assailant, but could not be positive. After the line-up, Miranda asked if the teenager and a second assault victim had identified him. "Yes, Ernie, they did," a detective replied.
12. ABA Special Commission on Criminal Justice in a Free Society, *Criminal Justice in Crisis* (1988), p. 28.
13. Charles Fried, *Order and Law* (1990), p. 46.
14. The case is *Davis v. United States* (1994).
15. The case is *Withrow v. Williams* (1993).
16. For background, see Richard L. Worsnop, "Police Brutality," *The CQ Researchers*, Sept. 6, 1991, pp. 633–656.
17. Walker, *op. cit.* (2d ed.), p. 197.
18. See *Ibid.*, pp. 232–234.
19. Cited in Worsnop, *op. cit.*, p. 644.
20. Cases cited in Randall Kennedy, *Race, Crime, and the Law* (1997), p. 152.

Kenneth Jost is a veteran legal-affairs journalist and *CQ Researcher* staff writer. He holds a law degree from Georgetown University, where he was editor of the *Georgetown Law Journal*. He is author of *The Supreme Court Yearbook* and a contributor to several legal periodicals.

Why Harlem Drug Cops Don't Discuss Race

Color Can Give Anonymity Undercover. But Looking Like a Suspect Has Its Risks.

By MICHAEL WINERIP

Friday, Feb. 25, at 5 p.m., there wasn't a single narcotics officer on the streets of Harlem. Everyone was being held inside on standby in case of a race riot. The Diallo verdict was about to come down.

On East 107th Street, at the police headquarters for Harlem narcotics, cops gathered around several televisions to watch the verdict, a couple of hundred plainclothes officers in two big rooms, maybe a third of them black and Hispanic. They appeared from interviews to be split racially, much as people had been by the O. J. Simpson case. The whites—officers like Sgt. Maria Brogli and Detectives Lee Macklowe and John Montes—hoped the four Diallo officers would be found not guilty. The blacks—detectives like Johnny Gonzalez and the undercovers Derrick and Rob—felt they should be found guilty on at least some counts. "Forty-one shots," said Derrick. "That's excessive."

Feelings ran deep. No case in recent years has hit the police closer to home. As Sergeant Brogli said, "There but for the grace of God...." Every officer with any sense, white or black, fears mistakenly shooting an unarmed man like Amadou Diallo. Talk about jamming up a career.

All eight members of Sergeant Brogli's narcotics team have stories about almost squeezing the trigger. In Detective Gonzalez's case, he remembers running after a drug dealer, Earl Thomas, on 143rd Street, and as he got close, the man dropped to the ground and with his back to Detective Gonzalez, reached into his waistband. "MAN WITH A GUN!" is what flashed through Detective Gonzalez's mind. In a split second, the detective had to decide: shoot, or jump him and risk being shot. He risked it. This time, Earl Thomas was reaching in to dump his drugs before being arrested.

"I almost shot an unarmed man in the back," said Detective Gonzalez. "It would've been the end of my career. I would have been like the Diallo cops."

But dark-skinned plainclothes officers have a second, more chilling fear: that someday, a white officer will accidentally shoot them. And that, they said, made them view the Diallo case differently.

Several years ago, before going undercover, Derrick recalls being in street clothes, on his way to work at the 63rd Precinct in Brooklyn, when he saw an elderly woman being robbed by two teenagers. He managed to get the woman into his car, subdue the attackers (though he had no handcuffs) and persuade a passer-by to call 911—an effort that would win him a hero's medal. But as he waited for backup, he was scared. Most officers at the 63rd were away at a funeral that day. He feared that the officers who showed up would not know him, and that he would be in danger—a black man in street clothes with a gun. Seeing a patrol car approach, he waved his police ID over his head and kept screaming: "I'm a cop! I'm a cop!"

Race colors everything for Harlem narcotics detectives. It lies beneath the surface in a dispute over tactics between a white sergeant and a black undercover detective. Race is out there in the neighborhood where Sergeant Brogli's team pits African-American informers against Dominican drug dealers. Race is in the police radio descriptions ("suspect is a dark-skinned Dominican, mid-20's ..."), and race amplifies the anger on the street when the police drive up and arrest yet another dark-skinned man.

The biggest police race case in New York City in years, Diallo—the 1998 killing of a black man standing in the doorway of his Bronx building by four panicky white policemen—touched every Harlem narcotics officer in the room that day to the core. And yet Sergeant Brogli's team had never discussed it. Cops do not discuss race. It's too risky. They need to get along.

As the Diallo verdict was read charge by charge that rainy February evening and it became evident that the four officers would be cleared on every count, Sergeant Brogli was so delighted she felt almost as if she had been personally exonerated, and Derrick was so bitter he could not stop pacing. But despite the enormous emotion of the moment, the whites did not cheer or whoop; the blacks showed no outrage. There was barely a sound in the room.

Working a Brown Neighborhood

When Sergeant Brogli sees a dozen brown-skinned Dominican men standing on the corner of 141st Street and Broadway in Harlem, she thinks, "Drug dealers."

"Most are involved in drugs, probably," she says. "That's the best assumption I can make."

And even though she is a five-foot-tall woman dressed in everyday clothes and driving an ordinary van, the moment they see her, they give the warning whistle that means "cops on the block, 5-0, policía."

"La Terrible," they whisper as she approaches. "La Bruja" ("the Witch").

The very visible, white Sergeant Brogli could not do her work without her undercover detectives, whose dark skin renders them invisible on these streets.

For five years Detective Johnny Gonzalez, himself Dominican-American, was an undercover for Sergeant Brogli, posing as a drug user, a brown man disappearing into a brown neighborhood. He'd buy the drugs, leave the scene, radio in a description of the dealer, and then Sergeant Brogli and her team of mainly white investigators would speed their vans up the street and grab that one man from the dozen on the corner.

So deft is the whole thing when done properly that dealers don't have a clue which person they sold to was the undercover cop. Often they don't figure it out until months later, when they go to trial and the undercover is there on the stand.

"Can I ask what you're taking me in for?" a surprised Victor Figueroa said when arrested during a buy-and-bust one evening in May as he stood at 141st Street and Hamilton Place with $2,650 in his pockets.

Sergeant Brogli always has the same answer: "You really don't know what you did? You'll find out."

Smart cops like Sergeant Brogli and Detective Gonzalez know how to use race wisely, how to turn race to their advantage to enforce the law.

For five years, Detective Gonzalez—nicknamed Johnny G.—returned over and over to the same five blocks, 140th to 145th Streets, sometimes making $5 "nick" buys, sometimes buying thousands of dollars in cocaine, and never was he found out. Among Harlem drug cops he is a legend, an easygoing, jokey, charming, streetwise man who, occasionally, when things went wrong, got in fistfights with dealers but took pride in never having used his gun. Dealers loved Johnny G. They invited him into their apartments, they kidded with him, their mothers fed him, their girlfriends flirted with him and most important, they trusted him, enough to sell him their drugs, more than 500 buys, hundreds of arrests, hundreds of guilty pleas and convictions.

On the streets, Johnny G. used whatever he could to get an edge. Usually he pretended to be African-American, acting as if he knew only English. Then the Spanish-speaking dealers would talk openly in front of him, sometimes spilling their secrets. But other times he bought from Dominican dealers who hated blacks, who would make blacks wait for their drugs, who would tell their steerers in Spanish, "Have all the monkeys stand over there."

"Then I'd be Dominican," said Detective Gonzalez. "To get done faster."

He was so smooth at switching it on and off, from Dominican to African-American, from cop to coke-head, that at times his wife, Sonia, would catch him slipping into a street character as he played with their two little sons and would gently remind him, "Johnny, you're home now, you're not working."

The Perils of Going In Cold

Detective Gonzalez may be Dominican, but when he sees those young Dominican men on that corner, he has the same reaction as Sergeant Brogli: "Ninety percent are working in drugs."

Still, he insists, he does not stoop to racial profiling. He would not go cold into a corner full of black and brown men and try to make a buy, he says, unless his investigators had gathered evidence that a specific dealer was operating there. They should be able to tell him whether the dealer is selling in grams or ounces, crack, coke or heroin, whether it's shiny "fish scale" or powdery, whether the brand name is New World Order or Bazooka, so he knows what to ask for.

That is where Detective Gonzalez draws the line between good police work and racial profiling. "It's insulting to walk up to a guy just because he's black or Dominican standing on a corner and say, 'Who's working?' That is the distinction he makes between using race fairly and misusing race.

At times, he says, white sergeants have told him, "Go over to that group of Domos and see who's working."

"You can't say no to a direct order," Detective Gonzalez said. "You just go up, walk past and tell the sergeant nothing's going on." A dozen black and Hispanic undercovers working with him in Harlem said in interviews that they had defied a sergeant's orders in the same way.

Among these undercovers, Sergeant Brogli is a favorite, the rare white sergeant with a reputation for listening to undercovers and speaking up for them. "Maria has a mouth on her," says Rob, one of her undercovers. On May 9, as the team put together a list of buy-and-bust locations, a white investigator, Lee Macklowe, said he had a tip that cocaine was being sold from a street-level window on 140th near Hamilton.

"Just bang on the window," he said. But Sergeant Brogli was upset. She made him call his informer. "Find out if they're selling nicks, grams, dimes," she said.

Later, the undercover making that buy, Nelson, quietly thanked her. "Way to go, Sarge," he said.

Going in cold increases the risk. Some narcotics officers, including

Sergeant Brogli, suspect that is what went wrong earlier this year when Patrick Dorismond, an unarmed black man, was killed during a buy-and-bust by an undercover near Times Square. It may have been a case, they say, of a narcotics team working late, one body short of the nightly quota of five arrests, approaching a group of black men cold and having it blow up in their faces.

Dark-skinned undercovers are touchy about racial profiling because most, including Detective Gonzalez, say that when off duty, in their neighborhoods or out driving, they have been targets of white officers. One undercover, Tyrone, says that while driving home from work to Brooklyn he gets stopped an average of one night a week. Two of Sergeant Brogli's black undercovers, Derrick and Rob, describe standing outside Rob's home in Brooklyn after work, having a beer, and being approached by a man who asked, "Who's working?"

Derrick and Rob didn't bother explaining to that plainclothes cop that they, too, were cops. They just shook their heads and waited until he left. "You know it's because we're black," Derrick said.

"You develop thick skin," Detective Gonzalez said. Besides, working with Sergeant Brogli for seven years—first as an undercover and for the last two years as an investigator—he has learned there are harder things than being a black policeman. "Females on the job have it worse," he said.

He thinks it is what makes Sergeant Brogli a fairer boss than most whites; a female officer knows what it's like being in the minority.

Lately, he has been worried that she may be leaving narcotics and he may be assigned a new sergeant. And in an office where the top boss, the captain, changes every few months, where conditions are so cheesy that officers have to bring in their own toilet paper and lock it in their desks, your sergeant is often your only protection.

A Trained Eye Sees Blue

Maria Brogli is no bleeding heart. She is an aggressive Italian-American cop who has tackled men resisting arrest and slammed others against walls, who has been kicked and punched, had her nose broken and a flowerpot dropped on her head, and still got the collar. She thinks race is overblown as a police problem, but will not watch "The Sopranos," the television series on the Mafia, because she feels it is biased against Italian-Americans.

Going up cold to blacks on a corner doesn't bother her because it's racial profiling. It bothers her because it's lazy and risky.

And she cannot abide laziness. In recent years, her team has ranked first or second, among the 45 units working northern Manhattan, for felony arrests, search warrants, drugs confiscated. While most sergeants are satisfied doing buy-and-busts, twice she has undertaken complex yearlong investigations that involved extensive wiretaps.

When asked about dealing with race on the job, she says, "I don't see black and white, I see blue." But she is not blind about blue. In the mid-1990's, during a scandal at the 30th Precinct, two informers fed her tips on corrupt officers. She drove the informers to the internal affairs office in Harlem, contributing to the convictions of Officers George Nova and Alphonso Compres.

She is a short, stocky, unglamorous 38-year-old woman who has attained respect in a department dominated by white men. Her lieutenant, James Byrne, likes to smoke a cigar in the van and offer comments on young female passers-by. ("Wouldn't you like to spoil that one?" is a favorite.)

She never expected to be a cop. After attending racially mixed Bronx public schools and scoring 1400 on her SAT, she was pre-med at New York University. But her father, a commercial photographer, suffered a stroke, and she needed a job to support the family. She applied in 1983.

A requirement then was clearing a five-foot wall—no easy task for a woman who *claims* to be five feet tall. She practiced, she prayed to St. Anthony, but on the first of two tries she failed. "There was a tall black instructor," she recalled. "He says: 'What's the matter, munchkin? You can get over the wall. When you're running, don't look at the wall, look beyond the wall.'"

That is a pretty fair metaphor for her rise in the department. As a rookie, she was repeatedly given the complaint room, traditional duty for women, typing forms. Whenever possible, she traded for patrol, working her way onto the streets. In 1990, after passing the sergeant's test, she was sent to the 28th Precinct in Harlem, hard duty for any white, let alone the first female supervisor assigned there. As is the rule on the force, a separate supervisor's locker room was provided, by moving a wall of lockers to partition off a corner of the women's room for her. "You could hear them laughing on the other side of the lockers and you're alone," she recalled. She learned to bang her locker when she entered, so cops on the other side knew she was no snoop.

In narcotics she gets impressive numbers, in part because no one puts in longer hours. A single woman living with her widowed mother, she often stays past midnight.

But her success also comes from pushing hard on the street. It is because of officers like Sergeant Brogli that men in this neighborhood learn always to carry identification. Though there is no law saying they must, they know if they don't, and are stopped, they can be hauled into the precinct for a few hours, their names run through the computer for outstanding warrants.

On May 9, her team did a buy-and-bust at 141st and Amsterdam, arresting Pedro Pereira and confiscating $1,374. Standing on the same corner was Juan Payano, 30. He didn't have drugs or much money. Nor did he have identification; he said he couldn't remember his address.

"He don't know where he lives?" Sergeant Brogli asked. "He's got no ID?"

"He says he's only been here 15 days and he's legal," said her senior detective, Felix Berrios, interpreting the Spanish.

"Does he know he can be arrested for no ID?" said Sergeant Brogli, who kept him standing there about 10 minutes. "Ask him if he wants to go to jail." He didn't. "Ask him where he lives again."

"Riverside between 136 and 137."

"Is he going to learn the building number now?" Sergeant Brogli asked.

"He says he'll never forget."

Later the sergeant said: "I wanted to see if he changed his story and got nervous and blurted anything out. I think he's lying through his teeth."

A Racial Chameleon

It is as if Johnny Gonzalez was raised to be an undercover. He grew up in a working-class Dominican family (his father was a welder, his mother a beautician), in Brownsville, a tough African-American section of Brooklyn where he would see Mike Tyson and Riddick Bowe on the streets. He attended P.S. 41, a black school, then went to I.S. 302, a Puerto Rican school, where his Spanish helped. "If you met me when I was in elementary school, you'd assume I was black," he says. "But with Puerto Rican kids I became Puerto Rican."

When he began dating Sonia, a Puerto Rican, her dad was nice until he realized this boyfriend was Dominican. "Dad would not answer the door," she said. "My father used to say, 'He's a Dominican man, they don't know how to treat Spanish women.' "

Sonia, who is also a cop, says her co-workers assume that Johnny is black. Sometimes even she teases him, "Johnny, what are you, anyway?"

He applied to the department in 1987, but failed the psychological test. At the time, the test was being challenged in court as biased against minorities; under an appeals proce-

dure, he was allowed to see a non-departmental psychologist, and was approved after a two-year delay.

The first whites he and his wife knew well were cops. A few years ago, he moved to Long Island for the schools; it took the family time to adjust. "There was a blond boy, Jimmy, across the street," Detective Gonzalez recalled. "When my son Mark saw him, he said: 'Dad, what's wrong with him? He doesn't have any color.' "

More Risks, More of the Time

When Sergeant Brogli needed a new undercover, she looked at photos of two black officers she had never met and picked one.

"It's like the N.B.A. draft," said Rob, a black undercover, who has been traded among narcotics teams a few times. "They say, 'Grab him, he's a big black body.'" There is a logic to it—the poorest neighborhoods tend to be black or Hispanic and often have the biggest street narcotics problems. A minority undercover is less conspicuous.

But it means that from Day 1, when a team is assembled, race enters the room. Narcotics headquarters looks as racially divided as a school cafeteria. The undercovers sit together. In their free time they play backgammon. They tend to be younger and city-bred; many own motorcycles.

The jobs they do are different, and that sets them apart, too. Most police work can be dangerous, but day in and day out, undercovers take more risks. Detective Gonzalez has been locked in a dealer's apartment with a gun to his head; he has had his jaw broken; he has been accused of being a cop several times by dealers and has had to lie his way out of booby-trapped apartments. Often, he has worked without a gun.

On the other hand, to protect their identities, undercovers are excused from the daily duties that

make police work miserable. They do not have to transport sick, angry or foul-smelling prisoners ("stinkies") to jail; execute search warrants; or do crowd control at events like the Diallo protests. They are not allowed to have their full names or photographs used in the press.

While other cops do grunt jobs, undercovers play backgammon. Resentment builds. Race isn't mentioned, but it's there. Returning from executing a tedious search warrant, Detective Macklowe noticed an undercover's car parked in the lot. "How do these kids afford BMW's?" he asked.

Detective Gonzalez would not let the comment pass. "They live at home," he said. "They're not carrying a big mortgage." Indeed, it is a constant gripe among undercovers that they get pushed for more buys by white bosses seeking more overtime to pay off their heavily mortgaged houses out by Exit 68 on the Long Island Expressway.

The two groups of officers do not always communicate well.

"O.K., this is how it's going to work," Sgt. Joe Simonetti said one day last summer, outlining a series of buy-and-busts. He told Nelson, who had been working as an undercover less than a year, to make two buys: a $10 crack buy and a $300 cocaine buy. Several veteran undercovers winced. To do a $10 buy, you dress down, like a crackhead; for the other buy you need to look groomed, moneyed. You can't be both at once.

When Sergeant Simonetti had finished giving orders, several from Sergeant Brogli's team working backup, including Detective Gonzalez, put on bulletproof vests, then piled into the elevator to head out. Just before the door closed Nelson rushed up. Detective Gonzalez could see fear in the young undercover's eyes. "He wants me to do both," Nelson said.

"That's crazy," said Detective Gonzalez. "It's your call. You have to know what's safe and watch out for yourself." As the elevator door shut, Nelson knew what to do.

Same Show, Nth Performance

Narcotics enforcement is a frustrating cat-and-mouse game between officers and dealers who, after years of crackdowns, are savvy about dividing and concealing each step of the operation. Rarely do the police get the drugs, the money and the dealer together. Repeatedly Sergeant Brogli's team arrests dealers, and the next day, standing in that very spot, there is someone else—or even the same person.

On Nov. 12, they executed a search warrant at the basement apartments at 605 West 141st St., where some tenants are so poor they live in luggage storage bins. In the room of Ramon Ortiz, the superintendent, Detective Rob Arbuiso found drug paraphernalia, including a scale; 100 plastic sandwich bags commonly used to package cocaine; and $132,750 in cash. The money was confiscated as drug profits. Mr. Ortiz was notified that he could reclaim it if he proved he had earned it legitimately; he never has. But they found no drugs, and Mr. Ortiz was quickly back on the street. His misdemeanor charge on paraphernalia possession is still pending.

Weeks later, they searched in the same building, hitting Apartment 21, which was leased to an elderly woman who had recently had a liver transplant.

"We're going to knock instead of banging down the door," Sergeant Simonetti said. "We don't want to give her a heart attack."

Inside, near a painting of the Virgin Mary, were two bedrooms that she sublet, both equipped with locks. In one room was a sleeping Dominican, who was forced into the hall in his underwear, cuffed and questioned. He told Detective Gonzalez he had no idea who lived in the other bedroom, had never seen anyone going or coming. In that sec-

ond bedroom officers found a plastic bag containing about $60,000 worth of cocaine. The old woman with the new liver said that she had never seen anyone go in or out of that room. And neither she nor the man in his underpants had a key for it.

As Lieutenant Byrne mulled over whom to arrest, a man rushed up the stairs. He said that his name was Alberto Rivera Jr., and that he was the old woman's son.

At first he said he lived there; when he heard why the police were there, he said he didn't. Detective Gonzalez asked if Mr. Rivera had an ID, and before he knew it, Mr. Rivera was reaching into his pants.

"Don't do that until I tell . . . " began Detective Gonzalez, but it was too late. Mr. Rivera was pointing a dark brown *wallet* at the detective, who started, then relaxed. "Don't be making any fast moves like that," the officer sighed.

In the end the lieutenant compromised. He said he doubted that charges against the old woman would stick and didn't want her dropping dead in the prisoner van; he was suspicious of the son but had nothing. So he decided on the man in underpants. "We don't want to be embarrassed going into the neighborhood and coming out with no one," the lieutenant said. "This sends a message." They would take him to the precinct, check for outstanding warrants, and then, if he was clean, let him go. All of which they did.

To cops, who often feel they're in a losing battle against the dealers, it's a way to apply some leverage, maybe persuade someone to inform; in the neighborhoods, it smacks of racial profiling.

On these streets, dark-skinned man are often stopped, questioned, then let go. On May 4, Sergeant Simonetti's team searched 601 West 141st Street, Apartment 41. As several officers entered the apartment, others detained 15 men standing on the nearby corner of 141st and Broadway. Inside the apartment, the cops reported a rare trifecta: They seized 1.5 kilos of cocaine and about $3,000, and arrested 18-year-old Jorge Rodriguez (who has

since fled and is being sought on a bench warrant).

Outside on the street, the police lined up the detained men against a wall to see if any had keys to Apartment 41. Sometimes this works; a few weeks before, on the same block, they caught two dealers this way. This time no one had a matching key. One man had a small amount of coke and was arrested; a second had $2,000 in cash and a Kenwood two-way radio. There was another Kenwood inside the apartment, but the frequency didn't match. He and the other 14 were let go after half an hour.

As the police searched the men, a mainly Dominican crowd gathered, joking with the cops. Pointing at the men on the corner, a young woman called out, "Why are you bothering them? They're just working," and the crowd and cops shared a laugh.

But just as often, the crowd turns nasty. Last August, Flor Blum was arrested for buying $35 of crack. When she realized she would be handcuffed and put in the prisoner van, she began screaming. In the back of the van, she hurled herself against the walls, slamming her body against Detective Gonzalez and his partner, Detective Scott Signorelli. "Please let me go, let me get out of here!" she screamed. "I'm phobic!"

They tried to calm her, but she kept screaming. "I need water! I have AIDS, sir! I swear, I don't want to do this! It's only a job to you. What do you care?" She began hacking up phlegm, spitting all over the back of the van. Detective Gonzalez could not tell: Was she high? Having an anxiety attack? Faking it? Might she go into cardiac arrest? That could end a cop's career fast. They stopped and bought her a bottle of Poland Spring, but she continued to scream and thrash so much, the van rocked. "My T-cells are going down! Please let me go, sir!" When they parked on 135th Street to try to calm her, a crowd gathered outside the rocking van. "What are they doing?" a woman asked. "Are they beating her?"

"They're beating her?" yelled a second woman. Suddenly there was a bang on top of the van; someone had hurled an egg off a roof at the police. Detective Gonzalez drove off. Ms. Blum screamed the whole way to the precinct. Later she apologized, saying, "I just get phobic." She was given a desk appearance ticket and took a taxi home. Ultimately, charges were dismissed.

All of this make narcotics officers feel bitter, as if it were the 1920's and they were reliving Prohibition. "Everyone sees this is a joke," said Jason, an undercover. "They know we ain't putting no dent in drugs."

Lieutenant Byrne, who oversees Sergeant Brogli's team, says the only answer is legalizing drugs. "In my humble opinion, we're doing nothing up here," he said after another long day of buy-and-busts.

There Goes the Neighborhood

It's supposedly common knowledge: black New Yorkers distrust the police. But on the streets where Sergeant Brogli works, the biggest supporters of the police are African-American. In the last 15 years, this neighborhood may have changed from primarily African-American to Dominican, but the citizens council that meets monthly at the local precinct, the 30th, is headed by an African-American, Hazel O'Reilly, and dominated by African-Americans. At council meetings it is mainly black residents who attend to ask for *more* police enforcement, *more* drug arrests, who want *more* people jailed for loitering and trespassing.

Detective John Montes, a Hispanic cop who walked a beat for two years before joining Sergeant Brogli's team, says his best informers here were black. On these streets, the African-Americans are frequently the older, better-established families who moved here in the 1950's. Many are middle-class government workers, small-business owners and professionals, and often

they are resentful that Spanish is now the primary language spoken in the Broadway shops; that able-bodied Dominican men line the sidewalks all hours of the day; and that the police consider the neighborhood drug trade, controlled by Dominicans, the worst in the city.

At a 30th Precinct meeting, an African-American homeowner asked that the police do loitering sweeps, calling in the National Guard if necessary. The woman, a single professional with a master's degree, complained in an interview about the Dominicans: "They hang out on the corners—they have so many children. When I go into one of their stores, I try to line up to buy something the American way, but it's all chaos, the Dominican customers all milling, they don't know how to go in order."

In a dozen interviews in their homes, African-Americans complained about Dominicans ruining the neighborhood, sounding very much like the Jews and Italians who once dominated this area and began leaving 40 years ago, complaining about the blacks moving in.

Citing fear of retribution from dealers, all but one refused to be cited by name. The one who allowed her last name to be used, Mrs. Roper, ran a beauty shop but moved "when the neighborhood started going down because of the Dominicans."

"We had a nice building, until we got a Dominican superintendent and every time an apartment came available, he'd put in some of them, and each one looked like a drug dealer," said Mrs. Roper, a great-grandmother and a member of the scholarship committee at her Baptist church. "They'd play their music so loud, and this one time, a Dominican boy ran into our place and stole the money for the electric and a gold chain. I tell you the Dominicans destroy everything."

Dominicans Take the Rap

Everyone at headquarters has a racial or ethnic identity and gets needled about it. Lee Macklowe, a Jew, is

introduced to a Jewish reporter as "a fellow member of the tribe." When Sergeant Simonetti treats his team to bagels, he lifts up a dark brown one and yells to Detective Luis Nieves-Diaz, a black-skinned Puerto Rican: "The pumpernickel's for you, Lou! Heh-heh!"

The one slur rarely spoken is "nigger." In a year's time, a reporter did not hear it. Whether that was because, as Sergeant Brogli says, this generation has been conditioned against it, or because, as Derrick, a black undercover, says, racial animosity still runs too deep to joke about the word, it seemed off-limits.

On the other hand, in these streets where most arrested for drugs are Dominican, it's open season on "Domos." Many are from poor, rural parts of their Caribbean island, where record-keeping isn't precise, and officers making arrests jokingly wonder if the Domo will know his birth date.

Sgt. Neil Nappi, who is white, was trying to help Sergeant Brogli's team persuade an arrested Dominican to give up information about a drug ring. In the midst of questioning him, Sergeant Nappi started talking about Dominican women. "They're beautiful, but big trouble," he said to another officer. "You don't want to knock 'em up. There's a couple of little redheaded Dominican kids running around, belong to guys at the 30th. Cops get their checks garnished, it breaks up marriages—they're dangerous." As the cop spoke the Dominican man stared at the floor; he provided no useful information that day.

But there are times when the stereotype is true—that the able-bodied dark-skinned man standing on the corner day after day is up to something—and playing all the obvious hunches may pay off for the police.

Last Sept. 10, Sergeant Brogli's team bought drugs on 141st Street. Soon the van pulled up, and while Hector Espinal stood among a group of Dominican men, Detectives Gonzalez and Montes quietly arrested and cuffed him.

"Why'm I getting locked up?" he asked. A woman with a baby said, "He's just standing here." In Mr. Espinal's pocket was a Progressive Labor Party flier, headlined "Racist Cops Kill Workers in Cold Blood."

Back at the 30th, doing the paperwork, two detectives could not agree on whether Mr. Espinal's eyes were hazel or brown. "Hector, look at me," said Sergeant Brogli, getting so close you could barely squeeze a dime between them. "Light brown," she said, and while she had his attention, she mentioned that he might be able to knock some prison time off by cooperating. She did not tell him that based on an investigation, they believed he belonged to a ring run by a dealer with the street name D. B.

"I'm not a drug dealer," Mr. Espinal said.

"We'll go upstairs and talk," Detective Berrios said.

They took him to a windowless interrogation room, where he sat at a table, one hand cuffed to the wall, and sipped a Poland Spring they had bought him. "I go up on that block, but I mind my business," Mr. Espinal said. "I'm not out there with anybody else. All I do is hang out there and smoke weed."

"We're telling you, you sold drugs," Sergeant Brogli said.

"Hector, I'm going to treat you like a man, not a boy," Detective Montes said.

"I don't work for anybody," Mr. Espinal repeated.

"One-shot offer," Sergeant Brogli said. "Talk now or the offer's gone."

"I don't know about sales," Mr. Espinal said. "I'm just trying to get it in my mouth."

"You have kids?" Detective Berrios asked. Mr. Espinal said he wasn't married.

"Yeah," Detective Berrios said. "but you got a kid, right?"

"Saturday he turned 1," Mr. Espinal said.

"You don't think about the kid now," Detective Berrios said, adding that Mr. Espinal could face 15 years. "You won't see him until he turns 17 possibly, and by that time he

could have him another daddy." They all stared while Mr. Espinal swigged Poland Spring. "What are you thinking about?" Sergeant Brogli asked.

"You doubt if we are telling you the truth," Detective Berrios said.

"I don't work with nobody," Mr. Espinal repeated.

"You have exactly one minute," Sergeant Brogli said.

Mr. Espinal mumbled something. The cinder-block room went dead as a tomb. Next time he said it loud and clear: He got his stuff from "some cat named D. B."

"So you get it from D. B.," Detective Montes said.

"D. B.'s that chubby kid," Mr. Espinal said. "I'm not big like you think. I just got a lot of years" in the stuff.

They said they knew he had to be a seller, an able-bodied man, with no steady job, hanging on the street.

"I don't got a lot of expenses," he said. "I stay with my mother, plus I had a legal job—back in '96."

"So you only make a couple of bucks," Sergeant Brogli said.

"Just to feed my child and my mother and my girlfriend and me," Mr. Espinal said. "Not to bring no guns, or no kilos."

"How you get in contact with him?" Detective Montes asked.

"On the block," Mr. Espinal said. "D. B. used to live with his girlfriend, but don't anymore."

"To feed you, your mother, your baby and your girl, he's got to be around a lot," Detective Montes said.

"Even his ex don't know where D. B. lives," Mr. Espinal said.

Detective Montes asked if D. B. lived with his mother.

"I don't be talking to that crackhead bitch," said Mr. Espinal (who has since been indicted on drug-selling charges and is facing trial).

Looking Out for Each Other

Members of a police team spend enormous amounts of time together. They discuss all forms of personal minutiae, including their dental work, their sleeping problems,

whether they're having regular bowel movements and which relatives they're not getting along with.

They do not discuss race. They did not discuss Diallo.

And yet when the verdict came down, from interviewing them separately it was clear that each group knew how the other felt. Neither could afford to offend the other; light and dark, they needed each other to get home safely at day's end.

And so, the eerie silence after the verdict.

Despite the racial divides in that room, at some point, most had helped out when others were jammed up. When Pete, one of the few white undercovers, was new, he had a terrible time making buys. His first month he did only two, well short of the five quota. Detective Gonzalez took him aside and gave him tips about blending in, like finding a group of druggies to stand in line with and taking care to hand over the money in the same wrist motion as the guy before you. But more than that, he leveled with Pete. He told him that as a white, he wouldn't be able to act like a brown Spanish guy. It helped Pete create his own character. Pete changed, from jivey white dude to homeless crackhead. His record is now 13 buys in a month.

On the other hand, Detective Gonzalez, a gifted street cop, is weak on writing skills and awful about finishing his paperwork. At one point Lieutenant Byrne threatened to dock him a few days, for work that was months overdue, and told Sergeant Brogli to stay out of it. ("I want to put the fear of God in him," the lieutenant said.) Even so, the sergeant called Detective Gonzalez at home late at night and gave him tips on writing the forms in his own words.

In the two years between Amadou Diallo's death and the announcement of the verdict, Sergeant Brogli spent perhaps 5,000 hours with Derrick and Detective Gonzalez. They may never have discussed the case, but she knew their hearts. "Derrick's thinking it could have been him standing in that doorway," Sergeant Brogli said after the verdict.

Those were the very words Derrick used when asked later. "It could have been us," he said. "It could've been an undercover."

Up the Ladder

Several weeks ago, the new civil service list for lieutenants came out. Sergeant Brogli has friends all over the department, and one who got an early peek called her at home: "Is this *Lieutenant* Brogli?"

"Ma!" she called out. "I made the list!"

The police bureaucracy moves in inscrutable ways, and it could be months before the promotion takes effect and she is transferred. Fearing her departure, Detective Gonzalez has been looking around. He is not a good test taker, did poorly on the sergeant's exam. Like a lot of blacks and Hispanics, he took the undercover job because it put him on a fast track for a detective's shield and higher pay. It is a common avenue for minorities who either aren't good test takers or don't want the responsibility of being a sergeant.

But at 35, after doing five years as an undercover and two years as an investigator, he says he feels too old to return to that life, and now the options are less glamorous. Ideally he would like to stay with Sergeant Brogli until she changes jobs, and he said to her, "Maria, if you just tell me to stay, I will."

That's what she wanted, too. She's crazy about Johnny G., even if his paperwork is a nightmare. But she knew he had a couple of offers pending and it would be unfair to ask. "The door that opens now may not be open later," she said, and they laughed because she sounded like one of those fortune cookies that come with the Chinese takeout they order on the overnight tour.

Out With Prejudice

Years ago, when Detective Gonzalez was on uniformed housing patrol in Red Hook, Brooklyn, white officers couldn't tell what he was by looking at him and were guarded until reading his name tag. "Then they'd say, 'Oh, you're Gonzalez—these blacks, aren't they like animals with all their kids?' "

"Now I'm in a Dominican neighborhood," he said. "I'll hear some sergeant, not knowing I'm around, talking about Domos this, Domos that."

"I had a white cop ask me, 'How many in your family are drug dealers?'" said Detective Gonzalez, who doesn't drink alcohol. "I told him, in my family, nobody."

If the police can be too quick to label, Detective Gonzalez says, they are only reflecting society.

On a warm afternoon, dressed as usual in plain clothes, he met downtown with a prosecutor about a case, then stopped in a deli near Chinatown for an iced tea. One sip and he nearly spit it out. He knew immediately it was the extra-sweet tea that heroin addicts on methadone often crave. "Sorry," said the Asian woman behind the counter, exchanging the drink. "This is junkie iced tea." An honest mistake? Or had she assumed he was a junkie from a nearby methadone clinic because he is brown-skinned?

You could go crazy trying to get to the bottom of every slight, says Detective Gonzalez, and he doesn't bother. He is an upbeat family man. His view of the narcotics officers he deals with each day: "There's not that much prejudice in the room."

A Poor Homeland

Making assumptions about Dominicans and drugs is not wholly an act of racism. Federal officials consider the Dominican Republic a major drug depot. In part that is because it is halfway between Colombia, where the cocaine is grown, and the United States, where it is snorted. And unlike Haiti on the other side of the island, the Dominican Republic shares a language with Colombia. But the most common reason that Dominicans join the drug trade, Detective Gonzalez says, is that most are very, very poor. He visits the island a few times a year to see his mother, who has retired there, and tells this story:

He is driving on the island with his 2-year-old son, Mark, when the car breaks down. There is a shack nearby, and he walks to it carrying Mark. Inside there is a single light bulb dangling from a cord. He asks the woman living there to use a phone. She takes down the number, and before he knows it he sees a boy running through the fields; the woman has sent her son to the nearest phone, a few miles away. Then she disappears out back and kills a chicken. She pulls plantains from a tree and makes the New York City detective and his boy a meal. A lost afternoon turns festive. Finally a mechanic arrives with the detective's mother, but when they try to give the woman money, she will not take it. She says it would be an insult.

Now every time he visits the island, he stops by her shack to drop off some small gift, like clothes his children have outgrown, and is greeted like a rich man.

"You drive around the D. R.," he said, "and in the middle of rows of shacks, you see one big house, a big car, a satellite dish, and you know it's drug money. These Dominican kids see it, too, and they have no other way and they take a chance. Most are not bad people. They come up humble, country people. It's a choice of living in a shack or getting something better for their families."

When Detective Gonzalez sees the brown men lined up on 140th Street, he thinks drug dealers, he says. But he also thinks of the bare light bulb and the boy running miles through the fields to the nearest phone.

Unit 4

Unit Selections

Key Points to Consider

❖ Is the American jury system in trouble? Defend your answer.

❖ In your view, is "jury nullification" ever justified? Why or why not?

❖ Is there an alternative to "getting tough on crime"?

 **Links** **www.dushkin.com/online/**

These sites are annotated on pages 4 and 5.

The courts are an equal partner in the American justice system. Just as the police have the responsibility of guarding our liberties by enforcing the law, the courts play an important role in defending these liberties by applying the law. The courts are where civilized "wars" are fought, individual rights are protected, and disputes are peacefully settled.

The articles in this unit discuss several issues concerning the judicial process. Ours is an adversary system of justice, and the protagonists, the state, and the defendant are usually represented by counsel.

Noting deficiencies in jury trials, the authors of "How to Improve the Jury System" recommend allowing jurors to take notes and submit written questions for witnesses. Focusing again on the jury, "Q: Should Juries Nullify Laws They Consider Unjust or Excessively Punitive?" explores the pros and cons of the issue. In "A Get-Tough Policy That Failed," John Cloud argues that mandatory sentencing is not working. He supports his position by citing former adherents who are now trying to reform sentences that can be ridiculously disproportionate to the crimes. Another serious problem, the unreliability of eyewitness evidence, is examined in "Looking Askance at Eyewitness Testimony." A much more dependable source of identification, DNA, is looked at from different perspectives in "DNA: Fingerprint of the Future?" and "The Creeping Expansion of DNA Data Banking."

The Judicial System

COMMENTARY

How to Improve the Jury System

by Thomas F. Hogan, Gregory E. Mize, and Kathleen Clark

The subject of the American jury system raises conflicting cultural sentiments. While the jury trial is revered as the most democratic institution in our society, a summons for jury service is dreaded as an unwelcome intrusion into our lives. Jury verdicts, respected because they are reached by a group of peers, are also ridiculed in recent high-profile trials.

Amid this cultural cognitive disconnect, however, there is no major movement to abolish the right to a trial by jury. Rather, across the country, communities and their courts are joining forces to fix the system. Recent efforts in Washington, D.C., Arizona, California, Colorado, New York, and other states have all focused on modernizing the jury system by making it more convenient, democratic, and educational for the jurors.

The ongoing jury reform experience in Washington, D.C., provides a look at jury service through the eyes of the juror and reveals that community-wide collaboration may be the most effective way to reconnect our actions and our values about the duty to serve.

In late 1996, the Council for Court Excellence assembled a committee and charged it with recommending improvements to the jury systems in Washington, D.C. Then, in February 1998, after a full year of study, the D.C. Jury Project published its comprehensive research report, which includes 32 specific recommendations to the bench and bar on how to modernize jury trials in the local and federal courts.

In the District of Columbia, where well-intentioned committees addressing worthy problems are hardly uncommon, nothing unusual has happened. Or has it? This report, entitled *Juries for the Year 2000 and Beyond,* may not become another denizen of the library shelf after all.

What makes the D.C. Jury Project's recommendations worthy of thoughtful consideration by the local and national legal communities? First and foremost, the quality of analysis regarding an impressive number of important issues in *Juries for the Year 2000 and Beyond* renders it both readable and well worth reading.

The revered constitutional institution of the jury trial, under recent media at-

tack, deserves a renewed opportunity to thrive. Modernization efforts such as this could be a good opportunity. Besides offering rather mundane and unexceptionable recommendations, such as improving the quality and scope of the juror source list and providing comfortable facilities for jurors, the report probes deep into the history of the jury selection process and takes a stand on the complex issue of peremptory challenges.

Second, the courts and the bar should consider the message in this report because of who the authors are. The 36 diverse members of the D.C. Jury Project, collaborating in a way not previously experienced by these authors, were able to avoid the typical chasm that exists between the legal and civic communities. When jurors, lawyers, and judges take the time to actually listen to one another, then their conclusions deserve special attention.

Substantive recommendations aside for a moment, one of the most gratifying and productive aspects of the D.C. Jury Project was the makeup of the committee. Instead of assembling a generic group composed entirely of like-

Improving the Jury System

There is a national movement to modernize the jury system and reconnect our actions and our values about the duty to serve.

Recommendations include improving the quality and scope of the juror source list and providing comfortable facilities for jurors.

Jurors need practical training and easier access to information about the particulars of the cases before them.

minded lawyers and judges, the Council for Court Excellence actively recruited citizens with jury service experience as well as academicians with an interest in the field. Additionally, attorneys and businesspeople from a variety of backgrounds and viewpoints were called upon. Federal and local trial judges were included. Court administrators and jury officers rounded out the group.

The diversity of professional experience and personal background among Jury Project members was not an effort to have token representatives on the committee. Rather, the wide range of viewpoints enhanced the effectiveness of the collaborative effort. Each member was respected for his own perspective, but everyone understood that the purpose was to reach common/higher ground for the good of the overall system.

Not unlike a jury deliberation, we went about our work methodically, setting aside, when our convictions allowed, personal interests or biases that would impede true progress. It was clear at the outset that the citizen-juror members of the group were the real experts among us.

Also like deliberating jurors, committee members accepted the challenge with honesty and integrity. They struggled at times with controversial issues and differences of opinion yet continued to search for the right answers—overcoming the destructive chasm that so often divides the civic and the legal communities. Because this uncommon level of commitment and vision came from such a diverse committee and because former jurors contributed so significantly to the conclusions, the bench and bar need to listen to their consumers by giving

careful consideration to all of the recommendations in *Jurors for the Year 2000 and Beyond.*

PEREMPTORY CHALLENGES

One lesson learned from this collaborative effort involves group dynamics. Since the committee comprised people who often sit opposite one another in the courtroom, perspectives and theories were bound to collide. Over time, though, committee members developed a sense of trust and respect for one another. Improper gamesmanship, cynicism, and distrust were replaced by year's end with a refreshing dose of candor and a willingness to listen. At no point in the process was this lesson in group dynamics more evident than in our discussion of jury selection and peremptory challenges.

Many members of the D.C. Jury Project believe that peremptory challenges should be abolished, and an overwhelming majority believe that if not eliminated, they should be drastically reduced.

Several two- or three-hour meetings were devoted to this topic, and the discussions were both enlightened and forthright. After much study, soul-searching, and listening to our juror colleagues, a majority of the Jury Project reached the conclusion that the peremptory challenge is inconsistent with the fundamental precepts of an impartial jury.

In *Batson v. Kentucky* (1986) and subsequent decisions over the past decade, the Supreme Court has affirmed the constitutional principle that peremptory strikes of jurors may not be exercised in our nation's trial

courts to discriminate against jurors based on their race or gender, and that parties are not constitutionally entitled to peremptory strikes. Justice Thurgood Marshall, concurring in the *Batson* decision, forcefully advocated ridding trials of peremptory strikes. "The decision today will not end the racial discrimination that peremptories inject into the jury-selection process," he wrote. "That goal can be accomplished only by eliminating peremptory challenges entirely.... Misuse of the peremptory challenge to exclude black jurors has become both common and flagrant."

Indeed, in the experience of most trial judges on the Jury Project, attorneys in both civil and criminal cases continue to exercise peremptory strikes in a manner that, at a minimum, suggests the appearance that prospective jurors are being peremptorily stricken on the grounds of race, gender, or both. The District of Columbia Court of Appeals, as well as numerous state and federal appellate courts throughout the nation, repeatedly have found that such discrimination routinely occurs.

It is important to note that the use and abuse of peremptory challenges leaves prospective jurors and the public in general with the perception that people are being arbitrarily and discriminatorily denied the opportunity for jury service. Such a perception inevitably undermines confidence in our courts and the administration of justice.

In *The Future of Peremptory Challenges*, the Court Manager 16 (1997), G. Thomas Munsterman, director of the Center for Jury Studies of the National Center for State Courts, writes:

The peremptory challenge is a curious feature of our jury system. Starting with randomly selected names from broadbased lists, we work hard to assemble a demographically representative panel from which to select a jury. We defend every step of the process used to arrive at that point. Then comes the swift sword of the peremptory challenge, cutting jurors from the panel with nary an explanation.

No one has recently written more thoroughly or compellingly of the need to eliminate peremptory challenges than Judge Morris Hoffman, a state trial judge in Denver, Colorado.

In *Peremptory Challenges Should Be Abolished: A Trial Judge's Perspec-*

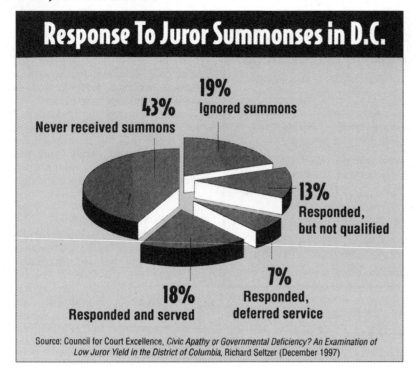

Response To Juror Summonses in D.C.

43% Never received summons

19% Ignored summons

13% Responded, but not qualified

18% Responded and served

7% Responded, deferred service

Source: Council for Court Excellence, *Civic Apathy or Governmental Deficiency? An Examination of Low Juror Yield in the District of Columbia*, Richard Seltzer (December 1997)

tive, 64 U. Chi. L. Rev. 809 (1997), Hoffman carefully traces the history of the peremptory challenge and demonstrates that it is not rooted in principles of fairness, impartiality, or protection of the rights of the accused; rather, it stems from "the now meaningless and quite undemocratic concept of royal infallibility," having been "invented two hundred years before the notion of jury impartiality" was conceived.

He also observes that "the Supreme Court has consistently and unflinchingly held that the peremptory challenge is neither a constitutionally necessary component of a defendant's right to an impartial jury, nor even so fundamental as to be part of federal common law."

Indeed, there was no discussion whatsoever of peremptory challenges in the *Federalist* papers or during the Constitutional Convention, and the Constitution is "utterly silent" on the matter. As Hoffman forcefully demonstrates, efforts to subvert constitutional rights, *not* to defend them, have invigorated and sustained the practice of peremptory challenges as the "last best tool of Jim Crow" in American trials. Such challenges provide "an incredibly efficient final racial filter" to keep African Americans off juries in the South and throughout the United States.

Against this background, Hoffman shows that peremptory challenges have never had a legitimate purpose and have none today. Their genesis in

England was to serve as a basis to excuse jurors for *cause.* Peremptory challenges are "decidedly undemocratic," are "susceptible to significant abuse by authorities," and are "inherently irrational." There is evidence that, notwithstanding the *Batson* decision and its progeny, they are used "in the same old way" they always have been used, "save for some nominal and meaningless extra hoops now required by *Batson.*"

Judge Hoffman concludes, as do many members of the D.C. Jury Project, that the peremptory challenge is inconsistent with fundamental precepts of an impartial jury because (1) it reflects an inappropriate distrust of jurors, causing "perfectly acceptable, perfectly fair and perfectly impartial prospective jurors to be excluded in droves" and to become frustrated and cynical about the justice system; (2) it improperly shifts the focus on jury selection from the individual to the group; and (3) it injects an inappropriate level of adversariness into the jury selection process, tending to result in the selection not of impartial jurors but of jurors who are biased for one side or the other.

The foregoing considerations have persuaded a substantial majority of the D.C. Jury Project that peremptory strikes should be eliminated or drastically reduced in the District of Columbia. The project is also persuaded, however, that if peremptory strikes are eliminated, it is vital to improve the ability to ascertain grounds for strikes

of jurors for cause. Relevant information about jurors should be obtained by (1) using a written questionnaire completed by all jurors and given to the court and parties upon the jury panel's arrival in the courtroom and (2) requiring that each juror be examined at least once during the voir dire process and attorneys be given a meaningful opportunity to ask follow-up questions of all jurors.

The process should be conducted so that no jurors will be called to the bench more than once. Moreover, to assure to the extent possible that prospective jurors who may be biased or partial are in fact stricken for cause, an expanded legal standard governing for-cause strikes should be established. It should mandate that when a prospective juror's demeanor or substantive response to a question during voir dire presents *any* reasonable doubt as to whether the juror can be fair and impartial, the trial judge shall strike the juror for cause at the request of any party, or on the court's own motion.

Throughout the report, the primary theme is that jurors need more institutionalized respect. When jurors arrive in a courtroom, we thank them for coming and remind them of their importance in the trial process. They are, we say with sincerity, the "other judges." Then, in more than a handful of instances, jurors and their needs are promptly forgotten. Our other actions—from the jury selection process throughout deliberations—send quite a different message about how important jurors really are.

No longer treated like judges, jurors are expected to endure a jury selection process that insults their intelligence and infects the entire judicial process with the stench of unfairness. They will likely spend countless hours waiting in the lounge or the jury room, often with no word of when they will be needed. During trial, we ask them to absorb complex and contradictory information, many times without the appropriate tools they need to fully understand and retain such information.

As Stephen Adler wrote in *The Jury,* "To build a better jury system, we need to grant jurors the perquisites of power: reasonable creature comforts, practical training in the nature of their endeavor, and easier access to information about the particulars of the cases before them." Fortunately, many judges in the District of Columbia and around the country have found ways to do this. In searching for ways to enhance the jury service experience and improve the quality of justice, the Jury Project learned from these judges.

For years, jurors have been viewed as passive recipients of often complex information. Recently, however, increasing numbers of judges and attorneys across the nation have recognized the juror education that takes place during trial.

Jurors, like students, need appropriate tools to make informed and rational decisions. We wouldn't send our children to school without pencils and paper. Why should jurors not have basic tools to do their important job? The Jury Project recommends that jurors be allowed to take notes and submit written questions for witnesses, that judges minimize sidebar conferences while the jury is in the room, that the court provide exhibit notebooks and interim summations in extended trials, and that judges offer to assist a jury that reports itself at an impasse.

How to efficiently incorporate these procedures into trials can be a part of every judge's training. What jurors want and need to do their job effectively is for such practices to be uniform throughout the court system. A citizen should have the same treatment no matter whose courtroom he reports to for jury service.

We recognize that receptivity to these recommendations will vary among those who read and ponder their contents. A recommendation may strike one person as unremarkable and a long-accepted custom, while another recommendation may appear radical or unreachable. The prime audience for one recommendation may be a juror administrator or data system designer. In other instances, a recommendation will be most relevant to a newer member of the bench or to a continuing legal education coordinator.

In any event, whether you are a jurist, policymaker, barrister, or citizen, we hope that you will engage yourself in this continuing project. In so doing, we believe, you will experience what we have: an opportunity to revisit important first principles of our jury system, join hands with a broad and talented spectrum of Washingtonians, and seek to make a genuine difference in the administration of justice in our courts. Welcome aboard.

Judge Thomas F. Hogan, of the U.S. District Court for the District of Columbia, and Judge Gregory E. Mize, of the D.C. Superior Court, are cochairs of the D.C. Jury Project. Kathleen Clark is a senior analyst for the D.C. Jury Project and is on the Council for Court Excellence.

Q: Should juries nullify laws they consider unjust or excessively punitive?

Yes: Juries can and should correct the overly broad use of criminal sanctions.

By Clay S. Conrad

Conrad is an appellate attorney in Houston, on the board of the Fully Informed Jury Association and author of Jury Nullification: The Evolution of a Doctrine.

Jury nullification occurs when a criminal-trial jury refuses to convict a defendant despite proof of guilt because the jurors believe the law is unjust or is being unjustly applied. According to studies, 3 to 4 percent of jury criminal trials involve jury nullification. There is no way to prevent jury nullification because juries never can be ordered to convict or be punished for acquitting someone. A jury acquittal, under the Constitution, is final.

Juries rarely nullify irresponsibly. Consider the acquittal of Sam Skinner, a California AIDS patient prosecuted for using marijuana. The marijuana helped counteract the devastating side effects of the drug AZT and kept Skinner from wasting away. Although Skinner admitted to the facts, the jury found him not guilty because they believed the prosecution was fundamentally unjust.

Sometimes juries find defendants guilty only of lesser offenses when they believe the punishment for the charged offense is excessive. In earlier times, British law made theft of 40 shillings or more a capital offense. Juries often undervalued property so as to spare the life of the accused—including one case in which a jury found ten £10 notes to be worth 39 shillings. Jack Kevorkian's latest trial involved just that sort of amelioration. The jury found him

guilty of second-degree murder despite the facts because they believed a conviction for first-degree murder would be too great.

Alternatively, it often is argued that race and prejudice lead to jury nullification more often than do considerations of justice. As common as that argument is, it doesn't hold water. During the 1960s in the trials of some who participated in crimes against civil-rights workers in the Deep South, it is true that juries returned "not guilty" verdicts. However, it also is true that sometimes prosecutors regularly refused to pursue those cases, police refused to investigate or testify honestly in them and judges eviscerated the cases through discretionary rulings. The juries rarely were given cases justifying conviction—and then were scapegoated for failings elsewhere in the system.

These contentions are proved by the fact that federal prosecutions for violations of civil-rights laws, involving the same cases, regularly ended in convictions—before juries selected from the same communities. Different judges, prosecutors and investigators—but the same jury pool. Obviously, any racist acquittals must be explained by something other than the juries.

A recent *National Law Journal* poll revealed that three in four Americans would nullify if they believed the court's instructions would lead to injustice. That only 3 to 4 percent of jury trials end in nullification verdicts shows that, in most cases, the law is just and justly applied. In exceptional, marginal or divisive cases, however, jurors often acquit in the interests of justice—just as the Founders of this country intended.

The Founders on both sides of the ratification debate believed trial by jury was necessary to prevent governmental overreaching. Thomas Jefferson said it was the only way to anchor government to constitutional principles. Alexander Hamilton said it was the surest protection of the people's liberties. Theophilus Parsons, first chief justice of Massachusetts, said in the Constitutional Convention: "The people themselves have it in their power effectually to resist usurpation, without being driven to an appeal to arms. An act of usurpation is not obligatory; it is not law; and any man may be justified in his resistance. Let him be considered as a criminal by the general government, yet only his fellow-citizens can convict him; they are his jury, and if they pronounce him innocent, not all the powers of Congress can hurt him; and innocent they certainly will pronounce him, if the supposed law he resisted was an act of usurpation."

Many important colonial trials ended in nullification. American jurors knew they could refuse to enforce unjust laws. Early jurors routinely were informed by courts of their right to try the law as well as the fact, and lawyers regularly argued the merits of the law to the jury. The independent role of juries was well-accepted in early American law.

It was not until the mid-19th century that courts began to question the jury's independent voice. Judges attempted to bind juries to their instructions and began prohibiting lawyers from arguing law to the jury. The Supreme Court allowed such practices to stand, and today many judges wrongly believe they are forbidden to allow jury nullification to be discussed in court.

American courts have not always been so reluctant to trust the conscientious judgments of juries. In the early years of this country, the Supreme Court itself occasionally heard cases with a jury. In 1794, Justice John Jay, for a unanimous Supreme Court, instructed a jury: "It may not be amiss, here, gentlemen, to remind you of the good old rule, that on questions of fact, it is the province of the jury, on questions of law, it is the province of the court to decide. But it must be observed that by the same law, which recognizes this reasonable distribution of jurisdiction, you have nevertheless a right to take upon yourselves to judge of both, and to determine the law as well as the fact in controversy. On this, and on every other occasion, however, we have no doubt, you will pay that respect, which is due to the opinion of the court: For, as on the one hand, it is presumed, that juries are the best judges of fact; it is, on the other hand, presumable, that the courts are the best judges of the law. But still both objects are lawfully within your power of decision."

> **A just society has to have just rules. Juries, by refusing to enforce unjust rules, can help improve the law and the society that it governs.**

These instructions meticulously delineate the roles of bench and jury. The court instructed the jury on a general rule, which allowed for exceptions. They admonished the jury to take their instructions with respect, yet acknowledged that the jury could not be bound by them. These instructions fostered juror independence and responsibility, not jury lawlessness or wanton disregard for the rights of the parties. Similar instructions could assist jurors in delivering fair, just verdicts today—making sure the law is applied in a manner in which the citizens of this country approve and giving us a legal system of which again we could be proud. The Fully Informed Jury Association, a Section 501(c)(3) [tax-exempt] educational organization with a mission to inform potential jurors of their right to nullify unjust laws, has provided model initiatives to allow for just such instructions. These initiatives have been introduced by legislators in more than a dozen states.

What would be the result of informing jurors about their power to nullify the law in the interests of justice? Perhaps better questions would be: Is the criminal law applied more or less fairly in 1999 than it was in 1799? Is it more or less a source of social divisiveness and tension? Has the criminal sanction been wrested from providing social protection to become a tool for social engineering?

Criminal law often is a divisive factor in society. The nonsensical distinctions between powder and crack cocaine; enormous penalties for many minor crimes; unfair sentencing favoritism given to snitches (who serve a small fraction of the time given their underlings); criminalization of "wetlands" violations; regulatory, licensing and administrative infractions; and the often-mechanical application of law favored by prosecutors have resulted in a hodgepodge of injustices strung together without rhyme or reason. Apologists who claim a society must have rules miss the point—a just society has to have just rules. Juries, by refusing to enforce unjust rules, can help improve the law and the society it governs.

Courts usually pretend injustices under law cannot occur. They can and too often do. As Judge Thomas Wiseman noted, "Congress is not yet an infallible body incapable of passing tyrannical laws." Occasionally, jurors follow their instructions, then leave court in tears, ashamed of their verdict.

This sort of thing is not supposed to happen in America. It isn't justice. If being a juror means anything, it should mean never having to say you're sorry. If the law is just and justly applied, jurors should be proud of their verdict and confident that any sentences meted out are well-deserved. Then we will engender respect for the law because, as Justice Louis Brandeis observed, for the law to be respected it first must be respectable.

What happens when a jury nullifies a law? One factually guilty person is acquitted in the interests of justice. If a particular law frequently is nullified, the legislature should bring the law into conformity with the judgment of the community. If the law is being misapplied, the legislature may make the law more specific or prosecutors may quit applying it overbroadly. The law is improved, and injustices are prevented.

Does jury nullification lead to anarchy—or is it democracy in action, allowing citizens to participate in the administration of justice? The concept that jury nullification is anarchy has been bandied about without analysis or justification in the face of juries being given nullification instructions for the first century of this country's existence without collapse into anarchy. Jury nullification does not eliminate law—it regulates it, allowing the people's perception of justice, not the government's, to prevail. It takes

a true authoritarian to call such vital citizen participation in governmental decisionmaking "anarchy."

Trial by jury, according to the Supreme Court, exists to prevent oppression by government. It is easy to see that an occasionally oppressive government does not like to have its powers limited. However, those of us who someday may find ourselves on the other side of the equation should be grateful that the Founders of this country had the foresight and wisdom to install this safety valve, this elegant and time-tested mechanism to anchor our government to the principles of its Constitution. It would be a disgrace to those same Founders to be unwilling to utilize this safety valve today, when circumstances indicate it would be appropriate to do so.

No: Don't give society's mavericks another tool to subvert the will of the people.

BY NANCY KING

King teaches law at Vanderbilt University and is author of the article, "Silencing Nullification Advocacy Inside the Jury Room and Outside the Courtroom."

Inviting jurors to acquit regardless of what the law says is attempting cure-all for the law's ills. But cultivating jury nullification is a mistake. Like the peddler's elixir, jury nullification is just as likely to produce unpleasant side effects as it is to bring relief. The most compelling reasons to be wary of the practice of jury nullification are the very arguments its advocates trot out in its defense—history, democracy, fairness, political change and the Constitution itself.

One does not have to look back far into history to find a good reason for discouraging jury nullification. True, the colonists embraced the jury's power as a weapon against the king's oppressive laws. And, we're reminded, juries bravely blocked prosecutions of those who resisted the Fugitives Slave Act, Prohibition and the Vietnam War draft. But jury nullification has not been neatly confined to the rejection of "bad" law or the release of "good" defendants. A much less appealing pattern of jury lawlessness is also prominent in our nation's history. For generations juries have refused to convict or punish those who clearly are guilty of violence against unpopular victims, particularly African-Americans. The Klan Act, barring Ku Klux Klan sympathizers from juries after the Civil War, was passed because juries were exercising their "independence" to ignore civil-rights statutes. In Texas after the Civil War,

prosecutors had to strike from juries those who "believe, morally, socially, politically, or religiously, that it is not murder for a white man to take the life of a [N]egro with malice aforethought." This is not a proud legacy. We should not assume that refusal to punish those who harm members of less popular groups is entirely behind us just because some juries, in some places, are more racially diverse than they used to be.

Racism, of course, is not the only risk. To invite nullification is to invite jurors to devise their own defenses to criminal charge. All three branches of government may have labored to eliminate similar considerations from the assessment of guilt. Juries have acquitted defendants in rape cases after concluding that the victims deserved to be raped because of the way they dressed or acted. Jurors may acquit protesters who trespass, damage property or harm others if they conclude the defendants were right to bypass lawful means of redress. Jurors may believe that reasonable doubt is not a strong-enough burden of proof and require fingerprints or eyewitnesses before convicting. They may decide that certain conduct by the police should be a complete defense, oblivious of efforts by legislators and judges to craft remedies and regulations for police misconduct. Now, as in the past, encouraging "good" nullification inevitably means encouraging "bad" nullification as well, because there is no way to second guess a jury's acquittal once delivered.

It is not feasible to try to separate "good" nullification from "bad." Even nullification advocates cannot agree on what type of nullification is acceptable. One supporter would require nullification instructions only in cases involving non-violent acts of civil disobedience where the defendant had "given serious thought" to legal means of accomplishing the same objective. Another would encourage jury pronouncements on the law only when the issue was the constitutionality of a criminal statute. A third insists that "true" nullification is limited to decisions "based on conscientious grounds." In a recent survey, college students were asked whether jury nullification included any combination of a set of possible reasons for acquittal, all of which the researchers believed were valid reasons for juries to nullify, such as,"The police wrongfully assaulted the defendant after he was arrested." When only 13 percent of those surveyed agreed that nullification included all of the reasons listed, the researchers concluded their subjects had a lot to learn about nullification. The response should suggest something else—that it is wishful thinking to assume that legislators or judges will be able to agree when jurors should ignore the law and when they should not.

One might support expanding the lawmaking role of the jury if one believes juries are an essential feature of our democracy, better at assessing whether a law is 'just" or "unjust" than democratically elected legislators. But juries probably are much worse at this task. Unlike legislators or electors, jurors have no opportunity to investigate or research the merits of legislation. Carefully stripped of those who know anything about the type of case or conduct at stake, juries are insulated from the information they would need to make reliable judgments about the costs and benefits, the justice or the injustices, of a particular criminal prohibition. Nor can jurors seek out information during the case. The so-called "safety valve" of jury nullification, which exempts a defendant here and there from the reach of a controversial law, actually reduces the pressure for those opposed to a truly flawed statute to lobby for its repeal or amendment and deprives appellate courts of opportunities to declare its flaws.

Nullification's supporters point out that legislatures cannot anticipate unfair applications of the laws they enact, so jury nullification is needed for "fine-tuning." But jurors are not in any better position than judges or prosecutors to decide which defendants should be exempted from a law's reach. Again, jurors probably are much worse at this function because they lack critical information. Any juror who actually knows the defendant is excused from the jury. Jurors only can speculate on the penalty that would follow from their verdict: Unless the defendant testifies (and most defendants do not), the jury will never hear him explain his side of the story nor learn whether he has a prior record. They may never learn, of evidence sup-

pressed because it was illegally obtained or because of other errors on the part of the prosecution. More importantly, because jurors decide only one case, they cannot compare the culpability of different defendants or assess the relative importance of enforcing a particular prohibition against a particular defendant. No doubt about it: Juries are excellent fact finders and lie detectors. But when facts are not in issue and guilt is clear, the ability of jurors to reach sound decisions about when the law should be suspended and when it should be applied is questionable at best.

Jury nullification sometimes is touted as an effective political tool for those who have failed at the voting booth and on the legislative floor. There are two problems with this argument. First, if a group is not influential enough to obtain favorable legislation, it is not likely to secure a majority in the jury box. At most, jurors with dissenting views succeed in hanging the jury. But hung juries are a political dead end.The defendant is not spared; he can be tried again and convicted. More importantly, as a recent recommendation in California demonstrates, rising hung-jury rates inevitably lead to proposals to eliminate the unanimity requirement, proposals that if adopted would shut down minority viewpoints more effectively than any instruction against nullification ever could.

Even if a politically unsuccessful group finds strength in some local jury boxes, should we really be heartened by the prospect of being stuck with the decision of 12 people who have been encouraged to ignore the pronouncements of the state or nation's elected representatives? If there is a concentrated population of homophobes, racists or anti-Semites in my state, I, for one, do not want judges and lawyers encouraging jurors drawn from these communities to apply their own standards—standards that may vary with the victim's sexual orientation, race or religion. Local dissent, of course, is not limited to group-based views. People disagree strongly about a variety of laws—laws against possessing weapons, euthanasia, driving after a couple of drinks, the use of marijuana, slapping one's wife or children around or the dumping of paint or oil. There are places well-suited for resolving these disagreements: the legislature and the polling booth. Our democratic process should not be jettisoned arbitrarily by an unelected group of citizens who need never explain themselves.

Finally, the Constitution does not support an enhanced law-making role for juries. Jurors have no personal constitutional right to disregard the law—otherwise, they would not be required to take an oath to obey it. Nor do defendants have constitutional right to insist that jurors be given the opportunity to disregard the law. True, judges cannot overturn a conviction or acquittal without the consent of the defendant (through appeal, motion or other-

> **Our democratic process should not be jettisoned so arbitrarily by an unelected group of citizens who need never to explain themselves.**

wise). But this rule is in place not because the Constitution considers the jury a superior lawmaker but because the Fifth Amendment prohibits the government from putting the defendant in jeopardy of life or limb more than once for the same offense. Judges also are barred from directing verdicts of guilt, but only because the Sixth Amendment guarantees to the defendant a jury's assessment of the facts.

Beyond what is necessary to protect these important interests of the accused, our refusal to tolerate jury nullification must not stray. Judges, for example, should continue to avoid seating jurors who cannot or will not promise to follow the judge's instructions; continue to prohibit argument and deny instructions concerning defenses not supported by the evidence; continue to instruct jurors about the law and require them to follow these instructions; and continue to prohibit nullification advocates from approaching jurors with nullification propaganda (just as they bar prosecution sympathizers from lobbying the jury for conviction). Although each of these practices is designed to prevent jury nullification, each is constitutional because the Constitution does not protect jury nullification itself. It protects a defendant's right to fact-finding by a jury and to the finality of a verdict.

Legislators and judges so far steadfastly have rejected repeated proposals to lower barriers to jury nullification because they understand that the costs of such changes would far outweigh any benefits they may bring. Other fundamental changes in our jury system, such as the Supreme Court's decision to ban race-based peremptory challenges as a violation of the equal-protection rights of potential jurors, have been preceded by sustained social, political and legal critique of the status quo. A similar groundswell to cede more power to those who sit in jury boxes in criminal cases has never existed and, fortunately, probably never will.

A Get-Tough Policy That Failed

Mandatory sentencing was once America's law-and-order panacea. Here's why it's not working

By JOHN CLOUD

REMEMBER LITTLE POLLY KLAAS? SHE was the 12-year-old Petaluma, Calif., girl whisked from a slumber party in 1993 and found murdered two months later. Her father Marc, horrified to learn that her killer was on parole and had attacked children in the past, called for laws making parole less common. He joined with others backing a "three strikes and you're out" law for California—no parole, ever, for those convicted of three felonies. Klaas went on TV, got in the papers, met the President—all within weeks after his daughter's body was found.

Then he began studying how the three-strikes law would actually work. He noticed that a nonviolent crime—burglary, for instance—could count as a third strike. "That meant you could get life for breaking into someone's garage and stealing a stereo," he says. "I've had my stereo stolen, and I've had my daughter stolen. I believe I know the difference."

Klaas began speaking against three strikes. But his daughter had already become a symbol for the crackdown on crime, and

DERRICK SMITH

The 19-year-old was accused in New York City of selling crack. Distraught at how many years he could get, he leaped out a window to his death

Likely sentence 15 years to life

California's legislature passed the three-strikes law. It now seems politically untouchable, despite horror stories like the one about a Los Angeles 27-year-old who got 25 years to life for stealing pizza. Last year two state senators tried to limit the measure to violent crimes, but the bill didn't make it out of committee. Governor Pete Wilson vetoed a bill simply to study the effects of the law.

Wilson probably knew what the study would conclude: while three-strikes laws sound great to the public, they aren't working. A growing number of states and private groups have scrutinized these and other "mandatory-minimum laws," the generic name for statutes forcing judges to impose designated terms. The studies are finding that the laws cost enormous amounts of money, largely to lock up such nonviolent folks as teenage drug couriers, dope-starved addicts and unfortunate offenders like the Iowa man who got 10 years for stealing $30 worth of steaks from a grocery store and then struggling with a store clerk who tackled him (the struggle made it a felony).

How much are we spending? Put it this way: mandatory minimums are the reason so many prisons are booming in otherwise impoverished rural counties across America. The U.S. inmate population has more than doubled (to nearly 2 million) since the mid-'80s, when mandatory sentencing became the hot new intoxicant for politicians. New York (the first state to enact mandatory mini-

mums) has sloshed $600 million into prison construction since 1988; not coincidentally, in the same period it has sliced $700 million from higher education. Americans will have to spend even more in the future to house and treat all the aging inmates. California has already filled its 114,000 prison beds, and double-bunks 46,000 additional inmates.

More important, mandatory minimums for nonviolent (and arguably victimless) drug crimes insult justice. Most mandatory sentences were designed as weapons in the drug war, with an awful consequence: we now live in a country where it's common to get a longer sentence for selling a neighbor a joint than for, say, sexually abusing her. (According to a 1997 federal report, those convicted of drug trafficking have served an average of almost seven years, nearly a year longer than those convicted of sexual abuse.) Several new books, including Michael Massing's *The Fix*, point out that the tough-on-drugs policies of the past 15 years haven't had much impact on the heart of the drug problem, abuse by long-term urban addicts.

PORSCHA WASICK

"Oh my, that's a long time!" the Ohio judge exclaimed on learning of the tough sentence awaiting this college student convicted of selling LSD in 1996

Sentenced to up to 25 years

Even the usually hard-line drug czar Barry McCaffrey has written that "we can't incarcerate our way out of the drug problem." He has urged Congress to reduce mandatory minimums for crack, which are currently 100 times as heavy as those for powdered coke and impact most on minority youth.

This injustice is most palpable on city streets. In places like New York there are more black and Hispanic kids in prison than in college. That injustice may have played a role in the fate of Derrick Smith, a New York City youth who in October faced a sentence of 15 years to life for selling crack. At the sentence hearing a distraught Smith told the judge, "I'm only 19. This is terrible." He then hurled himself out of a courtroom window and fell 16 stories to his death. "He didn't kill anyone; he didn't rob anyone," says his mother. "This happened because we are black and poor."

Worst of all, mandatory minimums have done little to solve the problems for which they were crafted. Casual drug use has declined since the 1970s, but the size of the addict population has remained stable. And even conservative criminologists concede that demographics (i.e., fewer young men) and better policing are more responsible for the dropping crime rate than criminals' fear of mandatory minimums. John DiIulio Jr., the Princeton professor who wrote a 1994 defense of mandatory sentencing for the *Wall Street Journal* with the charming headline LET 'EM ROT, now opposes mandatory minimums for drug crimes. He points out that more and more young, nonviolent, first-time offenders are being incarcerated—"and they won't find suitable role models in prison."

But even some older, repeat offenders are getting punishments that seem ridiculously disproportionate to their crimes. Consider Douglas Gray, a husband, father, Vietnam veteran and owner of a roofing business who bought a pound of marijuana in an Alabama motel for $900 several years ago. The seller turned out to be a police informant, a felon

fresh from prison whom cops paid $100 to do the deal. Because Gray had been arrested for several petty crimes 13 years earlier—crimes that didn't even carry a prison sentence—he fell under the state's "habitual offender" statutes. He got life without parole.

The good news is that a consensus is emerging among judges (including Reagan-appointee Chief Justice William Rehnquist), law enforcers and crime experts—among them many conservatives who once supported the laws—that mandatory minimums are foolish. The Supreme Court last week declined to hear a case challenging the California three-strikes law, but four Justices expressed concern about the law's effect and seemed to invite other challenges. A few brave politicians have gingerly suggested that the laws may be something we should rethink. Some states are starting to backtrack on tough sentencing laws:

■ **MICHIGAN** Last February former Republican Governor William Milliken called the "650 Lifer Law" his biggest mistake. The 1978 law mandated a life-without-parole term for possession with intent to deliver at least 650 g (about 1.4 lbs.) of heroin or cocaine. But though the law was intended to net big fish, few major dealers got hit. In fact, 86% of the "650 lifers" had never done time; 70% were poor. "A lot of them were young people who made very stupid mistakes but shouldn't have to pay for it for the rest of their lives," says state representative Barbara Dobb, the Republican who began a reform effort. In August, G.O.P. Governor John Engler signed a law allowing 650 lifers to be paroled after 15 years.

■ **UTAH** In March 1995, Republican senate president Lane Beattie, concerned about the excesses of mandatory minimums, introduced a bill to eliminate them in certain

cases. Worried about the political fallout, he did so near midnight on the last day of the legislative session. The bill passed quietly, without debate, but victims' groups noticed. Though a public outcry followed, the G.O.P. Governor said he agreed with the bill and refused to veto it.

■ **GEORGIA** In the final minutes of the 1996 legislative session, state lawmakers nixed mandatory life sentences for second-time drug offenders. State statistics showed that four-fifths of those serving life had hawked less than $50 in narcotics. Even state prosecutors backed the change.

■ **NEW YORK** John Dunne, a former Republican legislator who helped devise the Rockefeller Drug Laws, the mandatory-sentencing legislation promulgated in the 1970s by Governor Nelson Rockefeller, is lobbying to end them. "This was a good idea 25 years ago, but the sad experience is that it has not had an effect," says Dunne, who also served in the Bush Administration. "Behind closed doors, virtually everyone will say these drug laws are not working, but they cannot say that publicly."

Certainly no one in Washington is saying it publicly. The House Judiciary Committee didn't even hold hearings on the bill that created the current minimums, which coasted to victory just in time for the 1986 midterm elections. Congress and the President last year added a new mandatory minimum to the books: five years for 5 g of crystal meth, the crack of the '90s. Mandatory minimums remain political beasts, and it would probably take Nixon-goes-to-China leadership from a Republican to turn public opinion against them. Either that or more Jean Valjeans serving 10-year sentences for stealing steaks.

—With reporting by Andrew Goldstein and Elaine Rivera/New York, Viveca Novak and Elaine Shannon/Washington, Kermit Pattison/St. Paul and James Wilwerth/Los Angeles

2 million **Number of people behind bars in the U.S., including local jails—twice as many as a decade ago**

60% **Portion of federal prisoners jailed for drug crimes, up from 38% before mandatory-sentencing laws were passed in 1986**

36% **Portion of drug offenders who committed nonviolent, low-level crimes**

JEDONNA YOUNG

After 20 years in prison for heroin possession, she was ordered released on Friday under a new Michigan law allowing parole in drug cases

Sentenced to life, now freed

DOUGLAS GRAY

Alabama police caught him buying a pound of pot. Earlier petty crimes made him a "habitual offender"

Sentenced to life, no parole

Looking Askance at Eyewitness Testimony

Psychologists, showing how errors reach the courts, offer advice on handling such evidence

BY D. W. MILLER

RONNIE BULLOCK was sentenced to 60 years in jail for kidnapping and raping a young Illinois girl. Edward Honaker spent a decade in a Virginia prison for sexually assaulting a woman at gunpoint. Kirk Bloodsworth was shipped off to Maryland's death row for raping and strangling a 9-year-old girl.

All three of those men were convicted in part because eyewitnesses or victims firmly placed them at the scene of the crime. But not one of them was guilty. They were among the first convicts to be exonerated by DNA tests proving that someone else was responsible.

Some psychologists believe that such mistakes happen in thousands of courtrooms every year. But most crimes leave no DNA traces to rule out the innocent. For more than two decades, psychological researchers have asked, How could so many witnesses be wrong, and what can be done about it? Only recently have they seen their findings influence the way the criminal-justice system handles eyewitness testimony.

Psychologists have conducted hundreds of studies on errors in eyewitness identification. In some cases, of course, witnesses simply lie. But research has shown that flawed police procedures and the vagaries of memory often lead witnesses to identify the wrong person, and that credulous jurors too easily credit their testimony.

To those familiar with the mountain of evidence about the way the human mind works, that comes as no surprise. "Why should people make good eyewitnesses?" asks Gary L. Wells, a psychologist at Iowa State University who is widely considered the dean of eyewitness research. In the presence of danger, he says, "we're wired for fight or flight. What helped for survival was not a quick recall of details."

The findings of Mr. Wells and his colleagues are finally gaining currency in the halls of criminal justice. In part that is due to the gradual acceptance of expert testimony on eyewitness identification.

Far more crucial, however, is the growing roster of convicts cleared by DNA evidence. In 1996, the U.S. Department of Justice released a report on the first 28 known cases of DNA exoneration. After studying those and 12 subsequent cases, Mr. Wells discovered that mistaken eyewitness testimony had played a part in about 90 percent of the convictions.

MISSING THE KEY DETAILS

Concerned about the high rate of eyewitness error in the DNA cases, U.S. Attorney General Janet Reno invited him to a meeting in early 1997. As a result of their conversation, the department's National Institute of Justice asked Mr. Wells and five fellow scholars to join a panel of law-enforcement officials, criminal-defense lawyers, and prosecutors created to write guidelines for handling eyewitness testimony.

The guide, published in October, gave scholars the opportunity to show that human memory is not a highly reliable tool for determining guilt in the courtroom. For example, contrary to popular belief, people under stress remember events no better than, and often less well than, they do under ordinary circumstances. Witnesses also perceive time as moving more slowly during traumatic events. That, in turn, leads them to overestimate how much time they had to notice details, a key factor of their credibility in court. And studies have found that witnesses to a crime are so distracted by the presence of a

Gary L. Wells: "Why should people make good eyewitnesses?" In times of danger, "we're wired for fight or flight. What helped for survival was not a quick recall of details."

weapon—a phenomenon called "weapon focus"—that they remember little else with accuracy.

Researchers cannot ethically recreate the trauma of real crimes. But plenty of field research suggests that witnesses are apt to misidentify people.

For example, many studies have tested the ability of convenience-store clerks and bank tellers to recall customers they encountered in non-stressful situations. Around a third of the time, the employees wrongly identified faces from "lineups" that did not include the person they had actually met.

THE DETERIORATION OF MEMORY

In addition, all sorts of factors inhibit our ability to recognize and recall facial detail. For instance, psychologists have established that most of us have more difficulty recognizing people of a different race. And memory deteriorates very quickly over time.

Elizabeth F. Loftus, a psychologist at the University of Washington and a pioneer in research on false memory, has discovered that it's remarkably easy to alter one's recollection without realizing it. Human beings are highly susceptible to incorporating "post-event information"—newspaper articles, comments by police, conversations with other witnesses—into their recollections.

Witnesses also have been known to identify as criminals people they recognized from some other encounter, a process called "transference." In one bizarre example, an Australian psychologist and memory researcher named Donald Thomson was himself once identified by a rape victim as her attacker. Not only was his alibi airtight—he was being interviewed on live television at the time—but she had mistaken him for the rapist because she had seen his face on her television screen during the assault.

IMPROVING POLICE PROCEDURES

Of course, policymakers can't do much to improve the flaws in our memories. So scholars like Mr. Wells, who wanted to reduce eyewitness mistakes, began to focus on things that the justice system can control—particularly police procedures.

One of the biggest problems with eyewitness identification, researchers have found, is that uncertain witnesses are often prompted to finger the person whom police have detained, even when the suspect is not the same person they spotted at the scene. Witnesses viewing a lineup tend to assume that police have caught the person they saw. So they think their job is to find the face that most resembles the description they gave to police.

The police sometimes exacerbate that tendency by designing lineups poorly. Imagine a witness to a liquor-store robbery who says the robber was white, stocky, and bearded. Based on that description, the police identify a suspect and ask the witness to look at a lineup of live individuals or at a spread of photos (known as a "six-pack").

Too often, say researchers, the "distractor" faces used by police do not closely match the witness's description, or the suspect's photo looks different from the others. If the suspect stands out in any way—if his is the only color photo in the six-pack, for instance—the witness is far more likely to say, "That's the guy."

Lineups are also fraught with the possibility of mistaken identity, researchers report, because of our tendency to overlook differences in facial appearance among people not of our race. Not only are white witnesses, say, more likely to mistake one black suspect for another (and vice versa), but police officers may overestimate the degree to which the distractors they choose match the suspect's description.

Recently, Mr. Wells has raised the alarm about the way a witness's confidence can be manipulated. Witnesses are easily influenced during and after the lineup—by talking with other witnesses or police interviewers—to be more certain of their choice than their recall warrants. Police investigators, for example, may praise a witness for "picking the right guy" out of the lineup.

That taint frequently makes its way to the jury box. Understandably, jurors put a lot of stock in a witness who can point to the defendant and say, "He's the one. I'll never forget his face." But scholars have learned that the degree of confidence during trial is a poor predictor of a witness's accuracy. And, they warn, jurors ought to be particularly skeptical if they learn that a witness professed more confidence on the witness stand than in the squad room. Recall, they say, doesn't improve over time.

ASKING THE RIGHT QUESTIONS

Until recently, the criminal-justice system made little use of those findings. Defense lawyers, of course, have embraced and exploited them at least since the 1980's. But according to Brian L. Cutler, a psychologist at Florida International University, they have rarely been able to use the research to cross-examine eyewitnesses or police.

As Expert Witnesses, Psychologists Have an Impact—but Only a Case at a Time

UNTIL a few years ago, when the U.S. Department of Justice invited six psychologists to help reshape police procedures for eyewitness identification, scholars had only one way to influence criminal justice: one defendant at a time. Many have themselves testified to educate juries about the pitfalls of witness memory.

Like a lot of his colleagues, Gary L. Wells, a psychologist at Iowa State University who testifies four or five times a year, got into that line of research in part to save innocent defendants from false imprisonment, and to force police to improve methods for interviewing witnesses and identifying suspects. "There was a time 20 years ago when I was so naive as to think that all I had to do was document the problem and the police would change their procedures," he says. But eventually he decided that "the courtroom was never the place to have that kind of impact."

"Judges are reluctant to tell police how to do their jobs," he says. And judges tend to hew to the established view that juries are the arbiters of witness credibility.

That has been changing slowly. In 1993, the U.S. Supreme court ruled in *Daubert* v. *Merrell Dow Pharmaceuticals, Inc.* that new federal rules of evidence permitted a broader standard for allowing expert psychological testimony. Since then, says Solomon Fulero, a psychologist at Sinclair Community College, in Dayton, Ohio, several convictions have been overturned because the trial judge had not allowed such experts to testify.

Still, there's a limit to the broad change that scholars can effect by testifying. According to Mr. Wells, there just aren't that many experts: About 50 to 75 psychologists testify in court regularly, and only about 25 of them actually do original research in the field.

Furthermore, their services can be pricey. While rates vary widely, the psychologists themselves report fees of up to $3,500 a case, although most will take some clients *pro bono*.

WITNESS CREDIBILITY

In general, the experts try to avoid challenging the credibility of individual witnesses or the conduct of the police officers who worked with them. "The goal of the defense is to cast doubt on the credibility of a particular witness. But that's not my job," says Mr. Fulero, who was invited to join the Justice Department's eyewitness-testimony panel because of his courtroom experience, not his scholarly *vitae*. What he can testify to, he explains, is that "eyewitnesses are not as accurate, over all, as the jurors believe them to be."

Unfortunately for defendants, that means the research doesn't always help their cause.

"The deep problem," says James M. Doyle, a Boston defense lawyer who served on the panel, "is that the research is all statistical and probabilistic, but the trial process is clinical and diagnostic." In other words, a jury expects the experts to say whether a witness is right or wrong, when all an expert can really do is explain how to assess the odds.

Mr. Wells echoes many of his colleagues when he says that he's not really in it for the money. He was among the half-dozen scholars who helped to fashion the new Justice Department guidelines for handling eyewitness testimony. If they are widely adopted, he says, "we have no business in the courtroom on this issue. My purpose is to make expert testimony unnecessary."

He may get his wish. According to participants, prosecutors on the Justice Department panel were concerned that quick-witted defense lawyers would use the new guidelines to impeach eyewitness testimony.

Mr. Doyle, who has co-written a lawyer's guide to the research, *Eyewitness Testimony*, calls that a reasonable fear. In the past, his colleagues have had difficulty incorporating the science into their cross-examination techniques, because they haven't taken the trouble to understand the research methods, he says. Now they won't have to.

On the other hand, he doubts that's a bad thing. "One thing police and defense lawyers share is that we don't really want to deal with innocent people. It's not necessarily easier or better for me to represent innocent people. I would just as soon the police did their jobs."

—D. W. MILLER

"Defense lawyers have no special training—they don't know what questions to ask," says Mr. Cutler. "If they do ask the right questions, how well-equipped are jurors to evaluate the questions?" Unfortunately, jurors cling to a belief that "the way memory works is a matter of common sense," he says. "It just isn't so."

"People expect it's like videotape, that we attend equally well to everything out there," says Roy S. Malpass, a psychologist at the University of Texas at El Paso who served on the Justice Department panel. In fact, he says, "we're highly selective."

No one knows how often eyewitness error leads to false convictions, but some scholars have taken a stab at the question. In their book *Mistaken Identification: The Eyewitness, Psychology, and the Law* (Cambridge University Press, 1995), Mr. Cutler and Steven D. Penrod, of the University of Nebraska at Lincoln, do some courtroom calculations: If just 0.5 percent of America's yearly 1.5 million convictions for serious crimes are erroneous—a rate suggested by some studies—then other research allows the authors to infer that well over half of those defendants, or around 4,500 innocent people, are convicted on false eyewitness testimony.

All that may change now that the nation's top law-enforcement officials have created new guidelines for police conduct. The Justice Department report, "Eyewitness Evidence: A Guide for Law Enforcement," reads like a primer on eyewitness research. Among other things, it instructs investigators who assemble a lineup to:

■ Select "distractors" that match the witness's description, even simulating tattoos or other unusual features if necessary.

■ Remind the witness that the suspect they saw may not even be in the lineup, and that the lineup is intended to clear the innocent as much as it is to identify the guilty.

■ Avoid any comments that might influence the witness's selection.

■ Ask for and record the witness's degree of certainty immediately.

■ Photograph or film lineups to make the police more accountable to the defense.

Before they can take their new influence for granted, psychologists say, there is more to be done. For one thing, police officers and prosecutors need to be educated about the guidelines, which do not have the force of law. But Mr. Wells and others believe that both groups will embrace them once defense lawyers in the courtroom begin to hold the guidelines up as the gold standard of diligent police work.

NO DOUBLE-BLIND LINEUPS

The social scientists didn't win every battle. Despite their urgings, law-enforcement officials on the Justice Department panel batted down two key suggestions for improving police lineups. Research suggests that lineups are more accurate when they are double-blind—in other words, when the investigator in charge doesn't know which person is the suspect—and sequential—when the witness sees faces one at a time.

According to participants, police representatives nixed the former idea, because logistically it would be difficult to round up investigators who didn't know who the suspect was. More important, they said, it would be a tough sell to their fellow cops, because it smacks of mistrust and requires them to cede control of an investigation to someone else.

After scholars lost the battle to include double-blind procedures, participants say, they gave up on demanding sequential lineups. Without the first precaution, they explained, sequential lineups might be even more vulnerable to manipulation than simultaneous lineups are.

John Turtle, a panel member and a psychologist at the Ryerson Polytechnic Institute, in Toronto, believes that he has a high-tech solution to all those concerns. He has developed computer software that purports to take the bias out of the photo-spread lineups, which constitute about 80 percent of those in the United States and virtually all of those in Canada.

All a police investigator would need to do is scan a photo of the suspect into a computer and sit the witness down in front of the screen. The machine would then automatically choose photos of others who match the witness's description from a large database, and offer standardized, neutral instructions that wouldn't nudge the witness toward a particular response.

Psychologists deny they are imputing bad faith to police investigators. It's human nature, they say, to want your results to match your expectations. The scholars are simply urging police officers to treat their procedures for handling witnesses with all the care of scientific experiments. "Human memory is a form of trace evidence, like blood or semen or hair, except the trace exists inside the witness's head," says Mr. Wells. "How you go about collecting that evidence and preserving it and analyzing it is absolutely vital."

DNA: Fingerprint of the Future?

by Ronald Burns and Jason Smith
Texas Christian University

The President cringed as his physician, Connie Mariano, drew 4 milliliters of blood from his right arm. Dr. Mariano labeled the sample "K39" and sent it to the lab for DNA analysis and comparison to a sample of semen, Q3243, removed from Monica Lewinsky's navy blue dress. Later that evening, August 3, 1998, the analyses were finished and in the eyes of some Americans, so was President Clinton. The odds were roughly one in 7.8 billion that someone other than Clinton had stained Lewinsky's dress on February 28, 1997 (Sloyan, 1998). Such overwhelming odds were too convincing for the President to refute, and thus, he subsequently admitted his "inappropriate behavior" to the American public. Regardless of one's opinion regarding the "MonicaGate" fiasco, most would agree that the situation was largely impacted by DNA analysis.

DNA analysis is affecting every aspect of the criminal justice system, from the way evidence is collected to exonerating innocent people from long-term imprisonment. As such, it has played an integral role in our continuous search for justice, and promises to play an increasingly important function. However, as so often occurs with technological advancements, DNA testing has also provided several unexpected problems which could hamper the criminal justice system.

DNA and Crime Fighting

Since 1989, DNA analysis has aided in over 20,000 convictions (Gladwell 1995). DNA testing has been used most notably in cases involving sexual contact and abuse, including a case in Bloomington, Illinois where a 12-year old boy was walking home from junior high when an older boy led him into a factory. In the factory, the boy was forced into three sexual acts, bitten and beaten. The police recovered DNA evidence from the 12-year-old and linked it to a 15-year-old boy in the area, who eventually was tried as an adult and imprisoned within weeks (Arney, 1995). DNA testing has also been used in highly publicized cases such as the O.J. Simpson trial in which DNA evidence positively linked Simpson to the crime scene. A drop of Simpson's blood was found near the bodies of Nicole Brown Simpson and Ronald Goldman, leading prosecutors to suggest that Simpson cut his hand while brutally slashing the victims' throats (Deutsch, 1995). This evidence was key in leading to Simpson's civil conviction. In 1996, 29 convictions were made with no leads other than DNA evidence (Butterfield, 1996).

DNA testing also provides the criminal justice system the welcomed opportunity to correct some of its mistakes. Consider, for example, the case of Kevin Lee Green, who arrived home on September 30, 1979 to find his house burglarized and his pregnant wife lying face down in her bed, covered in blood from a gunshot wound to the head. Ten hours later the child died, but his wife survived with extensive brain damage. For months, Green's wife could not remember the attack, but suddenly her memory returned and she identified the killer as Kevin Lee Green himself. On the strength of his wife's testimony Green was sentenced to life in prison. It was not until the advent of DNA testing that Green would receive his appeal. Sixteen years after his conviction, a computer linked the semen found on the bed sheets to a convicted rapist named Gerald Parker, and Mr. Green was released (Schoofs, 1997). While tragic, this story nevertheless highlights the benefits DNA analysis can provide the criminal justice system. In 1992 alone, twelve men convicted of rape were freed from prison when DNA testing suggested they were not guilty (Sauer, 1993), and an additional 28 men were released over the next two years. (Butterfield, 1996). The FBI and Scotland Yard reported that one-third of all suspects in rape cases are released before booking because DNA evidence exonerates them (Koshland, 1994). The FBI also reported that DNA testing had exonerated the primary suspect in 25% of the sexual assault cases referred to its crime lab (Butterfield, 1996).

DNA evidence is also very effective in settling cases of disputed parentage. For example, upon in-depth examination, scientists have determined that Thomas Jefferson, the third president of the United States, had an illegitimate son with his slave-mistress Sally Hemings. For almost 200 years, this case has been disputed among researchers and now, through identification of a variant upon Jefferson's Y chromosome, the debate has been settled: Eston Hemings is actually a Jefferson (Boyd, 1998).

Problems Associated with DNA

Along with the benefits of DNA testing comes many social costs and responsibilities. As expected, DNA

From *Academy of Criminal Justice Science (ACJS) Today*, November/December 1999, pp. 1, 3-4. Reprinted with permission of the Academy of Criminal Justice Sciences.

analysis can be used for many things other than law enforcement. DNA not only identifies individuals, but also identifies problems within that individual. Gene codes have been found that predispose individuals to heart disease, Alzheimer's, cancer, alcoholism, and many other dangerous diseases (Schoofs, 1997). There have also been controversial claims that a gene common to all homosexuals has been discovered (Evenson, 1993).

Concern has been shown towards insurance companies' reactions to genetic predispositions. If such groups learned of risk factors, would they unnecessarily be more selective about whom to insure? Would such traits enable insurance companies to deny coverage altogether? Insurance companies would surely not want a client who is at significant risk for cancer, given that the medical bills are immense for such a disease. Companies' knowledge of employees with predispositions to alcoholism or homosexuality may also present problems.

Intimate and personal details such as those contained in the human genetic code open the door for widespread discrimination. An example of this discrimination involves the Air Force Academy's refusal to admit cadets that carried the gene for sickle cell anemia during the 1970's. Because only African-Americans carry this gene, and it is very common among them, the ulterior motive behind this policy likely involved racism (Schoofs, 1997).

Geneticists have continuously searched for the infamous "criminal gene," a gene that theoretically predisposes a person to crime. The results of such research could mark a perilous step toward a society in which carriers of "criminal genes"—regardless of whether or not they have violated the law—are monitored, controlled, or perhaps even genetically "cured" (Schoofs, 1997). The concept of repairing a gene is not too far fetched, as scientists have already successfully completed the operation in mice (Solomon et. al.,

1996). However, the problem with gene repair is that each gene may code for many different traits, so by repairing one "bad" trait, one may inadvertently affect many other "good" traits. History suggests that the idea of monitoring and controlling people with specific traits, as amazing as it sounds, is possible. During the 1920's and 30's, crime and mental illness were assumed to have a genetic basis; consequently thousands of mentally ill patients were sterilized (Schoofs, 1997). Similarly, the Nazi idea of purifying the gene pool is part of the not-so-distant past. There are numerous phenotypic traits (i.e., external characteristics, such as skin or eye color) against which people discriminate, yet there are infinitely more genotypic traits (i.e., individual differences in the actual genetic code, such as the genes for Sickle Cell Anemia) to discriminate against. The intimate knowledge of our genetic makeup has been seen by some as a violation of our Fourth Amendment right against "unreasonable searches and seizures" (Schoofs, 1997). The government, fully aware of the potential dangers of disclosing genetic information of individuals to the public, has restricted access to the database to law enforcement only, and enforces this decision with a $100,000 fine for unauthorized disclosure of information (Pezzela, 1998).

One final concern with regard to the use of DNA testing involves tampering with evidence or incorrectly processing information, as in the instance of the OJ Simpson trial in which the Los Angeles Police Department allegedly tampered with evidence. Arguably, it would be quite simple for a police officer to collect false evidence, such as a pre-collected hair, skin or blood sample, and turn it over to the court as evidence collected from the crime scene. The jury would then be presented with concrete evidence linking the suspect to the crime scene, and a conviction would be likely. The ease with which DNA evidence

can be collected also allows it to be easily forged (Deutsch, 1995).

The Future of DNA

DNA testing is becoming cheaper, faster, and more accurate. It was estimated that from 1996 to 2001 the price per DNA analysis will drop from $700 to $10, and the time per analysis will decrease from months to seconds (Butterfield, 1996). Also, the accuracy of the analysis will improve through the use of short tandem repeats (STR), a new method of performing the test which examines 13 fragments of a person's DNA as opposed to the 3–6 fragments examined by previous methods. STR will increase the odds of an exact DNA match from 1 in a million to perhaps 1 in a trillion (Pezzela, 1998). It has been suggested that the system will soon be automated, simply requiring a technician to place a DNA sample in the machine, which will then provide a positive identification of a suspect in seconds (Leusner, 1993).

Headed by the FBI, an effort to create a national DNA database has begun. In addition to the millions of dollars already given to states and private companies to begin the DNA database, $9.7 million ($194,000 per state) was delegated this year to collect a "fingerprint" from all convicted sex offenders (Phillips, 1998). These DNA fingerprints will be filed in the FBI's newly created National Index System (NDIS). In December of 1997, eight states became charter members of the NDIS and by June 1998, all 50 states had entered. The system now contains 600,000 "fingerprints" and is growing rapidly. After only a few months of operation, the NDIS made roughly 400 matches which should likely assist in obtaining numerous convictions (Pezzella, 1998). Great Britain has had a DNA database since 1995, containing 360,000 samples that have already connected 28,000 suspects to crime scenes and linked 6,000 separate serial criminals (Pezzela, 1998).

In our continuous fight against crime, it is a relief to recognize a weapon that is successfully bringing criminals to justice and exonerating the innocent. But with this strong new weapon comes increased responsibility to refrain from abusing our power, as the costs could be quite severe. Nevertheless, many would argue that DNA testing will play a large role in the future of criminal justice. When asked if the DNA database was worth the risk, John Brown, manager of the NDIS, replied, "I think you would need to talk to a victim of a sexual assault or the family of a victim who died as the result of a murder to determine that" ("Legislation Points. . . ," 1994). DNA testing is arguably one of the greatest modern day advances affecting the criminal justice system and the future appears bright. In general, it's hard to dispute the benefits of a mechanism that provides access to information that, as recent as several years ago, was virtually unattainable. For the sake of the criminal justice system and society in general, we can only hope that such technological advances do not stop with DNA.

Works Cited

Arney, S. (1995, November 30). DNA 'fingerprint' points to suspect in B-N sexual assault. *The Pantagraph Bloomington, IL*. p. A1.

Boyd, R. (1998, November 1). DNA test: Jefferson had child with slave. *Sunday Star-News - Wilmington, NC*, pp. A1, A5.

Butterfield, F. (1996, June 16). DNA tests expected to get wider use as nationwide database is developed *The News & Observer Raleigh. NC*, p. A9.

Deutsch, L. (1995, May 5). DNA appears to tie Simpson to killing site. *The Patriot Ledger Quincy, MA*, p. 31.

Evenson, B. (1993, October 17). The dilemmas of DNA magic, Will be able to keep genetic data to ourselves? *The Toronto Star*, p. H6.

Gladwell, M. (1995, May 21). DNA 'Fingerprinting' Comes of Age//Blood Tests Leave Little To Dispute. *Chicago Sun-Times*, p. 28.

Koshland, D. (1994, August 19). The DNA fingerprint story. *American Association for the Advancement of Science*, p. 1015.

Legislation points to creating DNA fingerprinting registry. (1994, September 9). *San Antonio Express-News*.

Leusner, J. (1993, June 1). DNA: The Fingerprint of the Future. The analysis of deoxyribonucleic acid has become a key to link suspects to crime scenes. *Orlando Sentinel*, p. B1.

Pezzella, M. (1998, October 19). FBI DNA dragnet to track fugitives in 50 states. *Biotechnology Newswatch*, p. 1.

Phillips, J. (1998, September 15). 50 States Receive About $9.7 Million To Improve DNA and Fingerprint Identification System. *PR Newswire*.

Sauer, M. (1993, February 28). GENETIC JUSTICE? Expert witnesses don't agree on the use of DNA as evidence, and neither do judges. *The San Diego Union Tribune*, p. D1.

Schoofs, M. (1997, November 18). Genetic Justice. *The Village Voice*, p. 44.

Sloyan, P. (1998, September 24). Specimen K39': For Clinton, Smoking Gun/ Blood sample may be as damaging as Nixon tape. *Newsday*. p. A67.

Solomon, E., & Berg, L., & Martin, D., & Villee, C. (1996). *Biology*. Orlando, FL: Saunders College Publishing.

Stanfield, F. (1996, February 4). Attorneys to put DNA test on trial. The defense for slaying suspect Joseph Rolle will ask a judge for information to discredit the high-tech tool. *The Orlando Sentinel*, p.1.

The Creeping Expansion of DNA Data Banking

By Barry Steinhardt

I want to explain my fears about the creeping expansion of DNA data banking and the uses that this information will be put to. I want to explain what those fears are based on and to challenge those who advocate the use of DNA evidence in the criminal justice system to prove me wrong—to demonstrate that the lid can be firmly kept on Pandora's box.

Let me start with a point that I hope we can all agree on. Drawing a DNA sample is not the same as taking a fingerprint. Fingerprints are two-dimensional representations of the physical attributes of our fingertips. They are useful only as a form of identification. DNA profiling may be used for identification purposes, but the DNA itself represents far more than a fingerprint. Indeed, it trivializes DNA data banking to call it a genetic fingerprint; in Massachusetts, lawmakers have specifically rejected that term.[1]

I understand that the CODIS system[2] contains only a limited amount of genetic information compiled for identification purposes. But the amount of personal and private data contained in a DNA specimen makes its seizure extraordinary in both its nature and scope. The DNA samples that are being held by state and local governments can provide insights into the most personal family relationships and the most intimate workings of the human body, including the likelihood of the occurrence of over 4,000 types of genetic conditions and diseases. DNA may reveal private information such as legitimacy at birth and there are many who will claim that there are genetic markers for aggression, substance addiction, criminal tendencies and sexual orientation.

And because genetic information pertains not only to the individual whose DNA is sampled, but to everyone who shares in that person's blood line, potential threats to genetic privacy posed by their collection extend well beyond the millions of people whose samples are currently on file.

It is worth bearing in mind, too, that there is a long, unfortunate history of despicable behavior by governments toward people whose genetic composition has been considered "abnormal" under the prevailing societal standards of the day.

Genetic discrimination by the government is not merely an artifact of the distant past. During the 1970s, the Air Force refused to allow healthy individuals who carried one copy of the sickle-cell gene to engage in flight training, even though two copies of the gene are needed for symptoms of sickle-cell disease to develop. This restriction was based upon the then untested (and now known to be incorrect) belief that people with a single such gene could display symptoms of sickle-cell disease under low oxygen conditions, even though they would not actually have sickle-cell disease.[3]

Genetic discrimination by private industry is becoming increasingly commonplace as well. A 1997 survey conducted by the American Management Association found that six to ten percent of responding employers (well over 6,000 companies) used genetic testing for employment purposes.[4] The Council for Responsible Genetics, a nonprofit advocacy group based in Cambridge, Mass., has documented hundreds of cases in which healthy people have been denied insurance or a job based on genetic "predictions."

In short, there is a frightening potential for a brave new world where genetic information is routinely collected and its use results in abuse and discrimination.

Now, I am certainly aware that the primary purpose of forensic DNA databases like CODIS is identification and that the profiles are of 13 loci that currently provide no other information. However, I reject the term "junk DNA" because as the Human Genome Project and other studies continue those loci may well turn out to contain other useful genetic information.

The question then is why I am skeptical that we can hold the line and ward off the brave new world of genetic determinism?

In general, I am skeptical because of the long history of function creep. Of databases, which are created for one discrete purpose and, which despite the initial promises of the their creators, eventually take on new functions and purposes. In the 1930s promises were made that the Social Security numbers would only be used as an aid for the new retirement program, but over the past 60 years they have gradually become the universal identifier which their creators claimed they would not be.

Similarly, census records created for general statistical purposes were used during World War II to round up innocent Japanese Americans and to place them in interment camps.

We are already beginning to see that function creep in DNA databases. In a very short time, we have witnessed the ever-widening scope of the target groups from whom law enforcement collects DNA and rapid fire proposals to expand the target populations to new and ever greater numbers of persons.

In a less than a decade, we have gone from collecting DNA from convicted sex offenders—on the theory that they are likely to be recidivists and that they frequently leave biological evidence—to data banks of all violent offenders; to all persons convicted of a crime; to juvenile offenders in 29 states and now to proposals to DNA test all arrestees.

I am skeptical because too many state statutes allow evidence which has been purportedly collected only for identification purposes, to be used for a variety of other purposes. The Massachusetts law that the ACLU is challenging, for example, contains an open-ended authorization for any disclosure that is or may be required as a condition of federal funding and allows for the disclosure of information, including personally identifiable information for "advancing other humanitarian purposes."[5]

I am skeptical because there are proponents of these DNA database laws who continue to cling to notions of a genetic cause of crime. In 1996, the year before the Legislature's enactment of the law authorizing the Massachusetts DNA database, the Legislature commissioned a study to research the biological origins of crime that focused on the genetic causes.

That report specifically focused on genes as the basis for criminal behavior, stating: The report foresaw a future where "genetics begin . . . to play a role in the effort to evaluate the causes of crime," and even cited two articles regarding the debunked "XYY syndrome."[6]

I am skeptical too because too many holders of DNA data refuse to destroy or return that data even after the purported purpose has been satisfied.

The Department of Defense, for example, has three million biological samples it has collected from service personnel for the stated purpose of identifying remains or body parts of a soldier killed on duty. But it keeps those samples for information for *50 years*—long after the subjects have left the military. And the DOD refuses to promulgate regulations which assure that no third parties will have access to the records. Isn't it likely that once the genetic information is col-

lected and banked, pressures will mount to use it for other purposes than the ones for which it was gathered, such as the identification of criminal suspects or medical research? In fact, on several occasions, the FBI has already requested access to this data for purposes of criminal investigations near military bases.

Similarly, many state laws do not require the destruction of a DNA record and/or sample after a conviction has been overturned or—in the case of Louisiana's incipient law—do not require that a person arrested for a crime of which he is not convicted automatically has his DNA records expunged.

The existence of private DNA databases in testing laboratories and government offices, that operate outside the relatively strict CODIS framework, also gives me reason for concern and skepticism.

I am also skeptical, when I hear from Professor Barry Scheck of discussions he has had with law enforcement officials who are considering DNA "dragnets" of neighborhoods or classes of people without informed consent. And I am particularly distressed by the trumpeting of the British model, with its expansive testing and where in one case all the young male inhabitants of a whole village were required to submit to blood or saliva tests.

And I am made more skeptical by sloppy practices that indicate that too few jurisdictions take seriously their obligations under the data bank regime to carefully preserve and test the samples that they do have. Only two state statutes, for example, mandate outside proficiency testing of DNA labs.

In short, the trend is away from limited-purpose forensic data banks. The purposes and target populations are growing and the trend is ominous.

Compounding this problem is that there are few laws, and certainly none at the federal level, which prohibit genetic discrimination by employers, insurers or medical care providers. More and more DNA is being collected, and with the advances in genetic research that make that DNA more and more valuable, instances of discrimination and misuse will grow as well.

Now let me turn to the specific question of DNA data collection from arrestees. Aside from supporting my suspicions that we will see an ever-widening circle of DNA surveillance, these proposals are fundamentally unfair, they violate the Constitution and even from a law enforcement perspective they are not practical—at least not at the moment.

Let's start with what I thought would be the obvious. Arrest does not equal guilt and you shouldn't suffer the consequences of guilt until after you have been convicted. The fact is that many arrests do not result in a conviction.

For example, a national survey of the adjudication outcomes for felony defendants in the 75 largest counties in the country revealed that in felony assault cases, half the charges were dismissed outright, and in 14 percent of cases, the charges were reduced to a misdemeanor.

A study released by the California State Assembly's Commission on the Status of African American Males in the early 1990s revealed that 64 percent of the drug arrests of whites and 81 percent of Latinos were not sustainable, and that an astonishing 92 percent of the black men arrested by police on drug charges were subsequently released for lack of evidence or inadmissible evidence.

Indeed, there is a disturbing element of racial disparity that runs throughout our criminal justice system that can only be compounded by the creation of databases of persons arrested but not convicted of crimes.

Racial profiling and stereotyping is a reality of our criminal justice system. One study of police stops on a strip of interstate in Maryland gives some insight into the nature of the problem. Over several months in 1995, a survey found that 73 percent of the cars stopped and searched were driven by African-Americans, while they made up only 14 percent of the people driving along the interstate. While the arrests rates were about the same for whites and persons of color (approximately 28 percent), the disproportionate number of stops of minorities resulted in a disproportionate number of persons of color being arrested.

Now I make no secret of the ACLU's opposition to DNA data banking, even for convicted felons. We have argued and will continue to argue in cases like *Landry*[7] in Massachusetts that these are intrusive, unreasonable searches made without the individualized suspicion required by the Fourth Amendment and analogous provisions of state constitutions. But even if you accept the rulings that DNA data banking for convicted felons is permissible, either because a special need is present where persons have been convicted of crimes with high recidivism rates and the presence of biological evidence like sexual assaults, or that convicted felons have a diminished expectation of privacy, neither of those circumstances apply to persons who have simply been arrested.

To find otherwise is to equate arrest with guilt and to empower police officers, rather than judges and juries, with the power to force persons to provide the state with evidence that harbors many of their most intimate secrets and those of their blood relatives. Under the current circumstances of mistrust, that is an especially chilling notion for a New Yorker.

Take, for example, the "diminished expectations" argument on which most of the post-conviction DNA testing cases rest. Under this doctrine, the rights of persons who have been convicted of crimes become "diminished," only to the extent that those rights are "fundamentally inconsistent"[8] with the "needs and exi-

gencies" of "the regime to which they have been lawfully committed."[9]

It cannot be argued that forcing arrestees to provide blood samples serves any legitimate security concern, even if they are in pre-trial detention. There are ample other means of confirming their identity. Nor by definition can DNA samples be used to insure compliance with any specified term of post-conviction supervised release. Put simply, these persons have not been convicted of any crime and may never be.

The only possible justification is investigatory and if law enforcement has reason to suspect an individual arrestee then it can and should seek a warrant.

If the special-exception doctrine makes any sense in the context of the post-convicted, it is based on the assumption that they have been found to have committed a crime where the recidivist rate is high and the presence of biological evidence is likely. How can you justify forced testing of a person arrested for jaywalking, or taking part in a political demonstration under that doctrine?

Now let me turn to the most practical of considerations—indeed the only consideration that gives me reason to hope that we will not move further down the path of DNA surveillance. As I read the literature, the single greatest obstacle to implementation of existing DNA data bank regimes is the large backlog of unprocessed samples. If I read the literature correctly, there is a backlog of 450,000 unprocessed samples and only 38,000 have been processed.[10]

There were 15 million arrests last year. From the law enforcement perspective does it really make sense to put the next dollars into collecting and processing samples for persons who have never been convicted of a crime; let alone a crime of the sort where DNA evidence is most likely to be probative. Wouldn't it make more sense to put scarce resources into processing the samples you already have and will generate in the future under the existing programs.

Let me say that I would love to be proved wrong. I would be more than happy to find that my fears are misplaced and that the civil liberties community is wrong about the likely future. If the advocates of DNA data banking can, in fact, restrict the uses of the data to forensic identification, if the data banks only cover persons convicted of a small number of crimes like sexual assault, if testing practices and data security are improved, all to the better. I won't mind being wrong. Pandora's box can be closed.

But the stakes are high and the risks are great. Every expansion of the data banks and every new use for the data increases those risks. The Commission has an obligation not just to assist law enforcement, but to protect the privacy interests of all Americans.

We may not agree on what has come before, but I hope you will agree that if the line is not held here, it may never be held at all.

Endnotes

1. *Commonwealth v. Curnin*, 409 Mass. 218, 219 n. 2 (1991) (rejecting the use of the phrase " 'DNA fingerprinting" because (1) it tends to trivialize the intricacies of the processes by which information for DNA comparisons is obtained (when compared to the process of fingerprinting) and (2) the word fingerprinting tends to suggest erroneously that DNA testing of the type involved in this case will identify conclusively, like real fingerprinting, the one person in the world who could have left the identifying evidence at the crime scene.").

2. Combined DNA Index System, "[a] collection of databases of DNA profiles obtained from evidence samples from unsolved crimes and from known individuals convicted of particular crimes. Contributions to this database are made through State crime laboratories and the data are maintained by the FBI." Jeremy Travis & Christopher Asplen, National Commission on the Future of DNA Evidence, NCJ Pub. No. 177626, Postconviction DNA Testing: Recommendations for Handling Requests 67 (1999).

3. F. Donald Shapiro & Michelle L. Weinberg, *DNA Data Banking: The Dangerous Erosion of Privacy*, 38 Clev. St. L. Rev. 455, 480 n. 132 (1990).

4. American Management Association, Workplace Testing & Monitoring (1997), *quoted in* Rosemary Orthmann, *Three-Fourths of Major Employers Conduct Medical and Drug Tests,* Employment Testing—Law & Policy Reporter (Jul. 1997).

5. Mass. Gen. Laws Ann. ch. 22E, § 10 (West 1999).

6. "Questions Concerning Biological Risk Factors for Criminal Behavior" (1996), *cited in* Brief of Amicus Curiae, Council for Responsible Genetics, *Landry v. Harshbarger* (No. SJC-07899), http://www.aclu.org/court/landry/harshbarger_crg.html.

7. *Landry v. Attorney General*, 429 Mass. 336 (1999) *cert. denied,* 68 U.S.L.W. 3153 (U.S.Mass. Jan 10, 2000) (No. 99–359) (holding that involuntary collection of DNA samples from persons subject to Massachusetts' DNA statute did not result in unreasonable search and seizure under the 4th Amendment and the State Constitution).

8. *Hudson v. Palmer*, 468 U.S. 517, 523 (1984).

9. *Wolff v. McDonnell*, 418 U.S. at 555–556 (1974).

10. National Commission on the Future of DNA Evidence, *CODIS Offender Database Backlog Reduction Discussion* (last modified Jan. 17, 2000) http://www.ojp.usdoj.gov/nij/dnamtgtrans3/trans-k.html.

Barry Steinhardt, Esq., is the Associate Director, American Civil Liberties Union.

This article is based on the author's testimony before the National Commission on the Future of DNA Evidence on Monday, March 1, 1999. Transcripts of his and other testimony before the Commission are available on line at http://www.ojp.usdoj.gov/nij/dna.

Unit 5

Unit Selections

Key Points to Consider

❖ What reform efforts are currently under way in the juvenile justice system?

❖ What are some recent trends in juvenile delinquency? In what ways will the juvenile justice system be affected by these trends?

❖ Is the departure of the juvenile justice system from its original purpose warranted? Why or why not?

 **Links**   **www.dushkin.com/online/**

These sites are annotated on pages 4 and 5.

Although there were variations within specific offense categories, the overall arrest rate for juvenile violent crime remained relatively constant for several decades. Then, in the late 1980s, something changed, bringing more and more juveniles charged with a violent offense into the justice system. The juvenile justice system is a twentieth-century response to the problems of dealing with children in trouble with the law or children who need society's protection.

Juvenile court procedure differs from the procedure in adult courts because juvenile courts are based on the philosophy that their function is to treat and to help, not to punish and to abandon, the offender. Recently, operations of the juvenile court have received criticism, and a number of significant Supreme Court decisions have changed the way that the courts must approach the rights of children.

Despite these changes, however, the major thrust of the juvenile justice system remains one of diversion and treatment rather than adjudication and incarceration, although there is a trend toward dealing more punitively with serious juvenile offenders. This unit's opening essay addresses the issue of young people becoming killers. In "Why the Young Kill," Sharon Begley maintains that a particular biology leads to tragic results. The next

essay, "Young Women in the Juvenile Justice System," Jay Zaslaw points out that the needs of girls in the juvenile justice system are different from those of boys. Typical approaches to dealing with delinquent behavior in young men simply do not work with young women. In the essay entitled "Racial Disparities Seen as Pervasive in Juvenile Justice," another perspective of juvenile justice is raised. Fox Butterfield points out that at every step of the juvenile justice system black and Hispanic youths are treated more severely than white teenagers charged with comparable crimes.

The court of law that is known as youth court is the subject of the next essay, "Youth Court of True Peers Judges Firmly." Teenagers arrested on misdemeanor charges, are judged, quite literally, by a jury of their peers. In the article that follows, "Juvenile Justice: A Century of Experience," Steven Drizin contends the juvenile court is one of the most important contributions the United States has made to the world. The next essay, "The Maximum Security Adolescent," asserts that the juvenile justice system is currently being dismantled, with more and more teenagers incarcerated alongside adults.

The unit closes with an article that cites current trends in juvenile crime and identifies reforms needed to improve the probation experience in "Juvenile Probation on the Eve of the Millennium."

WHY THE YOUNG KILL

**Are certain young brains predisposed to violence?
Maybe—but how these kids are raised can either save them
or push them over the brink. The biological roots of violence.**

BY SHARON BEGLEY

THE TEMPTATION, OF COURSE, IS TO SEIZE on one cause, one single explanation for Littleton, and West Paducah, and Jonesboro and all the other towns that have acquired iconic status the way "Dallas" or "Munich" did for earlier generations. Surely the cause is having access to guns. Or being a victim of abuse at the hands of parents or peers. Or being immersed in a culture that glorifies violence and revenge. But there isn't one cause. And while that makes stemming the tide of youth violence a lot harder, it also makes it less of an unfathomable mystery. Science has a new understanding of the roots of violence that promises to explain why not every child with access to guns becomes an Eric Harris or a Dylan Klebold, and why not *every* child who feels ostracized, or who embraces the Goth esthetic, goes on a murderous rampage. The bottom line: you need a particular environment imposed on a particular biology to turn a child into a killer.

It should be said right off that attempts to trace violence to biology have long been tainted by racism, eugenics and plain old poor science. The turbulence of the 1960s led some physicians to advocate psychosurgery to "treat those people with low violence thresholds," as one 1967 letter to a medical journal put it. In other words, loboto-

mize the civil-rights and antiwar protesters. And if crimes are disproportionately committed by some ethnic groups, then finding genes or other traits common to that group risks tarring millions of innocent people. At the other end of the political spectrum, many conservatives view biological theories of violence as the mother of all insanity defenses, with biology not merely an explanation but an excuse. The conclusions emerging from interdisciplinary research in neuroscience and psychology, however, are not so simple-minded as to argue that violence is in the genes, or murder in the folds of the brain's frontal lobes. Instead, the picture is more nuanced, based as it is on the discovery that experience rewires the brain. The dawning realization of the constant back-and-forth between nature and nurture has resurrected the search for the biological roots of violence.

Early experiences seem to be especially powerful: a child's brain is more malleable than that of an adult. The dark side of the zero-to-3 movement, which emphasizes the huge potential for learning during this period, is that the young brain also is extra vulnerable to hurt in the first years of life. A child who suffers repeated "hits" of stress—abuse, neglect, terror—experiences physical changes in his brain, finds Dr. Bruce

Perry of Baylor College of Medicine. The incessant flood of stress chemicals tends to reset the brain's system of fight-or-flight hormones, putting them on hair-trigger alert. The result is the kid who shows impulsive aggression, the kid who pops the classmate who disses him. For the outcast, hostile confrontations—not necessarily an elbow to the stomach at recess, but merely kids vacating en masse when he sits down in the cafeteria—can increase the level of stress hormones in his brain. And that can have dangerous consequences. "The early environment programs the nervous system to make an individual more or less reactive to stress," says biologist Michael Meaney of McGill University. "If parental care is inadequate or unsupportive, the [brain] may decide that the world stinks—and it better be ready to meet the challenge." This, then, is how having an abusive parent raises the risk of youth violence: it can change a child's brain. Forever after, influences like the mean-spiritedness that schools condone or the humiliation that's standard fare in adolescence pummel the mind of the child whose brain has been made excruciatingly vulnerable to them.

In other children, constant exposure to pain and violence can make their brain's system of stress hormones unresponsive, like a keypad that has been

 From *Newsweek*, May 3, 1999, pp. 32-35.

pushed so often it just stops working. These are the kids with antisocial personalities. They typically have low heart rates and impaired emotional sensitivity. Their signature is a lack of empathy, and their sensitivity to the world around them is practically nonexistent. Often they abuse animals: Kip Kinkel, the 15-year-old who killed his parents and shot 24 schoolmates last May, had a history of this; Luke Woodham, who killed three schoolmates and wounded seven at his high school in Pearl, Miss., in 1997, had previously beaten his dog with a club, wrapped it in a bag and set it on fire. These are also the adolescents who do not respond to punishment: nothing hurts. Their ability to feel, to react, has died, and so has their conscience. Hostile, impulsive aggressors usually feel sorry afterward. Antisocial aggressors don't feel at all. Paradoxically, though, they often have a keen sense of injustices aimed at themselves.

Inept parenting encompasses more than outright abuse, however. Parents who are withdrawn and remote, neglectful and passive, are at risk of shaping a child who (absent a compensating source of love and attention) shuts down emotionally. It's important to be clear about this: inadequate parenting short of Dickensian neglect generally has little ill effect on most children. But to a vulnerable baby, the result of neglect can be tragic. Perry finds that neglect impairs the development of the brain's cortex, which controls feelings of belonging and attachment. "When there are experiences in early life that result in an underdeveloped capacity [to form relationships]," says Perry, "kids have a hard time empathizing with people. They tend to be relatively passive and perceive themselves to be stomped on by the outside world."

These neglected kids are the ones who desperately seek a script, an ideology that fits their sense of being humiliated and ostracized. Today's pop culture offers all too many dangerous ones, from the music of Rammstein to the game of Doom. Historically, most of those scripts have featured males. That may explain, at least in part, why the murderers are Andrews and Dylans rather than Ashleys and Kaitlins, suggests Deborah Prothrow-Smith of the Harvard School of Public Health. "But girls are now 25 percent of the adolescents arrested for violent crime," she notes. "This follows the media portrayal

RISK FACTORS

Having any of the following risk factors doubles a boy's chance of becoming a murderer:

- **Coming from a family with a history of criminal violence**
- **Being abused**
- **Belonging to a gang**
- **Abusing drugs or alcohol**

Having any of these risk factors, in addition to the above, triples the risk of becoming a killer:

- **Using a weapon**
- **Having been arrested**
- **Having a neurological problem that impairs thinking or feeling**
- **Having had problems at school**

of girl superheroes beating people up," from Power Rangers to Xena. Another reason that the schoolyard murderers are boys is that girls tend to internalize ostracism and shame rather than turning it into anger. And just as girls could be the next wave of killers, so could even younger children. "Increasingly, we're seeing the high-risk population for lethal violence as being the 10- to 14-year-olds," says Richard Lieberman, a school psychologist in Los Angeles. "Developmentally, their concept of death is still magical. They still think it's temporary, like little Kenny in 'South Park'." Of course, there are loads of empty, emotionally unattached girls and boys. The large majority won't become violent. "But if they're in a violent environment," says Perry, "they're more likely to."

There seems to be a genetic component to the vulnerability that can turn into antisocial-personality disorder. It is only a tiny bend in the twig, but depending on how the child grows up, the bend will be exaggerated or straightened out. Such aspects of temperament as "irritability, impulsivity, hyperactivity and a low sensitivity to emotions in others are all biologically based," says psychologist James Garbarino of Cornell University, author of the upcoming book "Lost Boys: Why Our Sons Turn Violent and How We Can Save Them." A baby who is unreactive to hugs and smiles can be left to go her natural, antisocial way if

frustrated parents become exasperated, withdrawn, neglectful or enraged. Or that child can be pushed back toward the land of the feeling by parents who never give up trying to engage and stimulate and form a loving bond with her. The different responses of parents produce different brains, and thus behaviors. "Behavior is the result of a dialogue between your brain and your experiences," concludes Debra Niehoff, author of the recent book "The Biology of Violence." "Although people are born with some biological givens, the brain has many blank pages. From the first moments of childhood the brain acts as a historian, recording our experiences in the language of neurochemistry."

There are some out-and-out brain pathologies that lead to violence. Lesions of the frontal lobe can induce apathy and distort both judgment and emotion. In the brain scans he has done in his Fairfield, Calif., clinic of 50 murderers, psychiatrist Daniel Amen finds several shared patterns. The structure called the cingulate gyrus, curving through the center of the brain, is hyperactive in murderers. The CG acts like the brain's transmission, shifting from one thought to another. When it is impaired, people get stuck on one thought. Also, the prefrontal cortex, which seems to act as the brain's supervisor, is sluggish in the 50 murderers. "If you have violent thoughts that you're stuck on and no supervisor, that's a prescription for trouble," says Amen, author of "Change Your Brain/ Change Your Life." The sort of damage he finds can result from head trauma as well as exposure to toxic substances like alcohol during gestation.

Children who kill are not, with very few exceptions, amoral. But their morality is aberrant. "I killed because people like me are mistreated every day," said pudgy, bespectacled Luke Woodham, who murdered three students. "My whole life I felt outcasted, alone." So do a lot of adolescents. The difference is that at least some of the recent school killers felt emotionally or physically abandoned by those who should love them. Andrew Golden, who was 11 when he and Mitchell Johnson, 13, went on their killing spree in Jonesboro, Ark., was raised mainly by his grandparents while his parents worked. Mitchell mourned the loss of his father to divorce.

Unless they have another source of unconditional love, such boys fail to develop, or lose, the neural circuits that control the capacity to feel and to form healthy relationships. That makes them hypersensitive to perceived injustice. A sense of injustice is often accompanied by a feeling of abject powerlessness. An adult can often see his way to restoring a sense of self-worth, says psychiatrist James Gilligan of Harvard Medical School, through success in work or love. A child usually lacks the emotional skills to do that. As one killer told Garbarino's colleague, "I'd rather be wanted for murder than not wanted at all."

THAT THE LITTLETON MASSACRE ENDED in suicide may not be a coincidence. As Michael Carneal was wrestled to the ground after killing three fellow students in Paducah in 1997, he cried out, "Kill me now!" Kip Kinkel pleaded with the schoolmates who stopped him, "Shoot me!" With suicide "you get immortality," says Michael Flynn of John Jay College of Criminal Justice. "That is a great feeling of power for an adolescent who has no sense that he matters."

The good news is that understanding the roots of violence offers clues on how to prevent it. The bad news is that ever more children are exposed to the influences that, in the already vulnerable, can produce a bent toward murder. Juvenile homicide is twice as common today as it was in the mid-1980s. It isn't the brains kids are born with that has changed in half a generation; what has changed is the ubiquity of violence, the easy access to guns and the glorification of revenge in real life and in entertainment. To deny the role of these influences is like denying that air pollution triggers childhood asthma. Yes, to de-velop asthma a child needs a specific, biological vulnerability. But as long as some children have this respiratory vulnerability—and some always will— then allowing pollution to fill our air will make some children wheeze, and cough, and die. And as long as some children have a neurological vulnerability—and some always will—then turning a blind eye to bad parenting, bullying and the gun culture will make other children seethe, and withdraw, and kill.

With ADAM ROGERS, PAT WINGERT *and* THOMAS HAYDEN

Young Women In The Juvenile Justice System

BY JAY G. ZASLAW

Overview

In the 1990s the issues of young women in the juvenile justice system have received their overdue and necessary attention. Vicki Burke, the founder of Practical Academic Cultural Education (PACE), a Florida based young women's day treatment program and Meda Chesney-Lind, among others, articulated the need for unique approaches to meet the needs of young women in the juvenile justice system.

The people who have labored endlessly over the years working with adolescent young women realize that girls in the juvenile justice system are different. Typical approaches to deal with their delinquent behavior used with young men do not work. As a probation officer for over 20 years, this author experienced frustration. Young women are sassy, defiant, have special problems and they just do not care. Probation officers employed the "one for 10" rule: "If you take this one girl from my caseload, I will take ten of your boys."

The court and probation departments tend to "sexualize" their behavior. For example, if a boy stays out all night, "boys will be boys," but if a girl does it, she was having sex. It was not uncommon for girls to be detained and be ordered to have gynecological exams (Odem and Schlossman, 1991). Judges detained them for their own protection (Girls Incorporated, 1996). This practice was impacted, however, by the establishment of the Juvenile Justice and Delinquency Prevention Act of 1974, and the mandates of the Office of Juvenile Justice and Delinquency Prevention.

Nina Siegal (1995), in her work with young women in San Francisco, observed that they spent more time in detention for fewer and less serious offenses than boys, because of a dearth of resources available to them. It is not unusual for young women to spend six to nine months in detention awaiting a placement bed.

The issues that make young women difficult to work with are the same ones that are gratifying in helping them. They are emotional, honest and they respond to relationships. To enjoy the challenge of working with the young female offender, one must understand their uniqueness.

Even though young women are different in many ways, the juvenile justice response to them, in some ways, needs to be similar to that of boys. Young women involved in the juvenile justice system have committed crimes. They have victims and owe their communities a debt. In addition, they need to develop social, vocational and academic competencies. Also, the public needs to be protected from their continued victimization.

Trends Of The Young Female Offender

According to Shay Bilchik, OJJDP Administrator, young women are entering the juvenile justice system at a younger age. They are also increasing in number for more serious crimes (U.S. Department of Justice Report, 1996). This study revealed that between 1989 and 1993, arrests of young women more than doubled. Property crimes during that period rose by 22 percent for young women and dropped by 3 percent for young men. Twenty percent of all juvenile assaults were committed by young women, an increase of 87 percent. The use of secure detention for young women rose during that period, by 23 percent and by 47 percent for property crimes.

Meda Chesney-Lind documents (The Female Offender, 1997) that historically, research on the female offender is lacking. She writes that the work of Jessie Bernard (cited in Smith, 1992) revealed a phenomenon

From *Perspectives*, Winter 1999, pp. 33-38. Reprinted with permission from the American Probation and Parole Association.

117

known as the "stag effect." That is, scholars would rather study the romance and fascination of the male "outlaw." The problems of young women and crime were simply ignored.

Chesney-Lind documents research conducted on the social histories of women in prison that the effects of victimization led to bad choices. She states that in order to accurately view the increase in crimes committed by young women, we must look at it in the context of gender. She believes that therapeutic responses must address a world that has been unfair to women and especially those of color and poverty (The Female Offender, 1997).

The following facts were revealed in a study done by the American Correctional Association (1990) regarding young women in the juvenile justice system:

- 61.2 percent were physically abused (over ½ were minorities);
- 50 percent were physically abused 11 times or more;
- 54.3 percent were also sexually abused; and
- 33 percent were sexually abused 11 times or more.

Historically, young women have been arrested and held in secure detention more than young men. This trend decreased by the mandates of the JJDP Act, but now again is on the rise. Since 1985 status offenses of young women have risen by 18 percent and curfew by 83 percent (FBI, 1995). The study also reveals that, in cases of abuse that started at age nine or younger, 80 percent of those young women ran away, 39 percent 10 times or more. In 53.8 percent of those cases, they attempted suicide.

The juvenile justice response to status offenses, in some cases revictimizes young women. As Chesney-Lind details, it is crucial to view this behavior in the context of their lives. Running away and staying out beyond curfew is a survival mechanism. Who wants to return to an intolerable situation?

It is this author's experience that young women who are placed in residential facilities and bond to the program staff will run away or "act out" when they are about to be returned home. They will also use run away behaviors to avoid closeness. Viewing these behaviors in the context of their experiences, young women have difficulty trusting adults. If success means returning to abuse and victimization, they tend to run or act out. To arrest and commit them to a more restrictive program is to stifle the survival instinct that has kept them safe.

This process is known as "bootstrapping." It occurs when the juvenile justice system labels a status offense as a delinquent offense because of the context in which it was committed. For example, if a young woman runs away from a residential or commitment program, she has violated a court order and therefore is charged with the delinquent act of escape. Another example in which this author is familiar involves juveniles accused of domestic violence for crimes previously considered "incorrigibility" or being beyond the control of parents. Police in Tucson, Arizona, took juveniles into custody for family conflicts because a program for juvenile domestic violence existed (Zaslaw, 1989).

Bootstrapping occurs most with young women. According to a study conducted by Girls Incorporated (1996), 19 percent of young women and less than 3 percent of boys were incarcerated for status offenses. Also, twice as many young women were detained for violation of probation or parole than boys. The juvenile justice system further victimizes minority young women. In Virginia, where 26 percent of the juvenile offender population are minority young women, over one-half were held in secure facilities (Task Force on Juvenile Offenders, 1991).

For young women, "self-defeating behaviors" are defined partially as sexual promiscuity, which is not true for boys (Wellhorn, 1988).

Bootstrapping was addressed by the legislature in 1992, making it more difficult to detain juveniles in secure detention for committing status offenses. Revisions now require that juveniles receive due process and that all resources, short of detainment, were exhausted in each case, for violations of court orders. The revised act now requires a written report be submitted by the court in each case, to document that no option exists, short of incarceration when a status offender is detained.

In a study conducted in Hillsborough County at their Juvenile Assessment Center on 2,104 juveniles (Dembo et. al, 1995) found that young women's delinquent behavior related to victimization and survival on the streets. They found that boys' delinquency related to delinquent lifestyles.

For boys, street gang membership meets needs of belonging, security, self-esteem, respect and thrill-seeking. Gangs exist to help young men and women cope with chaotic, violent and economically deprived lives. They offer acceptance and antisocial career paths such as selling drugs. Gangs provide a counter-culture that meets the same needs successful juveniles and adults meet through pro-social avenues. The street gang offers a vehicle to survive and escape the dismal future their members face (Huff, 1990).

Young women join gangs for a variety of reasons (Joe and Chesney-Lind, 1995). Young Latinos in Las Cholas, a San Fernando Valley set, rejected traditional values of the Latino culture, playing the roles of wife and mother (Harris, 1988). African American young women learned to defend themselves from abusive men and attacks on their integrity (Fishman, 1995).

Regarding issues of substance abuse, young women and young men use alcohol and drugs for different reasons. Young men tend to abuse substances for thrills and in support of delinquent lifestyles. Young women tend to use substances for escape and self-medication (Inciarodi, J. Lockwood and Pottiger, 1993).

Despite the picture of gloom drawn in this section, hope exists through creative programming that addresses young women within their communities and cultures. Interventions, a female adolescent treatment program in Chicago, addresses the disease of chemical dependency through education and treatment. Issues such as abuse, eating disorders and depression are worked through in educational and therapy groups. The program also offers young women educational testing, vocational training, sex education and AIDS prevention and programming to build self-esteem. Their approach is unique to the needs of young women.

The PACE program in Florida combines accredited education, non-traditional career planning, substance abuse treatment, pregnancy prevention, self-esteem, cultural awareness and health education. It also offers counseling, life management skills, meaningful community restoration projects and etiquette training. The executive director of PACE, Dr. LaWanda Ravoira, continued the tradition of the program by developing the curriculum through the input of the young women. PACE is a non-profit program which has survived through partnerships developed within local communities.

The state of Florida's Department of Juvenile Justice (DJJ) has a program called Girls Initiative. The purpose is to promote effective gender-specific programming and implement policies and practices that prohibit gender bias in placement, treatment and services rendered. The department launched its campaign, Listen to Girls. A coalition of DJJ employees and providers has worked on a local district and state level to implement the initiative. A video tape and workbook have been developed to insure that the campaign is successful and consistent.

A program in Oregon called Teen Pregnancy Prevention developed through the Oregon Action Agenda, 1997 was developed at the governor's request, to solidify teen pregnancy prevention efforts by local and state partners. This community project linked young men and young women, parents, schools, communities, government and health services. The purpose is to support positive values, build social skills and teach responsible sex education. It also encourages postponing sexual involvement, gives access to contraceptives and teaches legal issues. The project is a realistic approach to teenage sexuality.

In addition, the work of Girls' Incorporated, formerly the Girls' Club of America, has pioneered research efforts in the area of removing gender bias in systems dealing with young women. It has been involved in the challenge grants funded by OJJDP to prevent and treat young women in the juvenile justice system. Twenty-three states are currently participating in the challenge grant process.

Treatment Overview

In light of the research, diversion, day treatment and residential programs for young women need to be ho-

"Many programs for young women fail because they tend to ignore the importance of relationships. They use the same approaches with young women as they do young men. Although discipline and structure are necessary, the significance of relationships sometimes is lost in the pursuit of respect and discipline."

listic and comprehensive. Until recently, most programs were written to serve young women or young men with the same "boiler plate" approach.

Young women in the juvenile justice system have a myriad of complex problems to address. Many of them have been sexually and physically abused and tend to see bleak futures, unhappiness and continued victimization. Therefore, effective treatment requires dedicated people and a rich staff development curriculum. Typically, day treatment and residential programs are grossly under funded. In order to run a quality program, staff members need to be compensated and trained well. It is not easy to take the abuse and resistance of young women. Juvenile justice systems and their providers must recognize this when setting up or contracting for services.

The roles of female and male staff members should be clearly defined. Females model self-sufficient, assertive and confident behavior. They dress appropriately, not provocatively or like they are "going to war." Males model respect for the young women and female staff members. Many of these young women have no experience seeing adults in their lives in this context.

The interactions between the male and female staff members should respect boundaries. Although many of these young women need affection, a "no touch" policy should be employed. There are some instances that a hug is appropriate; however, an abused young woman may interpret it differently. Boundary training is essential to understand this issue.

The role of the male is critical to the treatment process. Young women need to know that they can be respected by men. They also need to experience that not all men are like the ones that have hurt them or like the boys to which they have formerly attached themselves. They need to learn that they can be loved and taken care of without sacrificing their dignity.

Young women respond to positive, non-sexual relationships with caring adults. This is the most critical issue in gender specific programming. When a young man acts out, he may need some time in isolation to reflect on the situation. With young women, a crisis situation is a prime opportunity to build a relationship. The content of any program is contingent upon the process of building the relationship. Young women will learn from adults whom they trust.

Young women also respond to cognitive approaches that utilize verbal expression. They also respond to experiential learning approaches, artistic expression, role playing and social activities. Again, young women are extremely abusive and disruptive at times and will resist participation in program components. This process needs to be recognized and expected. Patience, consistency and the development of strong non-sexual bonds with adults are the keys to breaking this resistance. Their unwillingness to comply with adult requests should be viewed as a survival skill.

Many programs for young women fail because they tend to ignore the importance of relationships. They use the same approaches with young women as they do young men. Although discipline and structure are necessary, the significance of relationships sometimes is lost in the pursuit of respect and discipline.

Program Components

Essential to an effective gender specific program is an accurate needs assessment and treatment planning process. In 1997 Cook County Illinois, in partnership with the National Council on Crime and Delinquency (NCCD) developed an instrument to measure the risk and needs of young women involved in the juvenile justice system. The instrument was created through research on young women, using demographic data, arrest information, prior services and outcome measures. A study of characteristics and social history identified necessary services and the risk to the public (Ereth and Healy, 1997).

Solutions for young women should focus on programming that deals with young women in the context of their lives. Strategies should address gender issues such as victimization, economic deprivation, cultural issues and unequal opportunities (Austin, et al, 1992).

Female Sexuality

Because many young women in the juvenile justice system have been sexually abused, dealing with sexual issues is the cornerstone of effective gender specific programming. Issues such as postponing sexual involvement, sexually transmitted diseases, pregnancy and birth control need to be addressed. In addition, sexual harassment, normal female sexuality and receiving affection without sex need to be included. Almost all young women will become or are mothers, so child rearing is another important focus. Using computerized dolls that simulate infant's behavior such as "Baby Think It Over" are effective teaching tools. They also show young women that raising children isn't always fun.

Young women typically do not reveal issues of victimization, although some information can be gathered from social histories and one-on-one needs assessments. For those young women who have documented histories of sexual abuse, "survivor" treatment is absolutely necessary. Sometimes, however, young women will not discuss it and it takes a trained intervention team to notice behaviors that indicate sexual abuse. Relationships with staff members who are adequately trained will foster the healing process. Key issues include:

- Defining sexual abuse.
- Addressing "Was I sexually abused?"
- It wasn't my fault.
- Coping with sexual abuse.
- How do I deal with the perpetrator?
- What are my rights?
- What are the laws?
- Surviving sexual abuse.
- Having a normal sex life.
- Breaking the pattern. How do I stop myself from abusing others?

This component will help young women realize that sexuality is a healthy part of life when it is an expression of love. They also will learn that they have the right to say no.

Counseling and Mental Health Services

Through a comprehensive needs assessment process, therapeutic issues for each young woman should be identified and addressed in individual and group counseling. In addition to treatment, delinquent behavior and victimizing others should be confronted.

Family counseling is important, ideally, but realistically many of the young women have families that will not participate and others should not return home. In one program run by Ramsay Youth Services, a mother said, "If you want me to write to my daughter, send me self-addressed stamped envelopes." For that program, this lack of involvement is the rule, not the acception. Family issues should be dealt within the context of other interventions.

Criminal Thinking Patterns

Young women and young men in the juvenile justice system tend to act from a victim stance. They see themselves as victims of a system that requires them to do things. They tend to blame others, assume the worst, mislabel and minimize behavior and use self-centered thinking. In addition, according to Arnold Goldstein, they have 12 problem areas including lying, fronting, using drugs and authority problems that need to be confronted. Those criminal thinking patterns need to be broken for young men and young women to become responsible for their actions. Robert Ross and Elizabeth Fabiano as well as Goldstein have used cognitive restructuring successfully. It should be a part of all juvenile treatment programs. Whatever cognitive model is used can be implemented by probation officers, case managers or youth care workers. Creative ways of teaching prosocial thinking include using puzzles, board games and role playing techniques.

Anger Management

Most young women in the juvenile justice system have problems with anger. The management of anger is a necessary component of successful programming. An effective model developed by Albert Ellis focuses on changing irrational beliefs. He breaks down aggressive responses to situations into the antecedent event, the belief and consequent event (ABC). This allows young women to realize that nobody makes them angry. They can work on changing belief systems and strategies to avoid explosive reactions. The EQUIP model developed by Arnold Goldstein (et al) utilizes Ellis' approach but adds the monitoring of physiological cues to recognize the onset of an angry response. The EQUIP program includes a 10 session anger management program.

Accredited Education

Most young women in the juvenile justice system do not see a future, let alone the value of education. An educational component must be creative and individualized for young women to be responsive. Strategies such as Peer Response Groups, Listen-Think-Pair-Share, Jigsaws and Thematic Education are such approaches. Computerized teaching, role playing and using materials that interest young women will stimulate their quest for knowledge. Critical to the teaching process is utilizing instructors that are patient, creative and know the problems that young women face. Also important is building gender and cultural pride.

Social Skills Development

Young women need to develop the ability to succeed in the community. Skills in budgeting, goal setting, conflict resolution, nutrition, dealing with authority, time structuring, etc. are necessary. In addition, special areas of need include social etiquette, assertiveness, self-examination for breast cancer, functioning in a male oriented culture, issues of domestic violence, and negotiation

"Solutions for young women should focus on programming that deals with young women in the context of their lives."

skills need to be developed. Because young women respond to cognitive approaches, role playing techniques and participatory learning strategies, they should be included in the process of teaching social skills.

Pre-Vocational and Vocational Skill Development

Areas of need for pre-vocational training include following directions, interest and strength assessment, interviewing and resume writing, time management and dependability. A comprehensive gender specific program will stress non-traditional career development. Guest speakers, one-to-one mentors and subcontracts with women (physicians, maintenance companies, teachers, etc.) will provide opportunities for young women to realize they can be the doctor as well as the nurse.

The same is true for vocational training. Young women should be provided the opportunity to learn whatever trade or career path they choose. Community partnerships developed through networking can allow chances for young women to learn about business and all possibilities of the world of work. While in a juvenile justice program, young women can begin to experience the necessities required to pursue their chosen career paths. Strategies such as job shadowing, female mentors and guest speakers will create a sense of optimism and hope.

Expressive Arts

Young women learn and gain self-esteem from outside sources. Expressing themselves through art projects, creative writing and drama will build feelings of self-worth. A residential setting should have the creative efforts of young women proudly displayed.

A teen theater in which young women express feelings about contemporary gender issues and the traumas of their lives through dramatic presentations is a creative way to deal with post traumatic stress. It provides a vehicle to share their inner confusion in a less threatening context. They can create and act out their real situations in the format of a play.

Substance Abuse Treatment

Young women use substances for the purpose of self-medication. It provides a survival or escape mechanism from the pain of the past and present while it shields them for the bleakness of the future. Strategies to address this should be incorporated with building self-esteem, competency development and therapies to deal with the issues from which they are trying to escape. This is accomplished through the implementation of the complete model.

Also necessary, is a strong educational and treatment approach that realistically deals with their chemical dependency. Although using drugs is symptomatic of deeper problems, the use of alcohol and other drugs is life threatening and needs to be addressed. Traditional 12-Step recovery models have proven effectiveness with adults, but may not be the best approach for adolescents. A model developed by Dr. Robert Schwebel, entitled "The Seven Challenges," is a realistic process (Schwebel, 1990). He treats chemical dependency by acknowledging young men and young women use substances for reasons that make sense to them. He also realizes that there needs to be a reason to give up their addiction. Dr. Schwebel understands that adolescents are not ready to commit to abstinence. Giving up the use of alcohol and other drugs and relapse prevention are the goals of substance abuse treatment not the prerequisites.

Eating Problems and Self-Esteem

Young women tend to develop eating disorders because of their lack of self-esteem. The media further complicates this by portraying beauty in the context of the "Barbie Syndrome." Programming should address self-esteem through all the aforementioned components. Young women with severe eating problems need to deal with them in the context of their mental health services.

Young Women and Restorative Justice

Young women in the juvenile justice system present a complex situation. Not only does programming need to address their unique and special needs, it also has to provide public protection and hold them accountable to their victims and communities.

Short term public protection is accomplished through hardware secure facilities, intensive staff supervision and highly structured activities. In the long term, the public is protected by young men and young women developing competencies and becoming accountable for their victimization of people and communities.

The Restorative Justice Model identifies three clients: the offender, victim and community. All have responsibilities and roles as partners in dealing with juvenile crime (Bazemore and Day, 1996). The offender (male and female) need opportunities to pay restitution, perform meaningful community restoration and to develop acceptable prosocial avenues to success (Zaslaw, 1996). Avenues to success include education and training resources, career paths, acceptable peer groups and oppor-

tunities to complete court sanctions. Without them, young men and young women usually will return to their historical behaviors.

Strategies for young men and young women need to address the physical, emotional and material harm they have caused others and include the following:

- **Payment of Restitution -** Opportunities need to be created within facilities and the community for young men and young women to earn money and compensate victims for material losses suffered.
- **Victim/Offender Mediation -** A process to determine actual losses, amount to be repaid and strategies to earn money for restitution need to be negotiated.
- **Family/Group Conferencing -** This involves bringing together the victim and his/her friends and family members with the offender and his/her family members to discuss the physical, emotional and material harm caused. It is an opportunity to vent feelings and develop what should be done about it.
- **Victim Apology -** The offender should apologize to the victim directly or through victim advocates. It should include an empathetic statement of how the victim must have felt to be violated.
- **Victim Awareness Curriculum -** Young women need to learn the impact of their victimizing acts on others. A victim awareness curriculum for young women is difficult because so many of them have also been victimized. Cognitive approaches utilizing role playing and interaction with victims is suggested.
- **Victim Impact Panels -** Young women should meet with victim groups of crimes similar to the ones they have committed. Victims of burglary, domestic violence, Mothers Against Drunk Drivers (MADD), Parents of Murdered Children, etc., can come to the facility or common meeting place to discuss the process of victimization. This is a powerful process and participants should be screened because of the victimization some young women have suffered.

Victims, because they are one of the three clients, have a role to play in the juvenile justice process. They can participate in the victim/offender mediation and family/group conferencing process. Another role victims can play is that of a victim surrogate or advocate. A victim surrogate is one that plays the role of a victim in a specific case because the actual victim chooses not to participate. A victim advocate represents the need of a particular victim in a case. He/she updates the victim on progress in the case and represents the victim's concerns.

Examples of input include issues of restitution payments, testifying actively in all court procedures relevant to his/her case and choosing what type of community restoration a young man or young women should perform. They also can provide ongoing input to the court on how their needs have been met. Another role the victim can perform is to participate in Victim Impact Panels.

Because young women in the juvenile justice system have victimized the community through costs associated with court processing, placement in services, etc., they should participate in meaningful community restoration projects. These projects need to have significance to the young women and the community. They also provide opportunities to develop competencies and healthy relationships with adults.

Examples of projects include building or repairing houses for the needy, building shelters for victims of abuse, landscaping or other services for the elderly, volunteering in a day care facility (if appropriate), tutoring other young women and other options defined through community partnerships.

To develop the necessary network of community partners, certain strategies are recommended. One of the strongest bonds to the community is the advisory board. Members can be sought from business and civic groups, youth serving agencies, schools, law enforcement, prosecutors, the interfaith network and other stakeholders in the community. A critical component of the community advisory board is the involvement of the young women. The board can be instrumental in providing training, job-shadowing, paying jobs, mentors, restoration projects, program advisory, community supervision and much more.

Contacts within the community can be developed by the board, partnerships with the juvenile justice system and other task force involvement. In addition, the staff members' contacts can open many other avenues to success.

Essential to every juvenile justice program's success is the evaluation of the program components, staff members and the young men and young women participating in it. Goals such as helping the youth in the program from further juvenile justice or criminal involvement and engaging in high risk behaviors are measurable through re-arrest records and longitudinal studies. Objectives such as increases in academic gains, drug resistance skills, cognitive skills development and social skills can be measured through pre and post testing. The staff can be evaluated by utilizing performance appraisals that clearly identify the contract components and each staff members' duties. Program accountability can be measured by evaluation if prescribed services are being provided and by the success of the young men and young women enrolled in the program.

References

American Correctional Association (1990). The Female Offender. What Does the Future Hold. *Washington, D.C.*

Austin, J., Bloom, B. and Donahue, T. (1992). Female Offenders in the Community: An Analysis of Innovative Strategies and Programs. *Washington, D.C., NIC, NCCD.*

Bazemore, G. Day, S. Restoring the Balance: Juvenile and Community Justice. Juvenile Justice. A Journal of The Office of Juvenile Justice and Delinquency Prevention. *Volume III. Number 1. pp. 3–14.*

Chesney-Lind, Meda. The Female Offender, Girls, Women and Crime. *Sage Publications, 1997, pp. 10–23.*

Dembo, J.S., Sue, C.C., Borden, P. and Manning, D. (1995). "Gender Differences in Service Needs Among Youths Entering a Juvenile Assessment Center. A replication study." *Paper presented at the annual meeting of the Society of Social Problems, Washington, D.C.*

Ereth, J., Healy, T. Cook County Juvenile Offenders Risk Study. *Jan. 1997.*

Federal Bureau of Investigation (1995). Crime in the United States. *Washington, D.C. U.S. Department of Justice.*

Fishman, L.T. (1995). The Vice Queens. An Ethnographic Study of Black Female Gang Behaviors. The Modern Gang Leader, *pp. 83–92. Los Angeles. Roxbury.*

Girls Incorporated. Prevention and Parity: Girls in Juvenile Justice. *Indianapolis. Girls Incorporated National Resource Center.*

Harris, M.G. (1988). Cholos: Latino Girls and Gangs. *New York. AMS Press.*

Huff, R. (Ed.) (1990). Gangs in America. *Newbury Park, CA., (SAGE)*

Inciardi, J., Lockwood, D. and Pottiger, A.E. (1993). Women and Crack Cocaine. *New York. Macmillan.*

Joe, K.A. and Chesney-Lind, M. "Just Every Mother's Angel: An Analysis of Gender and Ethnic Variations in Youth Gang Membership. *Gender and Society. Volume 9, Number 4, August, 1995. pp. 408–431.*

Odem, M.E. and Schlossman, S. (1991). Gardens of Virtue: The Juvenile Court and Female Delinquency in early 20th Century, *Los Angeles. Crime and Delinquency, 37, 186–203.*

Schwebel, R. Saying No Is Not Enough. *New York. Newmarket Press. 1990.*

Siegal, N. (1995, October 4). Where the Girls Are. *San Francisco Bay Guardian, pp. 19–20.*

Smith, D.E. (1992). Whistling Women: Reflections on Rage and Nationality. *W.K. Carroll, L. Chustausen-Ruffman, R.E. Currie and D. Harrison (Eds.). Fragile Truths: 25 Years of Sociology and Anthropology in Canada. Ottawa: Carleton University Press.*

Task Force on Juvenile Offenders (1991). Young Women in Virginia's Juvenile Justice System: Where Do They Belong? *R. Ahmand, VA Department of Youth and Family Services.*

U.S. Department of Justice. Office of Justice Programs. Female Offenders in the Juvenile Justice System, Statistics Summary, *September, 1996.*

Weithorn, L.A. (1988). Mental Hospitalization of Troublesome Youth: An Analysis of Skyrocketing Admission Rates. *Stanford Law Review, 40, 773, 838.*

Zaslaw, J. Ballance, G. The Sociolegal Response: A New Approach to Juvenile Justice in the 90s. *Corrections Today. Feb., 1996, pp. 74–76.*

Zaslaw, J. "Stop Assaultive Children: Project SAC Offers Hope for Violent Juveniles." *Corrections Today. February, 1989, pp. 48–50.*

Jay Zaslaw currently works for Ramsey Youth Services at the Gulf Coast Treatment Center in Ft. Walton Beach, Florida, developing restorative justice and gender specific programs. Prior to this, he served as a probation officer for Plina County Juvenile Court in Tucson, Arizona.

RACIAL DISPARITIES SEEN AS PERVASIVE IN JUVENILE JUSTICE

A SNOWBALLING EFFECT

Study Finds Minority Youths Are Treated More Harshly Throughout the Process

By FOX BUTTERFIELD

Black and Hispanic youths are treated more severely than white teenagers charged with comparable crimes at every step of the juvenile justice system, according to a comprehensive report released yesterday that was sponsored by the Justice Department and six of the nation's leading foundations.

The report found that minority youths are more likely than their white counterparts to be arrested, held in jail, sent to juvenile or adult court for trial, convicted and given longer prison terms, leading to a situation in which the impact is magnified with each additional step into the juvenile justice system.

In some cases, the disparities are stunning. Among young people who have not been sent to a juvenile prison before, blacks are more than six times as likely as whites to be sentenced by juvenile courts to prison. For those young people charged with a violent crime who have not been in juvenile prison previously, black teenagers are nine times more likely than whites to be sentenced to juvenile prison. For those charged with drug offenses, black youths are 48 times more likely than whites to be sentenced to juvenile prison.

Similarly, white youths charged with violent offenses are incarcerated for an average of 193 days after trial,

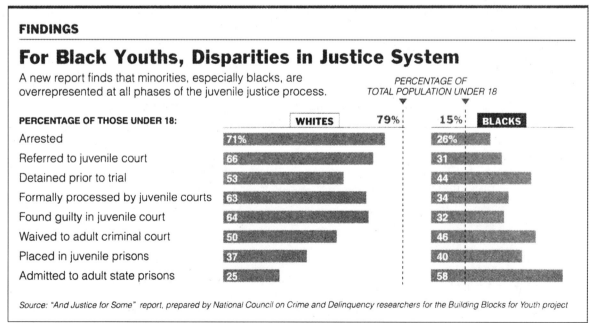

FINDINGS

For Black Youths, Disparities in Justice System

A new report finds that minorities, especially blacks, are overrepresented at all phases of the juvenile justice process.

PERCENTAGE OF TOTAL POPULATION UNDER 18

PERCENTAGE OF THOSE UNDER 18:	WHITES	79%	15%	BLACKS
Arrested	71%		26%	
Referred to juvenile court	66		31	
Detained prior to trial	53		44	
Formally processed by juvenile courts	63		34	
Found guilty in juvenile court	64		32	
Waived to adult criminal court	50		46	
Placed in juvenile prisons	37		40	
Admitted to adult state prisons	25		58	

Source: "And Justice for Some" report, prepared by National Council on Crime and Delinquency researchers for the Building Blocks for Youth project

The New York Times

but blacks are incarcerated an average of 254 days and Hispanics are incarcerated an average of 305 days.

"The implications of these disparities are very serious," said Mark Soler, the president of the Youth Law Center, a research and advocacy group in Washington who also is the leader of the coalition of civil rights and youth advocacy organizations that organized the research project.

"These disparities accumulate, and they make it hard for members of the minority community to complete their education, get jobs and be good husbands and fathers," Mr. Soler said.

The report, "And Justice for Some," does not address why such sharp racial imbalances exist. But Mr. Soler suggested that the cause lay not so much in overt discrimination as in "the stereotypes that the decision makers at each point of the system rely on." A judge looking at a young person, Mr. Soler said, may be influenced by the defendant's baggy jeans or the fact that he does not have a father.

In the past, when studies have found racial disparities in the number of adult black or Hispanic prison inmates, critics have asserted that the cause was simply that members of minorities committed a disproportionate number of crimes. That may be true, Mr. Soler said, but it does not account for the extreme disparities found in the report, nor for disparities at each stage of the juvenile justice process.

"When you look at this data, it is undeniable that race is a factor," Mr. Soler said.

The report, the most thorough of its kind, is based on national and state data initially compiled by the Federal Bureau of Investigation; the Office of Juvenile Justice and Delinquency Prevention, a Justice Department agency; the Census Bureau and the National Center for Juvenile Justice, the research arm of the National Council of Juvenile and Family Court Judges. The report was written by Eileen Poe-Yamagata and Michael A. Jones, senior researchers with the National Council on Crime and Delinquency, in San Francisco.

An unusual feature of the report is that its costs were underwritten by the Justice Department and several leading foundations: the Ford Foundation; the MacArthur Foundation; the Rockefeller Foundation; the Walter Johnson Foundation; the Annie E. Casey Foundation, which specializes in issues relating to young people; and the Center on Crime, Communities and Culture of George Soros's Open Society Institute.

Hugh B. Price, the president of the National Urban League, said that "this report leaves no doubt that we are faced with a very serious national civil rights issue, virtually making our system juvenile injustice."

Mr. Soler and the coalition that put the report together want Congress to give the Justice Department at least $100 million to reduce racial disparities and require states to spend a quarter of their federal juvenile justice grants on the issue.

A spokesman for Representative Bill McCollum, the Florida Republican who is the chairman of the House Judiciary Committee's Subcommittee on Crime, said he would have no comment because he had not seen the report. Mr. McCollum sponsored a bill last year that would have increased the number of juveniles tried in adult court.

Nationally, the report found that blacks under the age of 18 make up 15 percent of their age group, but 26 percent of those young people arrested, 31 percent of those sent to juvenile court, 44 percent of those detained in juvenile jails and 32 percent of those found guilty of being a delinquent. Similarly, young blacks account for 46 percent of all juveniles tried in adult criminal courts, 40 percent of those sent to juvenile prisons and 58 percent of all juveniles confined in adult prisons.

Youth Court Of True Peers Judges Firmly

By SOMINI SENGUPTA

Baseball caps and do-rags are dutifully removed while court is in session. The prosecutor is a deliberative, soft-spoken young man of 16 with a crown of cornrows. The defense lawyer is 16, too, only recently out of jail on a charge of attempted murder. On the six-member jury sits a girl with searing eyes and the memory of juvenile jail still fresh in her mind. And when the accused, a gawky 15-year-old charged with graffiti writing and weapons possession, rattles off the names of gangs he has a "beef" with at school, the courtroom congregation nods and murmurs knowingly.

This is not a high school moot court, where students pretend to be players in a court of law. This is a court of law, a small, quiet experiment in which Bronx teen-agers arrested on misdemeanor charges and even minor felonies—anything from graffiti writing to small-time robberies and drug sales—are judged, quite literally, by a jury of their peers.

They are all first-time defendants. They are referred here by a probation officer or a judge, as an alternative to prosecution in the city's overtaxed Family Court, where children under 16 are tried.

The teenagers who run the Bronx Youth Court, begun two years ago by youths organizing inside the city's juvenile jail, see their mission as what the United States Constitution guarantees: a speedy trial before a jury of one's peers.

Most of them have been through the juvenile justice maze, what they universally call "the system." They know well the inside of a juvenile jail (19 months in the case of Francisca Martinez, 16, the defense lawyer, known in Youth Court as youth advocate). They know how slowly the Family Court can move (three and a half months in detention for one juror, Latoya Orr, accused of stabbing another girl, until a judge ruled in her case).

The court seems to derive its credibility from the youths' firsthand knowledge of the system.

"I never got to talk to my lawyer the way I wanted to," said Miss Martinez, who was convicted of stabbing a girl. "I wanted to be there for somebody, being that nobody was there for me."

The effectiveness of such youth courts is largely unproved, but they have sprung up across the country in the last decade, spurred by frustration with the juvenile justice system.

Today, there are about 650 youth courts nationwide, compared with 50 in 1991, according to the Justice Department's Office of Juvenile Justice and Delinquency Prevention.

They handle mostly nonviolent first-time defendants: children accused of shoplifting, vandalism and other crimes unlikely to be prosecuted otherwise.

"There's a feel-good quality to them," said Jeffrey Butts, a senior research associate with the Urban Institute, a research organization in Washington, who is conducting a national evaluation of youth courts for the Justice Department.

That same quality gives experts like Mr. Butts a sense of déjà vu.

"A hundred years ago, we invented juvenile court to get kids out of the bureaucratic criminal court system," he said. "Now we're inventing youth courts to get them out of juvenile court, or to create alternatives."

There are four such courts in New York City. Two were created by the state, in Harlem and in Red Hook, Brooklyn. A third, in Queens Village, was begun by civic leaders and the city corporation counsel's office, which prosecutes children in Family Court.

All but the Bronx court handle youths arrested for the smallest infractions. One-fourth of the cases tried in the

Brooklyn Youth Court, for example, involve truancy, which is not prosecuted in Family Court.

The Bronx Youth Court is unusual because, operating with the sanction of the city's Probation Department, it tends to judge more serious offenses—drug possession with intent to sell, robbery, weapons charges.

The idea is to steer the accused away from crime and provide some restitution. Among the judges, jurors and lawyers are those whose own sentences included serving in Youth Court.

Not many get off.

Of the roughly 70 youths who have appeared in the Bronx Youth Court in the last two years, only 2 have been, in effect, acquitted, and none have been arrested again, according to Youth Force, the youth-run community group that established the court.

The Probation Department does not keep statistics, though officials there say anecdotal evidence suggests that it is effective.

The other day, as the late afternoon sun streamed in through the barred windows at Youth Force's headquarters in the Mott Haven section of the Bronx, the court was weighing the case of a freshman at Columbus High School.

The police thought he had been a lookout for a graffiti crew. The defendant, who agreed to allow a reporter to attend his trial if his name was not used, said he had merely been standing on the sidewalk, trying to hail a cab, while his friends were "bombing" a wall with graffiti.

Questioning the defendant, the jurors homed in on certain details: the police had found a knife in his pocket, and he had missed nearly three months of school.

"Anybody who carries a knife in their pocket, if they get busted, there should be some sort of consequence," argued Dante Motes, the prosecutor, known in the court as a community impact assessor.

The defendant, removing his baseball cap at Miss Martinez's urging, said he felt unsafe at school. His friends had angered several gangs, and some friends had been shot a couple of weeks before. That was why he was skipping school, he said, and carrying a knife.

"People are looking to jump me, shoot me," he cried. "How you expect me to feel safe?"

Some jurors were skeptical. His friends were shot only two weeks ago, but he had missed school for several months. If he really felt unsafe, why not ask the principal for a transfer to another school?

What did he do in his spare time? Were there youth centers near his home? Why had he been hanging out with these friends, anyway?

So it went for nearly two hours as the jury tried to decipher the penal code and understand the defendant's life better.

His mother, they learned, was in Yugoslavia. He lived with his sister and brother in the Bronx. He was not in a gang. He was trying to transfer to another school. He liked to play football.

After deliberating for 20 minutes in a closed room upstairs, the jury found him "responsible" on two of four counts and sentenced him to a two-hour legal rights workshop (mandatory for all Bronx Youth Court defendants), four hours on a Youth Court jury and 16 hours working on a Youth Force project.

Such projects have included voter registration drives and undercover stings against stores that sell alcohol to minors.

What lasting effect, if any, this will have on the young man remains to be seen. Statistics on recidivism rates of Youth Court defendants are only anecdotal, but supporters of the Bronx Youth Court and others point to the alarmingly high recidivism rates in the juvenile justice system.

A recent study by the State Division of Criminal Justice Services, for example, found that 81 percent of the boys incarcerated in the state juvenile justice system were rearrested within three years of their release.

Organizers of the Bronx Youth Court like to tell their peers how they fared in the juvenile justice system. "From arrest through court through incarceration, we went through feeling confused, powerless and alone," reads a paragraph from a pamphlet given to all defendants. "Almost all of us came out of the system disillusioned, better criminals, less educated and without the resources needed to succeed."

JUVENILE JUSTICE
A CENTURY OF EXPERIENCE

STEVEN A. DRIZIN

Mr. Drizin is a professor at Northwestern University School of Law. From "The Juvenile Court at 100" by Steven A. Drizin, Judicature, *July/August 1999:*

On July 3, 1999, the first juvenile court in the world, founded in Chicago, Illinois, celebrated its 100th birthday. While few outside of Chicago marked this anniversary, I raised a glass to toast the court. For in the past year, as I have worked on activities to commemorate the Chicago court's centennial and immersed myself in its history, I have learned that the juvenile court is one of the most important and enduring contributions the United States has made to the world.

That my enthusiasm is not widely shared outside of Chicago is perhaps understandable. The juvenile court is among the most maligned of American institutions. Attacks on its legitimacy have accompanied it since its inception. Until recently, the court has managed to absorb these assaults and repeatedly transform itself to meet the concerns of critics. In the past 10 years, however, the relentless and heightened pounding of the court by its critics, notably politicians and prosecutors, has begun to take its toll.

Whether the court is able to reassert its legitimacy as it enters its second century is anybody's guess. But if history has proven anything, this much maligned institution has a strong self-preservation instinct. In fact, the court can draw on the lessons from its history as a source of strength in these seemingly desperate times.

LESSONS OF HISTORY

In order to understand the historical importance of the juvenile court, turn your mind's eye back to the turn of the twentieth century for a moment. Imagine what life was like for a small immigrant child, one of millions of such children who along with their parents came to the United States in great waves from Europe. Many lived in abject poverty, crammed in ghettoes and tenement houses. From about the age of seven or eight, they were forced to work to help supplement the family's income. Children often worked long hours in sweatshops, performing menial tasks for many hours at a time when environmentally hazardous factory conditions dotted the urban landscape.

School was a luxury most poor children simply could not afford. Time spent in the classroom meant time away from work and less food on the family table. When not at work or in school, they played in the alleys and the streets on which they lived; there were few if any parks and other public spaces specifically designed for children.

For many years, there was little outcry about these conditions because the world viewed children very differently from the way we've come to think of them. Children had no "rights." They were considered the "property" of their parents (in particular, their fathers) or, if orphaned, the "property" of the state. From about the age of 10 or 11, they were viewed simply as little adults. They even dressed the part. Photographs of children at the turn of the century show young boys in suits with caps and young girls in dresses and skirts—miniaturized versions of their parents.

When children got into trouble, the law treated them no differently than adults. Although children between the ages of 7 and 13 were presumed to be incapable of forming criminal intent, this presumption did not prevent authorities from locking them in adult jails pending trial.

John Altgeld, an aspiring young lawyer who would later become governor of Illinois, observed the prevailing treatment of juveniles in 1882 when he toured the House of Corrections in Chicago, also known as Bridewell. There, he discovered hundreds of children, including some as young as 8 years old, jailed alongside adults. All told, children under 18 made up slightly less than 10 percent of Bridewell's population.

The plight of these children outraged Altgeld. His lectures and writings inspired Jane Addams, Lucy Flower, Julia Lathrop, and others associated with Addams's Hull House to establish a better and more humane justice sys-

 From *Current*, November 1999, pp. 3-8. © 1999 by Steven A. Drizin.

tem for children. Their community organizing and coalition building led to the first juvenile court act in 1899 and the creation of a separate justice system for children, one premised on rehabilitation and individualized justice rather than the crippling punishments and one-size-fits-all sentencing policies of criminal court.

REDEFINING "CHILDHOOD"

The juvenile court was only the start of a remarkable run of child-centered reforms spearheaded by the Hull House women. Soon to follow were such other universal reforms as the child-labor laws; compulsory education laws; the construction of playgrounds, recreation centers, and parks for children; and pioneering work in the area of early childhood education.

These reforms helped redefine "childhood," creating an unprecedented and uniquely American vision of childhood as a sacred period in human life in which children and adolescents required the care and guidance of responsible adults. No longer did society view children as "mini-adults"; it accepted that they were qualitatively and developmentally different, which made them both less culpable for their actions and more amenable to intervention.

To the Chicago reformers, the last thing a civilized society should do to its children was to process and punish them like adults. They believed that government had a moral responsibility to act as "kind and just parents." In the context of a court system, this meant that children should receive individualized attention, under the watchful eyes of trained and sensitive judges and probation officers.

In addition to focusing on delinquent children, the first juvenile court catered to the needs of abused, neglected, and dependent children. Court proceedings were informal, non-adversarial, and closed to the public. The focus on the proceedings was less on whether the child had offended than on "why" and on "what" could be done to prevent reoffending. There were lawyers for neither the state nor the child—only a probation officer who functioned as the "eyes and ears of the court" and whose job was to put into action the treatment plans developed by the court and its experts. The stigmatizing language of the criminal court was rejected, and court records were eventually made confidential to protect children from long-term damage to their future prospects.

The reformers' ideas spread like wildfire, leading to the development of juvenile courts in 46 states, three territories, and the District of Columbia by 1925. Even more remarkable, in the days when there were few highways, let alone superinformation highways, and boat travel still surpassed air travel, the juvenile court movement quickly spread throughout the world. By 1925, Great Britain, Canada, Switzerland, France, Belgium, Hungary, Croatia, Argentina, Austria, India, the Netherlands, Madagascar, Japan, Germany, Brazil, and Spain had all established separate court systems for children. Today, every state has a separate court system for children, as do most nations throughout the world.

CRITICS LEFT AND RIGHT

America's juvenile court system remained largely unchanged throughout the first half of the twentieth century—except that the service functions of the court were gradually taken over by trained professionals rather than the volunteers and untrained staff who served the early courts. And first prosecutors and then defense attorneys began to make appearances in the court.

Then, in the mid 1960s, the juvenile court underwent a radical transformation. Critics from the right attacked the court for its inability to deal with a new breed of delinquent youth, a familiar refrain that would rear its head time and time again throughout the court's history. Critics from the left, caught up in the due process revolution of the 1960s, raised concerns that juvenile court proceedings were arbitrary and unfair and that the court was ignoring the rights of the children who appeared before it.

In a series of decisions in the late 1960s, beginning with the landmark *Kent v. United States* (1966) and *In re Gault* (1967) decisions, the U.S. Supreme Court ordered the juvenile court to protect children's due process rights and provide them with notice of the nature of the charges against them, attorneys to represent them in delinquency proceedings, the right to confront and cross-examine witnesses, and the privilege against self-incrimination.

One effect of the Court's rulings was the replacement of informal, non-adversarial court proceedings with more formal proceedings. After the dust had cleared, the juvenile court more closely resembled the adult criminal court—with the exception that juveniles did not have a constitutional right to a jury trial. Yet many of the protective trappings of the old court remained. Proceedings were largely closed to the public, juvenile records remained confidential, punishments were less severe than in the adult court, and the "best interests of the child" was still as paramount a concern as the "protection of the public."

In the last 20 years, however, particularly during the last decade, the juvenile court has undergone yet another radical transformation. First, critics from the left have zeroed in on the post-*Gault* juvenile court, decrying the "due process" afforded juveniles and calling for the abolishment of the juvenile court. Barry Feld, a University of Minnesota law professor, has led this charge, repeatedly pointing out that even after *Gault* many juveniles do not receive counsel or routinely waive the right to counsel, that the Supreme Court's refusal in *McKeiver v. Pennsylvania* (1971) to give juveniles the right to a jury trial has resulted in less accurate and often biased fact-finding, and that recent trends to criminalize the juvenile court have transformed the court from "its original model as a social service agency into a deficient criminal court that provides people with neither the positive treatment nor criminal procedural justice."

A PROBLEM OF PERCEPTION

In the late 1980s and early 1990s, an alarming increase in the number of juvenile homicides spurred academics like John DiIulio of Princeton and James Alan Fox of Northeastern University to predict a coming tidal wave of "remorseless and morally impoverished youth" because of projected increases in the youth population. These predictions, in turn, resurrected age-old concerns that the court was ill-equipped to deal with this new "breed" of delinquent. The new breed was even given a name: the "juvenile superpredator."

In response, state and federal politicians began to dismantle systematically the remaining protective elements of the juvenile court. Between 1992 and 1995, 41 states passed laws to make it easier to prosecute juveniles as adults. Language in juvenile codes stressing "rehabilitation" and "the best interests of the child" was replaced or augmented with language stressing "punishment" and the "protection of the public." Juvenile records, previously confidential, were made widely accessible, and juvenile proceedings, previously closed to the public, were opened in certain cases. Discretion was taken out of the hands of judges and given to prosecutors, resulting in less individualized justice and more decisions based solely on the nature of the charged offense.

These "reforms" have continued unabated despite the fact that juvenile crime has declined significantly in each of the past six years at the same time that the number of juveniles in the population has increased. These trends have completely discredited the "superpredator" theory and have caused some of the academics who supported it to back away from their earlier predictions.

But politicians continue to demagogue the juvenile crime issue, fueling public perception that there is still an epidemic and that the only way to stem the crime wave is to punish children ever more harshly. In the past three years, 43 states have tinkered further with their transfer laws, increasing the numbers of children tried as adults and housed in adult prisons. According to Amnesty International, some 200,000 children under the age of 18 were tried as adults last year. And some 18,000 children were housed in adult prisons, 3,500 of whom shared living spaces with adults. In defending his pending bill, which would allow 13-year-olds to be jailed with adults, Congressman Bill McCollum recently said of America's children, "They're the predators out there, they're not children anymore. They're the most violent criminals on the face of the earth."

The media are also partly responsible for this perception. Between 1993 and 1996, there was a 30 percent decline in homicides in America. You'd never know it if you watched the evening news. During that same period of time, there was a 721 percent increase in the number of homicides reported on the ABC, CBS, and NBC evening news. Less than one-half of one percent of America's kids were arrested for violent offenses in 1996. Yet two-thirds of the times children are depicted on the evening news, it is in connection with violence.

Factor in the proliferation of crime shows like "Cops" and "America's Most Wanted," entertainment "news" shows, talk radio, and other outlets pounding the steady drumbeat of kids and violence, and you have the makings of a massive misinformation campaign. It's no wonder that Americans believe that juveniles are responsible for 43 percent of all homicides when they're actually responsible for about 10 percent and that 84 percent of adults surveyed in 1996 believed that U.S. teens had committed more crimes that year than during the previous year.

The recent heightened assaults clearly have shaken the court to its roots. So much of the juvenile court founders' unique vision of children as possibility has been discarded—not because children have changed but because adults are no longer willing to devote the time, energy, and resources to guide children through adolescence and because it has become fashionable and politically advantageous to scapegoat all teens based on the actions of a disturbed few.

SAVING AN ENDANGERED SPECIES

How then can admirers and defenders of the court stop history from repeating itself? What can be learned from the court's history, and how can that be applied to get the court off the endangered species list?

Supporters of the court, including judges and court administrators, must do a better job marketing its successes to the public. The simple fact is that juvenile court success stories greatly outnumber its failures. Most children who get into trouble with the law never reoffend, and most whose crimes are so serious that they are referred to the court never come back after court intervention. The juvenile court is also more likely to impose sanctions on violent offenders than the adult court, although adult sanctions are more severe. Both of these statistics rebut the commonly held perception that public safety is not a priority for the juvenile court.

In commemoration of the court's centennial, the Justice Policy Institute and the Children and Family Justice Center of Northwestern University School of Law's Legal Clinic are telling the stories of 25 people who turned their lives around after getting arrested as kids in a new book, *Second Chance: 100 Years of The Children's Court*. In addition to the book, the two groups have jointly produced and disseminated two public service announcements featuring former offenders' success stories and highlighting the importance of giving children second chances.

Success stories are essential in this age of negative campaigning, when publicity about the court's failures [is] guaranteed to be front page news. For every Willie Horton, there are many more Bob Beamons. Supporters of the court must find ways to publicize these successes even though they may be harder to sell to the mainstream media than their negative counterparts.

But publicizing success stories is not a panacea the court's poor public image. The court and its supporters must also fight the misinformation campaign with good, solid empirical research that refutes the claims of the court's opponents. Court officials and supporters rarely tell the public, for example, that juveniles who are kept in juvenile court rather than transferred to adult court are less likely to recidivate. But it's true.

Nor do they inform the public about the horrors of putting children in adult prison: that children are eight times more likely to commit suicide, five times more likely to be sexually assaulted, and twice as likely to be assaulted by staff than if kept in a juvenile facility. Such information is out there and easily available, much of it from the government's own Office of Juvenile Justice and Delinquency Prevention. In order to ensure the court's survival, supporters must fight fire with fire and return every volley from the court's critics.

In addition to repairing its public image, the court must make sure to provide meaningful due process to the children and families it serves. The criticisms of the "abolitionists" must be addressed rather than ignored. Rather than decreasing due process protections for children, the court must provide enhanced protections. The right to counsel for children must be mandatory and nonwaivable, both in the stationhouses and in the courtrooms. The court should employ the best staff—including judges, mental health professionals, prosecutors, defenders, and probation officers—and must demand a first-class, rather than second-class justice for children. All who work at the court must rededicate themselves to the court's historic mission of holding children accountable for their actions in ways that will not cripple their life chances.

And the court must reach out to the communities that it serves—especially the poor and minority communities who make up the bulk of its constituents in urban centers—and find ways for community members to have a voice in the quality of justice dispensed by the court, whether as volunteer mentors or as trained mediators, peer jurors, or community panelists.

In 1925, at a conference marking the 25th anniversary of Cook County's Juvenile Court, Julia Lathrop, one of the Hull House women most responsible for the court's creation, wrote:

Perhaps it is not out of place to remind ourselves that it has been clear from the beginning that the great business of the court is intimately involved in the most delicate and complicated question of social life. The court cannot serve its end unless it is sustained by intelligent public interest and cooperation.

Part of the juvenile court's demise is attributable to misinformation about its failures, but part of it is due to its own inertia. If the court is to survive and flourish into the next century, its supporters must educate the public about its successes and begin not only to court but to shape the public's opinion about its continuing worth.

The Maximum Security Adolescent

The juvenile justice system, founded on the idea that childhood is a distinct stage of life, is being dismantled, with more and more teenagers imprisoned alongside adults. The tough-on-crime crowd has won, but what kind of society has been left behind?

By Margaret Talbot

When Jefferson Alexander Stackhouse was 3 years old, good luck entered his life for the first and maybe the last time. Abandoned as a 2-week-old infant by a schizophrenic mother, Jeff had lived by then in eight different foster homes. But in 1988, he was taken in by a woman who quickly made up her mind to love him and who adopted him two years later. The fact that Jeff came to her "with all his worldly possessions in one very small box" and called every adult female Mommy "not only broke but stole my heart," his adoptive mother, Leslie Stackhouse, says now. Leslie and her then husband, Norman, adopted two more "special needs" children, a girl named Christin and her brother, Casey, who had been taken away from abusive parents when they were toddlers. Leslie's training as a foster parent helped her to go slowly with all three, giving them time to trust her. Though Jeff was withdrawn at first, prone to banging his head against the wall and biting himself, he grew into a happy little boy with a powerful loyalty to his mother.

By the time he hit 14, though, Jeff was getting into the kind of scrapes that keep a mother up at night. Joe Wilson, a family friend who ran a driving school in town, thought Jeff was a good kid who was being picked on because he was small for his age. "I think he was trying to defend himself in a pretty tough neighborhood," Wilson says. Jeff and his friends in Glendale, a working-class Phoenix suburb of low-slung houses, wide boulevards and scruffy palm trees, sneaked out one hot summer evening after curfew to search for loose change in unlocked

cars. Jeff was caught and went through counseling in a juvenile crime deterrence program. A couple of months later, he and another friend stole a bike, which Jeff rode to school and returned later that day.

Then one night, after an argument with his mom, he stalked off down the street. When Leslie caught up with him, he shoved her. His 12-year-old sister was worried enough to call the police, who arrested Jeff for assault, and Leslie figured, "O.K., maybe this isn't so bad, maybe he'll learn a lesson." What Leslie really hoped was that some official would figure out a way to get her son psychological help. Jeff was troubled, she knew—school psychologists told her he had attention-deficit disorder and depression, and though he loved to read, he struggled in school. But Leslie, who works as a school bus driver, had never been able to afford a thorough evaluation for him.

By that time, Jeff was under a kind of house arrest imposed by the juvenile court—he wasn't supposed to leave home alone except to attend school. But on Feb. 23 of this year, he was arrested again. He and three other neighborhood kids his age had been "play boxing," as the police report termed it, at the school bus stop, and Jeff had given one of the boys a bloody lip. After the fight, the boy and his pals set out for Jeff's house, where they called him out on the lawn, got him in a headlock and punched him. Jeff ran into the house, found an unloaded antique shotgun that his mother kept in her closet and brought it out to wave at the other kids, shouting,

"Get off my property!" The three boys headed home in a hurry. No one was hurt, and two of the three did not even want to press charges.

But Jeff Stackhouse's worst luck so far was to have fallen afoul of the law at this particular moment in American judicial history, a moment when the century-old notion of children and adolescents as less culpable and more amenable to rehabilitation than adults has been giving way to an altogether different view. In this new and far harsher view, child criminals are virtually indistinguishable from adult criminals: they are just as capable of forming criminal intent, just as morally responsible, just as autonomous in their actions. Since 1992, 45 states, including Arizona, have passed or amended legislation making it easier to prosecute juveniles as adults. While judges in the juvenile system have always had the authority to send particularly brutal or chronic young offenders into the adult system, state legislatures have been making it easier for less serious wrongdoers to meet the same fate. Because of changes over the last decade, 15 states now grant prosecutors the sole discretion to transfer juveniles into adult court for certain categories of offenses. Twenty-eight states have statutes that automatically remove youths charged with particular crimes—many of them violent crimes, but some property and drug offenses as well—from the jurisdiction of the juvenile system. Though many states allow only children 14 and older to be prosecuted as adults, others have set younger minimum ages—10 in Vermont and Kansas—or no lower limit at all.

While these reforms were often motivated by such nightmarish cases as the school massacres in Jonesboro, Ark., or Littleton, Colo., they have cast a much wider net. Though 66 percent of the juveniles prosecuted as adults in 1994 were charged with violent offenses, according to a Bureau of Justice Statistics report, the remaining 34 percent were charged with property offenses, like burglary and theft, or with drug or public nuisance offenses. As a result, the number of youths under 18 held in adult prisons, and in many cases mixed in with adult criminals, has doubled in the last 10 years or so, from 3,400 in 1985 to 7,400 in 1997. Of the juveniles incarcerated on any given day, one in 10 are in adult jails or prisons.

Arizona is one of the states where prosecutors can bump a juvenile case into adult court at their own discretion. It is also a state with a number of mandatory sentencing laws. Jeff Stackhouse was charged as an adult on three separate counts of aggravated assault with a dangerous weapon. Since the boys Jeff pulled his unloaded gun on were all under 15, the prosecutor also had the option of classifying the assault as a so-called dangerous crime against children, and he did. If Jeff Stack-

house is convicted, he could be sentenced to a minimum of 30 years in prison.

Earlier this summer, the attorney assigned to him, a young public defender named Douglas Passon, was still hoping to get the case sent back to the juvenile court, which would most likely put Jeff in a juvenile detention facility until he is 18. That's a long shot; once a case is sent to adult court, it almost always stays there. Assuming Jeff remains in the adult system, the best-case scenario would be probation, which wouldn't get him any psychological counseling but would at least keep him out of the penitentiary. For now, the prosecutor has offered 10 years in an adult prison, which Passon thinks is no kind of deal at all. Still, he realizes "that at some point I may be asking Jeff to make up his mind about that. This is a kid who's not old enough to see an R-rated movie by himself, and we're telling him he's old enough to go to prison and get jumped in the showers. We're asking him to make decisions that will affect his entire life in ways he can't even imagine."

When you are 14, it's not easy to project yourself into the future with any sense of clarity; for Jeff Stackhouse, maybe that's a good thing. The present—which is to say, the Madison Street Jail in downtown Phoenix, a multistory building that resembles a particularly ugly parking garage—is overwhelming enough. I visited Jeff in jail one day in June, when it was 107 outside, but fluorescent-lighted and as weatherless as a casino inside. Jeff had been in jail since February. A jocular female guard escorted him into the room, and because I was accompanied by his lawyer, I was permitted to sit on the same side of the Plexiglas partition with him. When his mother comes, she has to sit on the other side, with the signs that say "No Kissing. No Hugging" in clear view, and as Jeff tells me, "she just cries and cries."

Jeff Stackhouse is short, with clear hazel eyes, a face still softened by puppy fat and no hint of a whisker. He wears a faded jail-issue jumpsuit, the old-fashioned black-and-white-striped kind, orange rubber thongs and handcuffs. He is soft-spoken and polite—sweet is the word, really. I had been wondering what somebody his

Jeff Stackhouse's misfortune was to have fallen afoul of the law at a moment when the century-old notion of children as less culpable and more amenable to rehabilitation than adults has been giving way to an altogether different view.

age missed most in jail, and that was the first question I asked him. He said he missed his mom, his sister and his dog.

Jeff is housed in a unit with other juveniles, but many of them are 17 and 18, and some are gang members. There are classes for the juveniles held here, but Jeff gets nervous leaving his cell. When he does, he says, "Guys hit me in the head or take my latrine supplies, tell me they're going to beat me up. And if I hit 'em back, then I'd get in trouble and I couldn't see my mom." He has asked to be put in protective custody, but so far his request has not been granted. And even when he feels brave enough to face school, he says it's "too easy. They're doing plurals and nouns and capitalization. Third-grade work. There was a guy here—I think he was on paint chips for a while. He didn't know what the letter Y was. I kind of felt sorry for him."

Jeff says there is nothing he has got used to about being in jail, but in some small way, I see, he has already adapted. He has a tattoo now, eked out on one thin wrist with battery acid, shampoo and a staple. It says C-A-S-E-Y, which was his brother's name. When Jeff was 7, Casey, then 5, drowned in a lake near Phoenix where their dad had taken the three kids for a fishing trip on the day before Mother's Day. Jeff saw it happen. Leslie and her husband split up after that—the accident drove them apart, she says, "because I was looking for Casey in the Bible, wondering what heaven was like for him, and my husband was looking for him in the bottle"—and Jeff has hardly seen his father since. In jail, Jeff had been dreaming about Casey, and in one dream he looked down at his hand and saw his brother's name there. When he got up that morning, he told his cellmate he was ready; he wanted a tattoo. Only he is still kid enough to be embarrassed about his decision. "It was kind of dumb because my mom got real mad about it," he says glumly.

As it happens, Jeff is not the only 14-year-old boy sitting in the Madison Street Jail that day. A boy named Marco is there, too, and has been for nearly a year. Like Jeff, he is the sort of kid who, not so long ago, would have been kept within the juvenile system and considered a candidate for psychological intervention rather than adult-style punishment. Before his arrest, on July 30, 1999, Marco, who is the oldest child of Mexican immigrants—his mother works for a furniture company and his father drives a forklift—had never been in any kind of trouble. He was a small, shy, bright boy who did well in school. Soon after he turned 14, however, Marco was arrested for sexually molesting his 7-year-old sister. His mother confronted him with the charge, and when he admitted his guilt, she turned her son in. "I told him that I was going to take my daughter to the doctor," she said in an interview with the police. "If the doctor diagnosed that he had abused her, I was going to have to turn him over to the police. . . . When you make a mistake, you have to pay for it."

I didn't meet Marco that day, but I talked to his lawyer, an energetic, no-nonsense woman named Frances Gray, who is 47 and came to the law after a career as a software programmer for Bell Atlantic. Gray liked Marco and was worried about his fate. "Charged in the adult system," she wrote me in an e-mail message after our meeting, "his offenses mandate adult prison—five years minimum" in the one adult facility in Arizona that takes juveniles. But, Gray wrote, the prison has "no counseling programs for juvenile sex offenders like my client. All of the research on juvenile sex offenders emphasizes the importance of, and amenability to, treatment for this vulnerable age group." In fact, the only thing prison could do for kids like Marco was to "segregate them so they don't get beaten up by the general population (all sex offenders are preyed upon in jails and prisons) until they turn 18 and are thrown to the 'wolves' in the adult sex offender treatment program."

When I talked to Gray, she had been assembling evidence about juvenile sex offenders in general and Marco in particular, and what she had found made her only more determined to get him into treatment in the juvenile system. In the first place, Marco admitted what he had done and showed remorse. "Please tell Mom and Dad that I'm sorry," he wrote to the victim, his sister Helena, on the night he was arrested. "I can't imagine the pain and hurt this is causing them. I hope that someday they will forgive me as well. Helena, I'm sorry I ever did this to you, especially for your being my sister. . . . You can't even imagine how bad and guilty I feel about what I did." In the second place, he had not fondled any other children, nor had he tried to lure any others to him with candy or other bribes. "He is a young man who is in need of therapeutic assistance," concluded a psychologist and sexual-abuse expert who evaluated him. "However, I do not see him as an individual who represents a high risk for subsequent victimization of others around him."

At home in the evenings, Gray couldn't get the case out of her mind. She feared that if Marco went to prison as a boy, he would emerge as a man beyond reach. "You tell kids, If you don't shape up, you go to prison. And then you have a first offense and you're sent to prison. What more can society hold over you?" She thought she had some good evidence about Marco's prospects for rehabilitation, and her research had convinced her that the majority of sexual offenses committed by adolescents were one-time events—especially if the kids got help. But she also knew that lawyers trying to keep juveniles out of adult prison were playing a much harder game now.

One hundred years ago, when progressive-era reformers first invented the idea of a separate justice system for juveniles, it was boys like Jeff and Marco they had in mind. Nearly everything about the newly created juvenile court, from its paternalistic ethos to its central tenet that juveniles were not to be confused with hardened criminals to its goal of sentencing "in the best interest of the child," represented a radical break with the past and a pledge of faith in the malleability of youth. Until then, children had been tried, sentenced, imprisoned and sometimes executed alongside adults.

The common-law tradition did offer some recognition that young children were different from adults. Children under 7 who committed crimes were presumed not to be responsible for them and could not be punished. But after that, the question of culpability got murkier. Those between the ages of 7 and 14 were generally thought to lack responsibility for their actions. Those between 14 and 21 were presumed capable of forming criminal intent and were therefore punishable. Yet as early as the 1820's, judges who had to sentence juveniles in criminal court worried openly about the implications of putting young people behind bars. Letting them off scot-free was neither morally nor socially acceptable, but sending them to jail or prison with adults was like consigning them, in the words of one judge, to a "nursery of vices and crimes, a college for the perfection of adepts in guilt."

By the turn of the century, these qualms had spread widely enough to make jury nullification a problem: jurors were acquitting young lawbreakers rather than imposing sentences that would lock them up with adults. At the same time, the emerging child-study movement and the new specialty of pediatrics helped popularize the idea that childhood was a distinct phase of life and that adolescents, in particular, moved through discrete developmental stages, which adults had a duty to try and understand. Like compulsory school-attendance laws and bans on child labor, the juvenile court was a product of this new approach to childhood. It was to be presided over by a judge in street clothes, not a black robe, seated at a desk, where he could easily put a reassuring arm around a troubled lad.

In 1899, Illinois established the first juvenile court; by 1925, 46 states had done the same. The idea of a justice system tailored for children sank deep roots in American culture. In fact, it was not until the late 1960's that the system came under any real questioning. Paradoxically, the assault was launched by the civil liberties left. Because the juvenile court was supposed to be helping the accused child and because it shielded his identity in a way the criminal court did not, it was liberated from the necessity for due process protections—the right to counsel, the right to confront witnesses, the privilege against self-incrimination and so forth. The trouble with this arrangement was that it offered the court nearly unlimited authority to confine youths while it devised cures for their antisocial behavior.

The civil liberties critique of the juvenile justice system found its most powerful expression in the Supreme Court's 1967 decision in the Gault case. On June 8, 1964,

Gerald Gault, a 15-year-old boy living in Gila County, Ariz., made an obscene phone call to his neighbor, one Mrs. Cook. (He wondered, quaintly enough, if she had "big bombers.") Mrs. Cook called the sheriff, who arrested the boy; his mother came home from work and found Gerald missing, with no explanation. At two subsequent hearings, Mrs. Cook never appeared, no other witnesses were sworn and no transcript made. Yet in the end, the judge ordered Gerald committed to a juvenile facility until his 21st birthday—even though the maximum sentence for an adult who committed the same crime would have been two months in jail or a $50 fine. When the Supreme Court acted on the case, it concluded in irate language that Gerald's constitutional rights had been breached by "a kangaroo court"—and extended to juveniles all due process rights except that of a jury trial.

Gault was a necessary reform for a system that had become too arbitrary. But instead of leading to further constructive reforms, it led to full-scale rebellion: Gault helped open the door to the dismantling of the juvenile justice system. It galvanized a liberal movement for emancipation of minors that cast them as rights-bearing autonomous citizens, barely distinguishable from adults. It also "energized the tough-on-crime constituency," says Steven Drizin, the supervising attorney at the Children and Family Justice Center at the Northwestern University School of Law. "The juvenile court has been fighting the sound bite ever since that if you give kids adult rights, you can give them adult time, too." Of course, kids, some of them anyway, weren't helping matters. A spike in the juvenile crime rate in the early 1990's and a cluster of school shootings in the latter years of the decade all created the impression that young people were getting away with murder.

Even after the juvenile crime rate fell precipitously in the late 90's, this sentiment continued to gain currency, as Franklin Zimring, a criminal-law professor at the University of California at Berkeley, points out, because "a punishment gap was opening between the adult and juvenile systems. The tough-on-crime crowd had won the war in the criminal system; now they looked at the juvenile court and said, 'Hey, we've got to make it look more like the adult version.'" Increasingly, the focus was on the offense, not the offender.

'Animals,' the judge told Jessica Robinson, convicted of robbing and assaulting her grandparents, 'don't treat their families the way you treated your family.'

"What I noticed," says Stephen Harper, an assistant public defender in Miami who has handled cases in which juveniles were transferred to the adult system, "is that there was much less curiosity about who a kid was, why he might have done what he did. Was there abuse in his background, neglect, a drug-addicted parent?" Indeed, as more and more states began transferring kids to adult court, it became clear that youth itself would not be considered a mitigating circumstance. There was no contemporary legal precedent for going easier on a 14-year-old than a 40-year-old in criminal court—that's what juvenile court had been for, after all. And in any case, the new mandatory sentencing laws left judges little opportunity for leniency.

The new attitude meant passing laws that allowed more and more kids to be sent to adult court at younger and younger ages—many of them poor, a disproportionate number of them black. It also meant breaking the old taboo against dispatching the young to adult prisons, those "nurseries of vices and crimes" that advocates of the juvenile court had long lamented.

When Jessica Robinson was 13, she took part in a crime that Judge Barbara Levenson called "horrible, vile" and one of the most "deeply saddening" cases she had ever heard in her courtroom. On July 12, 1997, animated by a vague plan to go to Disney World with their spoils, Jessica and two older teenagers robbed her grandparents in their Miami home. It was Jessica who knocked on the door, calling, "Grandma, I need to talk to you." Once inside, she and another girl ransacked the house, snatching up jewelry, cash, liquor and clothes, while the 16-year-old boy with them slashed the furniture and the hand of Jessica's grandfather. At one point, the boy led Jessica's grandparents onto a glassed-in porch, where he threatened to kill them. Neither of the victims was seriously harmed, but as her grandmother testified at Jessica's sentencing: "Me and her grandpa is not young anymore. Our lives have been destroyed. We are terrified to go to our door." And she added plaintively, "I would like to ask her: 'Why? Why, honey?'"

Though Jessica had not actually wielded the knife or herded the victims onto the porch, she was charged with assault and armed kidnapping as well as armed robbery and sentenced to nine years in an adult prison. Asked to apologize to her grandparents during the trial, she at first refused, then managed only an impassive "I'm sorry" at the sentencing. "Animals," Judge Levenson told her, "don't treat their families the way you treated your family."

Jessica's family had never been much of a haven. Her mother left her dad, whom she described to Jessica's lawyers as abusive, in 1986, when the girls were 3 and 6. "I was scared," she told Claudia Kemp, a student at the Florida State University College of Law who is working on an appeal for Jessica, "scared that either he would eventually kill me or I would have to kill him in order to protect myself and the children." The family moved from Austin, Tex., to Miami, and Jessica has not seen her father since.

In Miami, Jessica's mother found a one-bedroom apartment in a housing project for her and the girls and worked as a waitress on the night shift at Denny's. She told Kemp that she often felt exhausted and frustrated, and that when she did, she would hit Jessica with a belt or her hand. Still, until Jessica entered the seventh grade, she seems to have caused little trouble at school or at home. A family friend thought of her as "a very normal, sweet kid" who loved to swim, sing and ride her bike. At 13, though, Jessica started getting into fights at home—on one occasion, throwing a plate at her 16-year-old sister; on another, biting her mother's hand. According to juvenile records, she repeatedly ran away for weeks at a time, occasionally staying at the apartment of a drug dealer in his 20's named Shorty.

A psychologist who evaluated her after one of these incidents described her as a girl of average intelligence, "cooperative with the examiner," but suffering from a "severe conduct disorder." A psychiatrist thought Jessica was "extremely childish and coquettish." Both evaluators recommended that Jessica be placed in a secure residential treatment center where she could receive therapy and a more definitive diagnosis. Instead, she was released into her grandparents' care; and when she quarreled with them, too, her grandmother called the police and Jessica was arrested again. Jessica told Kemp that her motivation for helping to rob her grandparents stemmed from this fight, that she was driven by "nothing but revenge."

On July 30, 1998, Jessica arrived at Jefferson Correctional Institution, a women's prison with conspicuous gun towers and a tough reputation, located 30 miles east of Tallahassee. At 14, she was then the youngest female in the Florida correctional system and the object of considerable curiosity. In the dining hall or the exercise yard, other prisoners strained for a good look at her, this lethargic girl with big green eyes, dirty blond hair hanging straight down her back and a prison-issue uniform that billowed over her slight frame. Within her first few weeks at Jefferson, Jessica tried to commit suicide. For a long time, her lawyers say, she seemed genuinely confused about the parameters of prison life. She kept asking them if she could just go out for a couple of hours with them—to the beach or to Taco Bell, maybe—and come back that night.

In prison, Jessica has found surrogate mothers to replace the real one who has yet to visit her incarcerated daughter. Jessica's first mother was a stocky, gray-haired woman named Susanne Manning, who was serving a 25-year term for embezzlement. Manning had a 13-year-old son of her own on the outside, and she pushed Jessica to do her homework, bought her snacks, read her "The Little Mermaid" and kept her out of fights when

Any child 14 or younger is too unformed, too vulnerable, too easily swayed, too limited in his understanding of the criminal process to be subjected to it in full force.

she could. "An embezzler is about the most trustworthy type you can find in prison," says Paolo Annino, a lawyer with the Children's Advocacy Center at the Florida State University College of Law who is representing Jessica in her appeal. "It's a lot better than having some slasher take you under her wing."

In October of last year, however, Jessica was transferred to Dade County Correctional Institution, near Miami. Her "family" at Dade is larger and more elaborate than it was in Tallahassee—it includes women whom Jessica calls her grandparents, great-grandparents, uncles, cousins, sisters, brothers. It is also considerably rougher, and for this reason, it is easy to see how a girl could settle into a life not just of crime but of truly depraved crime. The woman Jessica now refers to as Mommy, a beautiful, blue-eyed, heavily tattooed 29-year-old with the nickname Blackie, is serving a life sentence for murder. She and a male accomplice robbed two elderly people and cut their throats with a machete. The other Dade prisoner who wanted to be Jessica's mommy—they staged a sort of custody battle—stole an elderly man's checks with an accomplice, who then beat the man to death.

At Dade, Jessica isn't going to class anymore to get her G.E.D. "In a juvenile facility, you're required to attend school; in an adult prison, you're not," Kemp says. "Jessica's a teenager, and she finds a lot of reasons not to." She goes to her prison family for advice now. They don't think much of school, but in their way, they spoil her. On her 16th birthday, they made Jessica a cake out of Pop-Tarts and melted chocolate bars from the canteen; they buy her cigarettes; they think her street-girl swagger is cute. "She gets a lot of attention," says Kemp. "It's a mixed-up world in there, and there's a value to being associated with her."

Annino and Kemp are trying to get Jessica transferred to a juvenile facility where she can receive psychological counseling and an education. When Annino first met Jessica, he concluded his interview by asking, as he asks all his clients, what she wanted from her association with him. Jessica "looked up sort of sleepily and said, 'Milk,'" Annino recalls. "She wanted more milk than she was getting in the prison diet, which is based on the nutritional needs of an adult. I have an 8-year-old at home, and that

really struck me." As for Kemp, she is 47, with three daughters of her own, and says she couldn't help feeling protective of her client. "When you first meet her, she seems very defiant. She's got this heavy street accent. But when you spend time with her, you see she's still such a child. She whines; she fidgets. She wants your attention; she wants to be taken care of; she wants you to tell her to take her medication." Miami is a long way from Tallahassee, though, and her lawyers hardly ever see Jessica in person anymore.

If their appeal fails, Jessica will get out of prison when she is 22. She will have no education beyond the sixth grade, no job skills, no friends her age and no experience of ordinary, unincarcerated life after the age of 13. What she will have is a felony record—unlike the juvenile courts, adult courts do not preserve anonymity—and a collection of "mothers" and mentors, among whom a convicted embezzler is by far the most wholesome. She will have been raised by wolves, and then she will be released, like most juveniles convicted in adult court, when she is still young enough to commit many more crimes.

THE BODY OF RESEARCH ON JUVENILES IN ADULT PRISON is not especially large. Until recently, there weren't enough Jessica Robinsons to warrant systematic information-gathering. It isn't even all that easy to locate young inmates, in part because states have adopted different policies about how and where to house them. "The majority of states follow a practice of dispersing young inmates in the general prison population," says Dale Parent, a project director with the research firm Abt Associates in Cambridge, Mass., which is conducting a long-term study on juveniles in state prison systems. "They might not put a small, vulnerable adolescent in a cell with a sex offender, but other than that, they do not segregate the youth, and they have no separate programs for them. A few states have extreme segregation—physically separate housing units where youthful offenders have no contact with the adult population—or arrangements with the state juvenile facility where they spend a few years there and are transferred to prison on their 18th birthdays."

There are plenty of reasons to keep juvenile offenders away from the adult prison population. In general, young prisoners are more vulnerable than adults to sexual exploitation and physical brutalization. They are more likely than older inmates to commit suicide. They are more likely than young people in juvenile detention facilities to be physically assaulted and to return to a life of crime when they are set free.

None of this should come as any surprise. Prison populations are not only older, larger and more criminally experienced than juvenile detention populations, they are also more violent. (Nearly 50 percent of prison inmates are violent offenders, while only 20 percent of juvenile training school residents are.) Prisoners tend to be much more idle than juveniles in detention. Only one-third of state prison inmates work more than 34 hours a week, and only half take classes. In juvenile facilities, on the other hand, kids spend most of the day in school, vocational-training, group counseling, substance abuse programs and the like and are encouraged to form bonds with their counselors and teachers. When Donna Bishop, a professor of criminology at Northeastern University, interviewed minors in juvenile and adult facilities in Florida, she concluded that youths in prison "spent much of their time talking to more skilled and experienced offenders who taught them new techniques of committing crime and methods of avoiding detection."

An earlier study that Bishop and Charles Frazier conducted in Florida points to the effects of such environments on recidivism. Thousands of young offenders are sent to criminal court in Florida each year. But because so many of those transfers come about at the discretion of prosecutors, thousands of other juveniles, charged with equally serious crimes, are not. Bishop and Frazier were thus able to match by age, race, gender, current charges and past criminal record 2,738 juveniles who had been prosecuted as adults with 2,738 who had stayed in the juvenile system. Over a period of up to two years, they found that 30 percent of the teenagers prosecuted in criminal court were rearrested; the figure for those who had gone through the juvenile system was 19 percent. Transfers also proved more likely to be arrested for more serious offenses.

For all these reasons, many prison and jail officials would rather they never had to deal with youthful inmates at all. "We don't want juveniles locked up with adults," says Ken Kerle, the managing editor of American Jails magazine, the official publication of the American Jails Association. "I don't think we're doing the country any good by going back to Square 1 and chucking the whole idea of a separate system for juveniles. You can't handle kids like you handle adults. They're mercurial; they've got a lot of emotional growing-up to do. They need education, they need exercise and they need guards who have some insight into them. Put 'em in adult facilities, and they come out worse than when they went in."

Last year, the American Correctional Association, the professional organization that represents prison staffs, passed a resolution in favor of limiting transfers from juvenile to criminal court as sharply as possible, holding youthful offenders only where they can be entirely separate from adults and developing new training in adolescent psychology for those prison officials who are forced to manage the very young. Corrections-industry journals, meanwhile, have been particularly blunt when it comes to laying out the practical dilemmas of treating children as adults. "If inmates under the age of 18 are housed with the general population," a writer in Corrections Today asked recently, "does this mean adult systems should treat them like adults in every way or does it mean that special considerations should be made to

their questionable adult status? Can a youthful offender be sold tobacco products? . . . Can an incarcerated juvenile file a child-abuse complaint against prison officials?" These are far from hypothetical questions. "Unless a parent or guardian signs permission for it," says Elisa Corrado, a social worker who works with imprisoned juveniles in Miami, "they can't get a Tylenol. They're still minors, even if they're in adult prison."

IF WE ARE GOING TO KEEP PROSECUTING JUVENILES AS ADULTS, one thing it would surely be useful to know is what children can understand, at different ages, about the criminal process. To what degree can a child at 10 or 12 or an adolescent at 14 or 15 be expected to participate in his or her own defense? Is immaturity, like insanity or mental retardation, a form of incompetence—an effective limitation on a defendant's capacity to comprehend the charges and proceedings against him? When the Supreme Court asserted in its 1962 decision in Gallegos v. Colorado that "a 14-year-old boy, no matter how sophisticated. . . is not equal to the police in knowledge and understanding . . . and is unable to know how to protect his own interests or how to get the benefits of his constitutional rights," there may have been a general consensus that this was true. But now many judicial experts on both left and right hold a vision of children as competent legal decision-makers, reared on cop shows and Court TV and casually familiar with their due-process rights and how to demand them.

These questions acquire a particular poignancy when it comes to the investigative stage of a crime, during which young suspects are interviewed by the police. Children, especially those 12 and under, are much more likely to waive their rights. (In one study, 90 percent of juvenile suspects waived their rights to silence and to counsel, compared with 60 percent of adults.) And they are much more likely to say what they think adults want to hear, especially if they think it means they can go home soon. The 7- and 8-year-old boys accused of sexually assaulting and killing 11-year-old Ryan Harris in Chicago two years ago—and later cleared of all charges—were enticed to confess over a McDonald's Happy Meal. An 11-year-old boy who now says he falsely confessed to murdering his elderly neighbor wanted to get the police interview over with so he could go home to his younger brother's birthday party. "Kids confess all the time," says Mara Siegel, a deputy public defender in Phoenix. "They talk to the police all the time. It can drive you crazy."

Mark Chaffin, a pediatrician and psychologist at the University of Oklahoma Health Sciences Center, agrees that children are particularly vulnerable to offering false confessions. "Tendencies like wanting to please, wanting to say what they think the adult authority figure wants to hear or misunderstanding the situation," he says, all leave children at risk. "I think law-enforcement officials know how to interview people who are mentally retarded or psychotic," he adds. "But there's not a lot of specific training about how you interview a 10-year-old suspect."

A few states require the presence of an "interested adult"—usually a parent—when a child is being interrogated, but most do not. So what should be done? "My recommendation," says Thomas Grisso, a forensic psychologist at the University of Massachusetts Medical School, "is that kids 14 or under who are being questioned should have at least a parent available. Even if they don't have good relationships with their parents, the parents are still the people they look to for their buffer, their protection."

By the age of 14, several studies have shown, most children can accurately explain the purpose of trials and the role of judges and juries and can offer reasonably accurate definitions of a right. Children under 14, however, have a much weaker grasp on these concepts. Studies that have looked at juveniles' understanding of specific Miranda rights have found that adolescents 15 and older generally comprehend them about as well as adults, but that younger children frequently misconstrue them. According to Grisso, many children understood "the right to remain silent" to mean "they should remain silent until they were told to talk." To one boy who took Grisso's Miranda comprehension test, the right to remain silent simply meant "don't make noise."

Recent insights from neuroscience tend to support the notion that teenagers really are different from adults, and in precisely the ways anyone who has ever been a teenager might think. Researchers at the National Institutes of Mental Health have used brain imaging, for example, to show that both the frontal lobe and the corpus callosum, the cable of nerves connecting the left and right sides of the brain, are still underdeveloped in adolescence. And they surmise that until those parts of the brain have fully matured, they can contribute to greater impulsiveness and wider and more frequent mood swings. "Teenagers," Jay Giedd of the N.I.M.H. said in a speech last year, "don't utilize inhibitory pathways as well as their parents do to moderate their impulses." (To which their parents, anyway, might say, "Duh.")

Still, we are unlikely to return to an era when the juvenile system held sway over all lawbreakers under 18. And besides, limbically challenged or not, a 17-year-old clearly isn't as deserving a candidate for leniency as, say, a 12-year-old. Laurence Steinberg, a Temple University psychologist who heads a research project on adolescent development and juvenile justice, would rather see the law adopt more subtle dividing lines. "Most people older than 16 are not greatly distinguishable from adults on the relevant competencies—the ability to think through future consequences, for example," he says. "On the other hand, people 13 and under really do not have these abilities. For them, adult court should not be an issue."

The tricky ages, says Steinberg, are 14, 15 and sometimes 16. In that age range, some adolescents—especially those with emotional or learning difficulties, which would include many kids in the criminal justice system—are childlike in important respects, while others are quite mature.

There will always be some juveniles who deserve to be tried and punished in the adult system, either because their crimes are particularly coldblooded or because they have been given repeated chances to reform and repeatedly failed to do so. Even some of the staunchest advocates for juveniles concede that a few of them are irredeemably dangerous. "I'm a believer that there is true evil in the world," Darrow Soll, a former public defender and prosecutor in Phoenix told me. "I'm not so foolish as to think that every child can be saved just because of their age. But an effort has to be made. There are a few who you say no juvenile system in the world is going to be able to save. But in my experience, those are definitely the exceptions."

The majority of young offenders dabble in crime and grow out of the urge to do so. "Self-report studies indicate that most teenage males engage in some criminal conduct," notes Elizabeth Scott, a law professor, in a recent essay, "leading criminologists to conclude that participation in delinquency is 'a normal part of teen life.'" And think about it for a minute: did you ever do anything illegal as a teenager? (Yes, drugs and booze count.)

"I had juvenile referrals when I was a kid," says Soll, who is now a criminal defense attorney with a posh Phoenix firm. "And if I came into the system now, I'd probably be incarcerated. I wouldn't have gotten into the military. I wouldn't have gotten an education. I sure wouldn't have entered the bar." One of Soll's oddest moments as a public defender came when he was called upon to represent a 15-year-old boy charged in criminal court and facing a possible four-year prison sentence for stealing a golf cart and setting it on fire. "What was weird about it was that I had done virtually the same thing when I was that age," says Soll. He is 34 and a natty dresser with a bemused, cherubic face and a roster of well-heeled clients. But he grew up working class in Glendale, Jeff Stackhouse's neighborhood.

"O.K., in my case, I took the golf cart and drove it into the pool at school—big prank," Soll explains. "But I went to court, and I had this Roy Bean-type judge who said, 'Son, in the old days I could have sent you into the Army, and I can't now, but that's what I'd do with you.' And I did go into the Army, and I became a paratrooper, and it was a great educational experience for me and a lot of other rough-and-tumble kids like me. A whole lot better than fending off gangs in the state pen. If I'd done that today, I'd have a felony conviction and they wouldn't even let me in the Army." He whistles under his breath. "Boy, you don't want to be the parent of a teenager these days."

Last month, I visited Phoenix again. Jeff was still in jail, though in protective custody at last. Not much had changed for him, though he seemed a little more comfortable and, with a sprinkling of acne on his chin, a little older. Marco, on the other hand, was 24 hours away from being moved to prison in Tucson. Having pleaded guilty to two counts of attempt to molest, he had been sentenced to five years in prison. His lawyer, Frances Gray, had to see him one last time, to fill out some paperwork, so she invited me to come along.

When Gray and I enter the visiting room, Marco is waiting for us, slumped over on a molded plastic chair, staring at his feet. This is the first time I have met him in person. He has big, dark, scared-looking, myopic eyes; he ought to be wearing glasses, but they're broken. After a brief and awkward introduction, he mumbles: "Miss Gray, they've changed my status. I'm not minimum security anymore. Do you know how come?"

The lawyer, wearing a floral-print blouse and a black cardigan against the air-conditioned chill, has her back to us while she writes. "Well, Marco, you've been sentenced," she says crisply. "You're not presumed innocent anymore. You're considered a greater escape risk."

"Oh," he says. "I thought maybe it was something I did, but I couldn't think what."

We're quiet for a while, trying to avoid the slack-jawed stares of three guys in the visiting room behind us, who have their noses literally pressed against the window. "Miss Gray," says Marco, softly. "You know what I've heard about prison? I've heard that everything's really racial there—that they make you join a gang, even if you don't want to. The guards say, 'You want to go with the Mexicans or what?' There's a guy here, he's 15, he made a bad mistake. He told people he's half black and half Mexican. Now, when he goes to prison, everybody's going to beat him up."

As she turns around to face him, Gray reminds Marco that she is not his lawyer anymore.

"You're not?"

"No, now you'll be assigned an appeal lawyer by the public defender's office. But that doesn't mean you can't write to me. Keep studying, O.K.? Get your G.E.D. Stay out of trouble in there. Because if you do, you have a chance of making some kind of life for yourself when you get out. O.K.?"

Before we go, I ask Marco if he thinks jail, where he has been for more than a year—his family never could muster the $9,600 bail—has changed him. "Yeah," he says. "It's hard to explain. I know how to start a fight now, let's put it that way." He doesn't say anything for a while, and then he adds: "When I first came here, I didn't know what to do. I didn't even know there was a Madison Street Jail. Now when the new guys come, they look at me like I'm supposed to tell them what to do, like I'm the old-timer."

I don't know quite what to say to Marco when we leave, so, lamely, I say, "Good luck." The automatic doors close behind us, and crisp, no-nonsense Frances Gray bursts into tears. "You see, they don't know, these kids don't know, and I do. They think the worst of it is being locked up. When I first saw Marco, he was this petrified little kid. All he wanted was to go home. Now all he can think about is, How many days, how many hours do I have to be in prison? He doesn't know the worst of it is when he gets out, and he's a convicted sex offender and he can't get a job and he can't be around anyone under 18, and he can't live with his family because he can't be around his sister."

We walk outside, into the glare of downtown Phoenix. I'm thinking that nothing good is going to come of sending Jeff or Marco to prison. Some older adolescents—16- and 17-year-olds, especially—do belong in adult court. Others in that age range would be good candidates for an innovative strategy called blended sentencing, which is now being used in 19 states. Under this practice, young offenders serve their time in juvenile facilities until they are 18 or 21, but have an additional sentence in adult prison hanging over them if officials think they still pose a danger. But any child 14 or younger—and make no mistake, it is children we are talking about—is too unformed, too vulnerable, too easily swayed, too limited in his understanding of the criminal process to be subjected to it in full force.

"You know," Gray says, "I was a public defender in Virginia for a while, and I sometimes had to work in the juvenile court there, and I hated it—the wishy-washiness of it, the endless hearings. Now, here I am dealing with kids where they were never meant to be, in criminal court, where none of us are prepared to deal with them. And I would give my front teeth—my front teeth—to have a situation where there wasn't a final disposition, where you weren't sealing some kid's fate forever."

Margaret Talbot is a contributing writer for the magazine and a fellow at the New America Foundation.

Juvenile Probation on the Eve of the Next Millennium

BY RONALD P. CORBETT JR.

JUDGE JUDITH SHEINDLIN, supervising judge for the Manhattan Family Court, published in 1996 her perspective on the state of affairs in juvenile justice, titled *Don't Pee on My Leg and Tell Me It's Raining*. Judge Sheindlin's views, graphically implied in the title, include a repudiation of the social causation approach to juvenile delinquency and a call for a return to an ethic of self-discipline and individual accountability. From the vantage point of over twenty years experience as a juvenile judge, Sheindlin sees a system that can "barely function" (p. 5), trading in empty threats and broken promises. Juvenile courts in her view have avoided assigning blame for wrongdoing and have thereby encouraged a lack of individual responsibility, leaving young offenders with ready excuses for their predatory behavior and completely without fear of any consequences. The system must "cut through the baloney and tell the truth," starting with the "total elimination of probation" (p. 61) in favor of a greater reliance on police surveillance and increased incarceration. While more extreme than most, Sheindlin's damning critique of the juvenile justice system is of a piece with a number of recent treatments of the system, both journalistic and

From *Perspectives*, Fall 2000, pp. 22-30. Reprinted with permission from the American Probation and Parole Association.

academic. A brief synopsis of each suggests a system in a severe state of crises:

- In *No Matter How Loud I Shout*, Edward Humes (1996), a Pulitzer prize winning author, presents an inside view of the workings of the Los Angeles Juvenile Court. Describing the system generally as "broken, battered and outgunned" (p. 371), Humes echoes Sheindlin's theme of a widespread sense of immunity among juvenile offenders, perpetuated by a system that dispenses wrist slaps and apple bites in lieu of real sanctions. Facing continuous delays instead of prompt justice, and infrequent phone contact from probation officers instead of the close supervision needed, the young offenders in Los Angeles quickly learn that they are beyond the reach of the law:

    That's how the system programs you. They let you go and they know that just encourages you, and then they can get you on something worse later on. It's like, they set you up. Of course, I'm to blame, too, for going along with it. I didn't have to do those things, I know that. But the system didn't have to make it so goddamn easy (Humes, 1996, p. 333).

- In *The State of Violent Crime in America*, the first report of the newly formed Council on Crime in America (1996), the juvenile system is portrayed as a revolving door where again the theme of the lack of consequences and the consequent emboldening of young offenders is struck. Chaired by former Attorney General Griffin Bell and well-known conservative intellectual William Bennett, the report illustrates the success of one jurisdiction (Jacksonville, Florida) with the increased use of adult punishments for serious juvenile offenders and generally calls for a sober realization that the juvenile justice system's traditional reliance on treatment interventions must give way to strategies based on incapacitation and punishment.

- Finally, in *Screwing the System and Making It Work*, an ethnographic study of an unnamed juvenile court system, sociologist Mark Jacobs (1990) depicts a system whose principal intervention—community supervision—is demonstrably failing and whose state of disorganization and administrative weakness undermines any attempt at effective solutions. The few successes that Jacobs finds are accomplished in spite of the system by creatively evading the rules and regulations which otherwise frustrate all reasonable efforts. In the end, Jacobs concludes that the juvenile justice system fails because it attempts to solve problems of social breakdown through the largely ineffectual means of individual treatment plans.

Even granting that exposes will always earn publication more quickly than positive coverage, these four notable publications have such convergent findings that a conclusion regarding a crisis state for juvenile justice generally and juvenile probation specifically, seems inescapable. What then should be done? What initiatives might be undertaken in probation that would set juvenile justice on a more promising course, earning it back a measure of public trust and genuine impact on the lives of young offenders? This article will attempt an answer to those questions by first reviewing the scope of the work of juvenile probation and current trends in juvenile crime, then reviewing what has been learned about successful correctional interventions and how those lessons can be applied to juvenile probation, concluding with an examination of a new model for juvenile justice that can incorporate the findings of research in a context that values the rights and expectations of offenders, victims and society.

Juvenile Probation in the United States

In a review of juvenile probation nationally published in March 1996 by the Office of Juvenile Justice and Delinquency Prevention, Torbet reports an annual caseflow of nearly 1.5 million delinquency cases, resulting in some 500,000 juveniles under probation at any one time. Juvenile probation officers have caseloads averaging 41 offenders, with much higher numbers typifying urban locations.

Duties of juvenile probation officers are multiple but chiefly fall into the following three categories:

- **Intake, Screening and Assessment**—Juvenile probation officers are charged with the responsibility in many jurisdictions of determining which juveniles under arrest will proceed to a formal court process or instead be diverted to an informal process, if the offense involved is minor. In making this recommendation, the officer will obtain from the offender, his/her family and any social agencies involved with the juvenile at least a threshold amount of current status and background information involving such factors as school attendance, behavior at home and in the community, family relationships, peers, etc. A great deal of emphasis in screening will be placed on the circumstances of the offense and the previous record, if any. In addition to recommending for or against diversion, this intake process will yield pertinent information for the juvenile judge to utilize in making decisions regarding detention, bail, conditions of release, appointment of counsel and other matters.

"Trends within the juvenile probation system are ominous. The number of delinquency petitions increased 23 percent between 1989 and 1993, leading to a 21 percent increase in probation caseloads."

• **Pre-Sentence Investigations**—Probation officers play a crucial role in determining the most appropriate sentence or disposition to be imposed on the juvenile before the court. In preparing such reports, probation officers will begin by expanding information gathered at intake as well as reaching out to other officials, treatment personnel and family that may have useful information or perspectives bearing on the issue of an appropriate disposition. Pre-sentence reports will typically include as major sections a detailed examination of the facts and circumstances surrounding the offense and the juvenile's role in the incident; an elaborate social history, including any professional evaluations undertaken at the request of the court or the family; a summary of the impact of the delinquency on the victim(s) and their views regarding an appropriate disposition; and a discussion of the elements of an ideal disposition, including the alternatives available along with the probation officer's recommendation (National Center for Juvenile Justice, 1991).

• **Supervision**—The bulk of the work of juvenile probation officers is consumed in supervising youth placed by the courts on probation. This supervision includes both direct and regular contact with the offender (where resources permit) as well as collateral work with parents, schools, employers and agency personnel. It is the probation officer's responsibility to enforce the orders of the court in the form of victim restitution or curfews, to oversee the activities of the offender as much as possible, to uncover any lapses in behavior or company, and to insure that the juvenile takes advantage of all opportunities for addressing personal problems such as substance abuse or school failings. While the ideal is to insure full compliance with all the conditions of probation and to see that the juvenile leaves probation better equipped for a law abiding life than when supervision began, probation officers must also respond quickly to non-compliance and must move for revocation of probation and a more serious sentence when circumstances warrant.

In discharging this core function of supervision, effective probation must play many roles—police officer, counselor, family therapist, educator, mentor, and disciplinarian. It is the successful juggling of these multiple roles, assessing which is most appropriate in a given situation, that leads to the most effective practice.

Recent Trends

Trends within the juvenile probation system are ominous. The number of delinquency petitions increased 23 percent between 1989 and 1993, leading to a 21 percent increase in probation caseloads. At the same time, there has been no concomitant increase in resources provided to the juvenile courts, though the public demand for accountability and hard-nosed, intensive treatment of juveniles before the court has become most pronounced (Torbet, 1996).

More worrisome still is the worsening profile of the juveniles coming before the court. Even though most youth placed on probation are adjudicated for property offenses, the percent placed on probation for violent offenses has increased significantly in the last years. In 1989, 17 percent of those youth on probation were adjudicated for violent offenses; by 1993, that percentage had increased to 21 percent, which translates into nearly a 25 percent growth in the proportion of violent offenders on juvenile probation (Torbet, 1996).

This trend has changed the character of probation work for many juvenile officers, who now must reckon with safety issues of a new dimension. A Justice Department survey found that one-third of officers polled had been assaulted in the line of duty and that 42 percent reported themselves as being either usually or always concerned for their safety (Torbet, 1996).

This problem is amplified by the generally held view that today's juveniles have a degree of unprecedented cold-bloodedness and remorselessness. While difficult to quantify in terms of traditional research, it has been this author's experience that, pervading discussions within both probation and police circles, has been the theme of a growing and alarming lack of concern and emotion among young offenders for both the consequences to their victims or even themselves of their involvement in serious violence. This is the new face of juvenile crime and

"Murders by young people are still alarmingly high and, as the number of teenagers increases over the next several years, it will take hard work and good fortune to sustain the currently hopeful trend."

it is a major departure from past experience, leaving few reliable blueprints for action available to concerned officials. In this connection, James Q. Wilson, a professor of public policy at UCLA, has referred to "Youngsters who afterwards show us the blank, unremorseful stare of a feral, presocial being" (as quoted in DiIulio, 1996).

The Coming Plague—Juvenile Violence

In a column appearing in the New York Times in the summer of 1996, Princeton criminologist John DiIulio described the juvenile violence problems as "grave and growing" (p. A15). The following trends underline DiIulio's concern and provide further evidence of an explosion of juvenile violence that has the potential to overwhelm America's big cities.

- The number of juveniles murdered grew by 82 percent between 1984 and 1994;
- While most trends in adult arrests for violent crime are down since 1990, juvenile arrests for serious violence increased 26 percent by 1994, including a 15 percent increase in murder;
- Juvenile arrest rates for weapons violations nearly doubled between 1987 and 1994;
- In 1980, the number of juveniles murdered by firearm was 47 percent. By 1994, that percentage had increased to 67 percent (Snyder, et al., 1996).

Researchers have been able to attribute the greatest part of the increase in juvenile homicides to firearm-related murders. Al Blumstein (1996) has offered an analysis of this increase that traces its origins to the emergence of the crack cocaine trade in the mid 1980s and the acquisition of firearms that was a unique aspect of that emerging criminal enterprise. Young people who obtained guns originally for business purposes would also have them available in the event of other, more conventional types of conflicts among youth. The wider circulation and possession of firearms by the "players" caused other youth not involved in the drug trade to pick up guns for self-protection, as they did not wish to leave themselves at a tactical disadvantage. Related research confirms that though firearm related deaths among youth may be commonly seen as related to drug trade, in fact most such homicides are a byproduct of a violent argument rather than an event occurring during the commission of a crime (Pacific Center, 1994). It becomes plan then that strategies to reduce the most serious juvenile crime must address the issue of reducing gun possessions, an issue to be taken up later in this paper.

Two additional observations help frame in the future of juvenile violence. It is commonly accepted that rates of juvenile crime, including violence, are driven by a demographic imperative. That is, as the number of people in the crime-prone age bracket—the teens and early twenties—ebbs and flows, so generally does the crime rate (Fox, 1996). The bad news in this respect in that America is entering a 10–15 year span when the crime-prone age cohort will increase substantially. For example, by the year 2000, there will be a million more people between the ages of 14–17 than there were in 1995, of which roughly half will be male (Wilson, 1995a). By the year 2010, there will be 74 million juveniles under age 17 (DiIulio, 1996). These estimates have left DiIulio and others to project that juvenile participation in murder, rape and robbery will more than double by 2010.

However, the most recent data, while limited, is promising. During 1995, for the first time in ten years, the rate of juvenile homicide decreased for the second year in a row, by 15.2 percent (Butterfield, 1996). In a report issued by the U.S. Department of Justice, data gathered by the FBI revealed that the juvenile homicide rate, which reached an all time high in 1993, declined over the following two years by 22.8 percent. While a two-year trend is certainly encouraging, it is too soon to predict that the demographical forecast is inoperative. Murders by young people are still alarmingly high and, as the number of teenagers increases over the next several years, it will take hard work and good fortune to sustain the currently hopeful trend.

Lessons Learned About Effective Interventions

While one could hardly guess it from the current tone of relentless punitiveness pervading the debates on criminal justice policy, there has been a near exponential increase over the last 15 years in what is known with some significant confidence about the characteristics of effective correctional interventions. While the amount of public funds devoted to criminal research pales in comparison with that devoted to other forms of basic research (e.g., health issues), researchers have nonetheless made important advances in our understanding of the ingredients necessary to purposefully impact criminal and delinquent career (Petersilia 1990).

Canadian criminologists Don Andrews and Paul Gendreau have been at the leading edge of this research. By employing the relatively new statistical technique of mega-analysis, which allows for combining the results of multiple studies of a similar type to test the aggregate strength of a given intervention, Andrews and Gendreau (1990) have been able to identify key factors that can be utilized in the construction of correctional programs, factors which when used in combination can reduce recidivism by as much as 50 percent. Their research looked equally at juvenile and adult programs and found commonalities across the two groups. Effective programs had the following features:

• They were intensive and behavioral. Intensity was measured by both the absorption of the offenders' daily schedule and the duration of the program over time. Appropriate services in this respect will occupy 40–70 percent of the offenders' time and last an average of six months. Behavioral programs will establish a regimen of positive reinforcements for pro-social behavior and will incorporate a modeling approach including demonstrations of positive behavior that offenders are then encouraged to imitate;

• They target high risk offenders and criminogenic needs. Somewhat surprisingly, effective programs worked best with offenders classified as high-risk. This effect is strengthened if the program first identifies the presence of individual needs known to be predictive of recidivism (e.g. substance abuse, poor self-control) and then focuses on eliminating the problem. Targeting needs not proven to be related to criminal behavior (e.g. self-esteem) will not produce favorable results;

• Treatment modalities and counselors must be matched with individual offender types, a principle Andrews and Gendreau refer to as "responsivity." The program approach must be matched with the learning style and personality of the offender—a one-size-fits-all approach will fail. Taking care to compare the style of any therapist/counselor with the personality of the offender (e.g., anxious offenders should be matched with especially sensitive counselors) also is critical;

• They provide pro-social contexts and activities and emphasize advocacy and brokerage. Effective programs will replace the normal offender networks with new circles of peers and contacts who are involved in law abiding lifestyles. Success will be enhanced by aggressive efforts to link offenders with community agencies offering needed services. Most offenders will be unfamiliar with strategies for working the community and effective programs can serve as a bridge to facilitate a kind of mainstreaming of offenders (Gendreau, 1996).

Lipsey (1991) undertook a mega-analysis of some 400 juvenile programs and reached findings similar to those of Andrews and Gendreau. Lipsey's findings are impressive due to the much greater number of programs included in the analysis and the fact that he restricted his study to juvenile programs. In addition to those findings that parallel earlier results, Lipsey further discovered that skill building programs and those that were closely monitored, usually by a research team, for program implementation and integrity, were successful.

Effectiveness of Specific Programs
Traditional Probation

Despite the fact that it is clearly the treatment of choice for most juvenile offenders, there has been amazingly little major research on the effectiveness of regular probation (Clear and Braga, 1995). Targeted at only a small percentage of the overall probation population, researchers' monies and efforts have more commonly been devoted to more recent innovations such as intensive supervision, electronic monitoring or boot camps.

One noteworthy exception to this trend is a study published in 1988 by Wooldredge, in which he analyzed the impact of four different types of dispositions—including traditional probation—imposed by Illinois juvenile courts. This study of the subsequent recidivism of over two thousand delinquents found that lengthy probation supervision if combined with community treatment had the greatest effect in suppressing later recidivism, particularly when compared with incarceration or outright dismissal. Wooldredge concludes as follows:

> "While it appears that 'doing something' is [usually] better than 'doing nothing' for eliminating recidivism, this study suggests that differences in 'something' may also yield differences in recidivism rates. Specifically, two years of court supervision with community treatment is superior to any other sentence examined in this study for eliminating and [delaying] recidivism. On the other hand, sentences involving detention should be carefully considered in relating the types of delinquents they may be effective on" (Wooldredge, 1988, pp. 281, 293).

Juvenile Intensive Supervision

The concept of intensive probation supervision (IPS) was one of a new generation of strategies to emerge from the intermediate sanctions movement. First developed for adult offenders, IPS programs were intended to both provide an alternative to incarceration for appropriate offenders as well as to enhance the impact of supervision on high-risk probationers.

The concept spread to the juvenile domain quickly and spawned similar experimentation, though not nearly on the same scale as the adult programs. The program models emphasized reduced caseloads and, in contrast to similar efforts in the 1960s, put a premium on closer surveillance and monitoring, with reduced attention to treatment (Armstrong, 1991).

As with so much else in the juvenile correctional field, little reliable scientific evidence is available on program impact. The National Council on Crime and Delinquency (NCCD) undertook in the late '80s a review of some 41 programs and found that evaluative data of program sites was "generally non-existent" (Krisberg, et. al., 1989, p. 40). A similar conclusion was reached by Armstrong (1991) who found only five scientifically acceptable program evaluations and further criticized the absence of any apparent theoretical base for the programs.

Though useful research on juvenile IPS program is scarce, two studies produced at least minimally reliable results. In the New Pride Replication Project conducted between 1980 and 1984, ten newly established juvenile IPS programs located in both medium and large cities. The program, comprised of two six-month phases, was the first involving nearly daily contact which gradually decreased during the second phase. The programs supplemented this intensive supervision with heavy doses of alternative schooling, vocational training and job placement.

After gathering three years of outcome data, findings revealed no significant differences between the experiment and control groups (Palmer, 1992). A similar study by Barton and Butts (1990) on three juvenile IPS programs using random assignment found comparable results, though it was asserted that the IPS cost less than one-third the expense of incarceration.

More recently, an experiment was undertaken by the Toledo Juvenile Court in using IPS as a diversion from commitment to the state youth authority. Employing a mix of surveillance and treatment techniques, the program extended over six months and the research employed an 18 month follow-up period. Results found that there was no difference in subsequent recidivism between the IPS youth and a matched group committed to the Ohio Depart-

ment of Youth Services. Researchers concluded that the IPS program posed no grater threat to public safety, at approximately 20 percent of the cost of incarcerating the same youth (Weibush, 1993).

Violent Offenders

In light of the prospect of a growing number of violent juveniles, information specific to intervening with this particular offender is especially critical. Recent research includes one major evaluation of intensive supervision for violent juveniles, though it must be said that this program *followed* commitment to a small, secure juvenile facility for subsequent stays in community programs for several months. Consequently, it would be difficult to compare the population and prior experience to that of most juvenile probationers. The supervision focused on job placement, education, and to some lesser extent, family counseling and peer support.

In a two-year follow-up measuring for subsequent felony or violent arrests, no significant differences were found between program youth and a control group who were institutionalized for eight months and then placed on standard juvenile parole. Some evidence was found that sites which had stronger and/or consistently implemented treatment components produced better results (Palmer, 1992).

Juvenile Boot Camp

Boot camps have become a popular option on the continuum of sanctions for adult offenders so—as with IPS programs—it is not surprising that juvenile agencies have implemented their own versions. Such programs emphasize strong discipline, modeled on military programs and a strict physical conditioning regimen. The typical program is aimed at non-violent offenders, and involves a three month commitment followed by after-care (Peterson, 1996).

In 1992, the U.S. Justice Department's Office of Juvenile Justice and Delinquency Prevention (OJJDP) funded three new juvenile boot camps and undertook impact evaluations. The subsequent reports included the following findings:

- most participants completed the program;
- academic skills were significantly improved;
- a significant number of participants found jobs during aftercare; and
- no reduction in recidivism was found compared to a control group of youth who were institutionalized or placed on probation. (Peterson, 1996).

How Intensive is Intensive?

All of the programs reviewed above represent the characteristic efforts at recent reform in juvenile corrections and are alike in their emphasis on increased oversight of offenders, coupled in some instances (the more effective experiments) with increased rehabilitative services. They are also alike in having largely failed by the most important measure—recidivism.

Why has there been so little success? Ted Palmer, arguably the Dean of research in juvenile corrections, argues that their "intensive" programs have not been intensive enough, in light of the multiple needs presented by high risk offenders:

> "... given the interrelatedness of most serious, multiple offenders' difficulties and deficits, it is perhaps overly optimistic to expect fairly short-term programs to help most such individuals sort out and settle these matters once and for all, even if the programs are intensive." (Palmer, 1992, p. 112).

It may be that the system has been attempting to generate success on the cheap. To create expectations of turning very troubled youth from confirmed pathways of negative and predatory behavior—patterns developed over perhaps a decade of poor if not harmful rearing—through the application of concentrated service for a 6–12 month period, may be entirely unrealistic. To do the impossible, we have generally spent less than one-third the cost of institutionalizing these same youth.

Rather than congratulate ourselves for the short-term cost savings represented by diversion from incarceration to an intermediate sanction, we should think of making a substantial investment in the near term—something, let us say, more equivalent to the cost of a year's incarceration—in order to increase the chances of long-term significant savings represented by future imprisonments avoided. Americans, it has been often observed, are congenitally drawn to short-term strategies and addicted to quick returns on their investment. What has been found not to work in other domains (business, personal investment, etc.) may similarly prove self-defeating in juvenile justice.

Juvenile Transfer to Adult Court

One clear result of the growing violence committed by youth is an increased reliance on the "transfer" option—that is, the power of the system to move jurisdiction over juvenile offenders into adult court, to take advantage of the greater penalties available on the adult level. The popularity of the transfer option is reflected in both an increased number of cases where jurisdiction is waived (a 41 percent increase from 1989–1993) as well as legislative reforms aimed at making waivers more automated than discretionary (Howell, et al, 1996).

Studies conducted on the comparative effectiveness of handling similar offenders in adult versus juvenile court give the advantage to juvenile court where recidivism is the measure. Most studies indicate that juveniles imprisoned in adult facilities were more likely to be arrested following release.

In the making of criminal or juvenile justice policy, frequently political and ideological considerations will over-ride (if not totally ignore) the available empirical data. The move to transfer a greater number of juvenile offenders to adult court is not likely to abate; it is a specific reform that has become captive of the "get tough" philosophy that unquestionably holds sway in the current climate.

Five Steps Toward a Reformed Juvenile Probation
#1 Let Research Drive Policy

Despite an ever-growing body of research relevant to the formation of criminal justice policy, it remains remarkable how little empirical findings inform the design of programs in juvenile justice. As a result of this rather willful ignorance, the juvenile probation field can be found to embrace existing models for intervention (e.g. juvenile IPS) with scant if any evidence that such models work (Blumstein and Petersilia, 1995).

The field too often becomes enthralled by the latest fad and rushes to adopt it, irrespective of the evidence that it has or can work. Finkenauer (1982) has referred to this as the "panacea phenomenon" and it seems no less common fifteen years after he first identified this tendency.

This myopia on the part of correctional administrators has multiple explanations. Practitioners typically value the wisdom imparted by experience more than that contained in criminological journals. They prefer to consult their own intuition and gut instincts, more than any hard data. Secondly, the pertinent research is not as accessible as it might be. This is a product of the conventions of the academy, which rewards publication in criminological journals more so than writing done for the publications practitioners would read or consult. Thirdly, administrators and policy makers live and work in a politically charged atmosphere where consideration of "what works" is only one of the relevant considerations in developing policy. In the administrator's world, that which is congruent with the current political climate may indeed depart from what makes sense empirically.

Even allowing for the burden to survive the ideological wars, juvenile probation administrators could do a much better job of incorporating a research perspective into their decision making. This research-sensitive approach would take two forms: first, managers must realize that policy rarely needs to be created in a vacuum; that is, in setting policy in any particular direction, there will usually be some data bearing on the decision to be made. Becoming familiar with the techniques for adequately researching the literature and accessing the federal information services is crucial, which implies the staffing of at least a modest research division.

Secondly, all new initiatives should include a strong evaluation component. We have missed opportunities to learn from much previous experimentation because data was not kept in a way that facilitated any useful analysis (Palmer, 1992). All new programs should be seen as experiments, with clearly demonstrated time lines and methodologies for assessing impact. Juvenile probation agencies must become "learning organizations" (Senge, 1990) in which no course of action becomes institutionalized until its value is proven and feedback loops become a regular feature of the informational architecture of an agency.

Instead of viewing decisions about future programs as primarily a choice between hard or soft, tough or lenient, probation administrators should train themselves to think more in terms of smart versus dumb. "Smart" programs are those built on existing research with strong evaluation components. While not all programs sponsored by juvenile probation must meet this test absolutely (restitution programs are vital, irrespective of their impact on recidivism), juvenile probation will gain in credibility and impact as it gets "smarter."

#2 Emphasize Early Intervention

If juvenile probation were analogized to an investment strategy, the enterprise would be facing bankruptcy. In many respects, resources are allocated to that area (older, chronic offenders) where they are least likely to gain an impressive return. First offenders, by contrast, are all but ignored. Demonstrated incapacity for reform—not amenability to change—is what earns attention from the system. That must change.

Much has been learned in the past twenty years about the early precursors for chronic delinquency (Greenwood, 1995). We have learned for example, that children whose parents are cold, cruel and inconsistent in their parenting skills are at greatly increased risk for becoming enmeshed in the juvenile justice system.

So what? Is there anything that can be done about it? Yes! Models have been developed that work dramatically in training parents to more effectively supervise their own children themselves, reducing significantly their later delinquencies. In a report released in the spring of 1996, Rand Corporation researchers identified this form of parent training as being among the two or three most cost-effective strategies in terms of reduction in crime and delinquency (Greenwood, et al., 1996). An elaborate and highly tested model for this training, developed by the Oregon Social Learning Center, has been supported by repeated evaluations (Wilson, 1995b).

One collateral finding from this research, in fact from nearly all research on prevention, is that intervening earlier (in or before the primary grades) yields stronger results. Most delinquents enter the juvenile court in their early teens. Can they be reached earlier?

Quite apart from what schools and other communities can do with younger children, juvenile courts have access to young children encountered either as the subject of abuse and neglect petitions or as younger siblings of older delinquents. By reconceptualizing their mandate as intervening with families instead of solely with the convicted juvenile, courts can truly enter the prevention business in a viable way. The Rand report strongly suggests that a small amount spent on young children and their families earlier can save much more substantial costs later.

Intervening aggressively with abusive families would very likely repay itself many times over. Juveniles found guilty of the more serious crimes typically have long histories of abuse. A National Institute of Justice study found that an abused or neglected child has a 40 percent greater chance of becoming delinquent than other children (DiIulio, 1996).

Assessment instruments are now available to determine the ongoing risk for abuse within families as well as to predict the likelihood that patterns of abuse will change once an intervention has commenced (Gelles, 1996). Focusing attention on abusive families will pay off both in terms of child protection and delinquency prevention.

The Los Angeles Juvenile Court has undertaken a special project with first offenders who have the hallmarks of chronic delinquents. Instead of waiting for several arrests before intensive services are provided, the notion now will be that a greater investment earlier on targeted youth makes more sense (Humes, 1996). This preventive approach promises to work better and cost less.

#3 Emphasize the Paying of Just Debts

The public image of the juvenile court has been marred for decades now by the impression that it coddles vicious children and "treats" kids who are more deserving of punishment.

Probation administrators ignore this perception at their peril, as it undermines their credibility and diminishes their support. Both as a matter of justice and good correctional practice, juveniles should get their "just deserts" for harm done. Restitution and community service programs repay and restore victims and harmed communities and counter the prevalent notion that juvenile offenders are immune from any real penalties, an impression certainly re-enforced by Humes (1996) recent study of the Los Angeles Juvenile Court.

In his otherwise bleak and discouraging account, Humes relates the story of a program that places juvenile probationers in a school for disabled children where the probationer must discharge their community service responsibilities by caring for and feeding young children with major disabilities. A juvenile prosecutor describes the impact of the program as follows:

> *These are street thugs, serious offenders, some of the worst kids who come through here. Most of them have served time in camp or at the Youth Authority, and they're harder than ever. Then they end up feeding and bathing autistic and wheelchair-bound kids, working with them intensively, having these handicapped folks depending on them utterly. It works a kind of magic. It softens them. For the first time in their lives, someone is dependent on them. And it changes them. It's been going for four years, there's never been a problem, never anyone neglected or hurt. Rival gang members go there and work together side by side. Sometimes it seems like a miracle (p. 173).*

One of the most promising new paradigms in juvenile justice is the "Balanced and Restorative Justice Mode" developed by Gordon Bazemore of Florida Atlantic University and his colleagues. In a compelling design that attempts to simultaneously serve the just expectations of victim, community and offender alike, the following principle is enunciated: "When an offense occurs by the offender, an obligation incurs by the offender to the victim that must be fulfilled" (Maloney et al., 1995 p. 43).

All juvenile probationers—in the interests of justice, for the sake of any injured victims or communities, and, not insignificantly, for their own moral education—must be compelled to pay their just debts. In doing so, wounds heal, losses are restored, and the moral sentiments of the community are assuaged.

#4 Make Probation Character Building

In the parlance of traditional clinical assessments, most delinquents have been labeled as "character disordered." To many observers, this was a kind of "default" diagnosis that filled in the blank when no other form of mental illness seemed present.

Indeed, delinquents do seem lacking in what we refer to commonly as character, by which we generally mean habits of thought and action that reveal a fidelity to principles of integrity, good comportment, concern for others and self-control (Wilson, 1995b).

Neo-conservative perspectives on crime have brought the issue of character defects among delinquents and criminals to the foreground, in contrast to the medical model which attributed various "problems" and "illnesses" to offenders, deficiencies presumably beyond their control and therefore beyond their responsibility (Wilson, 1995a). Imparting bad character to delinquents would seem to imply greater responsibility for wrong-doing while also pointing to a different type of remediation.

Can a term of juvenile probation build character? As Wilson (1995b) suggests, we know little about how to inculcate character. Yet we have some clues. According to Aristotle, character is reflected not in some inner quality or virtue, but in a pattern of commendable actions which, in the doing, both build and reveal character.

In the Aristotelian sense then, juvenile courts can attempt to build character by compelling probationers to complete actions that youth of high character would undertake. Compensating for harm done, discussed above, is surely part of this. Regular attendance and good behavior at school would also reflect character in action. Obeying the reasonable requests of parents and respectable conduct at home and in the neighborhood would further exemplify character. If Aristotle was right that we become good, by doing good, requiring juvenile probationers to do good even though they may not seem or yet be good could, over time, build what we call character.

As Andrews and Kiessling (1980) found, effective probation officers model pro-social behavior. Juvenile probation officers must then see themselves as moral educators, who must constantly look for opportunities to exemplify good character to those they supervise. Every occasion where self-restraint is exercised in the face of a probationer's provocation, where kindness and courtesy is extended to a probationer's family in defiance of the juvenile's expectation, and every effort by the officer to insure fair treatment in dispositional and revocational proceedings are opportunities for character building and moral education.

If character is revealed in making moral decisions, then juvenile probation agencies could undertake more explicit strategies for moral development. Though more employed in educational than correctional settings, techniques for instilling a heightened moral sense have been used successfully in advancing the moral reasoning powers of young children (Lickona, 1992). Based on Lawrence Kohlberg's highly regarded theory of moral development, participants in the program are led through discussions of moral dilemmas where they must reconcile competing interests and reach just solutions. Research has shown that subjects can elevate their moral reasoning away from more selfish egocentric perspectives to broader, more altruistic and emphatic thinking.

This psychoeducational strategy would lend itself readily to the probation environment. In lieu of what is too often a rather mechanical and vacuous exchange with a probation officer once or twice each month, young offenders could participate in discussion groups led by trained probation officers with both offenders and staff likely feeling that they are engaged in a more productive experience.

#5 Prioritize Violence Prevention

In light of the growing rates of serious juvenile violence and with this trend expected to continue into the next decade (Fox, 1996), juvenile probation must focus on efforts it can undertake to suppress violent behavior.

As mentioned earlier, there is scant evidence that the more punitive strategies will have long term impact (It must be said that there are independent "just deserts" rationales for punishing seriously violent offenders, but this does not account for first offenders showing aggressive tendencies). Again drawing from efforts more commonly found in schools, some juvenile probation departments have undertaken violence prevention programs with juvenile probationers (Office of the Commissioner of Probation, 1995). These programs employ curricula designed to improve the social, problem-solving and anger-management skills of young offenders. While curricula vary, most employ an interactive, exercise-based, skill-building model that extends over an average of 10–15 sessions of an hour or so duration (Brewer, et al., 1996).

Evaluations conducted on such programs indicate that they are generally effective in improving social skills and as measured by their response to hypothetical conflict solutions (Brewer, et al., 1996). An evaluation of a program undertaken with juvenile probationers in Massachusetts demonstrated significant reductions in subsequent juvenile violence (Romano, 1996). More importantly, this program, sponsored by the Boston Juvenile Court for several years now, attests to the viability of such programming within the juvenile probation context.

Given the aforementioned growth in juvenile violence attributed to firearms, prevention programs targeted on this area warrant consideration. Unfortunately, very little has been done: "Programs that intervene with young people who use guns or have been caught with guns unfortunately are rare and in dire need of further development" (Office of Juvenile Justice and Delinquency Prevention, 1996, p. 16).

Nonetheless, initiating more efforts in this area make sense. Studies of handgun possession by youth indicate that handguns are more likely to be owned by individuals with a prior record of violent behavior, particularly where the gun is illegal (OJJDP, 1996). This suggests a real potential pay-off in targeting juvenile probationers.

Firearm prevention programs have been undertaken in several juvenile jurisdictions, though thus far, little evaluative information is available. Pima County Arizona Juvenile Court, for example, operates a course for youth who, though not chronic offenders, are before the court for offenses involving the carrying or firing of a gun or youth who have been identified as being at risk for firearm use. Parents are required to attend these educational sessions, where the law governing gun use and the dangers implicit in unauthorized use are explained (OJJDP, 1996).

Given the extent of the violence problem, further experimentation and evolution seems highly warranted. Moreover, a greater reliance on substantive group-work modalities offers a common-sense alternative to the traditional and exhausted model of one-on-one contact, cynically derided within the profession as "fifteen-minutes-of-avoiding-eye-contact-once-a-month."

The Prospects Ahead

The five reforms recommended above constitute a modest and therefore doable agenda, not one that would likely entail additional large expenditures but would rely on reallocating existing resources and redeploying current staff. Implementing them will not delivery utopian, crime-free communities in the next millennium, but we have reason to believe they would be worth the effort.

Progressive administrators will no doubt consider such initiatives, as well as others. As to the rest, a changing climate in governmental circles may compel the reluctant and unimaginative to undertake steps toward building a system both more effective and more congruent with public attitudes and expectations (Corbett, 1996). In the face of disturbing projections for future rates of youthful violence, immediate action would not seem premature.

References

Andrews, D., Kiessling, J., Robinson, D., & Mickus, S. (1986). The risk principle of case classification: An outcome evaluation with young adult probationers. Canadian Journal of Criminology, 28, 377–384

Blumstein, Alfred Ph.D., 1996. "Youth Violence, Guns, and Illicit Drug Markets." National Institute of Justice, January 1996.

Butterfield, Fox. (1996, August 9). After 10 years, juvenile crime begins to drop. *The New York Times.*

Council on Crime in America, The. 1996. The State of Violent Crime in America. Washington, D.C.

DiIulio, John J. Jr. (1996, July 31). Stop crime where it starts. *The New York Times.*

Finckenauer, J. (1982). *Sacred straight! and the panacea phenomenon.* Englewood Cliffs, NJ: Prentice Hall.

Fox, James Alan. 1996. Trends In Juvenile Violence—A Report to the United States Attorney General on Current and Future Rates of Juvenile Offending. Washington, D.C.: Bureau of Justice Statistics, United States Department of Justice.

Gelles, Richard J. 1996. *The Book of David.* New York: Basic Books.

Gendreau, Paul. 1996. "The Principles of Effective Intervention With Offenders." In *Choosing Correctional Options That Work,* ed. Alan T. Harland, California: Sage Publications, 117–130.

Greenwood, Peter W., K. Model, C.P. Rydell, J. Chiesa. 1996. *Diverting Children From A Life of Crime.* California: RAND.

Humes, Edward. 1996. *No Matter How Loud I Shout.* New York: Simon & Schuster.

Jacobs, Mark D. 1990. *Screwing the System and Making It Work.* Chicago: The University of Chicago Press.

Lickona, Thomas. 1991. *Educating for Character.* New York: Bantam Books

Krisberg, B., Rodriguez, O., Baake, A., Nuenfeldt, D., & Steele, P. (1989). Demonstration of post-adjudication, non-residential intensive supervision programs: Assessment report. San Francisco: National Council on Crime and Delinquency.

Maloney, Dennis M. and Mark S. Umbreit. 1995. "Managing Change: Toward A Balanced and Restorative Justice Model." *Perspectives,* Spring 1995, 43–46.

National Center for Juvenile Justice. 1991. Desktop Guide to Good Juvenile Probation Practice. Pittsburgh: National Juvenile Court Services Association.

Office of Juvenile Justice and Delinquency. "Reducing Youth Gun Violence: An Overview of Programs and Initiatives." Washington, D.C.: Office of Justice Programs: May 1996.

Palmer, Ted. 1992. *The Re-Emergence of Correctional Intervention.* California: Sage Publications.

Petersilia, Joan. 1991. "Policy Relevance and the Future of Criminology." Criminology, Vol. 29, 1–15.

Peterson, Eric. "Juvenile Boot Camps: Lessons Learned". *Juvenile Justice Bulletin.* Washington, D.C.: Office of Juvenile Justice and Delinquency Prevention: June 1996.

Romano, Linda. 1996. *Preliminary Evaluation Report: Violence Prevention Groups.* Newton: Romano & Associates.

Senge, Peter M. 1990. *The Fifth Discipline.* New York: DoubleDay Currency.

Sheindlin, Judy. 1996. *Don't Pee On My Leg and Tell Me It's Raining.* New York: Harper Collins Publishers, Inc.

Snyder, Howard N., M. Sickmund, E. Poe-Yamagata. 1996. "Juvenile Offenders and Victims: 1996 Update on Violence." Washington, D.C.: Office of Juvenile Justice and Delinquency.

Torbet, Patricia McFall. "Juvenile Probation: The Workhorse of the Juvenile Justice System." *Juvenile Justice Bulletin.* Washington, D.C.: Office of Juvenile Justice and Delinquency Prevention.

Wiebush, Richard G. 1993. "Juvenile Intensive Supervision: The Impact on Felony Offenders Diverted From Institutional Placement." *Crime & Delinquency* 39:68–89.

Wilson, James Q. 1995a. "Crime and Public Policy." In Crime, eds. James Q. Wilson, and Joan Petersilia. San Francisco: CS Press.

Wilson, James Q. 1995b. *On Character.* Washington: The AEI Press.

Wooldredge, J. (1988). Differentiating the effects of juvenile court sentences on eliminating recidivism. Journal of Research in Crime and Delinquency, 25 (3), 264–300.

Ron Corbett, Jr. is the Deputy Commissioner, Massachusetts Probation Department.

Unit 6

Unit Selections

Key Points to Consider

❖ What issues and trends are most likely to be faced by corrections administrators at the beginning of this new century?

❖ What are some of the reasons for overcrowding in our nation's prisons?

❖ Discuss reasons for favoring and for opposing the death penalty.

 **Links**   **www.dushkin.com/online/**

These sites are annotated on pages 4 and 5.

In the American system of criminal justice, the term "corrections" has a special meaning. It designates programs and agencies that have legal authority over the custody or supervision of persons who have been convicted of a criminal act by the courts. The correctional process begins with the sentencing of the convicted offender. The predominant sentencing pattern in the United States encourages maximum judicial discretion and offers a range of alternatives from probation (supervised, conditional freedom within the community), through imprisonment, to the death penalty.

Selections in this unit focus on the current condition of the U.S. penal system and the effects that sentencing, probation, imprisonment, and parole have on the rehabilitation of criminals. In the lead essay, "Reading, Writing, and Rehabilitation," the author describes efforts under way at Rikers Island, New York City's central jail complex, to enhance the schooling of its inmates. The *Newsweek* article that follows, "The Death Penalty on Trial," identifies severe problems with the administration of the ultimate penalty. The next essay discusses ex-offenders with nowhere to go when they are released from jail. They are the subject of Jeff Glasser's essay, "Ex-Cons on the Street." He contends the nation's get-tough-on-crime laws are fueling this phenomenon.

The essay that follows, "The Past and Future of U.S. Prison Policy: Twenty-Five Years After the Stanford Prison Experiment" by Craig Haney and Philip Zimbardo, contains a reflection on lessons learned in their Stanford Prison Experiment. It also includes suggested reforms for American corrections.

The concluding articles "Parole and Prisoner Reentry in the United States," parts one and two, discuss the "reinvention" of parole in the United States, as well as parole outcomes, recidivism rates, reform ideas, and promising programs.

Punishment and Corrections

Reading, Writing and Rehabilitation

Rikers Helps Inmates Whose Schooling Was Once Ignored

By JUAN FORERO

By his own account, Carlos Senquiz, 17, never had much use for school. But on a recent day, as he listened to his new teacher's lecture about "Hamlet" and its themes of suffering and pain, Mr. Senquiz came to realize that his own violent life in Queens closely mirrored those in Shakespeare's drama.

It was easy to see how: Mr. Senquiz, a high school dropout, had been shot in a street dispute, been arrested for a string of crimes and come from a family where an uncle once fatally stabbed another, an event Mr. Senquiz said was eerily similar to the death of Hamlet's father at the hands of his brother.

"I liked how the story went down," said Mr. Senquiz, who spends his days in a wheelchair, recuperating from the effects of a bullet that came inches from his spinal cord. "It's familiar to what happened to my uncles. I liked how the characters explained themselves, when they write the poetry, how it connects to everything that happens in the real world. When they say things, it's like it's real. It's not, like, fake. That's what I like about it."

Mr. Senquiz is an inmate on Rikers Island, New York City's central jail complex, which is known for the notoriety of its occupants rather than its educational programs.

But since 1996, when the Legal Aid Society filed a lawsuit calling on the city to expand educational services on Rikers, the Board of Education has started a variety of programs aimed at reaching school-age inmates who years ago would have been ignored. Although classes have been a part of life on Rikers for decades, school officials say that scores of inmates outside the general population, including those isolated for safety or discipline reasons, or hospitalized, like Mr. Senquiz, were long forgotten.

Everyone in Mr. Senquiz's class is recovering from gunshot wounds or serious illnesses at the North Infirmary Command annex. And most are looking at more than health problems. Mr. Senquiz, for instance, is facing a burglary charge in Queens. A classmate, Miguel Fortuna, is facing a murder rap. Willy Gomez was charged with drug dealing.

Recently, though, these young men have learned snippets of literature and reviewed basic social studies in a class started in January as part of the city's effort to educate more inmates. While some deficiencies remain—evidenced by a federal judge's ruling Jan. 7 ordering the city to devise a plan by April 14 to offer classes to all eligible inmates—school officials on Rikers say they have expanded services significantly since February 1998, when the fourth high school on the island, the Horizon Academy, opened.

Each school day, Horizon's 27 teachers carry their chalkboards and instruction books to the bedsides of AIDS patients, to the cells of potentially violent inmates segregated for infractions, to inmates isolated from the general population for their own safety. Instruction for the academy students (averaging 173 per day) takes place in small rooms converted into classes.

"It's the first time you have access to a dorm area, to where a student lives in jail," said Dolores Edwards Sullivan, 48, a veteran teacher in the state prison system who is a favorite among inmates because of her unflagging confidence and energetic teaching style. "You call them up and they come to the bars, and you teach them that way. It's been the sort of situation where we have virtually been breaking ground."

Rikers's four high schools cost $11.7 million annually, up from $7.7 million three years ago. This is not politically popular. After all, parents across the city have long complained about overcrowded classrooms and insufficient supplies.

But for prison education experts, the investment is viewed as smart public policy. "It is impossible to overstate the importance of education to young people who have gotten in trouble with the law," said Barbara Woodhouse, a University of Pennsylvania law professor and co-director of the Center for Children's Policy, Practice and Research. "Acquiring their high school degree can mean the difference between returning to society and playing a positive role as a citizen or becoming a career criminal."

At Rikers, Horizon teachers and administrators measure success in stories like that of Derrick Johnson, a 10th-grade dropout who earned his high school equivalency degree last year.

Mr. Johnson, who has a history of drug arrests in the Bronx and is awaiting trial on drug dealing charges, said it was not easy. He was confined to the chipped iron bars of the North Infirmary Command's D tier because officials considered him a flight risk. But he said he grabbed the opportunity when Ms. Sullivan proposed a course of study. "I thought, that's my chance. I needed it," he said. "It's time to grow up. I've done enough time, been arrested enough."

Mr. Johnson, 22, recounted how, with only the bars of his cellblock between them, he would review math with Gabriel Heller, one of Horizon's teachers, and discuss Claude Brown's "Manchild in the Promised Land" with another teacher, Marshall Johnson. Course work was completed under a bare light bulb in his tiny cell, amid the clutter of rap magazines like XXL and Vibe and a clothesline where wet T-shirts and socks hung.

Some days, lockdowns leave students in their cells and classes canceled.

When he finally passed his equivalency test after six months of study, Mr. Johnson was so overjoyed he wrote a letter to his teachers calling his accomplishment "the best experience I have ever had." He said he later went into his cell and began "crying for 10 minutes nonstop."

Yet inmates are also often ill prepared to learn. Twenty-five percent of all Rikers inmates read below a fifth-grade level, officials say. Forty percent of students require special education, though there are not enough specially trained teachers, said Gloria Ortiz, Horizon's principal. Others have mental or behavioral problems.

Teachers also have to contend with a rolling registry that sees students come and go constantly. At Horizon, nearly 1,500 students were enrolled last year, some of them for just a few weeks before they were released or sent to other prisons.

But Ms. Sullivan is not disheartened. Insisting that all her students can learn, she points to a big advantage of teaching at Rikers: small class sizes, often fewer than 10 students per teacher. "I teach my students as if they're all going to go to college," she said proudly, noting that 11 students at North Infirmary Command earned their high school equivalency diplomas last year.

Some of the students are not as optimistic. Mr. Senquiz, who said his days in a Manhattan high school were marred by fights and rowdy behavior, summed up his problems on a recent day as class wound down: "I learned something today. But in a couple of days, I'll forget, just forget it."

Another student, Damien Crooks, 20, who said he was shot by the police and is awaiting trial on a gun possession charge, is woefully behind, having only reached the ninth grade. His injuries make learning more difficult. "I can't really learn," Mr. Crooks said. "I have so much stuff going through my head, so much pain."

Mr. Heller, 23, who speaks fluent Spanish and teaches the classics and right angles with equal fervor, acknowledged the frustrations that can test a teacher's idealism. "You have only a couple of successes," he said. "In our classes, we have guys who don't speak English next to guys who don't know how to read, next to guys who are about to take their G.E.D.'s. It's a battle. It's a battle for the teachers and for the students."

Other obstacles come in the form of simple prison logistics. There are days when fights or other disturbances result in lockdowns, leaving students in their cells and classes canceled. There are times when correction officers are not available to escort inmates to classrooms. There are long waits at checkpoints between cellblocks.

"You go somewhere, you have to get searched before you leave," said David Mapp, 21, who earned his G.E.D. at Rikers before being released last year. "You have to get searched on your way back. You come back with one pencil too many, and you're in trouble."

Teachers are also irked by jail rules that bar them from meeting with inmates in the punitive segregation cells at the Otis Bantum Correctional Center, one of Rikers's 10 jails. At that jail, homework materials are delivered to the cells, and students then have to telephone teachers during prearranged hours.

Correction officials explain that while access to inmates is being improved, security comes first. "It is a jail setting," said Thomas Antenen, a Department of Correction spokesman. "That has to be kept in mind, and in a jail setting, security is a paramount concern."

THE DEATH PENALTY ON TRIAL

Special Report: DNA and other evidence freed 87 people from death row; now Ricky McGinn is roiling Campaign 2000. Why America's rethinking capital punishment.

BY JONATHAN ALTER

He STOOD AT THE THRESHOLD OF the execution chamber in Huntsville, Texas, 18 minutes from death by lethal injection, when official word finally came that the needle wouldn't be needed that day. The rumors of a 30-day reprieve were true. Ricky McGinn, a 43-year-old mechanic found guilty of raping and killing his 12-year-old stepdaughter, will get his chance to prove his innocence with advanced DNA testing that hadn't been available at the time of his 1994 conviction. The double cheeseburger, french fries and Dr Pepper he requested for dinner last Thursday night won't be his last meal after all.

Another galvanized moment in the long-running debate over capital punishment: last week Gov. George W. Bush granted his first stay of execution in five years in office not because of deep doubts about McGinn's guilt; it was hard to find anyone outside McGinn's family willing to bet he was truly innocent. The doubts that concerned Bush were the ones spreading across the country about the fairness of a system with life-and-death stakes. "These death-penalty cases stir emotions," Bush told NEWSWEEK in an exclusive interview about the decision. Imagine the emotions that would have been stirred had McGinn been executed, then proved innocent after death by DNA. So, Bush figured, why take the gamble?

"Whether McGinn is guilty or innocent, this case has helped establish that all inmates eligible for DNA testing should get it," says Barry Scheck, the noted DNA legal expert and coauthor of "Actual Innocence." "It's just common sense and decency."

Even as Bush made the decent decision, the McGinn case illustrated why capital punishment in Texas is in the cross hairs this political season. For starters, McGinn's lawyer, like lawyers in too many capital cases, was no Clarence Darrow. Twice reprimanded by the state bar in unrelated cases (and handling five other capital appeals simultaneously), he didn't even begin focusing on the DNA tests that could save his client until this spring. Because Texas provides only $2,500 for investigators and expert witnesses in death-penalty appeals (enough for one day's work, if that), it took an unpaid investigator from out of state, Tina Church, to get the ball rolling.

After NEWSWEEK shone a light on the then obscure case ("A Life or Death Gamble," May 29), Scheck and the A-team of the Texas defense bar joined the appeal with a well-crafted brief to the trial court. When the local judge surprised observers by recommending that the testing be done, it caught Bush's attention. The hard-line higher state court and board of pardons both said no to the DNA tests—with no public explanation. This time, though, the eyes of the nation were on Texas, and Bush stepped in.

But what about the hundreds of other capital cases that unfold far from the glare of a presidential campaign? As science sprints ahead of the law, assembly-line executions are making even supporters of the death penalty increasingly uneasy. McGinn's execution would have been the fifth in two weeks in Texas, the 132d on Bush's watch. Is that pace too fast? We now know that prosecutorial mistakes are not as rare as once assumed; competent counsel not as common. Since the Supreme Court allowed reinstatement of the death penalty in 1976, 87 death-row inmates have been freed from prison. With little money available to dig up new evidence and appeals courts usually unwilling to review claims of innocence (they are more likely to entertain possible procedural trial-court errors), it's impossible to know just how many other prisoners are living the ultimate nightmare.

So for the first time in a generation, the death penalty is in the dock—on the defensive at home and especially abroad for being too arbitrary and too prone to error. The recent news had prompted even many conservative hard-liners to rethink their position. "There seems to be growing awareness that the death penalty is just another government program that doesn't work very well," says Stephen Bright of the Southern Center for Human Rights.

When Gov. George Ryan of Illinois, a pro-death-penalty Republican, imposed a moratorium on capital punishment in January after 13 wrongly convicted men were released from Illinois's death row, it looked like a one-day event. Instead, the decision has resonated as one of the most important national stories of the year. The big question it raises, still unanswered: how can the 37 other states that allow the death penalty be so sure that their systems don't resemble the one in Illinois?

In that sense, the latest debate on the death penalty seems to be turning less on moral questions than on practical ones. While Roman Catholicism and other faiths have become increasingly outspoken in their opposition to capital punishment (even Pat Robertson is now against it), the new wave of doubts seems more hardheaded than softhearted; more about justice than faith.

The death penalty in America is far from dead. All is takes to know that is a glimpse of a grieving family, yearning for closure and worried about maximum sentences that aren't so long. According to the NEWSWEEK Poll, 73 percent still support capital punishment in at least some cases,

THEY'RE ON DEATH ROW. BUT SHOULD THEY BE?

Five cases where there may be big questions

Groups like the Death Penalty Information Center monitor cases of prisoners on death row whose guilt, the advocates believe, may not be beyond a reasonable doubt. A few top candidates, from the DPIC and others:

Gary Graham

Graham has been on death row in Texas for nearly 20 years for killing a man during a 1981 supermarket robbery. A 17-year-old at the time, he was convicted on the testimony of a single eyewitness who claimed she saw Graham from 30 to 40 feet away in a dark parking lot. Three other eyewitnesses could not make a positive identification of Graham at the crime scene. A store employee who said he saw the shooter fleeing told police Graham was not the killer—but he was never called to testify. And none of Graham's fingerprints or DNA was found at the scene. Last week the U.S. Supreme Court declined to hear his case; he is scheduled for execution June 22.

Joe Amrine

Amrine was sentenced to death for stabbing a man with an ice pick in a Missouri prison in 1985. The conviction was based on the testimony of two fellow prisoners who said they witnessed the murder. But the two told different stories, and both later said they had lied under pressure from a prison investigator.

Larry Osborne

Osborne—at 20 Kentucky's youngest death-row inmate—was convicted of killing an elderly couple by setting their house on fire when he was 17. His conviction was based primarily on statements from a 15-year-old friend, who Osborne's lawyer says was pressured to snitch by investigators. The friend then drowned before he could be cross-examined at the trial. There was no compelling physical evidence. An appeal is pending.

John Francis Wille

A drifter from Florida, Wille was convicted along with his girlfriend in the 1985 kidnapping and murder of an 8-year-old girl in Louisiana. Their convictions were based entirely on confessions they made at the time. (His girlfriend is currently serving a life sentence.) But Wille's lawyer claims they both have histories of false confessions. And he says the forensic evidence contradicts their stories.

John Spirko

Spirko was convicted in 1984 of killing the Elgin, Ohio, postmaster. But the chief witness against Spirko said he was only 70 percent sure of his identification. And records indicate that Spirko's codefendant was actually 600 miles away at the time of the crime. Evidence implicates others in the murder. Spirko remains on death row, but in 1995 a judge granted him an indefinite stay.

In the NEWSWEEK Poll, 73% support the death penalty, down slightly from five years ago; 38% say only the most brutal murderers should be executed.

FOR THIS NEWSWEEK POLL, PRINCETON SURVEY RESEARCH ASSOCIATES INTERVIEWED 750 ADULTS BY TELEPHONE JUNE 1–2. THE MARGIN OF ERROR IS +/– 4 PERCENTAGE POINTS. THE NEWSWEEK POLL © 2000 BY NEWSWEEK, INC.

But is a "vast majority" good enough when the issue is life or death? After years when politicians bragged about streamlining the process to speed up executions, the momentum is now moving the opposite way. The homicide rate is down 30 percent nationally in five years, draining some of the intensity from the pro-death-penalty argument. And fairness is increasingly important to the public. Although only two states— Illinois and New York—currently give inmates the right to have their DNA tested, 95 percent of Americans want that right guaranteed, according to the NEWSWEEK Poll. Close to 90 percent even support the idea of federal guarantees of DNA testing (contained in the bipartisan Leahy-Smith Innocence Protection bill), though Bush and Gore, newly conscious of the issue, both prefer state remedies.

The explanation for the public mood may be that cases of injustice keep coming, and not just on recent episodes of "The Practice" that (with Scheck as a script adviser) uncannily anticipated the McGinn case. In the last week alone Bush pardoned A. B. Butler after he served 17 years in prison for a sexual assault he didn't commit, and Virginia Gov. James Gilmore ordered new testing that will likely free Earl Washington, also after 17 years behind bars. All told, more than 70 inmates have been exonerated by DNA evidence since 1982, including eight on death row.

Death-penalty advocates often point out that no one has been proved innocent after execution. But the DNA evidence that could establish such innocence has frequently been lost by prosecutors with no incentive to keep it. In a recent Virginia case, a court actually prevented posthumous examination of DNA evidence. On the defense side, lawyers and investigators concentrate their scarce resources on cases where lives can be spared.

---

down only slightly in five years. Heinous crimes still provoke calls for the strongest penalties. It's understandable, for instance, how the families victimized by the recent shooting at a New York Wendy's that left five dead would want the death penalty. And the realists are right; the vast majority of those on death row are guilty as hell.

TO LIVE AND TO DIE

After a spate of well-publicized cases in which innocent men were sentenced to die, the nation's death-penalty debate seems to be taking on new urgency. Crime, after all, is down. But the annual total of executions in the United States is still rising, principally because appeals create long delays between a prisoner's sentencing and execution. A graphic history of the American way of death:

Inmates Executed Each Year in the United States

1930 155 EXECUTED

1930s Executions rise to an average 167 a year, the highest for any decade in U.S. history

1933 Giuseppe Zangara gets the death penalty for killing Chicago Mayor Anton Cermak during an assassination attempt on FDR. The execution takes place exactly 33 days after the shooting.

1935 199 EXECUTED

1942 147 EXECUTED

1953 62 EXECUTED

1953 Julius and Ethel Rosenberg, convicted of giving U.S. atomic-bomb secrets to the Soviet Union, become the first U.S. civilians to be executed for espionage

1957 65 EXECUTED

1966 Crime is down, the economy is up and public support for the death penalty falls to 42 percent in the Gallup poll

1968–76 0 EXECUTED

1972 In a landmark case, *Furman v. Georgia,* the U.S. Supreme Court effectively voids death-penalty laws

1976 The court rules that mandatory death-penalty laws are unconstitutional—but refuses to ban the death penalty altogether

1977 After a series of high-court rulings clarifying legal standards, executions resume after a 10-year pause. In Utah, convicted murderer Gary Gilmore is the first to die—by firing squad.

1982 Convicted in Texas of killing a man while trying to steal a car, Charles Brooks becomes the first person to be executed by lethal injection

1984 21 EXECUTED

1992 31 EXECUTED

1994 Timothy W. Spence, a Virginia rapist and murderer, becomes the first person to be executed in a case in which DNA evidence is pivotal

1995 New York reinstates the death penalty after Republican George Pataki is elected governor. Nationwide, the number of executions rises to 56, the highest total since 1957.

1997 74 EXECUTED

1998 Despite protests from supporters who claimed her religious beliefs had earned her clemency, Karla Faye Tucker becomes the first woman to be executed in Texas since the Civil War. Her crime: killing two people with a pickaxe.

1999 98 EXECUTED

1999 In St. Louis, Pope John Paul II calls for an end to the death penalty, and the U.N. Human Rights Commission passes a resolution urging a worldwide moratorium

They Shall Be Released

Since the 1970s, 87 inmates have been freed from death row because of problems or errors in the legal process. Common reasons for reversal include:

■ Key witnesses lied or recanted their testimony

■ Police overlooked or withheld important evidence

■ DNA testing showed someone else committed the crime

■ The defense lawyer was incompetent or negligent

■ Prosecutors withheld exculpatory evidence form the defense

World Leaders

In 1999, China easily led all nations with 1,077 executions, followed distantly by Iran (165), Saudi Arabia (103), Democratic Republic of the Congo (100) and the United States (98)

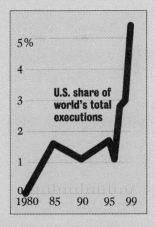

SOURCES: AMNESTY INTERNATIONAL, BUREAU OF JUSTICE STATISTICS, DEATH PENALTY INFORMATION CENTER. GRAPHIC BY STANFORD KAY AND KARL GUDE.

And while DNA answers some questions, it raises others: if so many inmates are exonerated in rape and rape-murder cases where DNA is obtainable, how about the vast majority of murders, where there is no DNA? Might not the rate of error be comparable?

Politics, for once, seems to be in the background, largely because views of the death penalty don't break down strictly along party lines. Ryan of Illinois is a Republican; Gray Davis, the hard-line governor of California, a Democrat. The Republican-controlled New Hampshire Legislature recently voted to abolish the death penalty; the Democratic governor vetoed the bill. Perhaps the best way to understand how the politics of the death penalty is shifting is to view it as a tale of two Rickys:

In January 1992, Arkansas Gov. Bill Clinton interrupted his presidential campaign to return home to preside over the execution of Ricky Ray Rector, a black man convicted of killing a police officer. Rector

The Executioner's Song Can Last for Years

How long death-row inmates must wait for execution varies sharply from state to state. Nebraska, where the delay averages 11.3 years, is slowest. But the interval between sentencing and execution is getting longer nationwide.

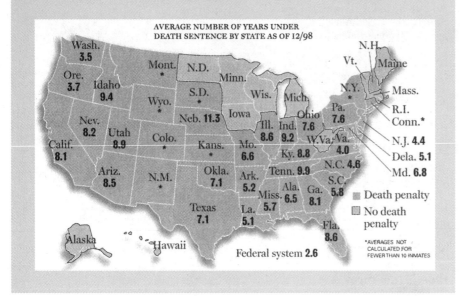

AVERAGE NUMBER OF YEARS UNDER
DEATH SENTENCE BY STATE AS OF 12/98

Wash. **3.5**
Ore. **3.7**
Mont. *
N.D. *
Minn.
N.H.
Vt.
Maine
Idaho **9.4**
Wyo. *
S.D. *
Wis.
Mich.
N.Y. *
Mass.
R.I.
Conn. *
Nev. **8.2**
Utah **8.9**
Neb. **11.3**
Iowa
Ill. **8.6**
Ind. **9.2**
Ohio **7.6**
Pa. **7.6**
N.J. **4.4**
Dela. **5.1**
Md. **6.8**
Calif. **8.1**
Colo. *
Kans. *
Mo. **6.6**
Ky. **8.8**
W.Va. Va. **4.0**
Ariz. **8.5**
N.M. *
Okla. **7.1**
Ark. **5.2**
Tenn. **9.9**
N.C. **4.6**
S.C. **5.8**
Miss. **5.7**
Ala. **6.5**
Ga. **8.1**
Texas **7.1**
La. **5.1**
Fla. **8.6**
Alaska
Hawaii
Federal system **2.6**

■ Death penalty
▢ No death penalty

*AVERAGES NOT CALCULATED FOR FEWER THAN 10 INMATES

had lobotomized himself with a bullet to his head; he was so incapacitated that he asked that the pie served at his last meal be saved for "later." By not preventing the execution of a mentally impaired man, Clinton was sending a strong message to voters: the era of soft-on-crime Democrats was over. Even now, Al Gore doesn't dare step out front on death-penalty issues.

Ricky McGinn's case presented a different opportunity for Bush. While the decision to grant a stay was largely based on common sense and the merits of the case, it was convenient, too. In 1999, Talk magazine caught Bush making fun of Karla Faye Tucker, the first woman executed in Texas since the Civil War. Earlier this year, at a campaign debate sponsored by CNN, the cameras showed the governor chuckling over the case of Calvin Burdine, whose lawyer fell asleep at his trial. In going the extra mile for McGinn over the objections of the objections of the appeals court and parole board, Bush looked prudent and blunted some of the criticism of how he vetoed a bill establishing a public defenders' office in Texas and made it harder for death-row inmates to challenge the system.

That system has scheduled 19 more Texas executions between now and Election Day. Gary Graham, slated to die June 22, was convicted on the basis of one sketchy eye-witness account when he was 17. The absence of multiple witnesses would make him ineligible for execution in the Bible ("At the mouth of one witness he shall not be put to death"—Deuteronomy

> Bush stayed McGinn's execution for political reasons, say **59%**, not because of evidence; **55%** say other governors also put politics first in capital cases

17:6); and Graham's age at the time he was convicted of the crime in 1981 would make him too young to be executed in all but four other nations in the world.

Americans might not realize how upset the rest of the world has become over the death penalty. All of our major allies except Japan (with a half-dozen executions a year) have abolished the practice. Only China, Iran, Saudi Arabia and Congo execute more than the United States. A draft version of the European Union's Bill of Rights published last week bars EU countries from extraditing a suspected criminal to a country with a death penalty. (If approved, this could wreak havoc with international law enforcement). Admission to the EU is now contingent on ending capital punishment,

which will force Turkey to abolish its once harsh death-penalty system.

The execution of juvenile offenders is a particular sore spot abroad. The United States has 73 men on death row for crimes committed when they were too young to drink or vote (mostly age 17); 16 have been executed, including eight in Texas. That's more than the rest of the world combined.

So far, opposition abroad has had little effect at home. What changed the climate in the United States was a series of cases in Illinois. The story traces back to the convictions of four black men, two of whom were condemned to die, for the 1978 murders of a white couple in the Chicago suburb of Ford Heights. In the early 1980s, Rob Warden and Margaret Roberts, the editors of a crusading legal publication called The Chicago Lawyer, turned up evidence that the four might be innocent. The state's case fell apart in 1996, after DNA evidence showed that none of the so-called Ford Heights Four could have raped the woman victim. It was only one case, but it had a scaring effect in Illinois for this reason: three other men confessed to the crime and were convicted of it. The original four were unquestionably innocent—and two of them had nearly been executed.

By then other Illinois capital cases were falling apart. Some of the key legwork in unraveling bum convictions came from Northwestern University journalism students. Late in 1998 their school hosted a conference on wrongful convictions. The event produced a stunning photo op: 30 people who'd been freed from death rows across the country, all gathered on one Chicago stage.

But it was another Illinois case, early in 1999, that really began to tip public opinion. A new crop of Northwestern students helped prove the innocence of Anthony Porter, who at one point had been just two days shy of lethal injection for a pair of 1982 murders. Once again, the issue in Illinois wasn't the morality of death sentences, but the dangerously sloppy way in which they were handed out. Once again a confession from another man helped erase doubt that the man convicted of the crime, who has an IQ of 51, had committed it.

By last fall the list of men freed from death row in Illinois had grown to 11. That's when the Chicago Tribune published a lavishly researched series explaining why so many capital cases were suspect. The Tribune's digging found that almost half of the 285 death-penalty convictions in Illinois involved one of four shaky components: defense attorneys who were later suspended or disbarred, jailhouse snitches eager to shorten their own sentences, questionable "hair analysis" evidence or black defendants convicted by all-white juries. What's more, in the weeks after those stories appeared, two more men were freed from death row. That pushed the total to 13—

HOW BUSH MADE THE CALL

A huddle with aides and a sharp sense of the media play

BY HOWARD FINEMAN

When the faxes arrived on the plane, the "body guy" didn't think the governor had to see them right away. Karen Hughes, George W. Bush's right hand, knew better. She'd checked in with Austin. Ricky McGinn's appeals were failing. The DNA issue was hot. The execution was set for 6 p.m. the next day. With Bush out of state, any reprieve technically was up to the acting governor, a Democrat who hoped to grant one. If Bush wanted to deny a reprieve, he'd have to rush home.

So in a car in Albuquerque last Wednesday morning, Bush focused intently on the case. He'd tentatively signed off on it 13 days before—but only as one of four cases in a two-hour briefing during a busy day at home for "state business." Now he read the faxes from his counsel, Margaret Wilson. He spoke to her by mobile phone, hashed things out with Hughes and made his call: yes, new DNA technology might well cast doubt on McGinn's guilt. Bush would tell the press that he was "inclined" to give a reprieve. The story made headlines, and McGinn was given a stay the next day.

The episode was revealing: a real-time example of Bush's leadership style. He sets and clings to broad goals, in this case "swift and just" execution of death-row inmates. He relies heavily on trusted aides—more than ever since he is holding one job while running for another. He has a visceral feel for the media and their discontents, and jumps ahead to the next safe spot.

Reviewing death-penalty cases, Bush says, is his "most profound" duty as governor, his "worst nightmare" the death of an innocent convict. But while executions are practically an industry in Texas, Bush doesn't think he needs to scrutinize the innards of the system he oversees. In a NEWSWEEK interview last week he didn't know how much the state pays attorneys to represent defendants on appeal—a figure reform groups have loudly complained is far too low. Nor did Bush think he should assume the likelihood of error or injustice. "I trust the juries," he said. He denied that the sheer volume of executions raised the risk of a nightmare mistake. "We take lots of time on these cases, " he said. "I'm talking about my staff, the attorney general's office and me."

But in Bush's intensely personal world, decision making is less about judging the facts than reading people. He asks his aides blunt questions and scrutinizes them for signs of uncertainty. It seems there were none in the mansion meeting of May 18, though reform advocates had been agitating about the case. It was press coverage—and the resultant involvement of DNA experts—that forced Bush's hand.

Bush denies that politics drove his decision—though 59 percent of voters in the NEWSWEEK Poll thought so. He also claimed not to care that the likes of well-known DNA expert Barry Scheck had descended on Texas. "With all due respect to Mr. Scheck, he had nothing to do with my decision," Bush said. "People like to read all kinds of motives into these things, and I understand that. These death-penalty cases stir emotions. But all I ever ask are two questions: is there doubt about guilt based on the evidence, and did the defendant have full access? In this case, there was doubt." But what about the next batch, and the one after that? After last week, chances are, the briefings will run a little longer.

But few are acting on it. In the wake of the Illinois decision, only Nebraska, Maryland, Oregon and New Hampshire are reviewing their systems. The governors of the other states that allow the death penalty apparently think it works adequately. If they want to revisit the issue, they might consider the following factors:

Race: The role of race and the death penalty is often misunderstood. On one level, there's the charge of institutional racism: 98 percent of prosecutors are white, and according to the NAACP Legal Defense Fund, they are much more likely to ask for the death penalty for a black-on-white crime than when blacks are the victims.. Blacks convicted of major violent offenses are more likely than white convicts to end up on death row. But once they get there, blacks are less likely than white death-row inmates to be executed because authorities

---

> ## 95% say states should permit DNA testing whenever it might prove guilt or innocence; 88% think Washington should require states to permit such testing

---

are on the defensive about seeming to target African-Americans. The result is both discrimination and reverse discrimination—with deadly consequences.

The risk of errors: The more people on death row, the greater chance of mistakes. There are common elements to cases where terrible errors have been made: when police and prosecutors are pressured by the community to "solve" a notorious murder; when there's no DNA evidence or reliable eyewitnesses; when the crime is especially heinous and draws large amounts of pretrial publicity; when defense attorneys have limited resources. If authorities were particularly vigilant when these issues were at play, they might identify problematic cases earlier.

Deterrence: Often the first argument of death-penalty supporters. But studies of the subject are all over the lot, with no evidence ever established of a deterrent effect. When parole was more common, the argument carried more logic. But nowadays first-degree murderers can look forward to life without parole if caught, which should

---

one more than the number of inmates Illinois had executed since reinstating the death penalty in 1977.

The Porter case and the Tribune series were enough for Governor Ryan. On Jan. 31, he declared a moratorium on Illinois executions, and appointed a commission to see whether the legal process for handling capital cases in Illinois can be fixed. Unless

he gets a guarantee that the system can be made perfect, Ryan told NEWSWEEK last week, "there probably won't be any more deaths," at least while he's governor. "I believe there are cases where the death penalty is appropriate," Ryan said. "But we've got to make sure we have the right person. Every governor who holds this power has the same fear I do."

THE CENTER OF THE STORM

McGinn gets a last shot to prove a lot of evidence wrong

BY MARK MILLER

Ricky McGinn is nobody's poster boy for ending capital punishment. Even before he got the death sentence for the 1993 rape and bludgeon murder of his 12-year-old stepdaughter, Stephanie Rae Flanary, McGinn, 43, had been tried and acquitted of murder in an unrelated case. He was once accused of rape—no charges were filed—and his daughter by a previous marriage has testified that McGinn molested her (again, he was not charged). He is also a key suspect in two unsolved murders of women that occurred in Brown County, Texas, in 1989 and in 1992.

Now McGinn's life may be hanging by a tiny fragment of hair—a pubic hair found in the victim's vagina during autopsy. Some time soon, this crucial piece of evidence will be subjected to mitochondrial DNA testing, a new lab technique. If the test proves the hair was McGinn's, his execution will be rescheduled and he will likely die later this year. But if the hair is someone else's, he may escape death and, possibly, get a new trial.

When McGinn was tried, the prosecution theorized that he killed the girl while raping her. Rape was the "aggravating circumstance" that persuaded the jury to impose the death penalty. Brown County District Attorney Lee Haney says McGinn was convicted of killing the girl on a compelling array of evidence that included a roofer's hammer that bore traces of Stephanie's blood and was found under a seat in McGinn's truck. Investigators also found blood in his Ford Escort, a drop of blood on his shoe and another drop on his shorts; all were type A positive, Stephanie's blood type.

But DNA testing at the time wasn't able to identify the pubic hair (prosecutors said it was "microscopically similar" to McGinn's) or to find DNA in a possible semen stain on Stephanie's shorts. The mitochondrial DNA testing will probably identify the hair, and another new DNA-analysis technique, known as STR (for short-tandem repeat) testing, may identify the semen.

McGinn still insists he was framed. He points out that the bloody hammer wasn't found during repeated searches of his truck by sheriff's deputies, implying that it was planted, and he cites a trial witness who said Stephanie's body wasn't in a culvert at a time when the authorities said it should have been there. He says testimony about the approximate time of death eliminates him as a suspect because he was already in custody. He also denies that he sexually abused his stepdaughter. "My wife kept me satisfied," he says. "I didn't need to go anywhere else, especially a 12-year-old girl." Those are hardly comforting words, but now McGinn will have a chance—and by law at least 61 days—to try to prove the rest of the evidence wrong.

72% say they are confident that those sentenced to death are guilty, but 82% agree at least a few innocent people have been executed since the '70s

in theory deter them as much as the death penalty. It's hard to imagine a criminal's thinking; "Well, since I might get the death penalty for this crime, I won't do it. But if it was only life in prison, I'd go ahead."

Inadequate counsel: Beyond the incompetent lawyers who populate any court-appointed system, Congress and the Clinton administration have put the nation's 3,600 death-row inmates in an agonizing Catch-22. According to the American Bar Association Death Penalty Representation Project, in a state like California, about one third of death-row inmates must wait for years to be assigned lawyers to handle their state direct appeals. And at the postconviction level in some states, inmates don't

have access to lawyers at all. The catch is that the 1996 Anti-Terrorism and Effective Death Penalty Act has a statute of limitations requiring that inmates file federal habeas corpus petitions (requests for federal court review) within one year after the end of their direct state appeal. In other words, because they have no lawyer after their direct appeals, inmates often helplessly watch the clock run out on their chance for federal review. This cuts down on frivolous appeals—but also on ones that could reveal gross injustice.

Fact-finding: Most states aren't as lucky as Illinois. They don't have reporters and investigators digging into the details of old cases. As the death penalty becomes rou-

tine and less newsworthy, the odds against real investigation grow even worse. And even when fresh evidence does surface, most states place high barriers against its use after a trial. This has been standard in the legal system for generations, but it makes little sense when an inmate's life is at stake.

Standards of guilt: In most jurisdictions, the judge instructs the jury to look for "guilt beyond a reasonable doubt." But is that the right standard for capital cases? Maybe a second standard like "residual doubt" would help, whereby if any juror harbors any doubt whatsoever, the conviction would stand but the death penalty would be ruled out. The same double threshold might apply to cases involving single eyewitnesses and key testimony by jailhouse snitches with incentives to lie.

Cost: Unless executions are dramatically speeded up (unlikely after so many mistakes), the death penalty will remain far more expensive than life without parole. The difference is in the upfront prosecution costs, which are at least four times greater than in cases where death is not sought. California spends an extra $90 million on its capital cases beyond the normal costs of the system. Even subtracting pro bono defense, the system is no bargain for taxpayers.

Whether you're for or against the death penalty, it's hard to argue that it doesn't need a fresh look. From America's earliest days, when Benjamin Franklin helped develop the notion of degrees of culpability for murder, this country has been willing to reassess its assumptions about justice. If we're going to keep the death penalty, the public seems to be saying, let's be damn sure we're doing it right. DNA testing will help. So will other fixes. But if, over time, we can't do it right, then we must ask ourselves if it's worth doing at all.

With JOHN MCCORMICK in Chicago, MARK MILLER in Livingston, Texas, and KEVIN PERAINO in New York

Ex-cons on the street

The crime crackdown produces a record flow of ex-offenders with nowhere to go

By Jeff Glasser

LAS VEGAS—Twenty-one days out of prison, convicted drug dealer Wodabá Ahkeem Jones has job prospects as bleak as the dusty urban landscape of this old, westside, working-class neighborhood. Five employers have rejected the three-time ex-felon. At $9 an hour, the part-time maintenance work he managed to find does not begin to pay the bills, which include $550 in monthly child support for his four kids. The stocky, 41-year-old former salesman wants to go straight, but he says the lack of opportunity has him contemplating a return to crime. "I ain't going to eat out of no can in a park," he says. "I'm going to do what I got to do to survive. I ain't going to rape no one, but I will do what's necessary to feed my family."

Jones's struggles are bitterly familiar to the legions of ex-felons returning to Sin City. Some 2,300 of 4,000 Nevada inmates released last year—part of a growing wave of prisoners being freed nationwide—were "dumped" onto city streets, Mayor Oscar Goodman says, with little more than $21 from the state and a free van ride. Michael "Muhammad" Staley, 36, lasted 90 days on the outside. The habitual criminal returned to the Strip last year after more than 11 years in prison. It was a disaster from the get-go: He had no job skills and no place to stay. His new girlfriend ended up pregnant. "I was frustrated so much that I laid on my bed and thought, 'Well, I wish I was back in prison,'" he says. His wish was granted when a parole

officer nabbed him after he was in a fight. "It's like a cub being taken out of the wilderness and then you throw him back in the wilderness when he's grown," he says from the familiar confines of Southern Desert Correctional Center shortly before being paroled again. "He doesn't know how to survive."

Five minutes away. The discharge of Staley and a record 585,000 other inmates this year raises serious public safety concerns. Communities will have to reabsorb a group larger than the entire 320,000 U.S. prison population in 1980. Two thirds of them will be rearrested for committing a crime within three years, at current national recidivism rates. More than 40 percent will end up back in prison. "Anybody who lives in a metropolitan area in the United States is going to be living within five minutes of tens of thousands of prisoners released from prison," says Leonard Sipes, a Maryland Department of Public Safety official.

The numbers are a consequence of the nation's get-tough-on-crime laws. The prison population grew by more than 60 percent in the 1990s, to nearly 1.9 million people. Crooks are serving longer sentences now, an average of 27 months, but 95 percent of them will eventually re-enter society. When they arrive home, most will report to parole officers responsible for dozens, if not hundreds, of parolees; 19 percent of the offenders, about 110,000 this year, will "max out," meaning they have completed their sentences and face no state su-

pervision. Often, these are the worst criminals, who have acted up in the penitentiary or failed to make parole because of the severity of their crimes. "It cries out for reform," says Stephen Rickman, who supervises federal "Weed and Seed" projects in 240 struggling urban neighborhoods. Otherwise, he warns, "you could see an explosive increase in crime."

Sobered by the statistics, criminal justice professionals are wrestling with ways to manage the felon influx. The Clinton administration has proposed a $145 million package to provide drug treatment, court supervision, and job training to returning offenders. Attorney General Janet Reno calls inmates' aftercare a "public safety" issue. "They're going to victimize [the community] again" in the absence of new programs, she tells *U.S. News*. "Why don't we stop it with a carrot-and-stick approach?" Skeptical police groups say the money would be better spent hiring more people to keep an eye on the lawbreakers. "What they need to do is put 50,000 to 60,000 additional parole and probation officers on the streets so we can monitor these people," says James Fotis, director of the Law Enforcement Alliance of America.

Across the country, 17 communities are devising pilot projects to reduce the recidivism rate. Nine of the test sites will set up "re-entry courts," where convicts will have to appear regularly before judges to earn their way back into society or

One city tries rebuilding lives

BALTIMORE—The seven ex-convicts hammering away in a dilapidated row house share a lifetime of splintered dreams. Ranging in age from 18 to 47, they are all former addicts or dealers with little education and few skills, the detritus of the drug-ravaged Druid Heights section. "If I wasn't working, I'd probably be out there selling drugs, whatever I need to get some money," says André Smothers, 18, who started stealing cars and dealing when he was 14.

Smothers and the others have jobs today because of a rare community development project. Recognizing that construction companies were not hiring unskilled workers with criminal pasts, community leaders decided to build their own construction crew. The workers rehabilitate abandoned or rundown houses that are then rented to low-income families. They earn $9-an-hour paychecks from the nonprofit Druid Heights Community Development Corp. More importantly, they learn how to frame houses, put up drywall, and do sheetwork. "We're creating a trained pool of men," says the organization's Kelly Little.

Many temptations. The three-year-old program addresses in a small way one of Druid Heights' biggest problems: how to handle returning offenders who know more about life behind bars than simple, every-day living. In 1998 alone, almost 900 ex-convicts were released into the neighborhood of less than 5,000 residents. The great majority—about three fourths if Druid Heights mimics national figures—have drug or alcohol problems. "For the majority of guys, when they're out a couple of weeks, the street get them," says André Fisher, a former addict and at 47, the "grandfather" of the crew. Guys fall back to what they know." Fisher says people re-entering society have to be reprogrammed. "You need to help with being on time, being taught the basics," he says. "A lot of them still don't have a clue about the boundaries."

Some ex-cons returning to Druid Heights may soon have an opportunity to get that kind of preparation. The area will be one of 17 in a public-private pilot program to reduce recidivism. In the Druid Heights version, 20 offenders will be trained in construction, food preparation, or computers. Money management, substance-abuse prevention, and life-skills classes will accompany the job instruction. If the program works, community leaders will ask for funds to expand it.

The experience of the construction crew suggests the task will not be easy. Four of the original six members fell back into drugs, Little says. But for those who stuck it out, there's been a payoff. When foreman Eric Lee, 41, returned from prison a recovering drug addict more than three years ago, he lived with his mother. Now he owns a home with his fiancée and just bought a black Chevy Blazer. "I'm really grateful somebody saw something in me when I always thought I was nothing," he says. "I found a new way to live."—*J.G.*

be sent back to prison. In western Iowa, the court will target the 22 percent of violent offenders, including sex felons, who have finished their sentences and refused treatment. Successful inmates will "graduate" into the community. Justice Department officials point to the nation's 300 drug courts as a successful model for such court supervision. Critics caution that this system could turn judges into super-parole officers and that mass re-entry courts could lead to greater prison populations if inmates fail to meet the courts' terms.

A more effective tactic, some community activists say, would be to establish programs in prisons, where they have a captive audience. Along with seven other jurisdictions, Nevada plans to test that idea at its Southern Desert correctional facility, a desultory fortress of buildings some 40 miles north of Las Vegas. Low-risk offenders will be required to draw up re-entry plans outlining where they will live, work, and get needed treatment. Mayor Goodman applauds the concept: "There should be alternative means to work with human beings other than to just throw them away like pieces of meat and then wait until the meat ages and let it come back into the community."

Surveillance is the alternative of choice in Lowell, Mass. Police have identified the 77 prisoners due back this year. "If each commits four or five crimes, that's a significant impact," says Ed Davis, Lowell's police chief. He says the department arrested the first two who came home "almost immediately" for larceny and drug offenses. They'll warn the others in coming months. "It seems to me 200 people in this city are committing all the crime," says Davis. "It's just a matter of getting them."

State response. Apart from the pilots, a number of states have designed programs to reduce recidivism. On July 1 Washington will become the first state to require that the corrections budget be divvied up based on the risk that ex-offenders represent to the community. In Maryland, 19,500 habitual drug offenders must submit to regular urinalysis in one of the nation's most ambitious drug-testing programs. The "Break the Cycle" initiative reduced drug use among participants by 53 percent and cut the recidivism rate by 23 percent. Florida has electronically monitored 778 released violent and sex offenders and has revoked just two for new felonies. Richard Nimer, a Florida corrections official, was among those who initially had privacy concerns about the big-brother technology. He's since decided it's well worth the $9.26 daily price tag per inmate: "The way you have to look at it is that these are people who have given up the rights they had with their crimes."

Some victims' rights advocates say even electronic monitoring isn't enough. "I don't think they should be let out," says Christine Long, 47. "I don't think rapists can change." She's speaking from a horrific perspective. In 1988, parolee Robert Blankenship broke into her Columbus home and raped her. The Ohio parole board had released him after he served 7½ years of a 15-to-75-year sentence on earlier rape convictions. Out on the streets, Blankenship was allowed to skip counseling because "the class was full," she later learned.

It's this kind of story that turns the public away from any programs for ex-offenders and makes it difficult for parole boards to predict how an inmate will react to freedom. Consider the case of convicted murderer Jimmy Keys, who will make parole in June. Southern Desert's warden, Sherman Hatcher, initially says Keys has as good a chance as any well-behaved inmate of successfully re-entering the Las Vegas community. "He's going to try much harder," he says. "He's learned a work ethic." Then he reconsiders. Keys hasn't crossed a street or driven a car in 15 years. He sports a curly perm and an early 1980s mesh cap. At the age of 42, he is a relic of another era. How will he react if he cannot follow his dream and become a stockbroker because of his criminal record? What will prevent him or any other released inmate with unreasonable expectations from snapping? "That's where the frustration sets in, when they set these lofty goals," Hatcher says. "They're setting themselves up for failure."

For many ex-convicts, a new start depends on trading the fast life for menial wages. One of the relatively few to make the trade is Noel Johnson, 33, who lived a thug's life for most of his adolescent and adult years. A former Crip from Compton with a "Gangster Man" tattoo, Johnson used to clear thousands of dollars a day selling drugs. Today, seven months fresh from a California prison, he feels lucky to make $8 an hour as a porter at a Las Vegas car dealership. "I had to put down my pride," says Johnson. "But I don't have to look over my back. When the police pull me over, I don't have to be nervous."

The Past and Future of U.S. Prison Policy

Twenty-Five Years After the Stanford Prison Experiment

Craig Haney
University of California, Santa Cruz

Philip Zimbardo
Stanford University

In this article, the authors reflect on the lessons of their Stanford Prison Experiment, some 25 years after conducting it. They review the quarter century of change in criminal justice and correctional policies that has transpired since the Stanford Prison Experiment and then develop a series of reform-oriented proposals drawn from this and related studies on the power of social situations and institutional settings that can be applied to the current crisis in American corrections.

Twenty-five years ago, a group of psychologically healthy, normal college students (and several presumably mentally sound experimenters) were temporarily but dramatically transformed in the course of six days spent in a prison-like environment, in research that came to be known as the Stanford Prison Experiment (SPE; Haney, Banks, & Zimbardo, 1973). The outcome of our study was shocking and unexpected to us, our professional colleagues, and the general public. Otherwise emotionally strong college students who were randomly assigned to be mock-prisoners suffered acute psychological trauma and breakdowns. Some of the students begged to be released from the intense pains of less than a week of merely simulated imprisonment, whereas others adapted by becoming blindly obedient to the unjust authority of the guards. The guards, too—who also had been carefully chosen on the basis of their normal–average scores on a variety of personality measures—quickly internalized their randomly assigned role. Many of these seemingly gentle and caring young men, some of whom had described themselves as pacifists or Vietnam War "doves," soon began mistreating their peers and were indifferent to the obvious suffering that their actions produced. Several of them devised sadistically inventive ways to harass and degrade the prisoners, and none of the less actively cruel mock-guards ever intervened or complained about the abuses they witnessed. Most of the worst prisoner treatment came on the night shifts and other occasions when the guards thought they could avoid the surveillance and interference of the research team. Our planned two-week experiment had to be aborted after only six days because the experience dramatically and painfully transformed most of the participants in ways we did not anticipate, prepare for, or predict.

These shocking results attracted an enormous amount of public and media attention and became the focus of much academic writing and commentary. For example, in addition to our own analyses of the outcome of the study itself (e.g., Haney et al., 1973; Haney & Zimbardo, 1977; Zimbardo, 1975; Zimbardo, Haney, Banks, & Jaffe, 1974) and the various methodological and ethical issues that it raised (e.g., Haney, 1976; Zimbardo, 1973), the SPE was hailed by former American Psychological Association president George Miller (1980) as an exemplar of the way in which psychological research could and should be "given away" to the public because its important lessons could be readily understood and appreciated by nonprofessionals. On the 25th anniversary of this study, we reflect on its continuing message for contemporary prison policy in light of the quarter century of criminal justice history that has transpired since we concluded the experiment.

When we conceived of the SPE, the discipline of psychology was in the midst of what has been called a "situational revolution." Our study was one of the "host of celebrated laboratory and field studies" that Ross and Nisbett (1991) referred to as having demonstrated the ways in which "the immediate social situation can overwhelm in importance the type of individual differences in personal traits or dispositions that people normally think of as being determinative of social behavior." Along with much other research conducted over the past two and one-half decades illustrating the enormous power of situations, the SPE is often cited in textbooks and journal articles as a demonstration of the way in which social contexts can influence, alter, shape, and transform human behavior.

Our goal in conducting the SPE was to extend that basic perspective—one emphasizing the potency of social situations—into a relatively unexplored area of social psychology. Specifically, our study represented an experimental demonstration of the extraordinary power of *institutional* environments to influence those who passed through them. In contrast to the companion research of Stanley Milgram (1974) that focused on individual compliance in the face of an authority figure's increasingly extreme and unjust demands, the SPE examined the conformity pressures brought to bear on groups of people functioning within the same institutional setting (see Carr 1995). Our "institution" rapidly developed sufficient power to bend and twist human behavior in ways that confounded expert predictions and violated the expectations of those who created and participated in it. And, because the unique design of the study allowed us to minimize the role of personality or dispositional variables, the SPE yielded especially clear psychological insights about the nature and dynamics of social and institutional control.

The behavior of prisoners and guards in our simulated environment bore a remarkable similarity to patterns found in actual prisons. As we wrote, "Despite the fact that guards and prisoners were essentially free to engage in any form of interaction . . . the characteristic nature of their encounters tended to be negative, hostile, affrontive and dehumanising" (Haney et al., 1973, p. 80). Specifically, verbal interactions were pervaded by threats, insults, and deindividuating references that most commonly directed by guards against prisoners. The environment we had fashioned in the basement hallway of Stanford University's Department of Psychology became so real for the participants that it completely dominated their day-to-day existence (e.g., 90% of prisoners' in-cell conversations focused on "prison"-related topics), dramatically affected their moods and emotional states (e.g., prisoners expressed three times as much negative affect as did guards), and at least temporarily undermined their sense of self (e.g., both groups expressed increasingly more deprecating self-evaluations over time). Behaviorally, guards most often gave commands and engaged in confrontive or aggressive acts toward prisoners, whereas the prisoners initiated increasingly less behavior; failed to support each other more often than not; negatively evaluated each other in ways that were consistent with the guards' views of them; and as the experiment progressed, more frequently expressed intentions to do harm to others (even as they became increasingly more docile and conforming to the whims of the guards). We concluded,

> The negative, anti-social reactions observed were not the product of an environment created by combining a collection of deviant personalities, but rather the result of an intrinsically pathological situation, which could distort and rechannel the behaviour of essentially normal individuals. The abnormality here resided in the psychological nature of the situation and not in those who passed through it. (Haney et al., 1973, p. 90)

In much of the research and writing we have done since then, the SPE has served as an inspiration and intellectual platform from which to extend the conceptual relevance of situational variables into two very different domains. One of us examined the coercive power of legal institutions in general and prisons in particular (e.g., Haney, 1993a, 1997b. 1997c, 1997d, 1998; Haney & Lynch, 1997). as well as the importance

of situational factors in explaining and reducing crime (e.g., Haney, 1983, 1994, 1995, 1997a). The other of us explored the dimensions of intrapsychic "psychological prisons" that constrict human experience and undermine human potential (e.g., Brodt & Zimbardo, 1981; Zimbardo, 1977; Zimbardo, Pilkonis, & Norwood, 1975) and the ways in which "mind-altering" social psychological dynamics can distort individual judgment and negatively influence behavior (e.g., Zimbardo, 1979a; Zimbardo & Andersen, 1993). Because the SPE was intended as a critical demonstration of the negative effects of extreme institutional environments, much of the work that grew out of this original study was change-oriented and explored the ways in which social and legal institutions and practices might be transformed to make them more responsive to humane psychological imperatives (e.g., Haney, 1993b; Haney & Pettigrew, 1986; Haney & Zimbardo, 1977; Zimbardo, 1975; Zimbardo et al., 1974).

In this article, we return to the core issue that guided the original study (Haney et al., 1973)—the implications of situational models of behavior for criminal justice institutions. We use the SPE as a point of historical departure to briefly examine the ways in which policies concerning crime and punishment have been transformed over the intervening 25 years. We argue that a series of psychological insights derived from the SPE and related studies, and the broad perspective that they advanced, still can contribute to the resolution of many of the critical problems that currently plague correctional policy in the United States.

Crime and Punishment a Quarter Century Ago

The story of how the nature and purpose of imprisonment have been transformed over the past 25 years is very different from the one that we once hoped and expected we would be able to tell. At the time we conducted the SPE—in 1971—there was widespread concern about the fairness and the efficacy of the criminal justice system. Scholars, politicians, and members of the public wondered aloud whether prisons were too harsh, whether they adequately rehabilitated prisoners, and whether there were alternatives to incarceration that would better serve correctional needs and interests. Many states were already alarmed about increased levels of overcrowding. Indeed, in those days, prisons that operated at close to 90% of capacity were thought to be dangerously overcrowded. It was widely understood by legislators and penologists alike that under such conditions, programming resources were stretched too thin, and prison administrators were left with increasingly fewer degrees of freedom with which to respond to interpersonal conflicts and a range of other inmate problems.

Despite these concerns about overcrowding, there was a functional moratorium on prison construction in place in most parts of the country. Whatever else it represented, the moratorium reflected a genuine skepticism at some of the very highest levels of government about the viability of prison as a solution to the crime problem. Indeed, the report of the National Advisory Commission on Criminal Justice Standards and Goals (1973), published at around the same time we published the results of the SPE, concluded that prisons, juvenile reformatories, and jails had achieved what it characterized as a "shocking record of failure" (p. 597), suggested that these institutions may have been responsible for creating more crime than they prevented, and recommended that the moratorium on prison construction last at least another 10 years.

To be sure, there was a fiscal undercurrent to otherwise humanitarian attempts to avoid the overuse of imprisonment. Prisons are expensive, and without clear evidence that they worked very well, it was difficult to justify building and running more of them (cf. Scull, 1977). But there was also a fair amount of genuine concern among the general public about what was being done to prisoners behind prison walls and what the long-term effects would be (e.g., Mitford, 1973; Yee, 1973). The SPE and its attendant publicity added to that skepticism, but the real challenge came from other deeper currents in the larger society.

The late 1960s saw the beginning of a prisoners' rights movement that eventually raised the political consciousness of large numbers of prisoners, some of whom became effective spokespersons for their cause (e.g., American Friends Service Committee, 1971; Jackson, 1970; Smith, 1993). Widely publicized, tragic events in several prisons in different parts of the country vividly illustrated how prisoners could be badly mistreated by prison authorities and underscored the potentially serious drawbacks of relying on prisons as the centerpiece in a national strategy of crime control. For example, just a few weeks after the SPE was concluded, prisoners in Attica, New York, held a number of correctional officers hostage in a vain effort to secure more humane treatment. Although national celebrities attempted to peaceably mediate the standoff, an armed assault to retake the prison ended tragically with the deaths of many hostages and prisoners. Subsequent revelations about the use of excessive force and an official cover-up contributed to public skepticism about prisons and doubts about the wisdom and integrity of some of their administrators (e.g., Wicker, 1975).

Legal developments also helped to shape the prevailing national Zeitgeist on crime and punishment. More than a decade before we conducted the SPE, the U.S. Supreme Court had defined the Eighth Amendment's ban on cruel and unusual punishment as one that drew its meaning from what Chief Justice Warren called "the evolving standards of decency that mark the progress of a maturing society" (*Trop v. Dulles*, 1958, p. 101). It is probably fair to say that most academics and other informed citizens anticipated that these standards *were* evolving and in such a way that the institution of prison—as the major organ of state-sanctioned punishment in American society—would be scrutinized carefully and honestly in an effort to apply contemporary humane views, including those that were emerging from the discipline of psychology.

Psychologists Stanley Brodsky, Carl Clements, and Raymond Fowler were engaged in just such a legal effort to reform the Alabama prison system in the early 1970s (*Pugh v. Locke*, 1976; Yackle, 1989). The optimism with which Fowler (1976) wrote about the results of that litigation was characteristic of the time: "The practice of psychology in the nation's correctional systems, long a neglected byway, could gain new significance and visibility as a result [of the court's ruling]" (p. 15). The same sentiments prevailed in a similar effort in which we participated along with psychologist Thomas Hilliard (1976) in litigation that was designed to improve conditions in a special solitary confinement unit at San Quentin (*Spain v. Procunier*, 1976). Along with other psychologists interested in correctional and legal reform, we were confident that psychology and other social scientific disciplines could be put to effective use in the creation and application of evolving standards inside the nation's prisons (see Haney & Zimbardo, 1977).

And then, almost without warning, all of this critical reappraisal and constructive optimism about humane standards and alternatives to incarceration was replaced with something else. The counterrevolution in crime and punishment began slowly and imperceptibly at first and then pushed forward with a consistency of direction and effect that could not be overlooked. It moved so forcefully and seemingly inexorably during the 1980s that it resembled nothing so much as a runaway punishment train, driven by political steam and fueled by media-induced fears of crime. Now, many years after the SPE and that early optimism about psychologically based prison reform, our nation finds itself in the midst of arguably the worst corrections crisis in U.S. history, with every indication that it will get worse before it can possibly get better. For the first time in the 200-year history of imprisonment in the United States, there appear to be no limits on the amount of prison pain the public is willing to inflict in the name of crime control (cf. Haney, 1997b, 1998). Retired judge Lois Forer (1994), in her denunciation of some of these recent trends, warned of the dire consequences of what she called the "rage to punish." But this rage has been indulged so completely that it threatens to override any of the competing concerns for humane justice that once served to make this system more compassionate and fair. The United States has entered what another commentator called the "mean season" of corrections, one in which penal philosophy amounts to little more than devising "creative strategies to make offenders suffer" (Cullen, 1995, p. 340).

The Radical Transformation of "Corrections"

We briefly recount the series of wrenching transformations that laid the groundwork for the mean season of corrections that the nation has now entered—the some 25 years of correctional policy that have transpired since the SPE was conducted. Whatever the social and political forces that caused these transformations, they collectively altered the correctional landscape of the country. The criminal justice system not only has become increasingly harsh and punitive but also has obscured many of the psychological insights on which the SPE and numerous other empirical studies were based—insights about the power of social situations and contexts to influence and control behavior. Specifically, over a very short period of time, the following series of transformations occurred to radically change the shape and direction of corrections in the United States.

The Death of Rehabilitation

A dramatic shift in correctional philosophy was pivotal to the series of changes that followed. Almost overnight, the concept that had served as the intellectual cornerstone of corrections policy for nearly a century—rehabilitation—was publicly and politically discredited. The country moved abruptly in the mid-1970s from a society that justified putting people in prison on the basis of the belief that their incarceration would somehow facilitate their productive reentry into the free world to one that used imprisonment merely to disable criminal offenders ("incapacitation") or to keep them far away from the rest of society ("containment"). At a more philosophical level, imprisonment was now said to further something called "just desserts"—locking people up for no other reason than they deserved it and for no other purpose than to punish them (e.g., von Hirsch, 1976). In fact, prison punishment soon came to be thought of as its own reward, serving only the goal of inflicting pain.

Determinate Sentencing and the Politicizing of Prison Pain

Almost simultaneously—and, in essence, as a consequence of the abandonment of rehabilitation—many states moved from indeterminate to determinate models of prison sentencing. Because indeterminate sentencing had been devised as a mechanism to allow for the release of prisoners who were rehabilitated early—and the retention of those whose in-prison change took longer—it simply did not fit with the new goals of incarceration. This shift to determinate sentencing did have the intended consequence of removing discretion from the hands of prison administrators and even judges who, studies showed, from time to time abused it (e.g., American Friends Service Committee, 1971). However, it also had the likely unintended consequence of bringing prison sentencing into an openly political arena. Once largely the province of presumably expert judicial decision makers, prison administrators, or parole authorities who operated largely out of the public view, prison sentencing had remained relatively free from at least the most obvious and explicit forms of political influence. They no longer were. Moreover, determinate sentencing and the use of rigid sentencing guidelines or "grids" undermined the role of situation and context in the allocation of punishment (cf. Freed, 1992).

The Imprisoning of America

The moratorium on new prison construction that was in place at the time of the SPE was ended by the confluence of several separate, powerful forces. For one, legislators continued to vie for the mantle of "toughest on crime" by regularly increasing the lengths of prison sentences. Of course, this meant that prisoners were incarcerated for progressively longer periods of time. In addition, the sentencing discretion of judges was almost completely subjugated to the various aforementioned legislative grids, formulas, and guidelines. Moreover, the advent of determinate sentencing meant that prison administrators had no outlets at the other end of this flow of prisoners to relieve population pressures (which, under indeterminate sentencing, had been discretionary). Finally, federal district court judges began to enter judicial orders that prohibited states from, among other things, cramming two and three or more prisoners into one-person (typically six feet by nine feet) cells (e.g., *Burks v. Walsh,* 1978; *Capps v. Atiyeh,* 1980). Eventually even long-time opponents of new prisons agreed that prisoners could no longer be housed in these shockingly inadequate spaces and reluctantly faced the inevitable: Prison construction began on an unprecedented scale across the country.

Although this rapid prison construction briefly eased the overcrowding problem, prisoner populations continued to grow at unprecedented rates (see Figure 1). It soon became clear that even dramatic increases in the number of new prisons could not keep pace. In fact, almost continuously over the past 25 years, penologists have described U.S. prisons as "in crisis" and have characterized each new level of overcrowding as "unprecedented." As the decade of the 1980s came to a close, the United States was imprisoning more people for longer periods of time than ever before in our history, far surpassing other industrialized democracies in the use of incarceration as a crime control measure (Mauer, 1992, 1995). As of June 1997, the most recent date for which figures are available, the total number of persons incarcerated in the United States exceeded 1.7 million (Bureau of Justice Statistics, 1998), which continues the upward trend of the previous 11 years, from 1985 to 1996, when the number rose from 744,208 to 1,630,940. Indeed, 10 years ago, long before today's record rates were attained, one scholar concluded, "It is easily demonstrable that America's use of prison is excessive to the point of barbarity, with a prison rate several times higher than that of other similarly developed Western countries" (Newman, 1988, p. 346). A year later, a reviewer wrote in the pages of *Contemporary Psychology:*

Figure 1
Number of Prisoners in the United States, 1970–1995

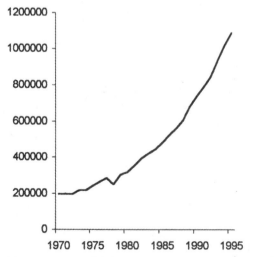

Note. Jail inmates are not included.

American prison and jail populations have reached historically high levels. . . . It is noteworthy that, although in several recent years the levels of reported crime declined, the prison and jail populations continued to rise. The desire for punishment seems to have taken on a life of its own. (McConville, 1989, p. 928)

The push to higher rates and lengths of incarceration has only intensified since then. Most state and federal prisons now operate well above their rated capacities, with many overcrowded to nearly twice their design limits. At the start of the 1990s, the United States incarcerated more persons per capita than any other modern nation in the world. The international disparities are most striking when the U.S. incarceration rate is contrasted to those of other nations with which the United States is often compared, such as Japan, The Netherlands, Australia, and the United Kingdom; throughout most of the present decade, the U.S. rates have consistently been between four and eight times as high as those of these other nations (e.g., Christie, 1994; Mauer, 1992, 1995). In fact, rates of incarceration have continued to climb in the United States, reaching the unprecedented levels of more than 500 per 100,000 in 1992 and then 600 per 100,000 in 1996. Although in 1990 the United States incarcerated a higher proportion of its population than any other nation on earth (Mauer, 1992), as of 1995, political and economic upheaval in Russia was associated with an abrupt increase in rate of incarceration, and Russia surpassed the United States. (Additional data on the abrupt growth in the U.S. prison population and international comparisons of incarceration rates can be found in the Appendix, Tables A1 and A2.)

The increase in U.S. prison populations during these years was not produced by a disproportionate increase in the incarceration of violent offenders. In 1995, only one quarter of persons sentenced to state prisons were convicted of a violent offense, whereas three quarters were sent for property or drug offenses or other nonviolent crimes such as receiving stolen property or immigration violations (Bureau of Justice Statistics, 1996). Nor was the increased use of imprisonment related to increased levels of crime. In fact, according to the National Crime Victimization Survey, conducted by the Bureau of the Census, a survey of 94,000 U.S. residents found that many fewer of them were the victims of crime during the calendar year 1995–1996, the year our incarceration rate reached an all-time high (Bureau of Justice Statistics, 1997b).

The Racialization of Prison Pain

The aggregate statistics describing the extraordinary punitiveness of the U.S. criminal justice system mask an important fact: The pains of imprisonment have been inflicted disproportionately on minorities, especially Black men. Indeed, for many years, the rate of incarceration of White men in the United States compared favorably with those in most Western European nations, including countries regarded as the most progressive and least punitive (e.g., Dunbaugh, 1979). Although in recent years the rate of incarceration for Whites in the United States has also increased and no longer compares favorably with other Western European nations, it still does not begin to approximate the rate for African Americans. Thus, although they represent less than 6% of the general U.S. population, African American men constitute 48% of those confined to state prisons. Statistics collected at the beginning of this decade indicated that Blacks were more than six times more likely to be imprisoned than their White counterparts (Mauer, 1992). By 1995, that disproportion had grown to seven and one-half times (Bureau of Justice Statistics, 1996). In fact, the United States incarcerates African American men at a rate that is approximately four times the rate of incarceration of Black men in South Africa (King, 1993).

All races and ethnic groups and both sexes are being negatively affected by the increases in the incarcerated population, but the racial comparisons are most telling. The rate of incarceration for White men almost doubled between 1985 and 1995, growing from a rate of 528 per 100,000 in 1985 to a rate of 919 per 100,000 in 1995. The impact of incarceration on African American men, Hispanics, and women of all racial and ethnic groups is greater than that for White men, with African American men being the most profoundly affected. The number of African American men who are incarcerated rose from a rate of 3,544 per 100,000 in 1985 to an astonishing rate of 6,926 per 100,000 in 1995. Also, between 1985 and 1995, the number of Hispanic prisoners rose by an average of 12% annually (Mumola & Beck, 1997). (Additional data on some of the disparities in imprisonment between Whites and Blacks in the United States can be found in the Appendix, Tables A3 and A4, and Figure A1.)

The Overincarceration of Drug Offenders

The increasingly disproportionate number of African American men who are being sent to prison seems to be related to the dramatic increase in the number of persons incarcerated for drug-related offenses, combined with the greater tendency to imprison Black drug offenders as compared with their White counterparts. Thus, although Blacks and Whites use drugs at approximately the same rate (Bureau of Justice Statistics, 1991), African Americans were arrested for drug offenses during the so-called war on drugs at a much higher rate than were Whites (Blumstein, 1993). The most recent data show that between 1985 and 1995, the number of African Americans incarcerated in state prisons due to drug violations (which were their only or their most serious offense) rose 707% (see Table 1). In contrast, the number of Whites incarcerated in state prisons for drug offenses (as their only or most serious offense) underwent a 306% change. In 1986, for example, only 7% of Black prison inmates in the United States had been convicted of drug crimes, compared with 8% of Whites. By 1991, however, the Black percentage had more than tripled to 25%, whereas the percentage of White inmates incarcerated for drug crimes had increased by only half to 12% (Tonry, 1995). In the federal prison system, the numbers of African Americans incarcerated for drug violations are shockingly high: Fully 64% of male and 71% of female Black prisoners incarcerated in federal institutions in 1995 had been sent there for drug offenses (Bureau of Justice Statistics, 1996).

Table 1

Change in Estimated Number of Sentenced Prisoners, by Most Serious Offense and Race, Between 1985 and 1995

Most serious offense	Total % change, 1985–1995	White % change, 1985–1995	Black % change, 1985–1995
Total	119	109	132
Violent offenses	86	92	83
Property offenses	69	74	65
Drug offenses	478	306	707
Public-order offenses[a]	187	162	229
Other/unspecified[b]	–6	–72	64

Note. Adapted from *Prisoners in 1996* (Bureau of Justice Statistics Bulletin NCJ 164619, p. 10), by C.J. Mumola and A.J. Beck, 1997, Rockville, MD: Bureau of Justice Statistics. In the public domain. [a]Includes weapons, drunk driving, escape, court offenses, obstruction, commercialized vice, morals and decency charges, liquor law violations, and other public-order offenses. [b]Includes juvenile offenses and unspecified felonies.

According to a historical report done for the Bureau of Justice Statistics (Cahalan, 1986), the offense distribution of federal and state prisoners—a measure of the types of crimes for which people are incarcerated—remained stable from 1910 to 1984. The classification of some offenses changed. For example, robbery is now included in the category of violent crime rather than being classified with property crimes, as it was in the past. Public order offenses, also called morals charges, used to include vagrancy, liquor law violations, and drug offenses. Drug offenses are no longer classified with public order crimes. Of course, not only have drug offenses been elevated to the status of their own crime category in national statistical compilations and their own especially severe legislated penalties, but there is also a "Drug Czar" in the executive branch and a large federal agency devoted exclusively to enforcing laws against drug-related crimes.

As we noted, the types and proportions of offenses for which people were incarcerated in the United States were highly consistent for the 75 years prior to 1984. For most of the 20th century, the U.S. prison population consisted of around 60–70% offenders against property, 13–24% offenders against persons (now called violent crime), around 20% public order–morals violations (which included drug offenses), and 10% other types of offenders (Cahalan, 1986).

However, these distributions have changed dramatically during the past 10 to 15 years. The federal government is now willing to incarcerate people for a wider range of criminal violations, and both state and federal prisoners remain incarcerated for longer periods of time. The number of violent offenders who are incarcerated has risen but not as steeply as the number of drug offenders who are now sent to prison. In 1995, 23% of state prisoners were incarcerated for drug offenses in contrast to 9% of drug offenders in state prisons in 1986. In fact, the proportion of drug offenders in the state prison population nearly tripled by 1990, when it reached 21%, and has remained at close to that level since then. The proportion of federal prisoners held for drug violations doubled during the past 10 years. In 1985, 34% of federal prisoners were incarcerated for drug violations. By 1995, the proportion had risen to 60%. (See Figure 2.)

We note in passing that these three interrelated trends—the extraordinary

Figure 2
Distribution of Offenses: State and Federal Prisons, 1985 and 1995

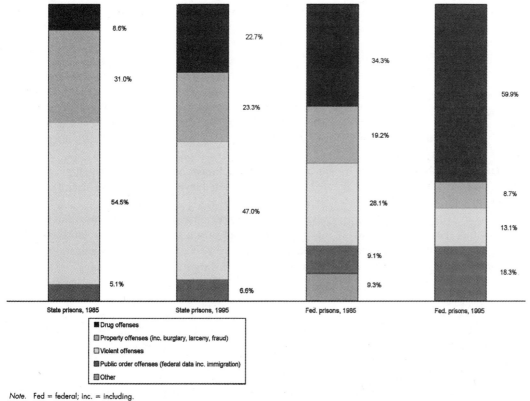

Note. Fed = federal; inc. = including.

increase in the numbers of persons in prison, the disproportionate incarceration of minorities, and the high percentage of persons incarcerated for drug offenses—reflect a consistent disregard of context and situation in the criminal justice policies of the past 25 years. The unprecedented use of imprisonment per se manifests a policy choice to incarcerate individual lawbreakers instead of targeting the criminogenic social conditions and risk factors that have contributed to their criminality. Sentencing models that ignore situation and context inevitably lead to higher rates of incarceration among groups of citizens who confront race-based poverty and deprivation and other social ills that are related to discrimination. The failure to address the differential opportunity structure that leads young minority group members into certain kinds of drug-related activities and the conscious decision to target those activities for criminal prosecution and incarceration, rather than to attempt to improve the life chances of the urban Black underclass, reflect dispositional— and discriminatory—views of crime control.

Moreover, excessive and disproportionate use of imprisonment ignores the secondary effects that harsh criminal justice policies eventually will have on the social contexts and communities from which minority citizens come. Remarkably, as the present decade began, there were more young Black men (between the ages of 20 and 29) under the control of the nation's criminal justice system (including probation and parole supervision) than the total number in college (Mauer, 1990). Thus, one scholar has predicted that "imprisonment will become the most significant factor contributing to the dissolution and breakdown of African American families during the decade of the 1990s" (King, 1993, p. 145), and another has concluded that "crime control policies are a major contributor to the disruption of the family, the prevalence of single parent families, and children raised without a father in the ghetto, and the 'inability of people to get the jobs still available' " (Chambliss, 1994, p. 183).

The Rise of the "Supermax" Prison

In addition to becoming dangerously overcrowded and populated by a disproportionate number of minority citizens and drug offenders over the past 25 years, many U.S. prisons also now lack meaningful work, training, education, treatment, and counseling programs for the prisoners who are confined in them. Plagued by increasingly intolerable living conditions where prisoners serve long sentences that they now have no hope of having reduced through "good time" credits, due to laws imposed by state legislatures, many prison officials have turned to punitive policies of within-prison segregation in the hope of maintaining institutional control (e.g., Christie, 1994; Haney, 1993a; Haney & Lynch, 1997; Perkinson, 1994). Indeed, a penal philosophy of sorts has emerged in which prison systems use long-term solitary confinement in so-called supermax prisons as a proactive policy of inmate management. Criticized as the "Marionization" of U.S. prisons, after the notorious federal penitentiary in Marion, Illinois, where the policy seems to have originated (Amnesty International, 1987;

Olivero & Roberts, 1990), one commentator referred to the "accelerating movement toward housing prisoners officially categorized as violent or disruptive in separate, free-standing facilities where they are locked in their cells approximately 23 hours per day" (Immarigeon, 1992, p. 1). They are ineligible for prison jobs, vocational training programs, and, in many states, education.

Thus, in the 25 years since the SPE was conducted, the country has witnessed the emergence of a genuinely new penal form—supermax prisons that feature state-of-the-art, ultra secure, long-term segregated confinement supposedly reserved for the criminal justice system's most troublesome or incorrigible offenders. Human Rights Watch (1997) described the basic routine imposed in such units: Prisoners "are removed from general population and housed in conditions of extreme social isolation, limited environmental stimulation, reduced privileges and service, scant recreational, vocational or educational opportunities, and extraordinary control over their every movement" (p. 14). (See also Haney, 1993a, 1997d, and Haney and Lynch, 1997, for discussions of the psychological effects of these special conditions of confinement.) By 1991, these prisons imposing extreme segregation and isolation were functioning in some 36 states, with many others in the planning stages (e.g., "Editorial," 1991). A newly opened, highly restrictive, modern "control unit" apparently committed the federal penitentiary system to the use of this penal form for some time to come (Dowker & Good, 1992; Perkinson, 1994). Thus, by 1997 Human Rights Watch expressed concern over what it called "the national trend toward supermaximum security prisons" (p. 13), noting that in addition to the 57 units currently in operation, construction programs already underway "would increase the nationwide supermax capacity by nearly 25 percent" (p. 14).

A constitutional challenge to conditions in California's supermax—one that many legal observers viewed as a test case on the constitutionality of these "prisons of the future"—resulted in a strongly worded opinion in which the federal court condemned certain of its features, suggesting that the prison, in the judge's words, inflicted "stark sterility and unremitting monotony" (*Madrid V. Gomez,* 1995, p. 1229) on prisoners and exposed them to overall conditions that "may press the outer bounds of what most humans can psychologically tolerate" (p. 1267) but left the basic regimen of segregation and isolation largely intact.

Here, too, the importance of context and situation has been ignored. Widespread prison management problems and gang-related infractions are best understood in systematic terms, as at least in large part the products of worsening overall institutional conditions. Viewing them instead as caused exclusively by "problem prisoners" who require nothing more than isolated and segregated confinement ignores the role of compelling situational forces that help to account for their behavior. It also overlooks the capacity of deteriorated prison conditions to continue to generate new replacements who will assume the roles of those prisoners who have been taken to segregation. Finally, the continued use of high levels of punitive isolation, despite evidence of significant psychological trauma and psychiatric risk (e.g., Grassian, 1983; Haney, 1997d; Haney & Lynch, 1997), reflects a legal failure to fully appreciate the costs of these potentially harmful social contexts—both in terms of immediate pain and emotional damage as well as their long- term effects on post-segregation and even post-release behavior.

The Retreat of the Supreme Court

The final component in the transformation of U.S. prison policy during this 25-year period came from the U.S. Supreme Court, as the Justices significantly narrowed their role in examining and correcting unconstitutionally cruel prison conditions as well as drastically redefining the legal standards that they applied in such cases. Ironically, the early constitutional review of conditions of confinement at the start of this historical period had begun on an encouraging note. Indeed, it was one of the things that helped fuel the early optimism about "evolving standards" to which we earlier referred. For example, in 1974, just three years after the SPE, the Supreme Court announced that "there is no iron curtain drawn between the Constitution and the prisons of this country" (*Wolff v. McDonnell*, 1974, pp. 556–567). Given the Warren Court's legacy of protecting powerless persons who confronted potent situations and adverse structural conditions, and the Court's legal realist tendencies to look carefully at the specific circumstances under which abuses occurred (e.g., Haney, 1991), hopes were raised in many quarters that a majority of the Justices would carefully evaluate the nation's worst prison environments, acknowledge their harmful psychological effects, and order badly needed reform.

However, a sharp right turn away from the possibility and promise of the Warren Court's view became evident at the start of the 1980s. The first time the Court fully evaluated the totality of conditions in a particular prison, it reached a very discouraging result. Justice Powell's majority opinion proclaimed that "the Constitution does not mandate comfortable prisons, and prisons which house persons convicted of serious crimes cannot be free of discomfort" (*Rhodes v. Chapman*, 1981, p. 349). None of the Justices attempted to define the degree of acceptable discomfort that could be inflicted under the Constitution. However, Powell used several phrases that were actually taken from death penalty cases to provide a sense of just how painful imprisonment could become before beginning to qualify as "cruel and unusual": Punishment that stopped just short of involving "the *unnecessary* and *wanton* infliction of pain" (p. 345, citing *Gregg v. Georgia*, 1976, p. 173) would not be prohibited, pains of imprisonment that were not "*grossly* disproportionate to the severity of the crime" (p. 345, citing *Coker v. Georgia*, 1977, p. 592) would be allowed, and harm that was not "*totally* without penological justification" (p. 345, citing *Gregg v. Georgia*, p. 183) also would be acceptable (italics added).

The Supreme Court thus set a largely unsympathetic tone for Eighth Amendment prison cases and established a noninterventionist stance from which it has rarely ever wavered. Often turning a blind eye to the realities of prison life and the

potentially debilitating psychological effects on persons housed in badly overcrowded, poorly run, and increasingly dangerous prisons, the Court developed several constitutional doctrines that both limited the liability of prison officials and further undermined the legal relevance of a careful situational analysis of imprisonment. For example, in one pivotal case, the Court decided that the notion that "overall prison conditions" somehow could produce a cruel and unusual living environment—a view that not only was psychologically straightforward but also had guided numerous lower court decisions in which overall conditions of confinement in particular prisons were found unconstitutional—was simply "too amorphous" to abide any longer (*Wilson v. Seiter*, 1991, p. 304).

In the same case, the Court decisively shifted its Eighth Amendment inquiry from the conditions themselves to the thought processes of the officials responsible for creating and maintaining them. Justice Scalia wrote for the majority that Eighth Amendment claims concerning conduct that did not purport to be punishment required an inquiry into prison officials' state of mind—in this case, their "deliberate indifference" (*Wilson v. Seiter*, 1991). Justice Scalia also had rejected a distinction between short-term deprivations and "continuing" or "systemic" problems of the sort that might have made state of mind less relevant. The argument here had been that evidence of systemic problems would obviate the need to demonstrate state of mind on the part of officials who had presumably known about and tolerated them as part of the correctional status quo. Scalia said instead that although the long duration of a cruel condition might make it easier to establish knowledge and, hence, intent, it would not eliminate the intent requirement.

Prison litigators and legal commentators criticized the decision as having established a constitutional hurdle for conditions of confinement claims that was "virtually insurmountable" and speculated that the impossibly high threshold "reflects recent changes in public attitudes towards crime and allocation of scarce public resources" (Hall, 1993, p. 208). Finally, in 1994, the Court seemed to raise the hurdle to a literally insurmountable level by explicitly embracing the criminal law concept of "subjective recklessness" as the Eighth Amendment test for deliberate indifference (*Fanner v. Brennan*, 1994). In so doing, the Court shunned the federal government's concern that the new standard meant that that triers of fact would first have to find that "prison officials acted like criminals" before finding them liable (*Farmer v. Brennan*, 1994, p. 1980).

This series of most recent cases has prompted commentators to speculate that the Supreme Court is "headed toward a new hands-off doctrine in correctional law" (Robbins, 1993, p. 169) that would require lower courts "to defer to the internal actions and decisions of prison officials" (Hall, 1993, p. 223). Yet, the narrow logic of these opinions suggests that the Justices intend to keep not only their hands off the faltering prison system but their eyes averted from the realities of prison life as well. It is difficult to avoid the conclusion that the Court's refusal to examine the intricacies of day-to-day existence in those maximum security prisons whose deteriorated and potentially harmful conditions are placed at issue is designed to limit the liability of those who create and run them.

Unfortunately, the U.S. Supreme Court was not the only federal governmental agency contributing to this retreat from the meaningful analysis of conditions of confinement inside the nation's prisons and jails. In April 1996, the U.S. Congress passed legislation titled the Prison Litigation Reform Act (PLRA) that significantly limited the ability of the federal courts to monitor and remedy constitutional violations in detention facilities throughout the country. Among other things, it placed substantive and procedural limits on injunctions and consent decrees (where both parties reach binding agreements to fix existing problems in advance of trial) to improve prison conditions. The PLRA also impeded the appointment of "special masters" to oversee prison systems' compliance with court orders and appeared to forbid the filing of legal actions by prisoners for mental or emotional injury without a prior showing of physical injury. Although the full impact of this remarkable legislation cannot yet be measured, it seems to have been designed to prevent many of the problems that have befallen U.S. prisons from ever being effectively addressed. Combined with the Supreme Court's stance concerning prison conditions, the PLRA will likely contribute to the growing tendency to avoid any meaningful contextual analysis of the conditions under which many prisoners are now confined and also to a growing ignorance among the public about the questionable utility of prison as a solution to the nation's crime problem.

Responding to the Current Crisis: Some Lessons From the Stanford Prison Experiment

Where has this series of transformations left the U.S. criminal justice system? With startling speed, national prison policy has become remarkably punitive, and correspondingly, conditions of confinement have dramatically deteriorated in many parts of the country. These transformations have been costly in economic, social, and human terms. At the beginning of the present decade, a stark fact about governmental priorities was reported: "For the first time in history, state and municipal governments are spending more money on criminal justice than education" (Chambliss, 1994, p. 183). In California, the corrections budget alone has now surpassed the state's fiscal outlays for higher education (e.g., Butterfield, 1995; Jordan, 1995). Despite this historic shift in expenditures and the unprecedented prison construction that took place during the past 25 years, many commentators still lament what has been referred to as the "national scandal of living conditions in American prisons" (Gutterman, 1995, p. 373). As we have noted and one reviewer recently observed, "For over a decade, virtually every contemporary commentary on corrections in the United States has reminded us that the system [is] in crisis" (Cullen, 1995, p. 338).

The dimensions of this crisis continue to expand and do not yet reflect what promises to be an even more significant boost in prison numbers—the effects of recently passed, so-called three-strikes legislation that not only mandates a life

sentence on a third criminal conviction but, in some states, also doubles the prison sentence for a second criminal conviction and reduces existing good-time provisions for every term (so that all prisoners actually are incarcerated for a longer period of time). This three-strikes legislation was written and rapidly passed into law to capitalize on the public's fear of violent crime (Haney, 1994, 1997b). Despite the fact that the crime rate in the United States has been declining for some time in small but steady increments, many of these bills were written in such a way as to cast the widest possible net—beyond violent career criminals (whom most members of the public had in mind)—to include nonviolent crimes like felony drug convictions and minor property offenses. As a consequence, a disproportionate number of young Black and Hispanic men are likely to be imprisoned for life under scenarios in which they are guilty of little more than a history of untreated addiction and several prior drug-related offenses. The mandate to create lifetime incarceration for so many inmates under circumstances where overcrowding precludes their participation in meaningful programs, treatment, and other activities is likely to raise the overall level of prisoners' frustration, despair, and violence. States will absorb the staggering cost of not only constructing additional prisons to accommodate increasing numbers of prisoners who will never be released but also warehousing them into old age (Zimbardo, 1994).

Remarkably, the radical transformations we have described in the nation's penal policy occurred with almost no input from the discipline of psychology. Correctional administrators, politicians, policymakers, and judicial decision makers not only ignored most of the lessons that emerged from the SPE but also disregarded the insights of a number of psychologists who preceded us and the scores of others who wrote about, extended, and elaborated on the same lessons in empirical studies and theoretical pieces published over the past several decades. Indeed, there is now a vast social science literature that underscores, in various ways, the critical importance of situation and context in influencing social behavior, especially in psychologically powerful situations like prisons. These lessons, insights, and literature deserve to be taken into account as the nation's prison system moves into the next century.

Here then is a series of propositions derived or closely extrapolated from the SPE and the large body of related research that underscores the power of situations and social context to shape and transform human behavior. Each proposition argues for the creation of a new corrections agenda that would take us in a fundamentally different direction from the one in which we have been moving over the past quarter century.

First, the SPE underscored the degree to which prison environments are themselves powerful, potentially damaging situations whose negative psychological effects must be taken seriously, carefully evaluated, and purposefully regulated and controlled. When appropriate, these environments must be changed or (in extreme cases) eliminated. Of course, the SPE demonstrated the power of situations to overwhelm psychologically normal, healthy people and to elicit from them unexpectedly cruel, yet "situationally appropriate" behavior. In many instances during our study, the participants' behavior (and our own) directly contravened personal value systems and deviated dramatically from past records of conduct. This behavior was elicited by the social context and roles we created, and it had painful, even traumatic consequences for the prisoners against whom it was directed.

The policy implications of these observations seem clear. For one, because of their harmful potential, prisons should be deployed very sparingly in the war on crime. Recognition of the tendency of prison environments to become psychologically damaging also provides a strong argument for increased and more realistic legal and governmental oversight of penal institutions in ways that are sensitive to and designed to limit their potentially destructive impact. In addition, it argues in favor of significantly revising the allocation of criminal justice resources to more seriously explore, create, and evaluate humane alternatives to traditional correctional environments.

Second, the SPE also revealed how easily even a minimalist prison could become painful and powerful. By almost any comparative standard, ours was an extraordinarily benign prison. None of the guards at the "Stanford Prison" were armed, and there were obvious limits to the ways in which they could or would react to prisoners' disobedience, rebellion, or even escape. Yet, even in this minimalist prison setting, all of our "guards" participated in one way or another in the pattern of mistreatment that quickly developed. Indeed, some escalated their definition of "role-appropriate" behavior to become highly feared, sadistic tormentors. Although the prisoners' terms of incarceration were extremely abbreviated (corresponding, really, to very short-term pretrial detention in a county jail), half of our prisoner-participants left before the study was terminated because they could not tolerate the pains of this merely simulated imprisonment. The pains were as much psychological— feelings of powerlessness, degradation, frustration, and emotional distress—as physical—sleep deprivation, poor diet, and unhealthy living conditions. Unlike our participants, of course, many experienced prisoners have learned to suppress such outward signs of psychological vulnerability lest they be interpreted as weakness, inviting exploitation by others.

Thus, the SPE and other related studies demonstrating the power of social contexts teach a lesson about the way in which certain situational conditions can interact and work in combination to produce a dehumanizing whole that is more damaging than the sum of its individual institutional parts. Legal doctrines that fail to explicitly take into account and formally consider the totality of these situational conditions miss this psychological point. The effects of situations and social contexts must be assessed from the perspective of those within them. The experiential perspective of prison inmates—the meaning of the prison experience and its effects on them—is the most useful starting point for determining whether a particular set of prison conditions is cruel and unusual. But a macroexperiential perspective does not allow for the parsing of individual factors or aspects of a situation whose psychological consequences can then be separately assessed. Thus, legal regulators and the psychological experts who assist them also must be sensitive to the ways in which different aspects

of a particular situation interact and aggregate in the lives of the persons who inhabit total institutions like prisons as well as their capacity to produce significant effects on the basis of seemingly subtle changes and modifications that build up over time. In contexts such as these, there is much more to the "basic necessities of life" than "single, identifiable human need[s] such as food, warmth or exercise" (*Wilson v. Seiter,* 1991, p. 304). Even if this view is "too amorphous" for members of the current Supreme Court to appreciate or apply, it is the only psychologically defensible approach to assessing the effects of a particular prison and gauging its overall impact on those who live within its walls.

In a related vein, recent research has shown how school children can develop maladjusted, aggressive behavior patterns based on initially marginal deviations from other children that get amplified in classroom interactions and aggregated over time until they become manifested as "problem children" (Caprara & Zimbardo, 1996). Evidence of the same processes at work can be found in the life histories of persons accused and convicted of capital crime (Haney, 1995). In similar ways, initially small behavioral problems and dysfunctional social adaptations by individual prisoners may become amplified and aggravated over time in prison settings that require daily interaction with other prisoners and guards.

Recall also that the SPE was purposely populated with young men who were selected on the basis of their initial mental and physical health and normality, both of which, less than a week later, had badly deteriorated. Real prisons use no such selection procedures. Indeed, one of the casualties of severe overcrowding in many prison systems has been that even rudimentary classification decisions based on the psychological makeup of entering cohorts of prisoners are forgone (see Clements, 1979, 1985). Pathology that is inherent in the structure of the prison situation is likely given a boost by the pathology that some prisoners and guards bring with them into the institutions themselves. Thus, although ours was clearly a study of the power of situational characteristics, we certainly acknowledge the value of interactional models of social and institutional behavior. Prison systems should not ignore individual vulnerabilities in attempting to optimize institutional adjustment, minimize behavioral and psychological problems, understand differences in institutional adaptations and capacities to survive, and intelligently allocate treatment and other resources (e.g., Haney & Specter, in press).

Third, if situations matter and people can be transformed by them when they go into prisons, they matter equally, if not more, when they come out of prison. This suggests very clearly that programs of prisoner change cannot ignore situations and social conditions that prevail after release if they are to have any hope of sustaining whatever positive gains are achieved during periods of imprisonment and lowering distressingly high recidivism rates. Several implications can be drawn from this observation. The first is that prisons must more routinely use transitional or "decompression" programs that gradually reverse the effects of the extreme environments in which convicts have been confined. These programs must be aimed at preparing prisoners for the radically different situations that they will enter in the free world. Otherwise, prisoners who were ill-prepared for job and social situations before they entered prison become more so over time, and the longer they have been imprisoned, the more likely it is that rapid technological and social change will have dramatically transformed the world to which they return.

The SPE and related studies also imply that exclusively individual-centered approaches to crime control (like imprisonment) are self-limiting and doomed to failure in the absence of other approaches that simultaneously and systematically address criminogenic situational and contextual factors. Because traditional models of rehabilitation are person-centered and dispositional in nature (focusing entirely on individual-level change), they typically have ignored the postrelease situational factors that help to account for discouraging rates of recidivism. Yet, the recognition that people can be significantly changed and transformed by immediate situational conditions also implies that certain kinds of situations in the free world can override and negate positive prison change. Thus, correctional and parole resources must be shifted to the transformation of certain criminogenic situations in the larger society if ex-convicts are to meaningfully and effectively adapt. Successful post-release adjustment may depend as much on the criminal justice system's ability to change certain components of an ex-convict's situation *after* imprisonment—helping to get housing, employment, and drug or alcohol counseling for starters—as it does on any of the positive rehabilitative changes made by individual prisoners during confinement itself.

This perspective also underscores the way in which long-term legacies of exposure to powerful and destructive situations, contexts, and structures means that prisons themselves can act as criminogenic agents—in both their primary effects on prisoners and secondary effects on the lives of persons connected to them—thereby serving to increase rather than decrease the amount of crime that occurs within a society. Department of corrections data show that about a fourth of those initially imprisoned for nonviolent crimes are sentenced a second time for committing a violent offense. Whatever else it reflects; this pattern highlights the possibility that prison serves to transmit violent habits and values rather than to reduce them. Moreover, like many of these lessons, this one counsels policymakers to take the full range of the social and economic costs of imprisonment into account in calculations that guide long-term crime control strategies. It also argues in favor of incorporating the deleterious effects of prior terms of incarceration into at least certain models of legal responsibility (e.g., Haney, 1995).

Fourth, despite using several valid personality tests in the SPE, we found that we were unable to predict (or even postdict) who would behave in what ways and why (Haney et al., 1973). This kind of failure underscores the possibility that behavioral prediction and explanation in extreme situations like prisons will be successful only if they are approached with more situationally sensitive models than are typically used. For example, most current personality trait measures ask respondents to report on characteristic ways of responding in familiar situations or scenarios. They do not and cannot tap into reactions that might occur in novel, extreme, or especially potent situations—like the SPE or Milgram's (1974) obedience paradigm—and thus have little predictive value when extrapolated to such extreme cases. More situationally sensitive models would attend less to characteristic ways of behaving in typical situations and more to the characteristics of the particular situations in which behavior occurs. In prison, explanations of disciplinary infractions and violence would focus more on the context in which they transpired and less on the prisoners who engaged in them (e.g., Wenk & Emrich, 1972; Wright, 1991). Similarly, the ability to predict the likelihood of reoffending and the probability of repeated violent behavior should be enhanced by conceptualizing persons as embedded in a social context and rich interpersonal environment, rather than as abstract bundles of traits and proclivities (e.g., Monahan & Klassen, 1982).

This perspective has implications for policies of crime control as well as psychological prediction. Virtually all sophisticated, contemporary accounts of social behavior now acknowledge the empirical and theoretical significance of situation, context, and structure (e.g., Bandura, 1978, 1991; Duke, 1987; Ekehammar, 1974; Georgoudi & Rosnow, 1985; Mischel, 1979; Veroff, 1983). In academic circles at least, the problems of crime and violence—formerly viewed in almost exclusively individualistic terms—are now understood through multilevel analyses that grant equal if not primary significance to situational, community, and structural variables (e.g., Hepburn, 1973; McEwan & Knowles, 1984; Sampson & Lauritsen, 1994; Toch, 1985). Yet, little of this knowledge has made its way into prevailing criminal justice policies. Lessons about the power of extreme situations to shape and transform behavior—independent or in spite of pre-existing dispositions—can be applied to contemporary strategies of crime control that invest more substantial resources in transforming destructive familial and social contexts rather than concentrating exclusively on reactive policies that target only individual lawbreakers (cf. Masten & Garmezy 1985; Patterson, DeBaryshe, & Ramsey, 1989).

Fifth, genuine and meaningful prison and criminal justice reform is unlikely to be advanced by persons who are themselves "captives" of powerful correctional environments. We learned this lesson in a modest but direct way when in the span of six short days in the SPE, our own perspectives were radically altered, our sense of ethics, propriety, and humanity temporarily suspended. Our experience with the SPE underscored the degree to which institutional settings can develop a life of their own, independent of the wishes, intentions, and purposes of those who run them (Haney & Zimbardo, 1977). Like all powerful situations, real prisons transform the worldviews of those who inhabit them, on both sides of the bars. Thus, the SPE also contained the seeds of a basic but important message about prison reform—that good people with good intentions are not enough to create good prisons. Institutional structures themselves must be changed to meaningfully improve the quality of prison life (Haney & Pettigrew, 1986).

Indeed, the SPE was an "irrational" prison whose staff had no legal mandate to punish prisoners who, in turn, had done nothing to deserve their mistreatment. Yet, the "psychologic" of the environment was more powerful than the benign intentions or predispositions of the participants. Routines develop; rules are made and applied, altered and followed without question; policies enacted for short-term convenience become part of the institutional status quo and difficult to alter; and unexpected events and emergencies challenge existing resources and compromise treatment in ways that persist long after the crisis has passed. Prisons are especially vulnerable to these common institutional dynamics because they are so resistant to external pressures for change and even rebuff outside attempts at scrutinizing their daily operating procedures.

These observations certainly imply that the legal mechanisms supposedly designed to control prison excesses should not focus exclusively on the intentions of the staff and administrators who run the institution but would do well to look instead at the effects of the situation or context itself in shaping their behavior (cf. *Farmer v. Brennan*, 1994). Harmful structures do not require ill-intentioned persons to inflict psychological damage on those in their charge and can induce good people with the best of intentions to engage in evil deeds (Haney & Zimbardo, 1977; Zimbardo, 1979a). "Mechanisms of moral disengagement" distance people from the ethical ambiguity of their actions and the painful consequences of their deeds, and they may operate with destructive force in many legal and institutional contexts, facilitating cruel and unusual treatment by otherwise caring and law-abiding persons (e.g., Bandura, 1989; Browning, 1993; Gibson, 1991; Haney, 1997c).

In addition, the SPE and the perspective it advanced also suggest that prison change will come about only when those who are outside of this powerful situation are empowered to act on it. A society may be forced to presume the categorical expertise of prison officials to run the institutions with which they have been entrusted, but this presumption is a rebuttable one. Moreover, to depend exclusively on those whose perspectives have been created and maintained by these powerful situations to, in turn, transform or control them is shortsighted and psychologically naive. This task must fall to those with a different logic and point of view, independent of and free from the forces of the situation itself. To be sure, the current legal retreat to hands-off policies in which the courts defer to the presumably greater expertise of correctional officials ignores the potency of prison settings to alter the judgments of those charged with the responsibility of running them. The SPE and much other research on these powerful environments teach that this retreat is terribly ill-advised.

Finally, the SPE implicitly argued for a more activist scholarship in which psychologists engage with the important social and policy questions of the day. The implications we have drawn from the SPE argue in favor of more critically and more realistically evaluating the nature and effect of imprisonment and developing psychologically informed limits to the amount of prison pain one is willing to inflict in the name of social control (Haney, 1997b, 1998). Yet, this would require the participation of social scientists willing to examine these issues, confront the outmoded models and concepts that guide crimi-

nal justice practices, and develop meaningful and effective alternatives. Historically, psychologists once contributed significantly to the intellectual framework on which modern corrections was built (Haney, 1982). In the course of the past 25 years, they have relinquished voice and authority in the debates that surround prison policy. Their absence has created an ethical and intellectual void that has undermined both the quality and the legitimacy of correctional practices. It has helped compromise the amount of social justice our society now dispenses.

Conclusion

When we conducted the SPE 25 years ago, we were, in a sense, on the cutting edge of new and developing situational and contextual models of behavior. Mischel's (1968) path-breaking review of the inadequacy of conventional measures of personality traits to predict behavior was only a few years old, Ross and Nisbett (1991) were assistant professors who had not yet written about situational control as perhaps the most important leg in the tripod of social psychology, and no one had yet systematically applied the methods and theories of modern psychology to the task of understanding social contextual origins crime and the psychological pains of imprisonment. Intellectually, much has changed since then. However, without the renewed participation of psychologists in debates over how best to apply the lessons and insights of their discipline to the problems of crime and punishment, the benefits from these important intellectual advances will be self-limiting. It is hard to imagine a more pressing and important task for which psychologists have so much expertise but from which they have been so distanced and uninvolved than the creation of more effective and humane criminal justice policies. Indeed, politicians and policymakers now seem to worship the very kind of institutional power whose adverse effects were so critically evaluated over the past 25 years. They have premised a vast and enormously expensive national policy of crime control on models of human nature that are significantly outmoded. In so doing, they have faced little intellectual challenge, debate, or input from those who should know better.

So, perhaps it is this one last thing that the SPE stood for that will serve the discipline best over the next 25 years. That is, the interrelated notions that psychology can be made relevant to the broad and pressing national problems of crime and justice, that the discipline can assist in stimulating badly needed social and legal change, and that scholars and practitioners can improve these policies with sound data and creative ideas. These notions are as germane now, and needed more, than they were in the days of the SPE. If they can be renewed, in the spirit of those more optimistic times, despite having lost many battles over the past 25 years, the profession still may help win the more important war. There has never been a more critical time at which to begin the intellectual struggle with those who would demean human nature by using prisons exclusively as agencies of social control that punish without attempting to rehabilitate, that isolate and oppress instead of educating and elevating, and that tear down minority communities rather than protecting and strengthening them.

REFERENCES

American Friends Service Committee. (1971). *Struggle for justice: A report on crime and punishment.* New York: Hill & Wang.

Amnesty International. (1987). *Allegations of mistreatment in Marion Prison, Illinois, USA.* New York; Author.

Bandura, A. (1978). The self system in reciprocal determinism. *American Psychologist, 33,* 344–358.

Bandura, A. (1989). Mechanisms of moral disengagement. In W. Reich (Ed.), *Origins of terrorism: Psychologies, ideologies, theologies, states of mind* (pp. 161–191). New York: Cambridge University Press.

Bandura, A. (1991). Social cognitive theory of moral thought and action. In W. Kurtines & J. Gewirtz (Eds.), *Handbook of moral behavior and development: Vol. 1. Theory* (pp. 45–102). Hillsdale, NJ: Erlbaum.

Blumstein, A. (1993). Making rationality relevant—The American Society of Criminology 1992 Presidential Address. *Criminology, 31,* 1–16.

Brodt, S., & Zimbardo, P. (1981). Modifying shyness-related social behavior through symptom misattribution. *Journal of Personality and Social Psychology, 41,* 437–449.

Browning, C. (1993). *Ordinary men: Reserve Police Battalion 101 and the final solution in Poland.* New York: Harper Perennial.

Bureau of Justice Statistics. (1991). *Sourcebook of criminal justice statistics.* Washington, DC: U.S. Department of Justice.

Bureau of Justice Statistics. (1996). *Sourcebook of criminal justice statistics, 1996.* Washington, DC: U.S. Department of Justice.

Bureau of Justice Statistics. (1997a, May). *Correctional populations in the United States, 1995* (NCJ 163916). Rockville, MD: Author.

Bureau of Justice Statistics. (1997b, November). *Criminal victimization 1996: Changes 1995–96 with trends 1993–96* (Bureau of Justice Statistics Bulletin NCJ 165812). Rockville, MD: Author.

Bureau of Justice Statistics. (1998, January 18). *Nation's prisons and jails hold more than 1.7 million: Up almost 100,000 in a year* [Press release]. Washington, DC: U.S. Department of Justice.

Burks v. Walsh, 461 F. Supp. 934 (W.D. Missouri 1978).

Butterfield, F. (1995, April 12). New prisons cast shadow over higher education. *The New York Times,* p. A21.

Cahalan, M. W. (1986, December). *Historical corrections statistics in the United States, 1850–1984* (Bureau of Justice Statistics Bulletin NCJ 102529). Rockville, MD: Bureau of Justice Statistics.

Capps v. Atiyeh, 495 F Supp. 802 (D. Ore. 1980).

Caprara, G., & Zimbardo, P. (1996). Aggregation and amplification of marginal deviations in the social construction of personality and maladjustment. *European Journal of Personality, 10,* 79–110.

Carr, S. (1995). Demystifying the Stanford Prison Study. *The British Psychological Society Social Psychology Section Newsletter, 33,* 31– 34.

Chambliss, W. (1994). Policing the ghetto underclass: The politics of law and law enforcement. *Social Problems, 41,* 177–194.

Christie, N. (1994). *Crime control as industry: Towards gulags, Western style?* (2nd ed.). London: Routledge.

Clements, C. (1979). Crowded prisons: A review of psychological and environmental effects. *Law and Human Behavior, 3,* 217–225.

Clements, C. (1985). Towards an objective approach to offender classification. *Law & Psychology Review, 9,* 45–55.

Coker v. Georgia, 433 U.S. 584, 592 (1977).

Cullen, F. (1995). Assessing the penal harm movement. *Journal of Research in Crime and Delinquency, 32,* 338–358.

Dowker, F., & Good, G. (1992). From Alcatraz to Marion to Florence: Control unit prisons in the United States. In W. Churchill & J. J. Vander Wall (Eds.), *Cages of steel: The politics of imprisonment in the United States* (pp. 131–151). Washington, DC: Maisonneuve Press.

Duke, M. (1987). The situational stream hypothesis: A unifying view of behavior with special emphasis on adaptive and maladaptive personality patterns. *Journal of Research in Personality, 21,* 239–263.

Dunbaugh, F. (1979). Racially disproportionate rates of incarceration in the United States. *Prison Law Monitor, 1,* 205–225.

Editorial: Inside the super-maximum prisons. (1991, November 24). *The Washington Post,* p. C6.

Ekehammar, B. (1974). Interactionism in personality from a historical perspective. *Psychological Bulletin, 81,* 1026–1048.

Farmer v. Brennan, 114 S. Ct. 1970 (1994).

Forer, L. (1994). *A rage to punish: The unintended consequences of mandatory sentencing.* New York: Norton.

Fowler, R. (1976). Sweeping reforms ordered in Alabama prisons. *APA Monitor, 7,* pp. 1, 15.

Freed, D. (1992). Federal sentencing in the wake of guidelines: Unacceptable limits on the discretion of sentences. *Yale Law Journal, 101,* 1681–1754.

Georgoudi, M., & Rosnow, R. (1985). Notes toward a contextualist understanding of social psychology. *Personality and Social Psychology Bulletin, 11,* 5–22.

Gibson, J. (1991). Training good people to inflict pain: State terror and social learning. *Journal of Humanistic Psychology, 31,* 72–87.

Grassian, S. (1983). Psychopathological effects of solitary confinement. *American Journal of Psychiatry, 140,* 1450–1454.

Gregg v. Georgia, 428 U.S. 153, 173 (1976) (joint opinion).

Gutterman, M. (1995). The contours of Eighth Amendment prison jurisprudence: Conditions of confinement. *Southern Methodist University Law Review, 48,* 373–407.

Hall, D. (1993). The Eighth Amendment, prison conditions, and social context. *Missouri Law Review, 58,* 207–236.

Haney, C. (1976). The play's the thing: Methodological notes on social simulations. In P. Golden (Ed.), *The research experience* (pp. 177– 190). Itasca, IL: Peacock.

Haney, C. (1982). Psychological theory and criminal justice policy: Law and psychology in the "Formative Era." *Law and Human Behavior, 6,* 191–235.

Haney, C. (1983). The good, the bad, and the lawful: An essay on psychological injustice. In W. Laufer & J. Day (Eds.), *Personality theory, moral development, and criminal behavior* (pp. 107–117). Lexington, MA: Lexington Books.

Haney, C. (1991). The Fourteenth Amendment and symbolic legality: Let them eat due process. *Law and Human Behavior, 15,* 183–204.

Haney, C. (1993a). Infamous punishment: The psychological effects of isolation. *National Prison Project Journal, 8,* 3–21.

Haney, C. (1993b). Psychology and legal change: The impact of a decade. *Law and Human Behavior, 17,* 371–398.

Haney, C. (1994, March 3). Three strikes for Ronnie's kids, now Bill's. *Los Angeles Times,* p. B7.

Haney, C. (1995). The social context of capital murder: Social histories and the logic of mitigation. *Santa Clara Law Review, 35,* 547–609.

Haney, C. (1997a). Psychological secrecy and the death penalty: Observations on "the mere extinguishment of life." *Studies in Law, Politics, and Society, 16,* 3–68.

Haney, C. (1997b). Psychology and the limits to prison pain: Confronting the coming crisis in Eighth Amendment law. *Psychology, Public Policy and Law, 3,* 499–588.

Haney, C. (1997c). Violence and the capital jury: Mechanisms of moral disengagement and the impulse to condemn to death. *Stanford Law Review, 46,* 1447–1486.

Haney, C. (1997d). *The worst of the worst: Psychological trauma and psychiatric symptoms in punitive segregation.* Unpublished manuscript, University of California, Santa Cruz.

Haney, C. (1998). *Limits to prison pain: Modern psychological theory and rational crime control policy.* Washington, DC: American Psychological Association.

Haney, C., Banks, W., & Zimbardo, P. (1973). Interpersonal dynamics in a simulated prison. *International Journal of Criminology and Penology, 1,* 69–97.

Haney, C., & Lynch, M. (1997). Regulating prisons of the future: A psychological analysis of supermax and solitary confinement. *New York Review of Law and Social Change, 23,* 101–195.

Haney, C., & Pettigrew, T (1986). Civil rights and institutional law: The role of social psychology in judicial implementation. *Journal of Community Psychology, 14,* 267–277.

Haney, C., & Specter, D. (in press). Legal considerations in treating adult and juvenile offenders with special needs. In J. Ashford, B. Sales, & W. Reid (Eds.), *Treating adult and juvenile offenders with special needs.* Washington, DC: American Psychological Association.

Haney, C., & Zimbardo, P. (1977).The socialization into criminality: On becoming a prisoner and a guard. In J. Tapp & F. Levine (Eds.), *Law, justice, and the individual in society: Psychological and legal issues* (pp. 198–223). New York: Holt, Rinehart & Winston.

Hepburn, J. (1973). Violent behavior in interpersonal relationships. *Sociological Quarterly, 14,* 419–429.

Hilliard, T. (1976). The Black psychologist in action: A psychological evaluation of the Adjustment Center environment at San Quentin Prison. *Journal of Black Psychology, 2,* 75–82.

Human Rights Watch. (1997). *Cold storage: Super-maximum security confinement in Indiana.* New York: Author.

Immarigeon, R. (1992). The Marionization of American prisons. *National Prison Project Journal, 7*(4), 1–5.

Jackson, G. (1970). *Soledad brother: The prison letters of George Jackson.* New York: Coward-McCann.

Jordan, H. (1995, July 8). '96 budget favors prison over college; "3 strikes" to eat into education funds. *San Jose Mercury News,* p. 1A.

King, A. (1993). The impact of incarceration on African American families: Implications for practice. *Families in Society: The Journal of Contemporary Human Services, 74,* 145–153.

Madrid v. Gomez, 889 F Supp. 1146 (N.D. Cal. 1995).

Maguire, K., & Pastore, A. (Eds.). (1997). *Sourcebook of criminal justice statistics 1996* (NCJ 165361). Washington, DC: U.S. Government Printing Office.

Masten, A., & Garmezy, N. (1985). Risk, vulnerability and protective factors in developmental psychopathology. In F. Lahey & A. Kazdin (Eds.), *Advances in clinical child psychology* (pp. 1–52). New York: Plenum.

Mauer, M. (1990). *More young Black males under correctional control in US than in college.* Washington, DC: The Sentencing Project.

Mauer, M. (1992). Americans behind bars: A comparison of international rates of incarceration. In W. Churchill & J. J. Vander Wall (Eds.), *Cages of steel: The politics of imprisonment in the United States* (pp. 22–37). Washington, DC: Maisonneuve Press.

Mauer, M. (1995). The international use of incarceration. *Prison Journal, 75,* 113–123.

Mauer, M. (1997, June). *Americans behind bars: U.S. and international use of incarceration, 1995.* Washington, DC: The Sentencing Project.

McConville, S. (1989). Prisons held captive. *Contemporary Psychology, 34,* 928–929.

McEwan, A., & Knowles, C. (1984). Delinquent personality types and the situational contexts of their crimes. *Personality & Individual Differences, 5,* 339–344.

Milgram, S. (1974). *Obedience to authority: An experimental view.* New York: Harper & Row.

Miller, G. (1980). Giving psychology away in the '80s. *Psychology Today, 13,* 38ff.

Mischel, W. (1968). *Personality and assessment.* New York: Wiley.

Mischel, W. (1979). On the interface of cognition and personality: Beyond the person-situation debate. *American Psychologist, 34,* 740–754.

Mitford, J. (1973). *Kind and usual punishment: The prison business.* New York: Knopf.

Monahan, J., & Kiassen, D. (1982). Situational approaches to understanding and predicting individual violent behavior. In M. Wolfgang & G. Weiner (Eds.), *Criminal violence* (pp. 292–319). Beverly Hills, CA: Sage.

Mumola, C. J., & Beck, A. J. (1997, June). *Prisoners in 1996* (Bureau of Justice Statistics Bulletin NCJ 164619). Rockville, MD: Bureau of Justice Statistics.

National Advisory Commission on Criminal Justice Standards and Goals. (1973). *Task force report on corrections.* Washington, DC: U.S. Government Printing Office.

Newman, G. (1988). Punishment and social practice: On Hughes's *The Fatal Shore. Law and Social Inquiry, 13,* 337–357.

Olivero, M., & Roberts, J. (1990). The United States Federal Penitentiary at Marion, Illinois: Alcatraz revisited. *New England Journal of Criminal and Civil Confinement, 16,* 21–51.

Patterson, G., DeBaryshe, B., & Ramsey, E. (1989). A developmental perspective on antisocial behavior. *American Psychologist, 44,* 329–335.

Perkinson, R. (1994). Shackled justice: Florence Federal Penitentiary and the new politics of punishment. *Social Justice, 21,* 117–132.

Pugh v. Locke, 406 F Supp. 318 (1976).

Rhodes v. Chapman, 452 U.S. 337 (1981).

Robbins, I. (1993). The prisoners' mail box and the evolution of federal inmate rights. *Federal Rules Decisions, 114,* 127–169.

Ross, L., & Nisbett, R. (1991). *The person and the situation: Perspectives of social psychology.* New York: McGraw-Hill.

Sampson, R., & Lauritsen, 1. (1994). Violent victimization and offending: Individual-, situational-, and community-level risk factors. In A. Reiss, Jr. & J. Roth (Eds.), *Understanding and preventing violence: Vol. 3. Social influences* (pp. 1–114). Washington, DC: National Research Council, National Academy Press.

Sandin v. Conner, 115 S. Ct. 2293 (1995).

Scull, A. (1977). *Decarceration: Community treatment and the deviant: A radical view.* Englewood Cliffs, NJ: Prentice Hall.

Smith, C. (1993). Black Muslims and the development of prisoners' rights. *Journal of Black Studies, 24,* 131–143.

Spain v. Procunier, 408 F Supp. 534 (1976), aff'd in part, rev'd in part, 600 F2d 189 (9th Cir. 1979).

Toch, H. (1985). The catalytic situation in the violence equation. *Journal of Applied Social Psychology, 15,* 105–123.

Tonry, M. (1995). *Malign neglect: Race, crime, and punishment in America.* New York: Oxford University Press.

Trop v. Dulles, 356 U.S. 86 (1958).

Veroff, J. (1983). Contextual determinants of personality. *Personality and Social Psychology Bulletin, 9,* 331–343.

von Hirsch, A. (1976). *Doing justice: The choice of punishment.* New York: Hill & Wang.

Wenk, E., & Emrich, R. (1972). Assaultive youth: An exploratory study of the assaultive experience and assaultive potential of California Youth Authority wards. *Journal of Research in Crime & Delinquency, 9,* 171–196.

Wicker, T. (1975). *A time to die.* New York: New York Times Books.

Wilson v. Seiser. 501 U.S. 294 (1991).

Wolff v. McDonnell, 418 U.S. 554, 556–7 (1974).

Wright, K. (1991). The violent and victimized in the male prison. *Journal of Offender Rehabilitation, 16,* 1–25.

Yackle, L. (1989). *Reform and regret: The story of federal judicial involvement in the Alabama prison system.* New York: Oxford University Press.

Yee, M. (1973). *The melancholy history of Soledad Prison.* New York: Harper's Magazine Press.

Zimbardo, P. (1973). On the ethics of intervention in human psychological research: With special reference to the Stanford Prison. Experiment. *Cognition, 2,* 243–256.

Zimbardo, P. (1975). On transforming experimental research into advocacy for social change. In M. Deutsch & H. Hornstein (Eds.), *Applying social psychology: Implications for research, practice, and training* (pp. 33–66). Hillsdale, NJ: Erlbaum.

Zimbardo, P. G. (1977). *Shyness: What it is and what to do about it.* Reading, MA: Addison-Wesley.

Zimbardo, P. G. (1979a). The psychology of evil: On the perversion of human potential. In T. R. Sarbin (Ed.), *Challenges to the criminal justice system: The perspective of community psychology* (pp. 142–161). New York: Human Sciences Press.

Zimbardo, P. G. (1979b). Testimony of Dr. Philip Zimbardo to U.S. House of Representatives Committee on the Judiciary. In J. J. Bonsignore et al. (Eds.). *Before the law: An introduction to the legal process* (2nd ed., pp. 396–399). Boston: Houghton Mifflin.

Zimbardo, P. G. (1994). *Transforming California's prisons into expensive old age homes for felons: Enormous hidden costs and consequences for California's taxpayers.* San Francisco: Center on Juvenile and Criminal Justice.

Zimbardo, P. G., & Andersen, S. (1993). Understanding mind control: Exotic and mundane mental manipulations. In M. Langone (Ed.), *Recover from cults: Help for victims of psychological and spiritual abuse* (pp. 104–125). New York: Norton.

Zimbardo, P. G., Haney, C., Banks, C., & Jaffe, D. (1974). The psychology of imprisonment: Privation, power, and pathology. In Z. Rubin (Ed.), *Doing unto others: Explorations in social behavior* (pp. 61–73). Englewood Cliffs, NJ: Prentice Hall.

Zimbardo, P. G., Pilkonis, P. A., & Norwood, R. M. (1975, May). The social disease called shyness. *Psychology Today,* pp. 69–70, 72.

Editor's note. Melissa G. Warren served as action editor for this article.

Author's note. Craig Haney, Department of Psychology, University of California, Santa Cruz; Philip Zimbardo, Department of Psychology, Stanford University.

We would like to acknowledge our colleague and coinvestigator in the original Stanford Prison Experiment, W. Curtis Banks, who died last year. We also acknowledge the assistance of Marc Mauer and The Sentencing Project, who granted permission to reprint Figure Al and helped us locate other sources of information, and Sandy Pisano, librarian at the Arthur W. Melton Library, who helped compile some of the data that appear in the tables and figures.

Correspondence concerning this article should be addressed to Craig Haney, Department of Psychology, University of California, Santa Cruz, CA 95064. Electronic mail maybe sent to psylaw@cats.ucsc.edu. Readers interested in the corrections system may contact the American Psychology–Law Society or Psychologists in Public Service, Divisions 41 and 18, respectively, of the American Psychological Association.

APPENDIX

Table A1

Number and Rate (Per 100,000 Resident Population in Each Group) of Sentenced Prisoners in State and Federal Institutions on December 31 (Not Including Local Jails)

Year	Total	Rate	Year	Total	Rate
1925	91,669	79	1960	212,953	117
1926	97,991	83	1961	220,149	119
1927	109,983	91	1962	218,830	117
1928	116,390	96	1963	217,283	114
1929	120,496	98	1964	214,336	111
			1965	210,895	108
1930	129,453	104	1966	199,654	102
1931	137,082	110	1967	194,896	98
1932	137,997	110	1968	187,914	94
1933	136,810	109	1969	196,007	97
1934	138,316	109			
1935	144,180	113	1970	196,429	96
1936	145,038	113	1971	198,061	95
1937	152,741	118	1972	196,092	93
1938	160,285	123	1973	204,211	96
1939	179,818	137	1974	218,466	102
			1975	240,593	111
1940	173,706	131	1976	262,833	120
1941	165,439	124	1977[a]	278,141	126
1942	150,384	112	1977[b]	285,456	129
1943	137,220	103	1978	294,396	132
1944	132,456	100	1979	301,470	133
1945	133,649	98			
1946	140,079	99	1980	315,974	139
1947	151,304	105	1981	353,167	154
1948	155,977	106	1982	394,374	171
1949	163,749	109	1983	419,820	179
			1984	443,398	188
1950	166,123	109	1985	480,568	202
1951	165,680	107	1986	522,084	217
1952	168,233	107	1987	560,812	231
1953	173,579	108	1988	603,732	247
1954	182,901	112	1989	680,907	276
1955	185,780	112			
1956	189,565	112	1990	739,980	297
1957	195,414	113	1991	789,610	313
1958	205,643	117	1992	846,277	332
1959	208,105	117	1993	932,074	359
			1994	1,016,691	389
			1995	1,085,363	411

Note. These data represent prisoners sentenced to more than one year. Both custody and jurisdiction figures are shown for 1977 to facilitate year-to-year comparison. Adapted from *Sourcebook of Criminal Justice Statistics 1996* (NCJ 165361,p. 518), by K. Maguire and A. Pastore (Eds.), 1997, Washington,DC: U.S. Government Printing Office. In the public domain.
[a]Custody counts. [b]Jurisdiction counts.

Table A2

Number and Rate (Per 100,000 Residents) of Adults in Custody of State and Federal Prisons and Local Jails

Year	Total custody	Federal prisons	State prisons	Local jails	Total rate[a]
1985	744,208	35,781	451,812	256,615	313
1990	1,148,702	58,838	684,544	405,320	461
1991	1,219,014	63,930	728,605	426,479	483
1992	1,295,150	72,071	778,495	444,584	508
1993	1,369,185	80,815	828,566	459,804	531
1994	1,476,621	85,500	904,647	486,474	567
June 30, 1995	1,561,836	89,334	965,458	507,044	594
December 31, 1995		89,538	989,007		
June 30, 1996	1,630,940	93,167	1,019,281	518,492	615

Note. Jail counts are for June 30; counts for 1994–1996 exclude persons who were supervised outside of a jail facility. State and federal prisoner counts for 1985 and 1990–1994 are for December 31. Adapted from *Sourcebook of Criminal Justice Statistics 1996* (NCJ 165361, p. 510), by K. Maguire and A. Pastore (Eds.), 1997, Washington, DC: U.S. Government Printing Office. In the public domain.

[a]Total number of adults held in the custody of state, federal, or local jurisdictions per 100,000 U.S. residents on July 1 of each reference year.

Figure A1

Percent of U.S. Adult Population in State or Federal Prisons or in Local Jails, by Race and Sex, 1984–1995

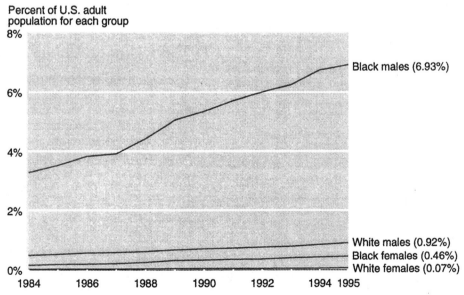

Note. Reprinted from *Correctional Populations in the United States, 1995* (NCJ 163916), by the Bureau of Justice Statistics, 1997, Rockville, MD: Author. In the public domain.

Table A3

Number of Adults Held in State or Federal Prisons or Local Jails, by Sex and Race, 1985–1995

	White		Black	
Year	Males	Females	Males	Females
1985	382,800	21,400	309,800	19,100
1986	417,600	23,000	342,400	19,900
1987	439,000	27,700	356,300	23,200
1988	469,200	32,600	407,400	28,000
1989	516,000	38,500	472,800	35,500
1990	545,900	39,300	508,800	38,000
1991	566,800	42,200	551,000	40,600
1992	598,000	44,100	590,300	42,400
1993	627,100	46,500	624,100	47,500
1994	674,400	51,800	676,000	52,300
1995	726,500	57,800	711,600	55,300

Note. Populations are estimated and rounded to the nearest 100. Adapted from *Correctional Populations in the United States, 1995* (NCJ 163916), by the Bureau of Justice Statistics, 1997, Rockville, MD: Author. In the public domain.

Table A4

Number of Adults Held in State or Federal Prisons or Local Jails Per 100,000 Adult Residents in Each Group, by Sex and Race, 1985–1995

	White		Black	
Year	Males	Females	Males	Females
1985	528	27	3,544	183
1986	570	29	3,850	189
1987	594	35	3,943	216
1988	629	41	4,441	257
1989	685	47	5,066	321
1990	718	48	5,365	338
1991	740	51	5,717	356
1992	774	53	6,015	365
1993	805	56	6,259	403
1994	851	61	6,682	435
1995	919	68	6,926	456

Note. Data are based on resident population for each group on July 1 of each year. Reprinted from *Correctional Populations in the United States, 1995* (NCJ 163916), by the Bureau of Justice Statistics, 1997, Rockville, MD: Author. In the public domain.

Parole and Prisoner Reentry in the United States

PART I*

BY JOAN PETERSILIA, PH.D

Introduction

PUBLIC ANGER AND FRUSTRATION OVER CRIME continue to produce significant changes in the American criminal justice system, but reforms focused on parole are among the most profound. Parole, which is both a procedure by which a board administratively *releases* inmates from prison and a provision for post-release *supervision*, has come to symbolize the leniency of the system, where inmates are "let out" early. When a parolee commits a particularly heinous crime, such as the kidnapping and murder of 13-year-old Polly Klaas by California parolee Richard Allen Davis, or the horrifying rape and murder of four-year-old Megan Kanka in New Jersey by a paroled sex offender, the public is understandably outraged and calls for "abolishing parole."

State legislatures have responded. By the end of 1998, 14 states had abolished early release by a parole board for all offenders, and several others had restricted its use. California still allows discretionary release by a parole board, but only for offenders with indeterminate life sentences (e.g., first-degree murder, kidnap for ransom) (Ditton and Wilson 1999). Even in states that have retained parole, parole boards have become more hesitant to grant it. In Texas, for example, 57 percent of all cases considered for parole release in 1988 were approved; but by 1998, that figure had dropped to just 20 percent (Fabelo 1999).

The argument for abolishing parole is that it will lead to longer prison sentences and greater honesty in sentencing decisions. George Allen, former Governor of Virginia, made abolishing parole a major campaign issue, and one of his first acts once elected Governor in 1994, was to eliminate that state's discretionary parole system for violent offenders. He wrote that:

> The principle that has guided our efforts is honesty. Easy-release rules prevented judges and juries from pre-empting the community's judgement about proper punishment for illegal conduct. Under the new law, judges do not have to play guessing games when imposing sentences. Police officers do not have to see the criminals out on the streets only a year after their last arrest. Criminals know they cannot beat the system. Crime victims and their families are finally seeing that justice is done (Allen, 1997:22).

But correctional experts argue that while abolishing parole may make good politics, it contributes to bad correctional practices—and ultimately, less public safety. As Burke (1995:11) notes, parole makes release from prison a privilege that must be earned. When states abolish parole or reduce the amount of discretion parole authorities have, they in essence replace a rational, controlled system of *"earned"* release for *selected* inmates, with *"automatic"* release for nearly *all* inmates. Proponents argue that the public doesn't understand the tremendous power that is lost when parole is abandoned. Through the exercise of its discretion, parole boards can actually target more violent and dangerous offenders for *longer* periods of incarceration.

Editors's Note: This is the first part of a two-part article. See next Annual Editions article for part two, which appeared in the Fall 2000 issue of Perspectives. Citations for both parts will be included at the end of [both articles].

From *Perspectives*, Summer 2000, pp. 32-46. © 2000 by the American Probation and Parole Association. Reprinted by permission.

Burke, (1995:11) writes:

> The absence of parole means that offenders simply walk out of the door of prison at the end of a pre-determined period of time, no questions asked. No human being asks the tough questions about what has been done to make sure this criminal is no longer a danger before he is released.

In fact, the case of Richard Allen Davis is a perfect example. The California Board of Prison Terms (the Parole Board) knew the risks he posed, and had denied him parole in each of the six instances where his case had been reviewed. But once California abolished discretionary parole release, the Board of Prison Terms no longer had the authority to deny release to inmates whose new standard sentence mandated automatic release after serving a set portion of their terms. Release dates were calculated by the computer for thousands of prisoners then in custody, and when it was determined that Mr. Davis had already served the amount of prison time that the new law required, he had to be released. Less than four months later, he murdered Polly Klaas. California parole officials suspect that had the state not abolished parole, Mr. Davis would have never been released (Burke 1995). Similarly, the case of the murderer of Megan Kanka was never heard by a parole board, rather he went out of prison under mandatory release.

Eliminating parole boards also means that several of its important ancillary purposes are also eliminated. Parole boards have the ability to "individualize sentencing," and as such can provide a review mechanism for assuring greater uniformity in sentencing across judges or counties. Parole boards can also take into account changes in the offender's behavior that might have occurred after he or she was incarcerated. Imprisonment can cause psychological breakdowns, depression or mental illnesses, and the parole board can adjust release dates to account for these changes. Finally, abolishing parole boards also eliminates the major mechanism by which overcrowded prisons can quickly reduce populations. As parole expert Vincent O'Leary once observed: "Most people start out reforming parole, but when you pull that string you find a lot more attached" (Wilson 1977:49).

A few states have not only abolished parole release, but have also considered abolishing parole supervision (often referred to as the "other" parole). In Maine, the legislature not only abolished the parole board but also abolished parole supervision. Similarly, when Virginia abolished parole release, they also abolished parole supervision. Unless the judge remembers to impose a split sentence with a term of probation to follow prison, when offenders leave prison in Virginia, they have no strings at all. If you abolish parole supervision along with parole release, you lose the ability to supervise or provide services to released inmates when they have the highest risk of recidivism and are most in need of services.

> *"The reality is that more than nine out of ten prisoners are released back into the community, and with an average (median) U.S. prison term served of 15 months, half of all inmates in U.S. prisons today will be back on the streets in less than two years."*
>
> —Beck, 1999

Several states that once abolished discretionary parole release have re-established its equivalent. North Carolina, which placed severe constraints on its parole commission in 1981, has gradually restored some of its previous discretion. Florida, which adopted sentencing guidelines in 1983 and abolished parole, has now returned the function under the new name, Controlled Release Authority. Colorado abolished discretionary parole release in 1979 and reinstated it six years later. Elected officials, along with law enforcement and corrections professionals, lobbied to reinstate parole release and supervision after data suggested that the length of prison sentence served had actually decreased following the elimination of parole, and the ability to provide surveillance or treatment of high-risk offenders had significantly declined. As Bill Woodward, then-director of the Division of Criminal Justice in Colorado, noted: "the problem with abolishing parole is you lose your ability to keep track of the inmates and the ability to keep them in treatment if they have alcohol and drug problems" (Gainsborough 1997: 12).

Today, all states except Maine and Virginia have some requirement for post-prison or parole supervision, and nearly 80 percent of all released prisoners in 1997 were subject to some form of conditional community or supervised release (Ditton and Wilson 1999). However, some states have changed its name to distance themselves from the negative image that "parole" has. For example, post-prison supervision is called "control release" in Florida, "community control" in Ohio, "supervised release" in Minnesota and the federal system, and "community custody" in Washington. Regardless of its name, however, parole supervision has changed significantly during the past decade, as national support for parole-as-rehabilitation has waned.

Parole officers readily admit they have fewer services to offer an ever-growing population of offenders. Safety and security have become major issues in parole services (Lynch, 1998), and parole officers are now authorized to carry weapons in two-thirds of the states (Camp and Camp 1997). Parole officers in most large urban areas are now more surveillance- than services- oriented, and drug testing, electronic monitoring and verifying curfews are the most common activities of many parole agents (Petersilia 1998b).

Parole was founded primarily to foster offender reformation rather than to increase punitiveness or surveillance. Abandoning parole's historical commitment to rehabilitation worries correctional professionals. The reality is that more than nine out of ten prisoners are released back into the community, and with an average (median) U.S. prison term served of 15 months, half of all inmates in U.S. prisons today will be back on the streets in less than two years (Beck 1999). The transition from prison back into the community is exceedingly difficult, and recidivism rates are highest in the first year following release. A study by the Bureau of Justice Statistics found that 25 percent of released prisoners are re-arrested in the first six months, and 40 percent within the first year (Beck and Shipley 1989).

To assist in this high-risk time period, parole has historically provided job assistance, family counseling and chemical dependency programs (although arguable, parole has never provided enough of these services). But, punitive public attitudes, combined with diminishing social service resources, has resulted in fewer services provided to parolees.

Until recently, the lines were drawn between tough-on-crime "abolitionists" and parole-as-rehabilitation "traditionalists." Politicians continued to shout "abolish parole," while corrections professionals asked for more money to invest in services and surveillance, and the two seemed worlds apart. Over the last year, however, politicians seem to be listening more closely to the professionals, as parole—or more precisely, *failure* on parole—is creating severe fiscal pressures on state prisons' budgets. A greater number of parolees are failing supervision and being returned to prison, and as a result, contributing disproportionately to prison crowding and the continued pressure to build more prisons. As New York Assemblyman Daniel L. Feldman recently put it: "Lock 'em up and throw away the key attitudes are coming back to haunt state legislators across the nation" (Carter 1998:2).

In California, for example, where 104,000 adults are now on parole (one out of every seven U.S. parolees), nearly 80 percent are failing to successfully complete supervision (Austin and Lawson 1998). Parole violators accounted for 65 percent of all California prison admissions in 1997, and 41 percent of prison admissions were for violations of the technical conditions of parole, rather than for the conviction of new crimes (Austin and Lawson 1998). It should be noted, however, that a technical violation does not mean the inmate was not engaged in criminal behavior. It may be that the inmate was arrested for a criminal charge but in lieu of prosecution, was revoked and returned to custody. In fact, the vast majority of these technical violations (82 percent) have an underlying criminal charge (Austin and Lawson 1998).

When revoked to prison, California inmates spend an additional three to four months in prison prior to being re-released (Little Hoover Commission 1998). Recent analyses suggest that such "high parole revocation rates presents an enormous waste of prison resources and does not fit the mission of a traditional state prison system (i.e. the long-term confinement of sentenced felons)" (Austin and Lawson 1998:13). California has, for the first time since abolishing parole release in 1977, called for a statewide reassessment of the state's parole services and revocation policies (Legislative Analysts Office 1998).

Parole, a system that developed in the U.S. more by accident than by design, now threatens to become the tail that wagged the correction's dog. Prison populations continue to rise, more offenders are required to be on parole supervision, where fewer services and work programs exist due to scarcity of resources (often diverted from parole services to fund prison expansion). A greater number of parole violations (particularly drug use) are detected through monitoring and drug testing, and parole authorities have increasingly less tolerance for failure. Revocation to prison is becoming a predictable (and increasingly short) transition in the prison-to-parole and back-to-prison revolving door cycle. Correctional leaders, joined by many elected officials, are increasingly asking: "Must they all come back?"

Of course, answering that question is exceedingly complex. We would need to know what kinds of programs reduce recidivism for offenders with different needs. Would more intensive surveillance lower recidivism, and how intense must it be to make a difference? What combination of conditions, surveillance and treatment would get the best results? Once we have identified programs that make a difference, we would have to ask a number of additional questions. For example, should we mandate that parolees participate in needed treatment, or simply make it available to those who volunteer? How long should parole last? Should some parolees be kept on "banked" caseloads, with no services or supervision, simply to expedite their return to prison if they commit new crimes? What difference does caseload size make, and which kinds of officers are more successful with which kinds of clients?

These are tough questions, and sound-bite attacks on parole aren't very helpful in answering them. We need to begin a serious dialogue aimed at "reinventing" parole in the U.S. so that it better balances the public's need to hold offenders accountable with the need to provide services to released offenders. To begin that dialogue, we need to first assemble information on what is known about parole in the U.S. That is the purpose of this essay.

Section I begins by describing sources of U.S. adult parole data. This essay does not describe juvenile data or practices. Section II discusses the early evolution of parole in the U.S., and its use in modern sentencing practices. This section reviews the dramatic changes in parole release that resulted from the nation's skepticism about the ability of prisons to rehabilitate. Section III describes the current parole population. It presents trend data on the growth of the parole population, and what are known about parolee's crimes, personal backgrounds and court-ordered conditions. It also presents data on the average size of parole caseloads, offender contact requirements and annual costs of supervision. Section IV is devoted to describing the offender's needs as he or she transitions to the community, and what services are available to meet these needs. This section also outlines the civil disabilities that apply to ex-convicts. Section V assesses parole outcomes, reviewing parole completion and recidivism rates. Section VI discusses some current thinking on how to reform parole, and identifies some of the more promising parole programs. Section VII presents concluding remarks. Note: Sections V-VII will appear in the Fall 2000 issue of *Perspectives*.

I. Sources of Parole Information

Various agencies within the U.S. Department of Justice collect most of the available information regarding current parole practices and parolee characteristics.

The National Institute of Corrections (NIC) has supported periodic surveys since 1990 that describe parole board practices in the U.S. (Rhine et al. 1991) and whether states currently have discretionary parole release (National Institute of Corrections 1995). The nation's major parole associations, the American Probation and Parole Association (APPA), the American Correctional Association (ACA) and the Association of Paroling Authorities, International (APAI) also have conducted periodic studies (Burke (1995), Rhine, Smith and Jackson (1991), and Runda, Rhine & Wetter (1994)). The Bureau of Justice Assistance (BJA) recently published a survey of state sentencing practices, including information on state's parole practices (Austin 1998).

Most of what we know about U.S. parolee characteristics comes from the Bureau of Justice Statistics (BJS), the statistical arm of the U.S. Department of Justice. Since the early 1980s, BJS has reported on the number of persons entering and exiting parole through its "National Corrections Reporting Program." This series collects data nearly every year on all prison admissions and releases and on all parole entries and discharges in participating jurisdictions.

The Bureau of Justice Assistance's "National Probation and Parole Reporting Program" gathers annual data on state and federal probation and parole counts and movements and the characteristics of persons under the supervision of probation and parole agencies. Published data include admissions and releases by method of entry and discharge. BJS also sponsors censuses, usually conducted every five to six years, describing the agencies that have control of persons serving a criminal sentence. The "Census of State and Local Probation and Parole Agencies," first conducted in 1991, gathers data on the agency organizational location, staffing, expenditures and programs. Finally, BJS conducts surveys of jail and prison inmates (usually done every five years), that ask offenders whether they were on parole at the time of the arrest that led to their current conviction.

Parole wasn't always such a minimal topic of data collection and research. Between 1965-1977, the National Council on Crime and Delinquency (NCCD) directed the "Uniform Parole Reports" project, which collected arrest, conviction and imprisonment data on parolees. Analyses of this data helped researchers to improve methods for predicting parolee behavior (Gottfredson, Hoffman and Sigler 1975). The NCCD data collection effort was discontinued in 1977, and no similar effort replaced it.

At about the same time, The U.S. Board of Parole undertook a major research study to develop parole guidelines, which incorporated offense seriousness and risk of recidivism (Gottfredson, Wilkins and Hoffman, 1978). This research tracked released federal prisoners, and used the recidivism data to create an actuarial device, which in turn, was applied to each inmate to create a "Salient Factor Score" (SFS). The SFS provided explicit guidelines for release decisions based on a determination of the potential risk of parole violation (Hoffman and DeGostin 1974). The SFS was adopted by the U.S. Parole Board in 1972, and remained in use until the abolition of parole at the federal level in 1997.

Beyond these early studies and the minimal descriptive data that is now collected, there has been scant attention paid parole from the research or scholarly community. We have very few parole program evaluations or research studies of the parole process and its impact on offenders. The National Institute of Justice (NIJ), the research arm of the U.S. Department of Justice, has funded most of what has been conducted, which includes evaluations of drug testing for high risk parolees in Texas (Turner and Petersilia 1992); intensive parole supervision in Minnesota (Deschenes, Turner and Petersilia 1995); work release in Washington (Turner and Petersilia 1996a); and the effects of providing work training and day programs to parolees (Finn 1998a; Finn 1998b; Finn 1998c).

Parole has never attracted much scholarly interest, although there are a few notable exceptions, for example (von Hirsch and Hanrahan 1979), (Bottomly 1990), (Rhine et al. 1991), (McCleary 1992), (Simon 1993), (Richards 1995), (Abadinsky 1997), (Lynch 1998) and (Cromwell and del Carmen 1999).

II. The Origins and Evolution of Parole in the U.S.

A Early Foundations and Growth of Parole

Parole comes from the word French word *parol*, referring to "word" as in giving one's word of honor or promise. It has come to mean an inmate's promise to conduct

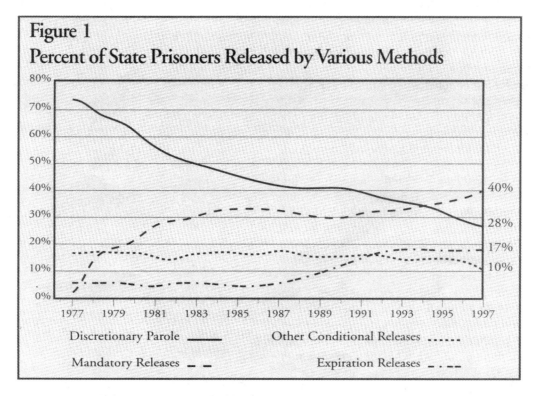

Figure 1
Percent of State Prisoners Released by Various Methods

Discretionary Parole ———   Other Conditional Releases ......

Mandatory Releases – –   Expiration Releases – . ––

Note: Discretionary paroles are persons entering the community because of a board decision. Mandatory releases are persons whose release from prison was not decided by a parole board. Includes those entering because of determinate sentencing statutes, good-time provisions, or emergency releases. Other conditional releases include commutations, pardons, and deaths. Expiration releases are those where the inmate has served his maximum court sentence. Source: Bureau of Justice Statistics, *National Prisoner Statistics,* selected years.

him or herself in a law-abiding manner and according to certain rules in exchange for release. In penal philosophy, parole is part of the general 19th-century trend in criminology from punishment to reformation. Chief credit for developing the early parole system is usually given to Alexander Maconochie, who was in charge of the English penal colony at Norfolk Island, 1,000 miles off the coast of Australia, and to Sir Walter Crofton, who directed Ireland's prisons (Cromwell and del Carmen 1999).

Maconochie criticized definite prison terms and developed a system of rewards for good conduct, labor and study. Through a classification procedure he called the mark system, prisoners could progress through stages of increasing responsibility and ultimately gain freedom. In 1840, he was given an opportunity to apply these principles as superintendent of the Norfolk Island penal settlement in the South Pacific. Under his direction, task accomplishment, not time served, was the criterion for release. Marks of commendation were given to prisoners who performed their tasks well, and they were released from the penal colony as they demonstrated willingness to accept society's rules. Returning to England in 1844 to campaign for penal reform, Maconochie tried to implement his reforms when he was appointed governor of the new Birmingham Borough Prison in 1849. However, he was unable to institute his reforms there because he was dismissed form his position in 1851 on the grounds that his methods were too lenient (Clear and Cole 1997).

Walter Crofton attempted to implement Maconochie's mark system when he became the administrator of the Irish Prison System in 1854. Crofton felt that prison programs should be directed more toward reformation, and that "tickets-of-leave" should be awarded to prisoners who had shown definitive achievement and positive attitude change. After a period of strict imprisonment, Crofton began transferring offenders to "intermediate prisons" where they could accumulate marks based on work performance, behavior and educational improvement. Eventually they would be given tickets-of-leave and released on parole supervision. Parolees were required to submit monthly reports to the police, and a police inspector helped them find jobs and generally oversaw their activities. The concepts of intermediate prisons, assistance and supervision after release were Crofton's contributions to the modern system of parole (Clear and Cole 1997).

By 1865, American penal reformers were well aware of the reforms achieved in the European prison systems, particularly in the Irish system. At the Cincinnati meeting of the National Prison Association in 1870, a paper by Crofton was read, and specific references to the Irish system were incorporated into the Declaration of Principles, along with other such reforms as indeterminate sentencing and classification for release based on a mark system. Because of Crofton's experiment, many Americans referred to parole as the Irish system (Walker 1998).

Zebulon Brockway, a Michigan penologist, is given credit for implementing the first parole system in the U.S. He proposed a two-pronged strategy for managing prison populations and preparing inmates for release: indeterminate sentencing coupled with parole supervision. He was given a chance to put his proposal into practice in 1876 when he was appointed superintendent at a new youth reformatory, the Elmira Reformatory in New York. He instituted a system of indeterminacy and parole release, and is commonly credited as the father of both in the United States. His ideas reflected the tenor of the times—a belief that criminals could be reformed, and that every prisoner's treatment should be individualized.

On being admitted to Elmira, each inmate (males between the ages of sixteen and thirty) was placed in the second grade of classification. Six months of good conduct meant promotion to the first grade—misbehavior could result in being placed in the third grade, from which the inmate would have to work his way back up. Continued good behavior in the first grade resulted in release. Paroled inmates remained under the jurisdiction of authorities for an additional six months, during which the parolee was required to report on the first day of every month to his appointed volunteer guardian (from which parole officers evolved) and provide an account of his situation and conduct (Abadinsky 1997). Written reports became required and were submitted to the institute after being signed by the parolee's employer and guardian.

Indeterminate sentencing and parole spread rapidly through the United States. In 1907, New York became the first state to formally adopt all the components of a parole system: indeterminate sentences, a system for granting release, post-release supervision and specific criteria for parole revocation. By 1927, only three states (Florida, Mississippi and Virginia) were without a parole system, and by 1942, all states and the federal government had such systems (Clear and Cole 1997).

The percentage of U.S. prisoners released on parole rose from 44 percent in 1940 to a high of 72 percent in 1977, after which some states began to question the very foundations of parole, and the number of prisoners released in this fashion began to decline (Bottomly 1990). As shown in Figure 1, just 28 percent of prison releases were paroled in 1997, the lowest figure since the federal government began compiling statistics on this issue (Dirron and Wilson 1999). Mandatory releases—the required release of inmates at the expiration of a certain time period—now surpass parole releases. And if one adds the "expiration releases," where the inmate is released after serving his full sentence, there is even a bigger imbalance between discretionary parole and mandatory release (28 percent vs. 57 percent).

Parole, it seemed during the first half of the 20th century, made perfect sense. First, it was believed to contribute to prisoner reform, by encouraging participation in programs aimed at rehabilitation. Second, the power to grant parole was thought to provide corrections offi-cials with a tool for maintaining institutional control and discipline. The prospect of a reduced sentence in exchange for good behavior encouraged better conduct among inmates. Finally, release on parole, as a "back end" solution to prison crowding was important from the beginning. For complete historical reviews, see (Simon, 1993) and (Bottomly 1990).

The tremendous growth in parole as a concept, however, did not imply uniform development, public support or quality practices. As (Bottomly 1990) wrote, "it is doubtful whether parole ever really operated consistently in the United States either in principle or practice." Moreover, Bottomly notes that parole-as-rehabilitation was never taken very seriously, and from its inception, prison administrators used parole primarily to manage prison crowding and reduce inmate violence.

Despite its expanded usage, parole was controversial from the start (Rothman 1980). A Gallup poll conducted in 1934 revealed that 82 percent of U.S. adults believed that parole was not strict enough and should not be as frequently granted (The Gallup Organization 1998). Today, parole is still unpopular, and a recent survey shows that 80 percent of Americans favor making parole more difficult to obtain (The Gallup Organization 1998). A comparable percentage is opposed to granting parole a second time to inmates who have previously been granted parole for a serious crime (Flanagan 1996). On the other hand, the public significantly underestimates the amount of time inmates serve, so their lack of support for parole reflects that misperception (Flanagan 1996).

Nonetheless, over time, the positivistic approach to crime and criminals—which viewed the offender as "sick" and in need of help—began to influence parole release and supervision. The rehabilitation ideal, as it came to be known, affected all of corrections well into the 1960s and gained acceptance for the belief that the purpose of incarceration and parole was to change the offender's behavior rather than simply to punish. As Rhine (1996) notes, as the rehabilitative ideal evolved, indeterminate sentencing in tandem with parole acquired a newfound legitimacy. It also gave legitimacy and purpose to parole boards, which were supposed to be composed of "experts" in behavioral change, and it was their responsibility to discern that moment during confinement when the offender was rehabilitated and thus suitable for release.

Parole boards, usually political appointees, were given broad discretion to determine when an offender was ready for release—a decision limited only by the constraints of the maximum sentence imposed by the judge. Parole boards—usually composed of no more than ten individuals—also have the authority to rescind an established parole date, issue warrants and subpoenas, set conditions of supervision, restore offenders' civil rights and grant final discharges. In most states, they also order the payment of restitution or supervision fees as a condition of parole release.

In the early years, there were few standards governing the decision to grant or deny parole, and decision-making rules were not made public. One of the long-standing criticisms of paroling authorities is that their members are too often selected based on party loyalty and political patronage, rather than professional qualifications and experience (Morse 1939).

In his book, *Conscience and Convenience,* David Rothman discussed the issue of discretionary decisions by parole boards. He reported that in the early 20th century, parole boards considered primarily the seriousness of the crime in determining whether to release an inmate on parole. However, there was no consensus on what constituted a serious crime. "Instead," Rothman wrote, "each member made his own decisions. The judgements were personal and therefore not subject to debate or reconsideration." (Rothman 1980:173) These personal preferences often resulted in unwarranted sentencing disparities or racial and gender bias (Tonry 1995). As has been observed, "no other part of the criminal justice system concentrates such power in the hands of so few" (Rhine et al. 1991:32-33).

Regardless of criticisms, the use of parole release grew, and instead of using it as a special privilege to be extended to exceptional prisoners, it began to be used as a standard mode of release from prison, routinely considered upon completion of a minimum term of confinement. What had started as a practical alternative to executive clemency, and then came to be used as a mechanism for controlling prison growth, gradually developed a distinctively rehabilitative rationale incorporating the promise of help and assistance as well as surveillance (Bottomly 1990:325).

By the mid-1950s, the indeterminate sentencing coupled with parole release was well entrenched in the U.S., such that it was the dominant sentencing structure in every state, and by the late 1970s, more than 70 percent of all inmates released were as a result of parole board discretionary decision. And in some states, essentially everyone was released as a result of the parole board decision-making. For example, throughout the 1960s, over 95 percent of all inmates released in Washington, New Hampshire and California were released on parole (O'Leary 1974). Indeterminate sentencing coupled with parole release was a matter of absolute routine and good correctional practice for most of the twentieth century.

But all that was to change during the late 1970s, gaining increasing strength in the 1980s and 1990s, when demands for substantial reforms in parole practice began to be heard.

B. Modern Challenges and Changes to Parole

The pillars of the American corrections systems—indeterminate sentencing coupled with parole release, for the purposes of offender rehabilitation—came under severe attack and basically collapsed during the late 1970s and early 1980s. This period in penology has been well documented elsewhere and will not be repeated here. For an excellent review, see (Reitz 1998).

In summary; attacks on indeterminate sentencing and parole release seem to have centered on three major criticisms. First, there was little scientific evidence that parole release and supervision reduced subsequent recidivism. In 1974, Robert Martinson and his colleagues published the now-famous review of the effectiveness of correctional treatment and concluded that: "With few and isolated exceptions, the rehabilitative efforts that have been reported so far have had no appreciable effect on recidivism" (Lipton, Martinson and Wilks 1975). Of the 289 studies they reviewed, just 25 (8.6 percent) pertained to parole, and yet their summary was interpreted to mean that parole supervision (and all rehabilitation programs) didn't work.

The National Research Council reviewed the Martinson data and basically concurred with the conclusions reached (Sechrest, White and Brown 1979). Martinson's study is often credited with giving rehabilitation the *coup de grace*. As Holt (1998) notes, once rehabilitation could not be legitimated by science, there was nothing to support the "readiness for release" idea, and therefore no role for parole boards or indeterminate sentencing.

Second, parole and indeterminate sentencing were challenged on moral grounds as unjust and inhumane, especially when imposed on unwilling participants. Research showed there was little relationship between in-prison behavior, participation in rehabilitation programs and post-release recidivism (Glaser 1969). If that was true, then why base release dates on in-prison performance? Prisoners argued that not knowing their release dates held them in "suspended animation" and contributed one more pain of imprisonment.

Third, indeterminate sentencing permitted authorities to utilize a great deal of uncontrolled discretion in release decisions, and these decisions were often inconsistent and discriminatory. Since parole boards had a great deal of autonomy and their decisions were not subject to outside scrutiny, critics argued that it was a hidden system of discretionary decision-making and led to race and class bias in release decisions (Citizens' Inquiry on Parole and Criminal Justice, 1974).

It seemed as if no one liked indeterminate sentencing and parole in the early 1980s, and the time was ripe for change. Crime control advocates denounced parole supervision as being largely nominal and ineffective; social welfare advocates decried the lack of meaningful and useful rehabilitation programs. Several scholars, for example, James Q. Wilson, Andrew von Hirsch, and David Fogel, began to advocate alternative sentencing proposals.

James Q. Wilson, an influential scholar, argued that if there was no scientific basis for the possibility of rehabilitation, then the philosophical rationale for making it the chief goal of sentencing should be abandoned. He urged instead a revival of interest in the deterrence and incapacitation functions of the criminal justice system.

He urged the abandonment of rehabilitation as a major purpose of corrections, and wrote: "Instead we could view the correctional system as having a very different function—to isolate and to punish. That statement may strike many readers as cruel, even barbaric. It is not. It is merely recognition that society must be able to protect itself from dangerous offenders. . . . It is also a frank admission that society really does not know how to do much else" (Wilson 1985: 193).

Andrew von Hirsch provided a seemingly neutral ideological substitute for rehabilitation (Holt 1998). He argued that the discredited rehabilitation model should be replaced with a simple nonutilitarian notion that sentencing sanctions should reflect the social harm caused by the misconduct. Indeterminacy and parole should be replaced with a specific penalty for a specific offense. He believed that all persons committing the same crimes "deserve" to be sentenced to conditions that are similar in both type and duration, and that individual traits such as rehabilitation or the potential for recidivism should be irrelevant to the sentencing and parole decision. He proposed abolishing parole and adopting a system of "just deserts" sentencing, where similarly situated criminal conduct would be punished similarly (von Hirsch 1976).

David Fogel advocated a "justice model" for prisons and parole, where inmates would be given opportunities to volunteer for rehabilitation programs, but that participation would not be required. He criticized the unbridled discretion exercised by correctional officials, particularly parole boards, under the guise of "treatment." He recommended a return to flat time/determinate sentencing and the elimination of parole boards. He also advocated abolishing parole's surveillance function and turning that function over to law enforcement (Fogel 1975).

These individuals had a major influence on both academic and policy thinking about sentencing objectives. Together they advocated a system with less emphasis on rehabilitation and the abolition of indeterminate sentencing and discretionary parole release. Liberals and conservatives endorsed the proposals. The political left was concerned about excessive discretion that permitted vastly different sentences in presumably similar cases, and the political right was concerned about the leniency of parole boards. A political coalition resulted, and soon incapacitation and "just deserts" replaced rehabilitation as the primary goal of American prisons.

With that changed focus, the indeterminate sentencing and parole release came under serious attack, and calls for "abolishing parole" were heard in state after state. In 1976, Maine became the first state to eliminate parole. The following year, California and Indiana joined Maine in establishing determinate sentencing legislation and abolishing discretionary parole release. As noted, by the end of 1998, 14 states had abolished discretionary parole release for all inmates. Additionally, in 21 states parole authorities are operating under what might be called a sundown provision, in that they have discretion over a small or diminished parole eligible population. Today, just fifteen states have given their parole boards full authority to release inmates through a discretionary process (see Table 1).

Likewise, at the federal level, the Comprehensive Crime Control Act of 1984 created the U.S. Sentencing Commission. That legislation abolished the U.S. Parole Commission, and parole was phased out from the federal criminal justice system in 1997. Offenders sentenced to federal prison, while no longer eligible for parole release, are now required to serve a defined term of "supervised release" following release from prison (Adams and Roth 1998).

One of the presumed effects of eliminating parole or limiting its use is to increase the length of prison term served. After all, parole release is widely regarded as "letting them out early." Time served in prison has increased in recent years, but it is attributed to the implementation of Truth-in-Sentencing Laws rather than the abolition of parole boards. BJS data reveal no obvious relationship between type of release (mandatory vs. parole board) and actual length of time spent in prison prior to release. For all offense types combined the mean (average) time served in prison for those released from state prison in 1996 through "discretionary" (parole) methods was 25 months served; whereas for those released "mandatorily," the average (mean) time served in prison was 24 months (Ditton and Wilson 1999). Allen Beck, Chief of Corrections Statistics at the BJS, recently observed that ending parole by itself "has had no real impact on time served" (Butterfield 1999:11).

Offenders are, however, spending greater amounts of time in prison and on parole. These longer time periods may make it more difficult for offenders to maintain family contacts and other social supports, thereby contributing to their social isolation upon release. As Table 2 shows, the average (mean) time served among released state prisoners for all types of offenders has increased from an average of 20 months in 1985 to 25 months in 1996. The median prison term served has increased from 14 months in 1985 to 15 months in 1996. Similarly, the length of time on parole supervision (for those successfully discharged) has increased, from an average of 19 months in 1985 to 23 months in 1996. The average time on parole for "unsuccessful exits" was 19 months in 1985 and 21 months in 1996 (Bureau of Justice Statistics 1998).

Even in states that did not formally abolish parole or restrict its use to certain serious offenses, the sentencing reform movement produced a significant diminution of parole boards' discretionary authority to release. Mandatory minimum sentencing policies now exist in every state and the federal government, and 24 states have enacted "Three Strikes, You're Out" laws that require extremely long minimum terms for certain repeat offenders (National Conference of State Legislatures 1996).

Perhaps most significantly, 27 states and the District of Columbia have established "truth-in-sentencing"

Table 1—Status of Parole Release in the U.S., 1998

	Parole Board Has Full Release Powers	Parole Board Has Limited Release Powers	If Parole Board Powers Are Limited, Crimes Ineligible for Discretionary Release	Discretionary Parole Abolished (Year Abolished)
Alabama	✔			
Alaska		✔		
Arizona				✔(1994)
Arkansas		✔		
California		✔	Only for indeterminate life sentence	
Colorado	✔			
Connecticut		✔	Murders, capital felonies	
Delaware				✔(1990)
Florida		✔	Certain capital/life felonies	
Georgia		✔	Several felonies	
Hawaii		✔	Punish. by life w/o parole	
Idaho	✔			
Illinois				✔(1978)
Indiana				✔(1977)
Iowa		✔	Murder 1, kidnap, sex abuse	
Kansas				✔(1993)
Kentucky	✔			
Louisiana		✔	Several felonies	
Maine				✔(1975)
Maryland		✔	Violent, or death pen. sought	
Massachusetts		✔	Murder 1	
Michigan		✔	Murder 1, 650+ g.cocaine	
Minnesota				✔(1980)
Mississippi				✔(1995)
Missouri		✔	Several felonies	
Montana	✔			
Nebraska		✔	Murder 1/life, kidnap/life	
Nevada	✔			
New Hampshire		✔	Murder 1	
New Jersey	✔			
New Mexico				✔(1979)
New York		✔	"violent felony offenders"	
North Carolina				✔(1994)
North Dakota	✔			
Ohio				✔(1996)
Oklahoma	✔			
Oregon				✔(1989)
Pennsylvania	✔			
Rhode Island	✔			
South Carolina	✔			
South Dakota		✔	None with life sentence	
Tennessee		✔	Murder 1/life, rapes	
Texas		✔	None of death row	
Utah	✔			
Vermont	✔			
Virginia				✔(1995)
Washington				✔(1984)
West Virginia		✔	No life without mercy	
Wisconsin		✔	No life without parole	
Wyoming	✔			
Total	15	21		14
U.S. Parole				✔(1984)

*Wisconsin abolished discretionary parole release in 1999 to go into effect on January 1, 2000 for crimes committed on or after that date.

Note: This information is from *Status Report on Parole, 1996. Results from an NIC Survey (1997)*, and updated with information from Ditton and Wilson, 1999.

Table 2 Time Served in Prison, Jail and on Parole, All Offense Types Combined, in months

	1985	1990	1996
Time Served in Jail Average (Mean)	6	6	5
Time Served in Prison Average (Mean)	20	22	25
Time Served on Parole	19	22	23
Total Months	44	50	53

Source: Data from the Burreau of Justice Statistic, *National Corrections Reporting Program*, 1985, 1990, 1996. Includes only offenders with a sentence of more than 1 year released for the first time on the current sentence. Time served on parole is for "successful" exits.

laws, under which people convicted of selected violent crimes must serve at least 85 percent of the announced prison sentence. To satisfy the 85 percent test (in order to qualify for federal funds for prison construction), states have limited the powers of parole boards to set release dates, or of prison managers to award good time and gain time (time off for good behavior or for participation in work or treatment programs), or both. Truth-in-sentencing laws not only effectively eliminate parole but also most "good time."(Ditton and Wilson 1999)

Even in the 15 jurisdictions that give parole authorities discretion to release, most of them utilize formal risk prediction instruments (or parole guidelines) to assist in parole decision-making (Runda, Rhine and Wetter 1994). Parole guidelines are usually actuarial devices, which objectively predict the risk of recidivism based on crime and offender background information. The guidelines produce a "seriousness score" for each individual by summing points assigned for various background characteristics (higher scores mean greater risk). Inmates with the least serious crime and the lowest probability of reoffending (statistically) would then be the first to be released and so forth. The use of such objective instruments helps to reduce the disparity in parole release decision-making, and has been shown to be more accurate than release decisions based on the case study or individualized method (Holt 1998). One half of U.S. jurisdictions now utilize formal risk assessment instruments in relation to parole release (Runda, Rhine and Wetter 1994).

III. A Profile of Parolees in the U.S.

A. Numbers of Parolees under Supervision

While discretionary parole release has declined, parole supervision remains in almost every state. And, as the size of the prison populations has risen, so too has the parole population. BJS reports that, at yearend 1997, there were 685,033 adults on parole in the U.S. Persons on parole represented 12 percent of the total 5.7 million persons who were incarcerated or on community supervision ("under correctional control") at yearend 1997 (Bureau of Justice Statistics 1998).

The growth in parole populations has slowed considerably in recent years; increasing just 1.3 percent in 1997, after growing 24 percent between 1990-1992. This is the smallest growth of any of the correctional populations and likely reflects a short-term lull in the growth of the parole population, primarily as a consequence of an increase in the average length of prison term being served as a result of truth-in-sentencing policies (Ditton and Wilson 1999).

Nearly a third (31.2 percent) of all persons on parole in the U.S. were in Texas or California. Texas led the nation with 109,437 adults on parole in 1997, followed by California with 104,409. In 1997, however, the parole population in Texas declined by 2.8 percent, while the California population increased by 4.9 percent. The District of Columbia has, by far, the greatest number of its resident population on parole supervision. In 1997, nearly 1.7 percent of all its residents were on parole supervision, compared to a national average of .03 percent (Bureau of Justice Statistics 1998).

B. Selected Characteristics of Parolees

As noted earlier, there is little available information on the characteristics of persons on parole. BJS reports some basic characteristics of those entering parole as part of its *National Corrections Reporting Program* series. In 1997, similar to other correctional populations, males constitute most of the parolee population (89 percent), although the percentage of female parolees increased from 8 percent in 1990 to 11 percent in 1997. The median age of the parolee population was 34 years, and the median education level was 11th grade, although 13 percent of parolees had an education level of below the 8th grade and an additional 45 percent, between the 9th and 11th grade level (Bureau of Justice Statistics 1997). These characteristics have remained fairly constant since the early 1980s.

The only parolee characteristic that has changed in recent years appears to be conviction crime. In 1988 30 percent of first entries to parole were convicted of violence, but in 1997 that figure had dropped to 24 percent. In 1985 just 12 percent of those persons released to parole were convicted of drug crimes, whereas in 1997 that was true for 35 percent of first releases to parole (Beck 1999).

Today, more than a third of all entrants to parole are convicted of drug related crimes (see Table 3).

Individual states sometimes publish descriptions of their parolees. For example, a recent report by the California Parole and Community Services Division reported the following (California Department of Corrections 1997):

- 85 percent of parolees were chronic substance abusers;
- 10 percent are homeless, but homelessness is as high as 30 to 50 percent in San Francisco and Los Angeles;
- 70-90 percent of all parolees were unemployed;
- 50 percent are functionally illiterate. Over half of all parolees read below the sixth grade level and therefore, could not fill out job applications or compete in the job market;
- 18 percent have some sort of psychiatric problem.

IV. The Reentry Process and Parole Supervision.

A. Administration of Parole Field Services

As noted earlier, parole consists of two parts: *parole boards that have the authority to decide when to release prisoners and parole field services* whose parole officers supervise offenders after their release. The major criticisms of parole release (e.g., lack of professionalism, unwarranted discretion and ineffectiveness) were also leveled at field supervision and caused major changes and reforms there as well.

One of the first and continuing reforms in parole field services have been to make them more independent of parole boards. Since the mid-1960s, states have increasingly moved parole field services away from being an arm of the parole board and into a separate agency. According to the American Correctional Association, the parole field service agency is housed under a separate agency in 41 states, usually in the state's department of corrections. Parole boards have responsibility for supervising parolees in only ten states (American Correctional Association, 1995).

Regardless of their administrative relationship, parole board directives heavily influence how parole agents carry out their duties and responsibilities. When setting the conditions of release, parole boards are in fact prescribing the goals it expects parole agents to pursue in the period of supervision. A 1997 survey by the Association of Paroling Authorities International shows that most parole boards are responsible for ordering community service, restitution, supervision fees, sex offender registration and treatment program participation (Association of Paroling Authorities International 1998). In addition, some parole boards also mandate drug testing, intensified supervision and participation in victim mediation programs.

Table 3: Conviction Offenses of Persons Entering Parole, Selected Years

Most serious offense First entries to parole supervision[*]					
	1988	1990	1992	1994	1996
All offenses	100%	100%	100%	100%	100%
Violent offenses	30.1	25.2	25.5	23.5	23.6
Homicide	3.8	3.0	2.7	2.3	2.1
Sexual assault	5.4	4.2	4.2	4.4	4.3
Robbery	13.7	11.2	10.7	8.7	8.9
Assault	6.3	5.8	6.6	6.9	6.0
Other violent	0.9	1.0	1.0	1.2	1.4
Property offenses	42.2	37.2	32.7	33.3	31.0
Burglary	20.8[*]	17.5	14.8	14.5	12.9
Larceny/theft	10.2	9.6	8.4	8.5	8.1
Motor vehicle theft	2.9	2.7	2.7	3.1	2.7
Fraud	5.1	4.6	3.9	4.2	4.3
Other property	3.2	2.8	2.9	3.0	3.0
Drug offenses	19.2	28.2	31.1	31.6	34.7
Possession	6.0	8.6	8.2	7.0	10.0
Trafficking	10.4	15.6	19.3	19.5	19.5
Other	2.8	4.0	3.6	5.1	5.2
Public-order offense	7.1	8.1	9.8	10.5	10.0
Weapons	1.9	1.8	2.2	2.4	2.7
DWI/DUI	—	3.0	3.7	3.5	3.2
Other public-order	—	3.3	3.9	4.6	4.2
Other offenses	1.4	1.3	1.2	1.1	0.6

Source: Bureau of Justice Statistics, *National Corrections Reporting Program*, 1988, 1990, 1992. Unpublished data for 1994 and 1996.

[*]Based on parole entries who were released for the first time on the current offense and who had a maximum sentence of more than 1 year.

—Not available.

In all states, the decision to revoke parole ultimately rests with the parole board. As such, parole boards set implicit and explicit criteria about which types of parole violations will warrant return to prison and, as such, heavily influence the types of behavior parole officers monitor and record. If, for example, failing a drug test is not a violation that will result in revocation to prison or any serious consequence by the parole board, parole agents will not administer drug tests as frequently since no consequence can be guaranteed (McCleary 1992). In this way, parole boards and parole field services are functionally interdependent.

B. Offender's Need for Services and Conditions of Parole Supervision

Persons released from prison face a multitude of difficulties in trying to successfully reenter the outside community. They remain largely uneducated, unskilled, and usually without solid family support systems—and now they have the added burden of a prison record and the distrust and fear that inevitably results. If they are African American and under age thirty, they join the largest group of unemployed in the country, with the added handicap of former convict status (Clear and Cole 1997). As Irwin and Austin write: "Any imprisonment reduces the opportunities of felons, most of whom had relatively few opportunities to begin with." (Irwin and Austin 1994:133)

Research has shown that parolees want the same things as the rest of us, although most believe they will not succeed (Richards 1995). Most aspire to a relatively modest, stable, conventional life after prison. "When I get out, I want to have my kids with me and have a good job so I can support them (Irwin and Austin 1994:126).

The public too would like them to succeed. But what assistance are parolees given as they re-enter our communities? Sadly, while inmates' need for services and assistance has increased, parole in some (if not most) states has retreated from its historical mission to provide counseling, job training, and housing assistance.

An excellent ethnographic study of parole officers in California concludes that while "rehabilitation" remains in parole's rhetoric, as a practical matter, parole services are almost entirely focused on control-oriented activities (Lynch 1998). Agents have constructed the prototypical parolee as someone who generally chooses to maintain an involvement with crime, who needs no more than an attitude adjustment in order to get on the right tract, and who does not need the agent to provide intervention and services to facilitate reform. As Lynch observes: "In this way, while parole may talk of the need and capability for reform among their clientele, the agency can absolve itself of the responsibility to provide it" (Lynch 1998:857). Even when traditional rehabilitative tools are available to agents (e.g., drug treatment and counseling) they "are treated as rehabilitative in discourse, but are often used for coercive control in practice"(Lynch 1998:860).

Services and Parole Conditions. Of course, what help parolees receive differs vastly depending on the state and jurisdiction in which they are being supervised. But as states put more and more of their fiscal resources into building prisons, fewer resources are available for parole services. And, as noted earlier, the public has become less tolerant and forgiving of past criminal transgressions, as well as more fearful of particular offenders (e.g., sex offenders). This sentiment has translated into both

> *"At least 1,200 inmates every year go from a secure housing unit at a Level 4 prison—an isolation unit, designed to hold the most violent and dangerous inmates in the system—right onto the street. One day these predatory innmates are locked in their cells for 23 hours at a time and fed all their meals through a slot in the door, and the next day they're out of prison, riding a bus home."*
>
> *—Schlosser 1998:51*

stricter requirements for release and stricter supervision as well as revocation procedures once released.

In California, for example, there are few services for parolees. There are only 200 shelter beds in the state for more than 10,000 homeless parolees, four mental health clinics for 18,000 psychiatric cases, and 750 beds in treatment programs for 85,000 drug and alcohol abusers (Little Hoover Commission 1998). Under the terms of their parole, offenders are often subjected to periodic drug tests. But they are rarely offered any opportunity to get drug treatment. Of the approximately 130,000 substance abusers in Californians prisons, only 3,000 are receiving treatment behind bars. And of the 132,000 inmates released last year in California, just 8,000 received any kind of pre-release program to help them cope with life on the outside. As was recently reported:

Inmates are simply released from prison each year in California, given nothing more than $200 and a bus ticket back to the county where they were convicted. At least 1,200 inmates every year go from a secure housing unit at a Level 4 prison—an isolation unit, designed to hold the most violent and dangerous inmates in the system—right onto the street. One day these predatory inmates are locked in their cells for 23 hours at a time and fed all their meals through a slot in the door, and the next day they're out of prison, riding a bus home. (Schlosser 1998:51)

The national picture is almost as disturbing. The Office of National Drug Control Policy (ONDCP) recently reported that 70-85 percent of state prison inmates need substance abuse treatment, however, just 13 percent will receive any kind of treatment while incarcerated(McCaffrey 1998).

All parolees are required to sign an agreement to abide by certain regulations. Conditions can generally be grouped into standard conditions applicable to all parolees and special conditions that are tailored to particular offenders. Special conditions for substance abusers, for example, usually include periodic drug testing. Standard conditions are similar throughout most jurisdictions, and violating them can result in a return to prison. Common standard parole conditions are:

- Report to the parole agent within 24 hours of release
- Not carry weapons
- Report changes of address and employment
- Not travel more than 50 miles from home or leave the county for more than 48 hours without prior approval from the parole agent
- Obey all parole agent instructions
- Seek and maintain employment, or participate in education/work training
- Not commit crimes
- Submit to search by the police and parole officers.

Some argue that we have created unrealistic parole conditions. Boards were asked in 1988 to indicate from a list of 14 items, which were standard parole conditions in their state. The most common, of course, was "obey all laws." However, 78 percent required "gainful employment" as a standard condition, 61 percent "no association with persons of criminal records," 53 percent "pay all fines and restitution," and 47 percent "support family and all dependents," none of which can consistently be met by most parolees (Rhine eral. 1991). Increasingly, the most common condition for probationers and parolees is drug testing. It is estimated that more than one-third of all community correctional clients have court-ordered drug testing conditions (Camp and Camp 1997).

In October 1998, the state of Maryland began ordering every drug addict released on parole or probation to report for urine tests twice a week in an ambitious attempt to force about 25,000 criminals statewide to undergo drug treatment or face a series of quick, escalating punishments. The project, known as "Break the Cycle," is based on the theory that frequent drug testing coupled with swift, graduated punishments for drug use will force more addicts off drugs than the threat of long jail terms or treatment programs alone ever could. The state anticipates that more than a million tests annually may be required to make the plan work, compared with the 40,000 tests the state administered last year (Pan 1998).

Seeing that the parolee lives up to this parole contract is the principle responsibility of the parole agent. Parole agents are equipped with legal authority to carry and use firearms, to search places, persons and property without the requirements imposed by the Fourth Amendment (i.e., the right to privacy), and to order arrests without probable cause and to confine without bail. The power to search applies to the household where a parolee is living and businesses where a parolee is working. The ability to arrest, confine and in some cases re-imprison the parolee makes the parole agent a walking court system (Rudovsky et al. 1988).

Parole Classification and Caseload Assignment. When a parolee first reports to the parole field office, they are usually interviewed for the purposes of being assigned to a caseload. Most jurisdictions rely on a formal approach to classification and case management with respect to parolee supervision. Such systems recognize that not all offenders are equal in their need for supervision. A recent parole survey found that 90 percent of the states use a classification system for assigning parolees to different levels of supervision (Runda, Rhine and Wetter 1994).

Most often, this assignment is based on a structured assessment of parolee risk and an assessment of the needs or problem areas that have contributed to the parolee's criminality. By scoring information relative to the risk of recidivism and the particular needs of the offender (i.e., a risk/need instrument) a total score is derived, which then dictates the particular level of parole supervision (e.g., intensive, medium, minimum, administrative). Each jurisdiction usually has established policies that dictate the contact levels (times the officer will meet with the parolee). These contact levels correspond to each level of parole supervision. The notion is that higher risk inmates and those with greater needs will be seen most frequently (e.g., on "intensive" caseloads). These models are described as "management tools," and are not as devices to reduce recidivism directly (Holt 1998).

Larger parole departments have also established "specialized caseloads" to more effectively supervise certain types of offenders. These offenders generally pose a particularly serious threat to public safety or present unique problems that may handicap their adjustment to supervision. Specialized caseloads afford the opportunity to match the unique skills and training of parole officers with the specialized needs of parolees. The most common specialized caseloads in the U.S. are those that target sex offenders and parolees with serious substance abuse problems, although as shown in Table 4, fewer than 4 percent of all parolees are supervised on specialized caseloads.

Cases are then assigned to parole officers and comprise an officer's caseload. Table 4 contains the latest information on these characteristics for U.S. parolees.

Table 4 shows that over 80 percent of U.S. parolees are supervised on regular caseloads, averaging 69 cases to 1 parole officer, in which they are seen face-to-face less than twice per month. Officers may also conduct "collateral" contacts, such as contacting family members or employers to inquire about the parolee's progress. Many parole officers are frustrated because they lack the time and resources to do the kind of job they believe is maximally helpful to their clients. Parole officers often

Table 4—Parole Caseload Supervision Level, Contact, and Annual Costs

Caseload Type	% of All Parolees	Average Caseload Size	Face to Face Contacts	Annual Supervision Cost
Regular	82%	69:1	1.6/month	$1,397
Intensive	14%	27:1	5.1/month	$3,628
Electronic Monitoring	0.7%	25:1	5.7/month	$3,628
Specialized	3.7%	43:1	4.4/month	$4,080

Source: Camp & Camp (1997)

complain that paperwork has increased, clients have more serious problems and caseloads are much higher than the 35 to 50 cases that have been considered the ideal caseload for a parole officer. However, there is no empirical evidence to show that smaller caseloads result in lower recidivism rates (Petersilia and Turner 1993).

One important implication of larger caseloads and the reduction in the quality of client supervision is the increased potential for lawsuits arising from negligent supervision (del Carmen and Pilant, 1994). In a 1986 case, the Alaska Supreme Court ruled that state agencies and their officers may be held liable for negligence when probationers and parolees under their supervision commit violent offenses (*Division of Corrections v. Neakok*, 1986). Thus, parole officers are increasingly at risk through tort actions filed by victims harmed by the crimes committed by their offender-clients. Some have argued that this legal threat will eventually force states to invest more heavily in parole supervision.

Parole Revocation. If parolees fail to live up to their conditions, they can be revoked to custody. Parole can be revoked for two reasons: (1) the commission of a new crime or (2) the violation of the conditions of parole (a technical violation). Technical violations pertain to behavior that is not criminal, such as the failure to refrain from alcohol use or remain employed.

In either event, the violation process is rather straightforward. Given that parolees are technically still in the legal custody of the prison or parole authorities, and as a result maintain a quasi-prisoner status, their constitutional rights are severely limited. When parole officers become aware of violations of the parole contract, they notify their supervisors who can rather easily return a parolee to prison.

Parole violations are an administrative function that is typically devoid of court involvement. However, parolees do have some rights in revocation proceedings. Two U.S. Supreme Court cases, *Morrissey v. Brewer* (1972), and *Gagnon vs. Scarpelli* (1973) are considered landmark cases of parolee rights in revocation proceedings. Among other things, *Morrissey* and *Gagnon* established minimum requirements for the revocation of parole boards, forcing boards to conform to some standards of due process. Parolees must be given written notice of the nature of the violation and the evidence obtained, and they have a right to confront and cross examine their accusers.

B. Changing Nature of Parole Supervision and Services

Historically, parole agents were viewed as paternalistic figures that mixed authority with help. Officers provided direct services (e.g., counseling). They also knew the community, and brokered services (e.g., job training) to needy offenders. As noted earlier, parole was originally designed to make the transition from prison to the community more gradual, and during this time, parole officers were to assist the offender in addressing personal problems, searching for employment and a place to live. Many parole agencies still do assist in these service activities. Increasingly, however, parole supervision has shifted away from providing services to parolees and more towards monitoring and surveillance activities (e.g., drug testing, monitoring curfews and collecting restitution).

A recent survey of 22 parole agencies shows that 14 provide job development help, seven offer detoxification services and 13 offer substance abuse treatment, yet all do drug testing (Camp and Camp 1997). Historically, offering services and treatment to parolees was commonplace but such services are dwindling.

There are a number of reasons for this shift. For one, a greater number of parole conditions are being assigned to released prisoners. In the federal system, for example, between 1987 and 1996, the proportion of offenders required to comply with at least one special supervision condition increased from 67 percent of entrants to 91 percent (Adams and Roth 1998). Parolees in state systems are also more frequently being required to submit to drug testing, complete community service and make restitution payments (Petersilia and Turner 1993).

Parole officers work for the corrections system, and if paroling authorities are imposing a greater number of conditions on parolees, then field agents must monitor those conditions. As a result, modern-day parole officers have less time to provide other services, such as counseling, even if they were inclined to do so.

It is also true that the fiscal crisis experienced in most states has reduced the number of treatment and job training programs in the community-at-large. Additionally, given the fear and suspicion surrounding ex-convicts, these persons are usually placed at the end of the waiting lists. The ability to broker services to parolees, given the scarcity of programs, has become increasingly difficult. If there is one common complaint among parole officers in the US, it is the lack of available treatment and job programs for parolees. At the end of the 1960s, when the country had more employment opportunities for blue collar workers than it does now, there was some movement to reduce the employment barriers. Studies revealed a full-time employment rate of around 50 percent for parolees (Simon 1993). Today, full time employment among parolees is rare.

The main reason, however, that services are not delivered to most parolees is that parole supervision has been transformed ideologically from a social service to a law enforcement system. Just as the prison system responded to the public's demands for accountability and justice, so did parole officers.

Feely and Simon (1992) argue that over the past few decades, a systems analysis approach to danger management has come to dominate parole, and that it has evolved into a "waste management" system rather than one focused on rehabilitation. In their model, those in the dangerous class of criminals are nearly synonymous with those in the larger social category of the underclass, a segment of the population that has been abandoned to a fate of poverty and despair. They suggest that a "new penology" has emerged, one that simply strives to manage risk by use of actuarial methods. Offenders are addressed not as individuals but as aggregate populations. The traditional correctional objectives of rehabilitation and the reduction of offender recidivism have given way to the rational and efficient deployment of control strategies for managing (and confining) high-risk criminals. Surveillance and control have replaced treatment as the main goals of parole.

Newly hired parole officers often embrace the surveillance versus rehabilitation model of parole, and embrace the quasi-policing role that parole has taken on in some locales. Twenty years ago, social work was the most common educational path for those pursuing careers in parole. Today, the most common educational path is criminal justice studies—an academic field spawned in the 1960s to professionalize law enforcement (Parent 1993). Parole agents began to carry concealed firearms in the 1980s. Firearms are now provided in most jurisdictions and represent a major investment of training resources, agent time and administrative oversight (Holt 1998).

The programming innovations likewise represent a theme of control and supervision rather than service and assistance. Parolees are held more accountable for a broader range of behavior including alcohol and substance abuse, restitution, curfews and community service.

As Irwin and Austin (1994:129) put it: "Instead of helping prisoners locate a job, find a residence or locate needed drug treatment services, the new parole system is bent on surveillance and detection. Parolees are routinely and randomly checked for illegal drug use, failure to locate or maintain a job, moving without permission, or any other number of petty and nuisance-type behaviors that don't conform to the rules of parole."

In addition to the limitations set out in the parole contract and enforced by the parole officer, parolees face a growing number of legal restrictions or "civil disabilities." Ironically, these civil disabilities often restrict the parolee's ability to carry out one of the most common parole requirements—that of remaining employed. The next section reviews the most common of these restrictions.

C. Civil Disabilities & Injunctions of Convicted Felons

While the services available to assist parolees have decreased, the structural obstacles concerning their behavior have increased. Under federal law and the laws of many states, a felony conviction has consequences that continue long after a sentence has been served and parole has ended. For example, convicted felons lose essential rights of citizenship, such as the right to vote and to hold public office, and may be restricted in their ability to obtain occupational and professional licenses. Their criminal record may also preclude them from parenting, be grounds for divorce and they may be barred from serving on a jury, holding public office and firearm ownership. These statutory restrictions or civil disabilities serve as punishments in addition to the conviction and sentence imposed by the court.

A recent survey shows that after a period where states were becoming less restrictive of convicted felons' rights, the "get tough movement" of the 1980s adds the effect of increasing the statutory restrictions placed on parolees. Between 1986 and 1996, stare legal codes reveal an increase in the extent to which states restrict the rights and opportunities available to released inmates (Olivares, Burton, & Cullen, 1996).

A complete stare-by-state survey of civil disabilities of convicted felons can be found in (Love and Kuzma 1996). These restrictions apply to all convicted felons and not separately to parolees. The most common restrictions are:

- **Right to vote.** Fourteen stares permanently deny convicted felons the right to vote, whereas most others temporarily restrict this right until the sentence has been fulfilled. Eighteen states suspend the right to vote until the offender has completed the imposed sentence of prison, probation or parole (and paid all fines). Colorado is typical in this regard, and states that the "right to vote is lost if incarcerated, and automatically restored upon completion of sentence, including parole." California denies the right to incarcerated offenders and parolees, yet allows probationers to vote. Fellner and Mauer (1998) estimate that 1.4 million black males, or 13.1 percent of the black male adult population, are currently or permanently not able to vote as a result of a felony conviction. While most states have procedures for regaining the right to vote, it often requires a gubernatorial pardon.

- **Parental Rights.** Nineteen states currently may terminate the parental rights of convicted felons, if it can be shown that a felony conviction suggests a parent's unfitness to supervise or care for the child. Oregon and Tennessee require that the parent be incarcerated for a specified length of time (three years in Oregon and two years in Tennessee).

- **Divorce.** The use of a felony conviction to permit divorce exists in 19 states. In 29 jurisdictions, a felony conviction constitutes legal grounds for divorce. In 1996, ten stares consider any felony conviction as sufficient grounds, whereas seven jurisdictions require a felony conviction and imprisonment to grant divorce.

- **Public Employment.** Public employment is permanently denied in six states: Alabama, Delaware, Iowa, Mississippi, Rhode Island and South Carolina. The remaining jurisdictions permit public employment in varying degrees. Of these states, ten leave the decision to hire at the discretion of the employer, while 12 jurisdictions apply a "direct relationship test" to determine whether the conviction offense bears directly on the job in question. But the courts have interpreted the "direct relationship" standard liberally. For example a California case (*Golde vs. Fox*) found that conviction of possession of marijuana for sale was substantially related to the business of real estate broker as it shows lack of honesty and integrity.

- **Each state has its own particular professions that have been restricted to ex-convicts.** In Colorado, for example, the professions of dentist, engineer, nurse, pharmacist, physician and realtor are closed to convicted felons. In California the professions of law, real estate, medicine, nursing, physical therapy and education are restricted. In Virginia the professions of optometry, nursing, dentistry, accounting, funeral director and pharmacy are professions generally closed to ex-felons.

- **Right to Serve as a Juror.** The right to serve as a juror is restricted permanently in 32 jurisdictions, and the remaining 20 states permit the right with consideration given to varying conditions. For example, ten states restrict the right only during sentence, while four jurisdictions impose an additional delay after sentence completion (e.g., from one year in the District of Columbia to ten years in Kansas).

- **Right to hold public office.** Seven states permanently deny elected office to persons convicted of specific crimes including bribery, perjury and embezzlement. Twenty states restrict the right to hold public office until the offender has completed his or her sentence of prison, probation or parole.

- **Right to own a firearm.** Thirty-one of 51 jurisdictions permanently deny or restrict the right to own or posses a firearm on any felony conviction. In contrast, the remaining 18 states deny the right to own or possess a firearm only for convictions involving violence.

- **Criminal Registration.** In 1986 only eight of 51 jurisdictions required offenders to register with a law enforcement agency upon release from prison. By 1998 every state required convicted sex offenders to register with law enforcement on release (Lieb, Quinsey and Berliner, 1998). These stare registration schemes, so-called "Megan's laws," vary considerably with respect to the crimes for which registration is required, the duration of the registration requirement, and the penalty for failure to register. Illinois, for example, requires sex offenders and those convicted of first-degree murder against a victim under 18 years old to register. The registration typically lasts for a period of several years, but may extend for the life of the offender for certain crimes. In addition, California now requires sex offenders to provide blood and saliva samples for DNA testing.

Jonathan Simon (1993) notes that these civil disabilities have the effect of creating an inherent contradiction in our legal system. He writes that different laws may serve different purposes, but they must not contradict one another. Yet, in the U.S., we spend millions of dollars to rehabilitate offenders and convince them that they need to obtain legitimate employment and then frustrate whatever was thereby accomplished by raising legal barriers that may bar them absolutely from employment and its rewards. He also notes that structural changes in the U.S. have taken their toll on the very population from which most parolees come, and have, in turn, impacted agents' ability to do their job. Most notably, the loss of a solid industrial base over the past few decades, which has traditionally supplied jobs among poorer inner-city communities, has left urban parolees with few opportunities, and left agents with fewer venues in which to monitor and supervise their clients (Lynch 1998).

References

Abadinsky, Howard. 1997. *Probation and Parole.* Upper Saddle River, New Jersey: Simon & Schuster.

Adams, William, and Jeffrey Roth. 1998. "Federal Offenders under Community Supervision, 1987–96." Washington, D.C.: Bureau of Justice Statistics.

Allen, George. 1997. "Abolishing Parole Saves Lives and Property." *Corrections Today* Vol. 59, No. 4:22.

American Correctional Association. 1995. *Probation and Parole Directory.* Lanham, Maryland: American Correctional Association.

Andrews, Don, and James Bonta. 1994. *The Psychology of Criminal Conduct.* Cincinnati, Ohio: Anderson Publishing.

Applegate, Brian, Frances Cullen, Michael Turner, and Jody Sundt. 1996. "Assessing Public Support for Three-Strikes-You're Out Laws: Global Versus Specific Attitudes." *Crime and Delinquency* 42:517–534.

Association of Paroling Authorities International. 1998. "APAI Survey of Parole Boards." Washington, D.C.

Austin, James, and Robert Lawson. 1998. "Assessment of California Parole Violations and Recommended Intermediate Programs and Policies." San Francisco: National Council on Crime and Delinquency.

Beck, Allen, and Bernard Shipley. 1989. "Recidivism of Prisoners Released in 1983." Washington, D.C.: Bureau of Justice Statistics.

Beck, Allen J. 1999. "Trends in U.S. Correctional Populations." Pp. 44–100 in *The Dilemmas of Corrections*, edited by Kenneth Haas and Geoffrey Alpert. Prospect Heights, Illinois: Waveland Press, Inc.

Bottomly, Keith A. 1990. "Parole in Transition: A Comparative Study of Origins, Developments, and Prospects for the 1990s." pp. 319–374 in *Crime and Justice: A Review of Research*, edited by Michael Tonry and Norval Morris. Chicago: University of Chicago Press.

Bureau of Justice Statistics. 1997. "National Corrections Reporting Program 1996." Washington, D.C.: Bureau of Justice Statistics.

Bureau of Justice Statistics. 1998. "Probation and Parole Populations 1997." Washington, D.C.

Burke, Peggy B. 1995. *Abolishing Parole: Why the Emperor Has No Clothes*. Lexington, Ky.: American Probation and Parole Association.

Burke, Peggy B. 1997. "Policy-Driven Responses to Probation and Parole Violations." Washington, D.C.: National Institute of Corrections, U.S. Department of Justice.

Butterfield, Fox. 1999. "Eliminating Parole Boards Isn't a Cure-All, Experts Say" in *New York Times*. New York, January 10, 1999:11.

California Department of Corrections. 1997. "Preventing Parolee Failure Program: An Evaluation." Sacramento, California.

Camp, Camille, and George Camp. 1997. *The Corrections Yearbook*. South Salem, New York: Criminal Justice Institute, Inc.

Carter, Beth. 1998. "Harbingers of Change." *Crime and Politics in the 1990's*: 1–8.

Citizens' Inquiry on Parole and Criminal Justice. 1974. "Report on New York Parole." New York City, New York: The Citizen's Inquiry.

Clear, Todd, and George Cole. 1997. *American Corrections*. Belmont, Ca.: Wadsworth Publishing.

Clear, Todd, and Ronald Corbett. 1999. "Community Corrections of Place." *Perspectives* 23:24–32.

Cromwell, Paul F. and Rolando del Carmen. 1999. *Community Based Corrections*. Belmont, Ca.: West/Wadsworth.

del Carmen, Rolando, and James Alan Pilant. 1994. "The Scope of Judicial Immunity for Probation and Parole Officers." *Perspectives* 18:14–21.

Deschenes, Elizabeth, Susan Turner, and Joan Petersilia. 1995. "A Dual Experiment in Intensive Community Supervision: Minnesota's Prison Diversion and Enhanced Supervised Released Programs." *The Prison Journal* 75.

DiIulio, John. 1997. "Reinventing Parole and Probation." *The Brookings Review*: 40–42.

Ditton, Paula, and Doris James Wilson. 1999. "Truth in Sentencing in State Prisons." Washington, D.C.: Bureau of Justice Statistics.

Fabelo, Tony. 1999. "Biennial Report to the 76th Texas Legislature." Austin, Texas: Criminal Justice Policy Council.

Feeley, Malcolm and Jonathan Simon. 1992. "The New Penology: Notes on the Emerging Strategy of Corrections and its Implications," 30 *Criminology*, 449–474.

Fellner, Jamie, and Marc Mauer. 1998. "Losing the Vote: The Impact of Felony Disenfranchisement Laws in the United States." Washington, D.C.: The Sentencing Project.

Finn, Peter. 1998a. "Chicago's Safer Foundation: A Road Back for Ex-Offenders." Washington, D.C.: National Institute of Justice.

Finn, Peter. 1998b. "Successful Job Placement for Ex-Offenders: The Center for Employment Opportunities." Washington, D.C.: National Institute of Justice.

Finn, Peter. 1998c. "Texas' Project RIO (Re-Integration of Offenders)." Washington, D.C.: National Institute of Justice.

Flanagan, Timothy. 1996. "Reform or Punish: Americans' Views of the Correctional System." in *Americans View Crime and Justice*, edited by Timothy Flanagan and Dennis Longmire. Thousand Oaks, California: Sage Publications.

Flanagan, Timothy, and Dennis Longmire (Eds.). 1996. *Americans View Crime and Justice: A National Public Opinion Survey*. Thousand Oaks, California: Sage Publications.

Fogel, David. 1975. *We Are the Living Proof*. Cincinnati, Ohio: Anderson.

Gainsborough, Jenni. 1997. "Eliminating Parole is a Dangerous and Expensive Proposition. *Corrections Today* Vol. 59, No. 4:23.

Glaser, Daniel. 1969. *The Effectiveness of a Prison and Parole System*. Indianapolis, Indiana: Bobbs-Merrill.

Golde v. Fox, 98 Cal.App. 3d 167, 159 California Reporter 864, 1st District 1979.

Gottfredson, Don, Peter Hoffman, and M. Sigler. 1975. "Making Parole Policy Explicit." *Crime and Delinquency*, January, pp. 7–17.

Gottfredson, Don, Leslie Wilkins, and Peter Hoffman. 1978. *Guidelines for Parole and Sentencing*. Lexington, MA: Health/Lexington.

Hoffman, Peter B., and Lucille K. DeGostin. 1974. "Parole Decision Making: Structuring Discretion." *Federal Probation* December.

Holt, Norman. 1998. "The Current State of Parole in America." Pp. 28–41 in *Community Corrections: Probation, Parole, and Intermediate Sanctions*, edited by Joan Petersilia. New York, N.Y.: Oxford University Press.

Irwin, John, and James Austin. 1994. *It's About Time: America's Imprisonment Binge*. Belmont, California: Wadsworth Publishing Company.

Institute of Medicine. 1990 (D.R. Gerstein and H.J. Harwood, eds.). *Treating Drug Problems: A Study of the Evolution, Effectiveness, and Financing of Public and Private Drug Treatment Systems*. National Academy Press, Washington, D.C.

Kleinknecht, William. 1997. "Juvenile authorities want satellite tracking for felons." in *The Star Ledger*, November 18: p. 7. New Jersey.

Legislative Analysts Office. 1998. "Reforming California's Adult Parole System." Sacramento.

Lieb, Roxanne, Vernon Quinsey, and Lucy Berliner. 1998. "Sexual Predators and Social Policy." in *Crime and Justice: A Review of Research*, edited by Michael Tonry. Chicago: University of Chicago Press.

Lipton, Douglas, Robert Martinson, and Judith Wilks. 1975. *The Effectiveness of Correctional Treatment and What Works: A Survey of Treatment Evaluation Studies*. New York: Praeger.

Little Hoover Commission. 1998. "Beyond Bars: Correctional Reforms to Lower Prison Costs and Reduce Crime." Sacramento, California.

Love, Margaret, and Kuzma. 1996. "Civil Disabilities of Convicted Felons: A State-by-State Survey." Washington, D.C.: Office of the Pardon Attorney.

Lynch, Mona. 1998. "Waste Managers? New Penology, Crime Fighting and the Parole Agent Identity." *Law and Society Review* 32, Vol. 4, 839–869.

McCaffrey, Barry. 1998. "Drug Treatment in the Criminal Justice System." Washington, D.C.: Office of National Drug Control Policy.

McCleary, Richard. 1992. *Dangerous Men: The Sociology of Parole*. New York: Harrow and Heston.

Morgan, Terry, and Stephen Marrs. 1998. "Redmond, Washington's SMART Partnership for Police and Community Corrections." Pp. 170–180 in *Community Corrections: Probation, Parole, and Intermediate Sanctions*, edited by Joan Petersilia. New York: Oxford University Press.

Morse, Wayne. 1939. "U.S. Attorney General's Survey of Release Procedures." Washington, D.C.: U.S. Department of Justice.

National Conference of State Legislatures. 1996. "Three Strikes' Legislation Update." Denver.

National Institute of Corrections. 1995. "Status Report on Parole, 1995." Washington, D.C.: U.S. Department of Justice.

O'Leary, Vincent (Ed.). 1974. *Parole Administration*. Chicago: Rand McNally Publishing.

Olivares, K., V. Burton, and F. Cullen. 1996. "The Collateral Consequences of a Felony Conviction: A National Study of State Legal Codes 10 Years Later." *Federal Probation* LX:10–18.

Pan, Philip. 1998. "Md. Orders Drug Tests for Addicts on Parole." Pp. 1 in *The Washington Post*. Washington, D.C.

Parent, Dale. 1993. "Structuring Policies to Address Sanctions for Absconders and Violators." in *Reclaiming Offender Accountability: Intermediate Sanctions for Probation and Parole Violators*, edited by Edward Rhine. Laurel, Maryland: American Correctional Association.

Parent, Dale, Dan Wentworth, Peggy Burke, and Becky Ney. 1994. "Responding to Probation and Parole Violations." Washington, D.C.: National Institute of Justice.

Petersilia, Joan. 1998a. "A Decade of Experimenting with Intermediate Sanctions: What Have We Learned?" Pp. 79–106 in *Perspectives on Crime and Justice*. Washington, D.C.: National Institute of Justice.

Petersilia, Joan. 1997. "Probation in America." in *Crime and Justice: An Annual Review of Research*, edited by Michael Tonry. Chicago, IL: University of Chicago Press.

Petersilia, Joan. 1998b. "Probation and Parole." in *The Oxford Handbook of Criminology*, edited by Michael Tonry. New York, New York: Oxford University Press.

Petersilia, Joan, and Susan Turner. 1993. "Intensive Probation and Parole." in *Crime and Justice: An Annual Review of Research*, edited by Michael Tonry. Chicago, IL: University of Chicago Press.

Prendergast, Michael, Douglas Anglin, and Jean Wellisch. 1995. "Treatment for Drug-Abusing Offenders Under Community Supervision." *Federal Probation* 66.

Reitz, Kevin. 1998. "Sentencing," Pp. 542–562 in *The Handbook of Crime and Punishment,* edited by Michael Tonry. New York, NY.: Oxford University Press.

Rhine, Edward, William Smith, Ronald Jackson, Peggy Burke, and Roger LaBelle. 1991. "Paroling Authorities: Recent history and current practice." Laurel, Maryland: American Correctional Association.

Rhine, Edward E. 1996. "Parole Boards." Pp. 342–348 in *The Encyclopedia of American Prisons,* edited by Marilyn McShane and Frank Williams. New York: Garland Publishing, Inc.

Richards, Stephen C. 1995. *The Structure of Prison Release: An Extended Case Study of Prison Release, Work Release, and Parole.* New York City: McGraw-Hill, Inc.

Rothman, David. 1980. *Conscience and Convenience: The Asylum and Its Alternatives in Progressive America.* Boston: Little, Brown.

Rubin, Edward. 1997. "Minimizing Harm as a Goal for Crime Policy in California." Berkeley, California: California Policy Seminar.

Rudovsky, David, Alvin Bronstein, Edard Koren, and Julie Cade. 1988. *The Rights of Prisoners.* Carbondale, IL: Southern Illinois University Press.

Runda, John, Edward Rhine, and Robert Wetter. 1994. "The Practice of Parole Boards." Lexington, Kentucky: Association of Paroling Authorities, International.

Schlosser, Eric. 1998. "The Prison Industrial Complex." Pp. 51–77 in *The Atlantic Monthly.*

Sechrest, Lee, Susan White, and Elizabeth Brown. 1979. *The Rehabilitation of Criminal Offenders: Problems and Prospects.* Washington, D.C.: National Academy of Sciences.

Sherman, Lawrence, Denise Gottfredson, Doris Mackenzie, John Eck, Peter Reuter, and Shawn Bushway. 1997. "Preventing Crime: What Works, What Doesn't, What's Promising." College Park, Maryland: University of Maryland.

Simon, Jonathan. 1993. *Poor Discipline: Parole and the Social Control of the Underclass, 1890–1990.* Chicago: The University of Chicago Press.

Smith, Michael, and Walter Dickey. 1998. "What If Corrections Were Serious About Public Safety?" *Corrections Management Quarterly* 2:12–30.

Sundt, Jody, Francis Cullen, Michael Turner, and Brandon Applegate. 1998. "What Will The Public Tolerate?" *Perspectives* 22:22–26.

The Gallup Organization. 1998. "Gallup Surveys Pertaining to Parole (special request)." New York City, New York.

Tonry, Michael. 1995. *Malign Neglect: Race, Crime, and Punishment in America.* New York: Oxford University Press.

Turner, Susan, and Joan Petersilia. 1992. "Focusing on High-Risk Parolees: An Experiment to Reduce Commitment to the Texas Department of Corrections. *The Journal of Research in Crime and Delinquency* 29:34–61.

Turner, Susan, and Joan Petersilia. 1996a. "Work Release in Washington: Effects on Recidivism and Corrections Costs." *The Prison Journal* 76.

Turner, Susan, and Joan Petersilia. 1996b. "Work Release: Recidivism and Corrections Costs in Washington State." Washington, D.C.: National Institute of Justice.

von Hirsch, Andrew. 1976. *Doing Justice: The Choice of Punishments.* New York: Hill and Wang.

von Hirsch, Andrew, and Kathleen Hanrahan. 1979. *The Question of Parole: Retention, Reform, or Abolition?* Cambridge, Massachusetts: Ballinger.

Walker, Samuel. 1998. *A History of American Criminal Justice.* New York: Oxford University Press.

Wilson, James. 1985. *Thinking About Crime.* New York: Basic Books.

Wilson, Rob. 1977. "Release: Should Parole Boards Hold the Key?" *Corrections Magazine* :47–55.

Joan Petersilia, Ph.D. is a Professor of Criminology Law & Society at the University of California in Irvine, California.

Parole and Prisoner Reentry in the United States

By Joan Petersilia, Ph.D.

PART II*

V. Recidivism and Crime Committed by Parolees

The most common question asked about parole is, "Does it work?" And by work, most mean whether persons granted parole refrain from further crime or reduce their recidivism. Recidivism is currently the primary outcome measure for parole, as it is for all corrections programs.

A. Prisoner Recidivism Rates

The most comprehensive study of state prisoner recidivism tracked 16,000 inmates released during 1983 in 11 states. The study found that overall, 63 percent of inmates were arrested for a felony or serious misdemeanor offense within three years of release from prison. In unpublished data from that cohort, Beck reports that 62.3 percent of those who were released "conditionally" (i.e., on parole) were rearrested within 3 years, whereas the figure was 64.8 percent for those who were released "unconditionally." About 47 percent of inmates were convicted of a new offense during the three years after release, and 41 percent returned to prison or jail for a

new offense or technical violation of their prison release (Beck and Shipley 1989).

The Beck and Shipley study is the best available to approximate the recidivism rates of parolees, but it has some limitations. Not all persons released from prison were officially on parole, however, in the early 1980s most were, so this data captures most parolee recidivism. Also, the study tracked inmates for a full 3-year period after release, and offenders may or may not have been officially on parole for all of that time period. The study was also conducted more than 15 years ago, and we know that parole policy has changed considerably since that time. Unfortunately, there are no U.S. record keeping systems that record the recidivism of parolees, and no more recent national prisoner follow-up studies.

B. Successful vs. Unsuccessful Completion of Parole

The Bureau of Justice Statistics (BJS), as part of its National Corrections Reporting Program, does collect data each year from every state about its parole population and how many of its parolees successfully complete parole. This data derives from parole agency records, not from the police, hence it may not capture all arrests. It is possible for an offender to be arrested, (a misdemeanor or low level felony, for example) and not be violated from parole. The event is therefore recorded as a "successful exit" from parole.

Editor's Note: This is the second part of a two-part article. See previous Annual Editions *article for part one, which appeared in the Summer 2000 issue of* Perspectives. *Citations for both parts are included at the end of the article.*

Figure 2
State Parole Outcomes, 1985-1997

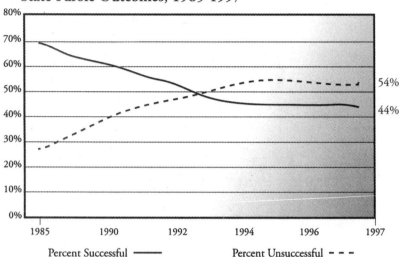

Percent Successful ———   Percent Unsuccessful - - -

Sources: Bureau of Justice Statistics, *Annual Parole Survey*, 1981, 1986-1997.

This data reveals a disturbing trend in that a majority of those being released to parole will not successfully complete their terms, and the percentage of unsuccessful parolees is increasing. As Beck (1999) recently reported, annual discharges from state parole supervision reveal a sharp drop in the number of parolees who successfully complete their term of community supervision. As a portion of all discharges from state parole supervision, offenders successfully completing parole declined from 70 percent in 1984, to 44 percent in 1996 (see Figure 2).

C. Parolees and Other "Conditional Releases" Return to Custody

Such high parole revocation rates are one of the major factors linked to the growing U.S. prison population. Since 1980, the percentage of conditional release violators who had originally left state prisons as parolees, mandatory releases and other type of releases subject to community supervision, has more than doubled from 16 percent to 33.8 percent (see Table 5).

In some states, the figures are even more dramatic. For example, in California, in 1997, over two thirds (64.7 percent) of all persons admitted to state prisons were parole violators. By comparison, in New York, the figure is 23 percent. In Texas, the state most comparable in prison population to California, the figure is 23 percent. A recent report concluded: "There is no question that California has the highest rate of parole violations in the nation. In terms of total numbers, California accounts for nearly 40% of all known parole violators that occur in the nation although it reflects less than 15 percent of the nation's parole population" (Little Hoover Commission 1998:23).

D. Contribution of Parolees to Crime

Another way to examine parole effectiveness is to look at the proportion of all persons arrested and in custody who were on parole at the time they committed their last crime. BJS conducts periodic surveys of persons arrested, in jail, in prison and on death row. This data show that 44 percent of all state prisoners in 1991 had committed their latest crimes while out on probation or parole (Figure 3).

Such high recidivism rates have led to the common perception that community supervision fails to protect the public and that nothing works. As DiIulio (1997:41) writes: "While formally under supervision in the com-

Table 5—Percent of Admitted Prisoners, Who were Parole Violators, Selected Years

State	1980	1985	1992	1997
New York	24.1	13.8	13.9	23.0
Pennsylvania	19.6	26.7	18.6	33.4
Ohio	18.5	21.1	16.6	19.6
Illinois	20.3	29.9	19.7	30.4
Michigan	16.6	23.5	25.8	28.3
North Carolina	10.6	5.8	17.4	23.6
Georgia	8.2	18.3	25.5	23.0
Florida	16.0	6.4	12.7	12.2
Texas	15.8	30.9	39.9	22.7
California	20.7	41.7	56.3	64.7
Average (All 50 States)	16.09	22.3	28.6	33.8
Average (Federal Only)	11.09	12.9	/	9.0
Average (State and Federal Combine)	**15.8**	**21.6**	**28.6**	**32.3**

Note: "/" means not reported.

Source: Bureau of Justice Statistics, *Correctional Populations in the United States,* 1980, 1985, 1992, and unpublished data from 1997.

munity, these prison inmate violations included more than 13,000 murders, some 39,0000 robberies and tens of thousands of other crimes. More than a quarter of all felons charged with gun crimes in 1992 were out on probation or parole."

Of course, it is important to remember that more than 80 percent of all parolees are on caseloads where they are seen less than twice a month, and the dollars available to support their supervision and services are generally less than $1,500 per offender—when effective treatment programs are estimated to cost $12,000 to $15,000 per year, per client (Institute of Medicine 1990). It is no wonder that recidivism rates are so high. In a sense, we get what we pay for, and as yet, we have never chosen to invest sufficiently in parole programs.

Nevertheless, most view this data as showing that the parole system is neither helping offenders nor protecting the public and that major reform is needed.

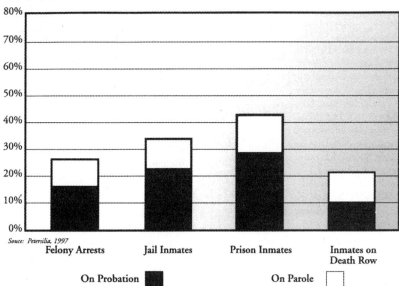

Figure 3
Who Is On Parole at Time of Arrest

Souce: Petersilia, 1997

Felony Arrests   Jail Inmates   Prison Inmates   Inmates on Death Row

On Probation ■   On Parole □

those neighborhoods where parolees live, and means forming active partnerships with local police, community members, offenders' families, neighborhood associations and other indigenous groups. Some refer to this as "neighborhood parole."

VI. Reinventing and Reinvesting in Parole

As Joe Lehman, currently Commissioner of the Washington Department of Corrections, told the author:

"We have a broken parole system. Part of the problem is that parole can't do it alone, and we have misled the public in thinking that we can—hence the frustration, and the cries to abolish parole. We don't need to abolish parole, but a new model is sorely needed."

Interviews recently conducted with U.S. correctional experts reveal a consensus that parole needs to be "reinvented," (a term commonly used) and that the new parole model should incorporate at least four components:

1) the identification of dangerous and violent parolees, for whom surveillance through human and technological means is a top priority;

2) the delivery of quality treatment (particularly substance abuse) and job training programs to the subgroup of offenders for whom research shows it could be most beneficial;

3) the establishment of intermediate sanctions and other means of diverting technical parole violators to community based alternatives and away from expensive prison cells; and

4) committing to a community-centered approach to parole supervision. This approach requires making a proactive commitment to managing offender risk in

A. Greater Monitoring of High-Risk, Violent Parolees

There can be no doubt that the public, aided by private industry, will continue to demand and receive an increase in the level of control over certain violent, predatory offenders in the community.

The most visible sign of this is the expanded registration of parolees, originally begun for sex offenses, but now expanding in terms of types of crimes and how accessible the information is to the public. Connecticut recently expanded its parolee registration to include kidnapping for sexual purposes, public indecency and fourth-degree sexual assault. On January 1, 1999, Connecticut's entire list was posted on the Internet. Florida and New Jersey also allow citizens to have complete access to inmate release information through an Internet site maintained by each state's Department of Corrections.

A New York City-based crime victim's advocacy group, using information from the State Department of Correctional Services, now places on the Internet the names of inmates soon to be *eligible* for parole from New York State prisons. In addition to including inmates' names, criminal background and parole eligibility dates, the Internet site includes press clippings of the crime if they are available. The site encourages citizens to contact the New York State Division of Parole with comments.

In California, the State Department of Justice developed a CD-ROM database with the pictures, names and

"The reality is that more than nine out of ten prisoners are released back into the community, and with an average (median) U.S. prison term served of 15 months, half of all inmates in U.S. prisons today will be back on the streets in less than two years." —Beck, 1999

whereabouts of the state's more than 50,000 registered sex offenders. Visitors to any local police station in the state are able to type in their ZIP codes and find out if a sex offender lives nearby. When the data was first released, many local newspapers published the pictures and addresses of local sex offenders. Los Angeles County just announced that since few residents are using the CD-ROMs, they would begin mass mailings to residents informing them of the location and names of sex offenders living in their neighborhoods. As of January 1, 1999, California school districts will also have direct access to the CD-ROM and permission to distribute the information directly to the public.

New York and California both also have 900-number hotlines set up to allow residents to check if someone is a registered sex offender. Before that, it was illegal for a law enforcement officer to notify citizens about a sex offender living in the neighborhood.

Sophisticated technology is also assisting police and parole officers to keep better track of parolees once in the community. As the Cold War wound down, the defense industry, along with the developing computer and electronic industries, saw the community correctional clientele as a natural place to put its energies—a growing market. Electronic monitoring, voice verification systems, cheap on-site drug testing and breathalyzers through the phone, all allowed community corrections the option of becoming more surveillance-oriented.

Since the mid-1980s, the electronic monitoring industry has continued to expand, and three states (Texas, Florida, New Jersey) now use global-positioning technology to determine when a parolee leaves his or her home or enters a restricted zone such as an area around a school or the neighborhood of a former victim.

These initiatives and programs are a far cry from the traditional social work approaches to probation and parole.

B. Delivering Appropriate Treatment and Work Training to Selected Parolees

The public seems to have isolated its fear and punitiveness to the violent, particularly sexual offender, and seems more willing to tolerate treatment programs for non-violent offenders, particularly substance abusers (Flanagan and Longmire 1996). Recent research reveals that the public favors both punishing and treating criminals, and their punitiveness tends to be reduced when they are provided with complex sentencing options and are informed about the high cost of incarceration (Applegate et al. 1996). A recent study found the public unwilling to tolerate regular probation for felons, but willing to tolerate, if not prefer, strict community based alternatives to prison when these sanctions are developed and applied meaningfully. For the crime of robbery with injury, for example, 50 percent of the respondents viewed a sanction between halfway house and strict probation acceptable. When the option of shock incarceration (prison followed by community supervision) is added, this figure rises to a full 63 percent (Sundt et al. 1998). The public seems open to tough community-based sanctions, and wants them to include both treatment and surveillance.

This softening of public attitudes seems to have resulted from knowledge about the high costs of prisons combined with emerging evidence that some treatment programs are effective, for some offenders, under certain empirically established conditions. This research has identified those principles that produce effective correctional interventions. The evidence indicates that well-designed and properly implemented programs incorporating these principles result in significant reductions in recidivism. The programs that are most successful include a strong behavior and cognitive skills development component (Andrews and Bonta 1994). Some of these programs have been effective in reducing the rearrest rates of parolees.

1. Drug and Alcohol Dependency Programs

A recent research summary of drug treatment effectiveness reported that a growing body of research shows that voluntary or mandatory drug treatment can reduce recidivism, especially when treatment is matched to offender needs (Prendergast, Anglin, & Wellisch, 1995). The most successful programs are based on social learning theory. These programs assume that criminal behavior is learned, so they try to improve offenders' interpersonal relations through vocational and social skill building, peer-oriented behavior programs, role playing and interpersonal cognitive skill training. Effective treatment programs must also continue assisting the offender for several months after program completion.

A program that attempts to do this, with noted success, is San Diego's Parolee Partnership Program (PPP), which is part of California's statewide Preventing Paroling Failure Program. The San Diego program, begun in 1992, provides substance abuse treatment for parolees in San Diego County. A private vendor operates the program using principles of client selection, managed care, case management, and case follow-up. The vendor subcontracts to provide outpatient, residential and detoxification treatment services and facilities. Support services (e.g., education and vocation training and transportation) are provided directly by the vendor or through referral to other community resource agencies. Typically, the time limit is 180 days of treatment. The participant is then assigned a recovery advocate who motivates the offender to continue in treatment for as long as necessary and keeps the parole agent aware of the parolee's progress. The program served about 700 offenders in fiscal year 1995–96 at a total cost of about $1.5 million (about $2,100 per parolee).

An evaluation of the program shows that the PPP was successful with its target group which was characterized as a hard to treat group, who on average had used drugs for about 11 years. The percentage of parolees placed in the PPP who were returned to prison was nearly 8 percentage points lower than the return rate for the statistically-matched comparison group, and this difference was statistically significant (California Department of Corrections 1997). Los Angeles County operates a similarly successful program. The success of these programs motivated the California State Legislature to increase funding for parole substance abuse programs in 1998-2000.

2. Employment and Job Training

Research has consistently shown that if parolees can find decent jobs as soon as possible after release, they are less likely to return to crime and to prison. Several parole programs have been successful at securing employment for parolees.

The Texas Re-Integration of Offenders Project (RIO) began as a two-city pilot program in 1985, and has become one of the nation's most ambitious government programs devoted to placing parolees in jobs (Finn 1998c). RIO has more than 100 staff members and 62 officers who provide job placement services to nearly 16,000 parolees each year in every county in Texas (or nearly half of all parolees released from Texas prisons

each year). RIO claims to have placed 69 percent of more than 100,000 ex-offenders since 1985.

RIO represents a collaboration of two state agencies, the Texas Workforce Commission, where the program is housed, and the Texas Department of Criminal Justice, whose RIO-funded assessment specialists help inmates prepare for employment and whose parole officers refer released inmates to the program. As the reputation of the program has spread, the Texas Workforce Commission has developed a pool of more than 12,000 employers who have hired parolees referred by RIO.

A 1992 independent evaluation documented that 60 percent of RIO participants found employment, compared with 36 percent of a matched group of non-RIO parolees. In addition, one year after release, RIO participants had worked at some time during more three-month intervals than comparison group members had. During the year after release, when most recidivism occurs, 48 percent of the RIO high risk clients were rearrested compared with 57 percent of the non-RIO high risk parolees and only 23 percent of high risk RIO participants returned to prison, compared with 38 percent of a comparable group of non-RIO parolees. The evaluation also concluded that the program continually saved the State money, more than $15 million in 1990 alone, by helping to reduce the number of parolees who would otherwise have been rearrested and sent back to prison (Finn 1998c).

These positive findings encouraged the Texas legislature to increase RIO's annual budget to nearly $8 million, and other states, Georgia for example, to implement aspects of the RIO model.

New York City's Center for Employment Opportunities (CEO) project is a transitional service for parolees consisting of day labor work crews. Assignment to a work crew begins immediately after release from prison, and while it is designed to prepare inmates for placement in a permanent job, it also helps to provide structure, instill work habits, and earn early daily income (Finn 1998b). Most participants are young offenders, released from prison boot camp programs, and are required to enroll as a condition of parole. The descriptive evaluation of this program shows that young parolees associated with it are more likely to be employed, refrain from substance use, and participate in community service and education while in the CEO program.

3. Multi-Service Centers

The Safer Foundation, headquartered in Chicago, is now the largest community-based provider of employment services for ex-offenders in the U.S. with a professional staff of nearly 200 in six locations in two states. The foundation offers a wide range of services for parolees, including employment, educational and housing. A recent evaluation shows that Safer has helped more than 40,000 participants find jobs since 1972, and nearly two-thirds of those placed kept their jobs for 30 days or more of continuous employment (Finn 1998a).

Another highly successful program for released prisoners is operated by Pioneer Human Services in Seattle, Washington, a private, non-profit organization. Pioneer Services provides housing, jobs, and social support for released offenders, but it also operates sheltered work-shops for the hard-to-place offender. It is different from other social-service agencies in that its program is funded almost entirely by the profits from the various businesses it operates and not through grants. They place a priority on practical living skills and job training. Most of their clients are able to maintain employment either in the free market or for Pioneer Services, and the recidivism rates are less than 5 percent for its work-release participants (Turner and Petersilia 1996b).

There are parole programs that work. One of the immediate challenges is to find the money to pay for them. Martin Horn, currently Commissioner of the Pennsylvania Department of Corrections, suggests using offender vouchers to pay for parole programs. At the end of the prisoner's term, the offender would be provided with vouchers with which he or she can purchase certain type of services upon release (e.g., drug and alcohol treatment, job placement, family counseling). Mr. Horn suggests giving $2,000 in service coupons for each of the two years following prison release. The offender can then purchase the services he feels he most needs. Mr. Horn's cost benefit analysis for this plan for the state of New York shows that it could save about $50 million per year—dollars that he says could then be invested in prevention programs instead of prison.

C. Intermediate Sanctions for Parole Violators

States are taking a new look at how they respond to violations of parole, particularly technical violations that do not involve, of themselves, new criminal behavior (Burke 1997). Several states are now structuring the court's responses to technical violations. Missouri opened up the Kansas City Recycling Center in 1988, a 41-bed facility operated by a private contractor to deal exclusively with technical violators who have been recommended for revocation. The pilot program proved so successful that the state took over operation and set aside a complete correctional facility of 250 beds for the program. Mississippi and Georgia use 90 day boot camp programs, housed in separate wings of the state prisons, for probation violators (for other program descriptions, see Parent et al. 1994). While empirical evidence as to the effects of these programs is scant, system officials believe that the programs serve to increase the certainty of punishment, while reserving scarce prison space for the truly violent. Importantly, experts believe that states with "intermediate" (non-prison) options for responding to less serious parole violations are able to reduce parolees' new commitments to prison, explaining the vast differences shown in Table 5.

D. "Neighborhood" Parole

One of the critical lessons learned during the past decade has been that no one program—surveillance or rehabilitation alone, any one agency, police without parole, parole without mental health, or any of these agencies without the community—can reduce crime, or fear of crime, on their own (Petersilia 1998a). Crime and criminality are complex, multi-faceted problems, and real long-term solutions must come from the community, and be actively participated in by the community and those who surround the offender. This model of community engagement is the foundation of community policing, and its tenants are now spreading to probation and parole.

This new parole model is being referred to as "neighborhood parole" (Smith and Dickey 1998), "corrections of place" (Clear and Corbert 1999), or "police-parole partnerships" (Morgan and Marrs 1998). Regardless of the name, the key components are the same. They involve strengthening parole's linkages with law enforcement and the community; offering a full-service model of parole; and attempting to change the offenders' lives through personal, family and neighborhood interventions. At their core, these models move away from managing parolees on conventional caseloads and towards a more activist supervision where agents are responsible for close supervision as well as procuring jobs, social support and needed treatment.

The "neighborhood parole" model has been most well thought out in Wisconsin, where the Governors' Task Force on Sentencing and Corrections recommended the program. Program proponents realize neighborhood-based parole will be more costly that traditional parole supervision, but are hopeful that reduced recidivism and revocations to prison will offset program costs. In 1998, the Wisconsin legislature allocated $8 million to fund and evaluate two countywide pilot projects (Smith and Dickey 1998).

VII. Concluding Remarks

Nearly 700,000 parolees are now doing their time on U.S. streets. Most have been released to parole systems that provide few services and impose conditions that almost guarantee their failure. Our monitoring systems are getting better, and public tolerance for failure on parole is decreasing. The result is that a rising tide of parolees is washing back into prison, putting pressure on states to build more prisons, which in turn, takes money away from rehabilitation programs that might have helped offenders while they were in the community. All of this means that parolees will continue to receive fewer services to help them deal with their underlying problems, assuring that recidivism rates and returns to prison remain high, and public support for parole remains low.

This situation represents a formidable challenge to those concerned with crime and punishment. The public will not support community based punishments until they have been shown to work, and they won't have an opportunity to work without sufficient funding and research. Spending on parole services in California, for example, was cut 44 percent in 1997, causing parole caseloads to nearly double (now standing at a ratio of 82-to-1). When caseloads increase, services decline, and even parolees who are motivated to change have little opportunity to do so. Job training programs are cut, and parolees often remain at the end of long waiting lists for community-based drug and alcohol treatment.

Yet crime committed by parolees is a real problem and there is every reason to be skeptical about our ability to reduce it significantly. Early parole research did not reveal any easy fixes, and the current parole population is increasingly difficult and dangerous. The public is skeptical that the experts know how to solve the crime problem and have increasingly taken matters into their own hands. Corrections officials report being increasingly constrained by political forces, and no longer able to use their own best judgements on crime policy (Rubin 1997). State officials feel that even a single visible failure of any parole program could readily become a political disaster for the existing administration. One notorious case was that of Willie Horton and the Massachusetts furlough program. The press often publicizes such cases to feed the public's appetite for news about the failure of the criminal justice system. Such negative news, and the fear of such negative news, often precludes any innovative parole reform efforts.

The challenge is to bring greater balance to the handling of parole populations by singling out those offenders who represent different public safety risks and different prospects for rehabilitation. The pilot parole programs described in Section VI are the first step, but it would help considerably if rigorous impact evaluations were always conducted. We don't know with any precision what impact parole has on an offender's recidivism, or what supervision conditions are helpful to the reintegration process.

It is safe to say that parole programs have received less research attention that any other correctional component in recent years. A congressionally mandated evaluation of state and local crime prevention programs included just one parole evaluation among the hundreds of recent studies that were summarized for that effort (Sherman et al. 1997). The author of this article has spent many years contributing to the evaluation literature on probation effectiveness but knows of no similar body of knowledge on parole effectiveness. Without better information, it is unlikely that the public will give corrections officials the political permission to invest in rehabilitation and job training programs for parolees. With better information, we might be able to persuade the voters and elected officials to shift their current preferences away from solely punitive crime policies and towards a sanctioning philosophy that balances incapacitation, rehabilitation and just punishment.

By the year 2000, the United States is predicted to have a record two million people in jails and prisons and more people on parole than ever before. If current parole revocation trends continue, more than half of all those entering prison in the year 2000 will be parole failures. Given the increasing human and financial costs associated with prison, investing in effective reentry programs may well be one of the best investments we make.

Author's Note: The author wishes to particularly thank Allen Beck, Chief Corrections Statistics Program, Bureau of Justice Statistics, U.S. Department of Justice, for his generous assistance in identifying and interpreting relevant parole data. Edward Rhine, Mike Tonry, Peggy Burke, Frances Cullen and Gail Hughes also made helpful comments on drafts of this article.

References

Abadinsky, Howard. 1997. *Probation and Parole.* Upper Saddle River, New Jersey: Simon & Schuster.

Adams, William, and Jeffrey Roth. 1998. "Federal Offenders under Community Supervision, 1987–96." Washington, D.C.: Bureau of Justice Statistics.

Allen, George. 1997. "Abolishing Parole Saves Lives and Property." *Corrections Today* Vol. 59, No. 4:22.

American Correctional Association. 1995. *Probation and Parole Directory.* Lanham, Maryland: American Correctional Association.

Andrews, Don, and James Bonta. 1994. *The Psychology of Criminal Conduct.* Cincinnati, Ohio: Anderson Publishing.

Applegate, Brian, Frances Cullen, Michael Turner, and Jody Sundt. 1996. "Assessing Public Support for Three-Strikes-You're Out Laws: Global Versus Specific Attitudes." *Crime and Delinquency* 42:517–534.

Association of Paroling Authorities International. 1998. "APAI Survey of Parole Boards." Washington, D.C.

Austin, James, and Robert Lawson. 1998. "Assessment of California Parole Violations and Recommended Intermediate Programs and Policies." San Francisco: National Council on Crime and Delinquency.

Beck, Allen, and Bernard Shipley. 1989. "Recidivism of Prisoners Released in 1983." Washington, D.C.: Bureau of Justice Statistics.

Beck, Allen J. 1999. "Trends in U.S. Correctional Populations." Pp. 44–100 in *The Dilemmas of Corrections*, edited by Kenneth Haas and Geoffrey Alpert. Prospect Heights, Illinois: Waveland Press, Inc.

Bottomly, Keith A. 1990. "Parole in Transition: A Comparative Study of Origins, Developments, and Prospects for the 1990s." pp. 319–374 in *Crime and Justice: A Review of Research*, edited by Michael Tonry and Norval Morris. Chicago: University of Chicago Press.

Bureau of Justice Statistics. 1997. "National Corrections Reporting Program 1996." Washington, D.C.: Bureau of Justice Statistics.

Bureau of Justice Statistics. 1998. "Probation and Parole Populations 1997." Washington, D.C.

Burke, Peggy B. 1995. *Abolishing Parole: Why the Emperor Has No Clothes.* Lexington, Ky.: American Probation and Parole Association.

Burke, Peggy B. 1997. "Policy-Driven Responses to Probation and Parole Violations." Washington, D.C.: National Institute of Corrections, U.S. Department of Justice.

Butterfield, Fox. 1999. "Eliminating Parole Boards Isn't a Cure-All, Experts Say" in *New York Times.* New York, January 10, 1999:11.

California Department of Corrections. 1997. "Preventing Parolee Failure Program: An Evaluation." Sacramento, California.

Camp, Camille, and George Camp. 1997. *The Corrections Yearbook.* South Salem, New York: Criminal Justice Institute, Inc.

Carter, Beth. 1998. "Harbingers of Change." *Crime and Politics in the 1990's:* 1–8.

Citizens' Inquiry on Parole and Criminal Justice. 1974. "Report on New York Parole." New York City, New York: The Citizen's Inquiry.

Clear, Todd, and George Cole. 1997. *American Corrections.* Belmont, Ca.: Wadsworth Publishing.

Clear, Todd, and Ronald Corbett. 1999. "Community Corrections of Place." *Perspectives* 23:24–32.

Cromwell, Paul F. and Rolando del Carmen. 1999. *Community Based Corrections.* Belmont, Ca.: West/Wadsworth.

del Carmen, Rolando, and James Alan Pilant. 1994. "The Scope of Judicial Immunity for Probation and Parole Officers." *Perspectives* 18:14–21.

Deschenes, Elizabeth, Susan Turner, and Joan Petersilia. 1995. "A Dual Experiment in Intensive Community Supervision: Minnesota's Prison Diversion and Enhanced Supervised Released Programs." *The Prison Journal* 75.

DiIulio, John. 1997. "Reinventing Parole and Probation." *The Brookings Review:* 40–42.

Ditton, Paula, and Doris James Wilson. 1999. "Truth in Sentencing in State Prisons." Washington, D.C.: Bureau of Justice Statistics.

Fabelo, Tony. 1999. "Biennial Report to the 76th Texas Legislature." Austin, Texas: Criminal Justice Policy Council.

Feeley, Malcolm and Jonathan Simon. 1992. "The New Penology: Notes on the Emerging Strategy of Corrections and its Implications," 30 *Criminology,* 449–474.

Fellner, Jamie, and Marc Mauer. 1998. "Losing the Vote: The Impact of Felony Disenfranchisement Laws in the United States." Washington, D.C.: The Sentencing Project.

Finn, Peter. 1998a. "Chicago's Safer Foundation: A Road Back for Ex-Offenders." Washington, D.C.: National Institute of Justice.

Finn, Peter. 1998b. "Successful Job Placement for Ex-Offenders: The Center for Employment Opportunities." Washington, D.C.: National Institute of Justice.

Finn, Peter. 1998c. "Texas' Project RIO (Re-Integration of Offenders)." Washington, D.C.: National Institute of Justice.

Flanagan, Timothy. 1996. "Reform or Punish: Americans' Views of the Correctional System." in *Americans View Crime and Justice,* edited by Timothy Flanagan and Dennis Longmire. Thousand Oaks, California: Sage Publications.

Flanagan, Timothy, and Dennis Longmire (Eds.). 1996. *Americans View Crime and Justice: A National Public Opinion Survey.* Thousand Oaks, California: Sage Publications.

Fogel, David. 1975. *We Are the Living Proof.* Cincinnati, Ohio: Anderson.

Gainsborough, Jenni. 1997. "Eliminating Parole is a Dangerous and Expensive Proposition. *Corrections Today* Vol. 59, No. 4:23.

Glaser, Daniel. 1969. *The Effectiveness of a Prison and Parole System.* Indianapolis, Indiana: Bobbs-Merrill.

Golde v. Fox, 98 Cal.App. 3d 167, 159 California Reporter 864, 1st District 1979.

Gottfredson, Don, Peter Hoffman, and M. Sigler. 1975. "Making Parole Policy Explicit." *Crime and Delinquency,* January, pp. 7–17.

Gottfredson, Don, Leslie Wilkins, and Peter Hoffman. 1978. *Guidelines for Parole and Sentencing.* Lexington, MA: Health/Lexington.

Hoffman, Peter B., and Lucille K. DeGostin. 1974. "Parole Decision Making: Structuring Discretion." *Federal Probation* December.

Holt, Norman. 1998. "The Current State of Parole in America." Pp. 28–41 in *Community Corrections: Probation, Parole, and Intermediate Sanctions,* edited by Joan Petersilia. New York, N.Y: Oxford University Press.

Irwin, John, and James Austin. 1994. *It's About Time: America's Imprisonment Binge.* Belmont, California: Wadsworth Publishing Company.

Institute of Medicine. 1990 (D.R. Gerstein and H.J. Harwood, eds.). *Treating Drug Problems: A Study of the Evolution, Effectiveness, and Financing of Public and Private Drug Treatment Systems.* National Academy Press, Washington, D.C.

Kleinknecht, William. 1997. "Juvenile authorities want satellite tracking for felons." in *The Star Ledger,* November 18: p. 7. New Jersey.

Legislative Analysts Office. 1998. "Reforming California's Adult Parole System." Sacramento.

Lieb, Roxanne, Vernon Quinsey, and Lucy Berliner. 1998. "Sexual Predators and Social Policy." in *Crime and Justice: A Review of Research,* edited by Michael Tonry. Chicago: University of Chicago Press.

Lipton, Douglas, Robert Martinson, and Judith Wilks. 1975. *The Effectiveness of Correctional Treatment and What Works: A Survey of Treatment Evaluation Studies.* New York: Praeger.

Little Hoover Commission. 1998. "Beyond Bars: Correctional Reforms to Lower Prison Costs and Reduce Crime." Sacramento, California.

Love, Margaret, and Kuzma. 1996. "Civil Disabilities of Convicted Felons: A State-by-State Survey." Washington, D.C.: Office of the Pardon Attorney.

Lynch, Mona. 1998. "Waste Managers? New Penology, Crime Fighting and the Parole Agent Identity." *Law and Society Review* 32, Vol. 4, 839–869.

McCaffrey, Barry. 1998. "Drug Treatment in the Criminal Justice System." Washington, D.C.: Office of National Drug Control Policy.

McCleary, Richard. 1992. *Dangerous Men: The Sociology of Parole.* New York: Harrow and Heston.

Morgan, Terry, and Stephen Marrs. 1998. "Redmond, Washington's SMART Partnership for Police and Community Corrections." Pp. 170–180 in *Community Corrections: Probation, Parole, and Intermediate Sanctions,* edited by Joan Petersilia. New York: Oxford University Press.

Morse, Wayne. 1939. "U.S. Attorney General's Survey of Release Procedures." Washington, D.C.: U.S. Department of Justice.

National Conference of State Legislatures. 1996. "Three Strikes' Legislation Update." Denver.

National Institute of Corrections. 1995. "Status Report on Parole, 1995." Washington, D.C.: U.S. Department of Justice.

O'Leary, Vincent (Ed.). 1974. *Parole Administration.* Chicago: Rand McNally Publishing.

Olivares, K., V. Burton, and F. Cullen. 1996. "The Collateral Consequences of a Felony Conviction: A National Study of State Legal Codes 10 Years Later." *Federal Probation* LX:10–18.

Pan, Philip. 1998. "Md. Orders Drug Tests for Addicts on Parole." Pp. 1 in *The Washington Post.* Washington, D.C.

Parent, Dale. 1993. "Structuring Policies to Address Sanctions for Absconders and Violators." in *Reclaiming Offender Accountability: Intermediate Sanctions for Probation and Parole Violators,* edited by Edward Rhine. Laurel, Maryland: American Correctional Association.

Parent, Dale, Dan Wentworth, Peggy Burke, and Becky Ney. 1994. "Responding to Probation and Parole Violations." Washington, D.C.: National Institute of Justice.

Petersilia, Joan. 1998a. "A Decade of Experimenting with Intermediate Sanctions: What Have We Learned?" Pp. 79–106 in *Perspectives on Crime and Justice.* Washington, D.C.: National Institute of Justice.

Petersilia, Joan. 1997. "Probation in America." in *Crime and Justice: An Annual Review of Research,* edited by Michael Tonry. Chicago, IL: University of Chicago Press.

Petersilia, Joan. 1998b. "Probation and Parole." in *The Oxford Handbook of Criminology,* edited by Michael Tonry. New York, New York: Oxford University Press.

Petersilia, Joan, and Susan Turner. 1993. "Intensive Probation and Parole." in *Crime and Justice: An Annual Review of Research,* edited by Michael Tonry. Chicago, IL: University of Chicago Press.

Prendergast, Michael, Douglas Anglin, and Jean Wellisch. 1995. "Treatment for Drug-Abusing Offenders Under Community Supervision." *Federal Probation* 66.

Reitz, Kevin. 1998. "Sentencing," Pp. 542–562 in *The Handbook of Crime and Punishment,* edited by Michael Tonry. New York, NY.: Oxford University Press.

Rhine, Edward, William Smith, Ronald Jackson, Peggy Burke, and Roger LaBelle. 1991. "Paroling Authorities: Recent history and current practice." Laurel, Maryland: American Correctional Association.

Rhine, Edward E. 1996. "Parole Boards." Pp. 342–348 in *The Encyclopedia of American Prisons,* edited by Marilyn McShane and Frank Williams. New York: Garland Publishing, Inc.

Richards, Stephen C. 1995. *The Structure of Prison Release: An Extended Case Study of Prison Release, Work Release, and Parole.* New York City: McGraw-Hill, Inc.

Rothman, David. 1980. *Conscience and Convenience: The Asylum and Its Alternatives in Progressive America.* Boston: Little, Brown.

Rubin, Edward. 1997. "Minimizing Harm as a Goal for Crime Policy in California." Berkeley, California: California Policy Seminar.

Rudovsky, David, Alvin Bronstein, Edard Koren, and Julie Cade. 1988. *The Rights of Prisoners.* Carbondale, IL: Southern Illinois University Press.

Runda, John, Edward Rhine, and Robert Wetter. 1994. "The Practice of Parole Boards." Lexington, Kentucky: Association of Paroling Authorities, International.

Schlosser, Eric. 1998. "The Prison Industrial Complex." Pp. 51–77 in *The Atlantic Monthly.*

Sechrest, Lee, Susan White, and Elizabeth Brown. 1979. *The Rehabilitation of Criminal Offenders: Problems and Prospects.* Washington, D.C.: National Academy of Sciences.

Sherman, Lawrence, Denise Gottfredson, Doris Mackenzie, John Eck, Peter Reuter, and Shawn Bushway. 1997. "Preventing Crime: What Works, What Doesn't, What's Promising." College Park, Maryland: University of Maryland.

Simon, Jonathan. 1993. *Poor Discipline: Parole and the Social Control of the Underclass, 1890–1990.* Chicago: The University of Chicago Press.

Smith, Michael, and Walter Dickey. 1998. "What If Corrections Were Serious About Public Safety?" *Corrections Management Quarterly* 2:12–30.

Sundt, Jody, Francis Cullen, Michael Turner, and Brandon Applegate. 1998. "What Will The Public Tolerate?" *Perspectives* 22:22–26.

The Gallup Organization. 1998. "Gallup Surveys Pertaining to Parole (special request)." New York City, New York.

Tonry, Michael. 1995. *Malign Neglect: Race, Crime, and Punishment in America.* New York: Oxford University Press.

Turner, Susan, and Joan Petersilia. 1992. "Focusing on High-Risk Parolees: An Experiment to Reduce Commitment to the Texas Department of Corrections. *The Journal of Research in Crime and Delinquency* 29:34–61.

Turner, Susan, and Joan Petersilia. 1996a. "Work Release in Washington: Effects on Recidivism and Corrections Costs." *The Prison Journal* 76.

Turner, Susan, and Joan Petersilia. 1996b. "Work Release: Recidivism and Corrections Costs in Washington State." Washington, D.C.: National Institute of Justice.

von Hirsch, Andrew. 1976. *Doing Justice: The Choice of Punishments.* New York: Hill and Wang.

von Hirsch, Andrew, and Kathleen Hanrahan. 1979. *The Question of Parole: Retention, Reform, or Abolition?* Cambridge, Massachusetts: Ballinger.

Walker, Samuel. 1998. *A History of American Criminal Justice.* New York: Oxford University Press.

Wilson, James. 1985. *Thinking About Crime.* New York: Basic Books.

Wilson, Rob. 1977. "Release: Should Parole Boards Hold the Key?" *Corrections Magazine* :47–55.

Joan Petersilia, Ph.D. *is a Professor of Criminology Law & Society at the University of California in Irvine, California.*

Appendix

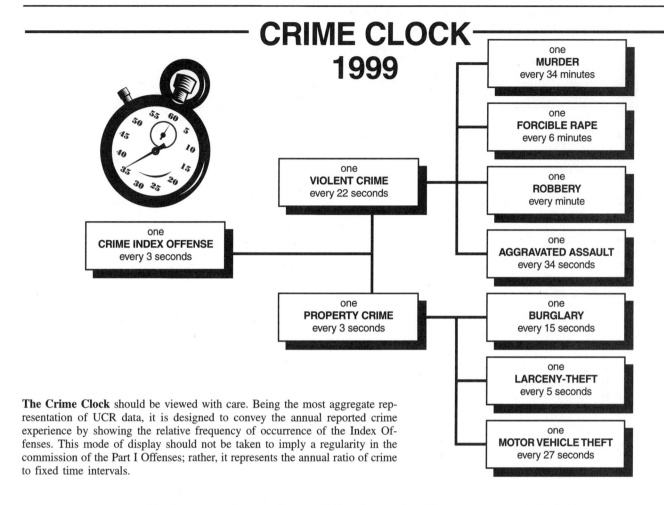

CRIME CLOCK 1999

one
CRIME INDEX OFFENSE
every 3 seconds

one
VIOLENT CRIME
every 22 seconds

one
PROPERTY CRIME
every 3 seconds

one
MURDER
every 34 minutes

one
FORCIBLE RAPE
every 6 minutes

one
ROBBERY
every minute

one
AGGRAVATED ASSAULT
every 34 seconds

one
BURGLARY
every 15 seconds

one
LARCENY-THEFT
every 5 seconds

one
MOTOR VEHICLE THEFT
every 27 seconds

The Crime Clock should be viewed with care. Being the most aggregate representation of UCR data, it is designed to convey the annual reported crime experience by showing the relative frequency of occurrence of the Index Offenses. This mode of display should not be taken to imply a regularity in the commission of the Part I Offenses; rather, it represents the annual ratio of crime to fixed time intervals.

Crime in the United States, 1999

The 1999 Crime Index total, estimated at 11.6 million offenses, is the lowest since 1978. This total represented the eighth consecutive annual decline in the Crime Index, which is down 7 percent from the 1998 number. The Nation's cities collectively recorded a 7-percent drop, with cities having populations of 25,000 to 99,999 recording the greatest decrease at 8 percent. Suburban counties registered an 8-percent Crime Index decline and rural counties a 7-percent downturn.

The 1999 national Crime Index total was 16 percent lower than in 1995 and 20 percent lower than in 1990.

Geographically, the Southern States, the most populous area of the Nation, accounted for 41 percent of the total volume of Crime Index offenses. The Western States comprised 23 percent of the total number; the Midwestern States, 22 percent; and the Northeastern States, 14 percent. The Western States showed a Crime Index decrease of 10 percent from the 1998 figures. The Northeastern States and the Midwestern States each were down 7 percent, and the Southern States registered a 5-percent decrease.

The monthly offense distribution shows the greatest number of Crime Index offenses occurred in August, and the fewest occurred in February.

Rate

The Crime Index rate for 1999 is the lowest—4,267 per 100,000 of the Nation's inhabitants—since 1973. By community type, cities outside metropolitan areas had a Crime Index rate of 4,561 offenses per 100,000 inhabitants, and metropolitan areas had a rate of 4,600 offenses per 100,000 inhabitants. Rural counties experienced a rate of 1,901 offenses per 100,000. The overall 1999 Crime Index rate dropped 8 percent from the 1998 level, 19 percent from the 1995 level, and 27 percent from the 1990 level.

Regionally, the South, the Nation's most populous region, had a Crime Index rate of 4,932 offenses per 100,000 inhabitants, the West registered 4,328, the Midwest noted 4,041, and the Northeast 3,233.

The rates in all four regions declined from 1998 to 1999. The Western region had an 11-percent downturn in Index crime, the Midwestern region showed an 8-percent fall, the Northeastern region had a 7-percent decline, and the Southern region dropped 6-percent.

Nature

Violent and property crimes together comprise the Crime Index. In 1999, violent crimes accounted for 12 percent of Crime

211

Table 1.—Index of Crime, United States, 1989–1998

Population[1]	Crime Index total[2]	Modified Crime Index total[3]	Violent crime[4]	Property crime[4]	Murder and non-negligent man-slaughter	Forcible rape	Robbery	Aggravated assault	Burglary	Larceny-theft	Motor vehicle theft	Arson[3]
					Number of Offenses							
Population by year:												
1989–248,239,000	14,251,400		1,646,040	12,605,400	21,500	94,500	578,330	951,710	3,168,200	7,872,400	1,564,800	
1990–248,709,873	14,475,600		1,820.130	12,655,500	23,440	102,560	639,270	1,054,860	3,073,900	7,945,700	1,635,900	
1991–252,177,000	14,872,900		1,911,770	12,961,100	24,700	106,590	687,730	1,092,740	3,157,200	8,142,200	1,661,700	
1992–255,082,000	14,438,200		1,932,270	12,505,900	23,760	109,060	672,480	1,126,970	2,979,900	7,915,200	1,610,800	
1993–257,908,000	14,144,800		1,926,020	12,218,800	24,530	106,010	659,870	1,135,610	2,834,800	7,820,900	1,563,100	
1994–260,341,000	13,989,500		1,857,670	12,131,900	23,330	102,220	618,950	1,113,180	2,712,800	7,879,800	1,539,300	
1995–262,755,000	13,862,700		1,798,790	12,063,900	21,610	97,470	580,510	1,099,210	2,593,800	7,997,700	1,472,400	
1996–265,284,000	13,493,900		1,688,540	11,805,300	19,650	96,250	535,590	1,037,050	2,506,400	7,904,700	1,394,200	
1997–267,637,000	13,194,600		1,636,100	11,558,500	18,210	96,150	498,530	1,023,200	2,460,500	7,743,800	1,354,200	
1998–270,296,000[5]	12,485,700		1,533,890	10,951,800	16,970	93,140	447,190	976,580	2,332,700	7,376,300	1,242,800	
1999–272,691,000	11,635,100		1,430,690	10,204,500	15,530	89,110	409,670	916,380	2,099,700	6,957,400	1,147,300	
Percent change, number of offenses:												
1999/1998	−6.8		−6.7	−6.8	−8.5	−4.3	−8.4	−6.2	−10.0	−5.7	−7.7	
1999/1995	−16.1		−20.5	−15.4	−20.5	−8.6	−29.4	−16.6	−19.0	−13.0	−22.1	
1999/1990	−19.6		−21.4	−19.4	−33.7	−13.1	−35.9	−13.1	−31.7	-12.4	−29.9	
					Rate per 100,000 Inhabitants							
Year:												
1989	5,741.0		663.1	5,077.9	8.7	38.1	233.0	383.4	1,276.3	2,171.3	630.4	
1990	5,820.3		731.8	5,088.5	9.4	41.2	257.0	424.1	1,235.9	3,194.8	657.8	
1991	5,897.8		758.1	5,139.7	9.8	42.3	272.0	433.3	1,252.0	3,228.8	659.9	
1992	5,660.2		757.5	4,902.7	9.3	42.8	263.6	441.8	1,168.2	3,103.0	631.5	
1993	5,484.4		746.8	4,737.6	9.5	14.1	255.9	440.3	1,099.2	3.032.4	606.1	
1994	5,373.5		713.6	4,660.0	9.0	39.3	237.7	427.6	1,042.0	3,026.7	591.3	
1995	5,275.9		684.6	4,591,3	8.2	37.1	220.9	418.3	987.1	3,043.8	560.4	
1996	5,086.6		636.5	4,450.1	7.4	36.3	201.9	390.0	944.8	2,979.7	525.6	
1997	4,930.0		611.3	4,318.7	6.8	35.9	186.3	382.3	919.4	2,893.4	506.0	
1998[5]	4,619.3		567.5	4,051.8	6.3	34.5	165.4	361.3	863.0	2,729.0	459.8	
1999	4,266.8		524.7	3,742.1	5.7	32.7	150.2	336.1	770.0	2,551.4	420.7	
Percent change, rate per 100,000 inhabitants:												
1999/1998	−7.6		−7.5	−7.6	−9.5	−5.2	−9.2	−7.0	−10.8	−6.5	−8.5	
1999/1995	−19.1		−23.4	−18.5	−30.5	−11.9	−32.0	−19.7	−22.0	−16.2	−24.9	
1999/1990	−26.7		−28.3	−26.5	−39.4	−20.6	−41.6	−20.7	−37.7	−20.1	−36.0	

[1] Populations are Bureau of the Census provisional estimates as of July 1, 1999, except 1990 which [is] the decennial census counts.
[2] Because of rounding, the offenses may not add to total.
[3] Although arson data are included in the trend and clearance tables, sufficient data are not available to estimate totals for this offense.
[4] Violent crimes are offenses of murder, forcible rape, robbery, and aggravated assault. Property crimes are offenses of burglary, larceny-theft, and motor vehicle theft. Data are not included for the property crime of arson.
[5] The 1998 figures have been adjusted.
All rates were calculated on the offenses before rounding.

Index offenses, and property crimes made up 88 percent. The property crime of larceny-theft had the highest volume of offenses reported to law enforcement, and the violent crime of murder had the lowest volume of offenses reported to law enforcement.

In 1999, the estimated total value of the stolen property for all Crime Index offenses was $15.2 billion. The greatest loss came from thefts of motor vehicles followed by the loss of televisions, radios, stereos, etc.; jewelry and precious metals; and currency, notes, etc.

There was a 36-percent recovery rate for monetary losses in connection with stolen property as reported to law enforcement agencies nationally in 1999. Stolen motor vehicles had the highest recovery percentages, trailed by livestock, clothing and furs, and firearms.

Law Enforcement Response

An estimated 2.3 million arrests were made for Index crimes by law enforcement agencies around the Nation, which resulted in a 21-percent clearance rate. Clearances can occur by arrest or by exceptional means when some element beyond law enforcement control precludes the placing of formal charges against the offender. The arrest of one person may clear several crimes, or several persons may be arrested in connection with the clearance of one offense.

The 1999 total Crime Index arrests fell 8 percent from 1998 arrest numbers. Adult arrests dropped 8 percent, and juvenile arrests declined 10 percent. Categorized by gender, male arrests fell 9 percent, and female arrests fell 7 percent.

Each offense in the Crime Index dropped in the number of persons arrested from 1998 to 1999. Arrests for murder were down 12 percent; forcible rape, 8 percent; robbery, 9 percent; and aggravated assault, 5 percent. Arrests for burglary sank 11 percent, larceny-thefts were down 9 percent, arrests for motor vehicle theft fell 6 percent and arrests for arson dipped 3 percent.

CRIME INDEX OFFENSES REPORTED

MURDER AND NONNEGLIGENT MANSLAUGHTER

DEFINITION
Murder and nonnegligent manslaughter, as defined in the Uniform Crime Reporting Program, is the willful (nonnegligent) killing of one human being by another.

Year	TREND Number of offenses	Rate per 100,000 inhabitants
1998	16,974	6.3
1999	15,533	5.7
Percent change	−8.5	−9.3

Volume

In 1999, the estimated number of persons murdered in the United States was 15,533, representing an 8-percent decrease from the 1998 estimate. The 1999 figure also represents a 28-percent decline in comparison to the 1995 estimate and a 34-percent decrease in contrast to the 1990 nationwide estimate.

When compared to 1998 figures, 1999 murder volumes in the Nation's cities collectively fell 7 percent. This decline ranged from 13 percent in cities with populations of less than 25,000 to 3 percent in those cities with populations of 250,000 and over. Declines of 12 percent in suburban counties and 10 percent in rural counties were also recorded.

Murder by Month
Percent distribution, 1995–1999

Months	1995	1996	1997	1998	1999
January	8.3	8.7	8.7	9.1	8.7
February	6.8	7.8	7.3	7.2	7.0
March	7.6	7.5	8.5	8.3	7.7
April	8.4	7.5	7.6	7.7	7.8
May	7.9	8.3	7.9	8.4	8.3
June	8.2	8.8	8.7	8.4	8.0
July	8.9	8.8	9.0	8.7	9.0
August	9.9	9.1	8.7	9.2	9.1
September	8.6	8.1	8.2	8.3	8.8
October	8.8	8.5	8.6	8.3	8.4
November	8.0	8.0	8.2	7.6	8.3
December	8.6	8.9	8.6	8.9	8.8

Considering the four regions of the Nation, 43 percent of murders were recorded in the South, the most heavily populated area of the country. The West and Midwest each accounted for 22 percent, and the Northeast accounted for 14 percent. All regions showed declines in the number of murders from 1998 to 1999. The greatest drop, 11 percent, was recorded in the South; the West followed, experiencing a decline of 8 percent. Decreases of 7 and 5 percent were recorded in the Midwest and in the Northeast, respectively.

Monthly distribution data indicate that murder was committed most frequently in August and least frequently in February.

Rate

The lowest national murder rate since 1966—5.7 murders per 100,000 inhabitants—was recorded in 1999, representing a 9-percent drop from the 1998 figure. Five- and 10-year trends indicate that the 1999 rate was 30 percent lower than in 1995 and 39 percent lower than in 1990.

Regionally, the South averaged 7 murders per 100,000 inhabitants; the West, 6 per 100,000; the Midwest, 5 per 100,000; and the Northeast, 4 per 100,000. All four of the geographic regions experienced decreases in murder rates when compared with 1998 figures. The South recorded a decline of 12 percent; the West, 9 percent; the Midwest, 7 percent; and the Northeast, 5 percent.

By community type, the Nation's metropolitan areas reported a 1999 murder rate of 6 victims per 100,000 inhabitants. Both rural counties and cities outside metropolitan areas recorded murder rates of 4 per 100,000 inhabitants.

Nature

Supplemental data were provided by contributing agencies for 12,658 of the estimated 15,533 murders in 1999. These supplemental data, submitted monthly, provide the age, sex, and race of both victims and offenders; the types of weapons used; the relationships of the victims to the offenders; and the circumstances surrounding the murders.

Based on 1999 supplemental data, 76 percent of murder victims were male. Persons aged 18 or older comprised the greatest percentage of victims, 88 percent. Half of the victims for whom race was known were white, 47 percent were black, and the remaining 3 percent were persons of other races.

Supplemental data were provided for a total of 14,112 murder offenders in 1999. Males comprised 90 percent of those offenders for whom gender was reported, and persons aged 18 or older constituted 90 percent of those for whom age was reported. Of those offenders for whom race was known, 50

Murder Victims by Race and Sex, 1999

Race of Victim	Total	Sex of Victims		
		Male	Female	Unknown
Total White Victims	6,310	4,489	1,818	3
Total Black Victims	5,855	4,734	1,121	—
Total Other Race Victims	329	251	118	—
Total Unknown Race	124	84	28	12
Total Victims[1]	12,658	9,558	3,085	15

[1]Total number of murder victims for whom supplemental homicide data were received.

percent were black, 47 percent were white, and the remainder were persons of other races.

Data suggest that the relationship among murder victims and offenders most often is intraracial. Figures based on one victim/one offender incidents in 1999 indicate that 94 percent of black murder victims were slain by black offenders and 85 percent of white murder victims were slain by white offenders.

FORCIBLE RAPE

DEFINITION
Forcible rape, as defined in the Uniform Crime Reporting Program, is the carnal knowledge of a female forcibly and against her will. Assaults or attempts to commit rape by force or threat of force are also included; however, statutory rape (without force) and other sex offenses are excluded.

Year	TREND Number of offenses	Rate per 100,000 inhabitants
1998	93,144	34.5
1999	89,107	32.7
Percent change	−4.3	−5.2

Volume

The estimated 89,107 forcible rapes reported to law enforcement agencies nationwide in 1999 represented the seventh consecutive annual decrease for this offense. The 1999 forcible rape total shows a 4-percent decline from the 1998 level, a 9-percent decrease from the 1995 level, and a 13-percent drop from the 1990 level.

By region, the South, the Nation's most populous region, recorded the highest portion of forcible rapes, 39 percent. The Midwest and West accounted for 25 and 23 percent, respectively, and the Northeast, 13 percent. Two-year trends for forcible rapes indicated 5-percent decreases in both the Northeast and Midwest, a 4-percent decline in the South, and a 3-percent decrease in the West.

According to monthly distribution figures, the highest number of forcible rapes occurred in July. The lowest number was reported during the month of December.

Rate

According to the Uniform Crime Reporting Program's definition, the victims of rape are always female. In 1999, an estimated 64 of every 100,000 females in the country were reported victims of forcible rape. The 1999 rate for forcible rape decreased 5 percent compared to the previous year's figures and declined 11 percent compared to the rate in 1995.

By community type, the forcible rape rate of 67 per 100,000 females recorded in the metropolitan areas represented the highest rate in the Nation. A rate of 66 per 100,000 females was recorded outside metropolitan areas, and a rate of 45 per 100,000 females was registered in rural counties. Although the metropolitan areas recorded the highest rate for forcible rape, over the past 10 years these areas experienced a 25-percent decline in rates. For the same 10-year timeframe, cities outside metropolitan areas and rural counties experienced increases of 3 percent and 2 percent, respectively.

Forcible Rape by Month
Percent distribution, 1995–1999

Months	1995	1996	1997	1998	1999
January	7.7	7.9	7.9	7.9	8.2
February	7.1	7.9	7.0	7.5	7.3
March	8.5	8.1	8.0	8.6	8.2
April	8.0	8.1	8.2	8.2	8.1
May	8.9	9.0	9.1	8.8	8.7
June	8.5	8.8	9.5	8.7	8.8
July	9.4	9.5	9.7	9.6	9.6
August	9.9	9.1	9.4	9.3	9.5
September	8.8	8.8	8.8	8.8	8.4
October	8.7	8.5	8.2	7.9	8.3
November	7.8	7.4	7.4	7.6	7.8
December	6.9	6.9	6.7	7.1	7.1

Of the four regions, the rate of 70 rapes per 100,000 females reported by the Southern States was the highest. Rates of 68 in the Midwestern States, 66 in the Western States, and 44 in the Northeastern States followed. Each of the regions experienced rate declines when compared to the 1998 figures. Rates in the South decreased 6 percent and in the Northeast, Midwest, and West rates fell 5 percent.

Over the last 10 years, all four regions have experienced declines in female forcible rape. The West reported a 24-percent decrease. The Northeast and the South demonstrated decreases of 21 and 20 percent, respectively. The Midwest reported a decline of 18 percent.

Nature

Rapes by force accounted for 89 percent of the total rapes in 1999. The remaining 11 percent were accounted for by attempts or assaults to commit forcible rape. Compared to the 1998 volume, the number of rapes by force in 1999 decreased by 6 percent. An 8-percent decrease in attempts to rape was noted nationwide.

Law Enforcement Response

Overall, law enforcement cleared 49 percent of the forcible rapes reported in 1999. Fifty percent of rapes reported in both suburban counties and rural counties were cleared. Collectively, cities reported a clearance rate of 49 percent.

Regionally, 1999 forcible rape clearance rates were 53 percent in the South, 52 percent in the Northeast, and 45 percent in both the Midwest and the West.

Juveniles (persons under 18 years of age) were involved in 12 percent of the total clearances for forcible rape nationwide. The percentage of juvenile involvement varied by community type, with 11 percent of clearances in the Nation's cities collectively. Rural counties experienced the greatest juvenile involvement, 16 percent, and suburban counties experienced 12 percent.

In 1999, law enforcement across the country arrested an estimated 28,830 persons for forcible rape. Of those arrested, 44 percent were under age 25 and 61 percent were white.

Compared to figures from 1998, an 8-percent decrease in the national arrest total for forcible rape was recorded in 1999. Arrests for forcible rape in both suburban and rural counties as well as the Nation's cities collectively, also declined by 8 percent.

ROBBERY

DEFINITION

Robbery is the taking or attempting to take anything of value from the care, custody, or control of a person or persons by force or threat of force or violence and/or by putting the victim in fear.

Year	TREND Number of offenses	Rate per 100,000 inhabitants
1998	447,186	165.4
1999	409,670	150.2
Percent change	−8.4	−9.2

Volume

Nationally, the 1999 estimated robbery total of 409,670 reported offenses was the lowest since 1973 and 8 percent lower than the 1998 figure. Collectively, cities across the Nation experienced an 8-percent decline with the largest drop, 12 percent, seen in cities with populations under 10,000. Suburban counties and rural counties also registered declines in the volume of robbery at 10 percent and 7 percent, respectively.

The Nation's most populous region, the Southern region, registered 37 percent of total reported robberies, the highest percentage among regions. The Western region accounted for 22 percent, the Northeastern region for 21 percent, and the Midwestern region for the remaining 20 percent. In comparing the 1998 figures with those for 1999, the number of robberies reported in all four regions decreased. Volumes fell 12 percent in the West, 8 percent in both the Northeast and the Midwest, and 7 percent in the South.

Five- and 10-year trends in the Nation's robbery volume indicate a 29-percent fall from the 1995 level and a 36-percent

Robbery by Month
Percent distribution, 1995–1999

Months	1995	1996	1997	1998	1999
January	8.6	9.2	9.2	9.5	9.0
February	7.3	8.0	7.6	7.5	7.2
March	8.0	8.1	7.9	8.0	7.6
April	7.5	7.5	7.6	7.6	7.7
May	7.8	7.9	8.2	7.9	8.1
June	8.0	7.9	8.0	7.7	8.0
July	8.5	8.5	8.6	8.5	8.7
August	8.9	8.6	8.8	8.7	8.8
September	8.5	8.2	8.5	8.5	8.2
October	9.3	8.6	8.8	9.0	8.8
November	8.7	8.4	8.2	8.3	8.6
December	8.9	9.1	8.6	8.8	9.3

drop from the 1990 volume. Robbery rates for 1995–1999, . . . steadily declined as well.

Distribution figures for robbery volume indicate that the most offenses occurred in December and the fewest occurred in February.

Rate

Nationally, there were 150 robberies for every 100,000 persons in 1999, a rate that was 9 percent lower than the rate for 1998. Metropolitan areas recorded a robbery rate of 180 per 100,000 inhabitants; cities outside metropolitan areas, 59; and rural areas, 17. The Nation's cities collectively experienced 220 robberies per 100,000 inhabitants, with cities of 1 million and over reporting 477 robberies per 100,000 inhabitants, the highest rate among the population groups. The robbery rates per 100,000 persons in suburban and rural counties were 67 and 15, respectively.

Regionally, the highest robbery rate was noted by the Northeast at 170 per 100,000 population. Rates recorded for other regions for 1999 include the South with a rate of 156, the West with a rate of 146, and the Midwest with a rate of 129. In comparing the 1999 robbery rates per 100,000 inhabitants with the 1998 figures, all regions showed declines: 13 percent in the West, 9 percent in the Midwest, and 8 percent in both the Northeast and the South.

Nature

In 1999, over $463 million were lost as the result of robbery offenses committed. The average dollar loss, $1,131, reflects a 15-percent increase from the 1998 figure. In 1999, the average dollar loss ranged from $620 taken during robberies of convenience stores to $4,552 per bank robbery. Despite the fact that the motive behind robbery is to obtain money or property, the nature of this crime involves force or the threat of force according to the Uniform Crime Reporting definition. Though monetary loss cannot possibly be equated with the serious personal injury often suffered by robbery victims, it does offer a means by which to measure the impact of this violent crime.

Robbery

Percent distribution by region, 1999

Type	United States Total	North-eastern States	Mid-western States	South-ern States	Western States
Total[1]	100.0	100.0	100.0	100.0	100.0
Street/highway	48.3	62.7	58.1	39.8	44.1
Commercial house	13.6	9.0	10.3	14.5	16.9
Gas or service station	2.2	1.4	2.8	2.3	2.3
Convenience store	6.0	4.1	3.6	8.6	5.6
Residence	12.2	11.6	9.1	16.4	9.2
Bank	2.0	1.3	1.6	1.5	3.0
Miscellaneous	15.8	9.9	14.5	16.8	19.0

[1]Because of rounding, percentages may not add to total.

All types of robbery decreased in 1999 when compared with the 1998 figures. Declines ranged from 5 percent for convenience store and residential robberies to 11 percent for those committed at gas or service stations. Of the total robbery types reported in 1999, those that occurred on streets and highways accounted for 48 percent; commercial and financial establishments, 24 percent; and residences, 12 percent. Miscellaneous types of robberies accounted for the remainder.

Strong-arm tactics were used in 42 percent of all robberies in 1999. Firearms were used in 40 percent, other dangerous weapons in 10 percent, and knives or cutting instruments in 8 percent. When comparing the 1999 figures against those for 1998, the use of weapons declined in all four weapon categories: strong-arm tactics, 9 percent; both firearms and knives and cutting instruments, 8 percent; and other dangerous weapons, 7 percent....

Law Enforcement Response

The national clearance rate for robbery in 1999 was 29 percent. Law enforcement agencies in rural counties reported the highest robbery clearance rate, 39 percent, and suburban county law enforcement agencies recorded 31 percent. The Nation's cities collectively had a robbery clearance rate of 28 percent, with law enforcement agencies in cities under 10,000 in population having the highest clearance rate among city types, 37 percent.

Regional robbery clearances were 31 percent in the Northeast, 29 percent in the South, 27 percent in the West, and 26 percent in the Midwest.

Juvenile offenders (those under the age of 18) were involved in 15 percent of all robbery clearances in 1999. By community type, this age group accounted for 16 percent of the robbery clearances in suburban counties, 15 percent in the Nation's cities overall, and 10 percent in rural counties. The greatest percentage of juvenile involvement for robbery occurred in cities with populations of 25,000 to 49,999, where juveniles accounted for 19 percent of robbery clearances.

Robbery arrests for 1999 were down 9 percent from the previous year's totals. Arrests of persons in the juvenile and adult age groups fell 14 percent and 8 percent, respectively. Rural counties registered a 15-percent decline in the number of arrests for robbery, and suburban counties recorded an 11-percent decrease. Collectively, cities reported a 9-percent decrease. By gender, male arrests declined 9 percent, and female arrests dropped 10 percent. Five- and 10-year trends indicate a 25-percent decrease in robbery arrests when 1999 figures are compared with robbery arrest figures for both 1995 and 1990.

Of those arrested for robbery in 1999, 62 percent were under 25 years of age. By gender, males accounted for 90 percent of arrestees. By race, blacks comprised 54 percent of robbery arrestees, whites for 44 percent, and all other races for the remainder.

AGGRAVATED ASSAULT

DEFINITION
Aggravated assault is an unlawful attack by one person upon another for the purpose of inflicting severe or aggravated bodily injury. This type of assault is usually accompanied by the use of a weapon or by means likely to produce death or great bodily harm.

Year	TREND Number of offenses	Rate per 100,000 inhabitants
1998	976,583	361.3
1999	916,383	336.1
Percent change	−6.2	-7.0

Volume

For the sixth consecutive year, reported aggravated assault figures showed a decline from the preceding year's figures. The 1999 estimated total of 916,383 aggravated assaults represented a 6-percent decrease from 1998 data for this offense, and the lowest measure since 1988. Aggravated assault comprised 64 percent of all the violent crimes in 1999.

All of the Nation's regions observed a decline in reported aggravated assaults. Forty-two percent of the aggravated assault volume occurred in the Southern Region, the Nation's most populous area. The Western Region followed with 23 percent, the Midwestern Region with 19 percent, and the Northeastern Region with 15 percent.

The highest volume of aggravated assaults, according to monthly distribution figures, occurred in July, and the lowest number was observed in February.

Collectively, the Nation's cities experienced a 7-percent drop in aggravated assault totals from 1998 to 1999. Among city population groupings, decreases ranged from 11 percent in cities with populations 25,000 to 49,999 to 5 percent in cities with 1 million and over inhabitants. The number of aggravated assaults in suburban counties and rural counties declined 6 percent and 4 percent, respectively. In those cities with populations of 250,000 and over, aggravated assault fell 6 percent when compared to the previous year's data.

Aggravated Assault by Month
Percent distribution, 1995–1999

Months	1995	1996	1997	1998	1999
January	7.6	7.8	7.5	7.9	7.9
February	7.0	7.4	7.0	7.0	7.0
March	8.1	8.0	8.3	8.1	7.9
April	8.3	8.1	8.2	8.3	8.3
May	8.8	8.9	9.3	9.1	9.0
June	8.8	9.1	9.0	8.9	8.7
July	9.4	9.4	9.5	9.4	9.5
August	9.4	9.3	9.4	9.4	9.2
September	8.9	8.6	8.8	8.7	8.6
October	8.7	8.5	8.4	8.3	8.7
November	7.5	7.4	7.5	7.4	7.7
December	7.4	7.6	7.2	7.4	7.5

Five- and 10-year trends for the country as a whole show aggravated assaults 17 percent lower than in 1995 and 13 percent below the 1990 figure.

Rate

Nationwide, there were 336 reported victims of aggravated assault per 100,000 inhabitants in 1999. The rate was 7 percent lower than in 1998 and represented a 20-percent drop from the 1995 rate. The 1999 rate was down 21 percent from the 1990 rate.

The rate in metropolitan areas, 363 per 100,000 inhabitants, was higher than the national average. Cities outside metropolitan areas experienced a rate of 307 and rural counties a rate of 177.

Compared to the preceding year's rates, 1999 aggravated assault rates were down in all regions. The aggravated assault rate was 401 per 100,000 inhabitants in the South, 347 in the West, 279 in the Midwest, and 271 in the Northeast. The West and Midwest each registered 10-percent drops;

Aggravated Assault, Types of Weapons Used
Percent distribution by region, 1999

Region	Total all weapons[1]	Fire-arms	Knives or cutting instruments	Other weapons (clubs, blunt objects, etc.)	Personal weapons
Total	100.0	18.0	17.8	35.3	28.9
Northeastern States	100.0	12.1	17.0	33.5	37.4
Midwestern States	100.0	20.8	18.0	34.7	26.4
Southern States	100.0	20.0	19.9	38.2	21.8
Western States	100.0	15.9	14.7	31.7	37.8

[1]Because of rounding, percentages may not add to total.

the Northeast decreased by 6 percent; and the South experienced a 4-percent decline.

Nature

Blunt objects or other dangerous weapons accounted for 35 percent of the weapons used in aggravated assaults in 1999. Twenty-nine percent of the assaults were committed with personal weapons such as hands, fists, and feet. Knives or cutting instruments and firearms each accounted for 18 percent of the weapons used.

Aggravated assaults decreased in all weapon categories when comparing 1999 to 1998 figures. Aggravated assaults with firearms fell by 12 percent; personal weapons (hands, fists, feet, etc.), 7 percent; knives and cutting instruments, 6 percent; and blunt objects or other dangerous weapons, 5 percent. . . .

Law Enforcement Response

Law enforcement agencies nationwide recorded a 59-percent aggravated assault clearance rate during 1999. Rural and suburban county law enforcement agencies cleared 64 and 62 percent, respectively, and law enforcement in cities collectively recorded 58 percent cleared. Among the city groupings, those cities with populations under 10,000 recorded the highest aggravated assault clearance rate at 65 percent.

Regionally, aggravated assault clearances were highest in the Northeast at 63 percent. The West recorded a clearance rate of 60 percent, followed by the Midwest at 59 percent, and the South with 58.

Law enforcement in both the Nation's cities and suburban counties had a juvenile clearance rate for aggravated assault of 12 percent. In rural counties the clearance rate was 10 percent.

Arrests for aggravated assault represented 76 percent of violent crime arrests in 1999. Sixty-three percent of the estimated 483,530 individuals arrested for this offense were white, 35 percent were black, and the remaining percent were comprised of all other races. Forty percent of aggravated assault arrestees were under the age of 25. Eighty percent of all persons arrested for aggravated assault were male.

Arrests for aggravated assault were down 5 percent in 1999 from the preceding year's total. Arrests were also down 5 percent for both adults and juveniles. The 5-year trend, 1995 to 1999, shows a decrease of 10 percent for total aggravated assault arrests. Adult arrest totals were also down 10 percent, and juvenile aggravated assault arrests decreased by 13 percent.

BURGLARY

DEFINITION
The Uniform Crime Reporting Program defines burglary as the unlawful entry of a structure to commit a felony or theft. The use of force to gain entry is not required to classify an offense as burglary.

	TREND	
Year	Number of offenses	Rate per 100,000 inhabitants
1998	2,332,735	863.0
1999	2,099,739	770.0
Percent change	–10.0	–10.8

Volume

The eighth consecutive annual decline in volume was recorded in 1999 for burglary offenses which were estimated at 2,099,739 nationwide and measured as the lowest since 1969. Regional distribution indicated that the most populous Southern States recorded the highest burglary volume, 44 percent. The Western States followed with 22 percent, the Midwestern States with 21 percent, and the Northeastern States with 13 percent.

In 1999, monthly figures revealed that the greatest number of burglaries occurred in August, and the lowest volume was recorded during February.

Compared to the 1998 volume figures, burglary declined 10 percent in 1999. By community type, at 11 percent the Nation's cities overall experienced the greatest decline, with cities with populations of 25,000 to 49,999 showing the greatest decline in burglary, 13 percent. Sururban counties showed a 10-percent decline and rural counties a 9-percent decrease.

In 1999, decreases from the previous year's burglary volumes were recorded in all four regions of the United States. The greatest decrease, 14 percent, was registered in the Western States. A 12-percent decline was recorded in the Northeastern States. The Midwestern and Southern States recorded burglary volume decreases of 9 and 8 percent, repsectively.

National 5- and 10-year trends indicate burglary was down 19 percent from the 1995 level and down 32 percent compared to the 1990 volume.

Rate

The national offense rate for burglary in 1999—770 offenses per 100,000 inhabitants—was the lowest since 1966. The rate was 11 percent lower than the 1998 figure, 22 percent under the 1995 figure, and 38 percent below the 1990 figure. The burglary rate in the metropolitan areas registered 802 offenses for every 100,000 in population; cities outside metropolitan areas recorded a rate of 783; and rural counties showed a rate of 551.

Regional comparisons demonstrate that the Southern States experienced the highest burglary rate, 959 offenses per 100,000

Burglary by Month
Percent distribution, 1995–1999

Months	1995	1996	1997	1998	1999
January	8.4	8.3	8.4	8.9	8.3
February	7.2	7.6	7.2	7.5	7.2
March	8.2	7.8	7.9	8.2	7.9
April	7.7	7.8	7.8	8.0	7.7
May	8.4	8.3	8.3	8.3	8.2
June	8.3	8.1	8.2	8.2	8.4
July	9.0	9.1	9.1	9.0	9.0
August	9.2	8.9	9.0	9.0	9.1
September	8.5	8.6	8.7	8.4	8.6
October	8.8	8.8	8.8	8.4	8.6
November	8.3	8.0	8.2	7.9	8.4
December	8.1	8.6	8.6	8.2	8.4

inhabitants. The Western States recorded a rate of 756, and the Midwestern States registered a rate of 701. The lowest rate, 520, was recorded in the North-eastern States. All regions indicated declines in rates compared to the previous year's numbers. The Western Region recorded a decline of 16 percent; the Northeastern Region recorded a 12-percent decline; and the Midwestern and the Southern Regions showed decreases of 10 percent and 9 percent, respectively.

Nature

Forcible entry was involved in 64 percent of all burglaries in 1999, 29 percent were unlawful entries (without force), and the remaining 7 percent were forcible entry attempts. Two of every 3 burglaries in 1999 were residential in nature. Offenses for which time of occurrence was reported showed that burglaries occurred more commonly during the day, 53 percent, than at night, 47 percent. Burglaries of residences occurred more frequently during daytime, 60 percent, than burglaries of nonresidences which occurred more frequently at night, 61 percent.

Although the 1999 average loss for both residential and nonresidential property burglary fell from the previous year, victims experienced an estimated loss of $3.1 billion. The average dollar loss per burglary was $1,458. Losses for residential offenses were recorded at $1,441 and for nonresidential burglaries at $1,490.

Both nonresidential and residential burglary volumes declined in 1999. Residential burglaries dropped 11 percent from the previous year's figure, and nonresidential burglary volume showed a 9-percent decline.

Law Enforcement Response

A 14-percent clearance rate was recorded for burglary offenses known to law enforcement in 1999. Regionally, the Northeast had a clearance rate of 16 percent; the South, 14 percent; the West, 13 percent; and the Midwest 12 percent.

Rural county law enforcement agencies cleared 16 percent of the burglaries reported in their jurisdictions. Law enforcement agencies in suburban counties cleared 14 percent, and those in cities collectively cleared 13 percent.

The higher percent of burglary offense clearances, 81 percent, involved adult offenders, and juvenile offenders (people under 18 years of age) were involved in the remaining 19 percent of clearances. The highest percent of juvenile clearances occurred in the Nation's smallest cities (under 10,000 in population), which recorded 25 percent. In suburban counties, the burglary clearance rate for juveniles was 21 percent. In both rural counties and cities collectively, juveniles accounted for 19 percent of clearances.

In the UCR Program, several persons may be arrested in connection with the clearance of one crime, or the arrest of one individual may clear numerous offenses. The latter is often true in cases of burglary for which an estimated 296,100 arrests were made in 1999.

In 1999, total burglary arrests were down 11 percent from the previous year's figure. Arrests of both juveniles and adults declined by 15 and 9 percent, respectively. An 11-percent decrease in burglary arrests for the Nation's cities overall was recorded for the same timeframe. Burglary arrests in rural counties declined 9 percent and in suburban counties decreased 14 percent.

At 87 percent of the total, males comprised the greater number of arrestees for burglary in 1999. By age, persons under the age of 25 made up the majority of arrestees, 63 percent. By race, whites accounted for 69 percent of all persons arrested for burglary, blacks for 29 percent, and other races for the remainder.

LARCENY-THEFT

DEFINITION

Larceny-theft is the unlawful taking, carrying, leading, or riding away of property from the possession or constructive possession of another. It includes crimes such as shoplifting, pocket-picking, purse-snatching, thefts from motor vehicles, thefts of motor vehicle parts and accessories, bicycle thefts, etc., in which no use of force, violence, or fraud occurs.

Year	TREND Number of offenses	Rate per 100,000 inhabitants
1998	7,376,311	2,729.0
1999	6,957,412	2,551.4
Percent change	−5.7	−6.5

Volume

Comprising 60 percent of the Crime Index total and 68 percent of the property crime total, larceny-theft was estimated at nearly 7 million offenses in 1999. Monthly distribution figures for 1999 demonstrate that larceny-thefts occurred most often in August and least often in February.

The Nation's most populous region, the South, accounted for 41 percent of the larceny-theft total in 1999. The Midwest accounted for 23 percent of the Nation's larceny-thefts; the West represented 22 percent; and the Northeast recorded 14 percent.

A decrease was registered in the number of incidents of larceny-theft in each of the country's geographic regions. The Western States reported a 9-percent drop in this offense; the Midwestern States recorded a 7-percent decrease; the Northeastern States noted a 5-percent decline; and Southern States reported a 4-percent drop.

In 1999, larceny-thefts decreased 6 percent nationwide when compared to the 1998 figure. Cities as a whole, suburban counties, and rural counties all reported drops of 6 percent. Among city population groups, those with 25,000 to 99,999 inhabitants showed the greatest decline in larceny-theft, 7 percent.

An examination of the long-term national trends indicated a decline of 13 percent when comparing 1999 larceny-theft totals to 1995 figures and a decrease of 12 percent when comparing 1999 totals to those in 1990.

Rate

When compared to the previous year's data, the 1999 larceny-theft rate of 2,551 per 100,000 population represented a 7-percent drop. The rate fell 16 percent below 1995 figures and 20 percent lower than 1990 rates. Rates for the Nation's community types revealed 3,151 offenses of larceny-theft per

Larceny-theft by Month
Percent distribution, 1995–1999

Months	1995	1996	1997	1998	1999
January	7.9	7.8	8.0	8.4	7.8
February	7.1	7.5	7.2	7.5	7.2
March	8.1	7.9	8.0	8.2	8.1
April	7.8	8.0	8.0	8.1	8.0
May	8.5	8.6	8.4	8.4	8.4
June	8.6	8.6	8.6	8.6	8.7
July	9.1	9.3	9.2	9.0	9.1
August	9.4	9.2	9.1	9.0	9.2
September	8.5	8.4	8.5	8.4	8.5
October	8.8	8.8	8.8	8.5	8.7
November	8.1	7.8	7.9	7.8	8.1
December	8.1	8.1	8.3	8.2	8.3

100,000 inhabitants in cities outside metropolitan areas, 2,727 in metropolitan areas, and 1,005 in rural counties.

All four geographic regions reported declines in the 1999 larceny-theft rate per 100,000 inhabitants. The West showed a 10-percent drop, the Midwest a 7-percent decline, and both the Northeast and the South reported 5-percent decreases. With respect to larceny-theft rates for 1999, the South reported a rate of 2,935 larceny-thefts per 100,000 population. The West registered a rate of 2,533. The Midwest experienced a rate of 2,517, and the Northeast recorded 1,901 per 100,000 inhabitants.

Nature

The average value of property stolen in 1999 as a result of larceny-theft was $678, up from the 1998 value of $632. The aggregate loss to victims, when applying the average value to the estimated number of larceny-thefts nationally, was over $4.7 billion for the year. This estimated dollar loss is considered conservative since many offenses in the larceny category never come to law enforcement attention, particularly if the value of the stolen goods is small. Losses over $200 accounted for 39 percent of reported larceny-thefts, and losses under $50 comprised 38 percent. The remaining 23 percent involved losses ranging from $50 to $200.

By type of larceny-theft, losses of goods and property reported stolen as a result of thefts from buildings averaged $1,015; from motor vehicles, $693; and pocket-picking and thefts of motor vehicle accessories, both averaged losses of $451. Purse-snatching resulted in an average loss of $392, thefts from coin-operated machines, $376 and thefts of bicycles, $338. Losses from shoplifting averaged $165.

Thefts of motor vehicle parts, accessories, and contents accounted for the largest segment of larceny-theft, 36 percent. Thefts from buildings and shoplifting both constituted 14 percent, and thefts of bicycles, 5 percent. The remainder of larceny-thefts were attributed to pocket-picking, purse-snatching, thefts from coin-operated machines, and all other types of larceny-thefts. The table below, left column provides the distribution of larceny-theft by type and geographic region.

Law Enforcement Response

In 1999, the national clearance rate for larceny-theft offenses was 19 percent. By community type, cities with populations from 10,000 to 24,999 accounted for the highest clearance rate, 23 percent. Law enforcement in the Nation's cities collectively cleared 20 percent of larceny-thefts, and those in rural counties recorded an 18-percent clearance rate. Law enforcement agencies in suburban counties reported a 17-percent clearance rate.

A review of the four regions reveals law enforcement agencies in the Northeast cleared 21 percent of reported larceny-theft offenses in 1999. Those in the other three regions, the Midwest, the South, and the West, each cleared 19 percent.

Larceny-theft clearances involving juveniles (persons under age 18), both nationally and in the Nation's cities collectively, were recorded at 23 percent. Juveniles comprised 21 percent of larceny-theft clearances in suburban counties, and 18 percent in rural counties. Cities with populations of 25,000 to 99,999 inhabitants showed the greatest juvenile involvement in larceny-theft with 26 percent.

During 1999, the number of persons arrested for larceny-theft fell 9 percent in comparison to the previous year's data. Arrests of males and females declined 10 percent and 8 percent, respectively. Arrests of juveniles dropped 10 percent during this same period, and arrests of adults decreased 9 percent.

The 5-year trend, 1995 to 1999, revealed that larceny-theft arrests declined 19 percent. The number of adult arrests decreased 18 percent during this timespan, and arrests of persons under the age of 18 fell 23 percent. Arrests of males were 22 percent lower when comparing 1999 totals to 1995 levels, and arrests of females were down 14 percent.

Larceny Analysis by Region
Percent distribution, 1999

Type	United States Total	North-eastern States	Mid-western States	Southern States	Western States
Total[1]	100.0	100.0	100.0	100.0	100.0
Pocket-picking	.6	1.9	.3	.4	.5
Purse-snatching	.6	1.1	.5	.4	.5
Shoplifting	14.4	14.4	13.0	13.3	16.6
From motor vehicles (except accessories)	25.7	23.9	23.9	23.9	29.7
Motor vehicle accessories	10.4	8.1	12.1	9.8	11.3
Bicycles	4.7	5.6	5.2	3.8	5.1
From buildings	13.6	18.2	15.3	11.5	13.2
From coin-operated machines	.7	.5	.5	.8	.7
All others	29.3	26.3	29.2	36.1	22.3

[1]Because of rounding, percentages may not add to total.

Larceny-theft accounted for 52 percent of arrests for all Crime Index offenses reported to law enforcement in 1999. Seventy-two percent of all arrests for property crimes were attributed to larceny-theft. Of those individuals arrested for larceny-theft, 46 percent were persons under 21 years of age, and 31 percent of the arrestees were under 18. Females were arrested for this offense more often than for any other and comprised 36 percent of larceny-theft arrestees.

Of the total number of persons arrested for larceny-theft offenses, 66 percent were white, 31 percent were black, and the remaining 3 percent were all other races.

MOTOR VEHICLE THEFT

DEFINITION
Defined as the theft or attempted theft of a motor vehicle, this offense category includes the stealing of automobiles, trucks, buses, motorcycles, motorscooters, snowmobiles, etc.

Year	TREND Number of offenses	Rate per 100,000 inhabitants
1998	1,242,781	459.8
1999	1,147,305	420.7
Percent change	-7.7	-8.5

Volume

The estimated 1.1 million thefts of motor vehicles that occurred in the United States during 1999 represented the lowest total since 1985. By region, the distribution of thefts showed the most populous region, the South, with 37 percent of the volume, the West with 27 percent, the Midwest with 21 percent, and the Northeast with 15 percent.

The 1999 figures show that the greatest number of motor vehicle thefts was recorded during the month of August, and the fewest thefts occurred in February.

A comparison of 1999 figures to the previous year's figures shows that motor vehicle thefts declined 8 percent nationally and 7 percent in cities collectively. Among city population groupings, those with populations of 250,000 to 499,999 and cities with populations of 25,000 to 49,999 experienced the greatest decline in motor vehicle theft, 9 percent. Decreases of 12 percent in suburban counties and 7 percent in rural counties were recorded during the same 2-year period.

Declines in the numbers of motor vehicle thefts from 1998 to 1999 were reported for all four regions. The greatest decline, a 12-percent drop, was reported in the Western States. The Northeastern States reported an 8-percent decrease; the Southern States, a 6-percent decline; and the Midwestern States, a 5-percent drop.

The volume of motor vehicle thefts in 1999 declined 22 percent from the 1995 volume and fell 30 percent from the 1990 figure.

Rate

The national rate of 421 motor vehicle thefts per 100,000 inhabitants recorded for the year was 8 percent lower than in

Motor Vehicle Theft by Month
Percent distribution, 1995–1999

Months	1995	1996	1997	1998	1999
January	8.6	8.8	9.0	9.1	8.5
February	7.5	8.0	7.6	7.9	7.3
March	8.2	8.2	8.2	8.5	8.0
April	7.8	7.9	7.9	7.9	7.7
May	8.2	8.1	8.2	8.3	8.0
June	8.1	8.0	8.1	8.1	8.2
July	8.6	8.8	8.7	8.7	8.8
August	9.0	8.6	8.7	8.8	9.1
September	8.4	8.2	8.3	8.3	8.5
October	8.9	8.6	8.6	8.4	8.7
November	8.5	8.3	8.2	7.9	8.5
December	8.3	8.6	8.3	8.1	8.7

1998. This figure is 25 percent below the 1995 rate, and 36 percent lower than the 1990 rate.

For every 100,000 inhabitants living in metropolitan areas, 486 motor vehicle thefts were reported in 1999. For the same period, motor vehicle theft rates of 224 per 100,000 population in cities outside metropolitan areas and 123 motor vehicle thefts per 100,000 inhabitants in rural counties were recorded. The highest rate of motor vehicle theft during the year—1,012 for every 100,000 inhabitants—was experienced in cities with populations 500,000 to 999,999. Cities with fewer than 10,000 inhabitants recorded a rate of 223 per 100,000.

Motor Vehicle Theft
Percent distribution by region, 1999

Region	Total[1]	Autos	Trucks and buses	Other vehicles
Total	100.0	74.6	18.7	6.6
Northeastern States	100.0	87.0	8.0	5.1
Midwestern States	100.0	79.4	13.5	7.2
Southern States	100.0	71.9	20.5	7.6
Western States	100.0	70.6	23.6	5.8

[1]Because of rounding, percentages may not add to total.

Regionally, the highest motor vehicle theft rate was recorded in the Western States at 506 per 100,000 people. The Southern States reported a rate of 439; the Midwestern States, a rate of 375; and the Northeastern States, a rate of 343 per 100,000 inhabitants. Compared to 1998 figures, all regions registered declines in 1999. The greatest drop, 13 percent, was recorded in the West. The Northeast reported a decrease of 8 percent, the South a decline of 7 percent, and the Midwest a drop of 6 percent.

Nature
Nationally, the value of motor vehicles stolen during 1999 was estimated at over $7 billion. The average value per vehicle was $6,104 at the time of theft. The recovery percentage for the value of vehicles stolen was higher than for any other property type. Relating the value of vehicles stolen to the value of those recovered resulted in a 67-percent recovery rate for 1999.

Seventy-five percent of all motor vehicles reported stolen during the year were automobiles, 19 percent were trucks or buses, and the remainder were other types of vehicles.

Law Enforcement Response
Law enforcement agencies across the Nation reported a 15-percent motor vehicle theft clearance rate in 1999. Motor vehicle theft clearance rates in the Nation's cities ranged from a 31-percent clearance rate in cities with less than 10,000 inhabitants to 9 percent in cities with populations of 1 million and over. Law enforcement agencies in rural counties reported a 30-percent clearance rate, and those in suburban counties reported an 18-percent clearance rate.

Regional clearance percentages for motor vehicle theft were 17 percent each for the Southern and Midwestern States, and 13 percent and 12 percent in the Northeastern and the Western States, respectively.

Persons in the under-18 age group were involved in 19 percent of the motor vehicle thefts cleared nationally. This group also comprised 20 percent of the motor vehicle thefts cleared in rural counties, 19 percent of those cleared in cities, and 18 percent of those cleared in suburban counties.

Of the estimated 142,200 arrests for motor vehicle theft in 1999, males accounted for 84 percent of those arrested. By race, 55 percent of the arrestees were white, 42 percent were black, and the remainder were of other races.

By age, the largest percentage of persons arrested for motor vehicle theft—67 percent—was persons under the age of 25. Though arrestees under the age of 18 accounted for 35 percent of the total in 1999, arrests of persons under age 18 were down 5 percent from 1998 levels. Arrests of juvenile females and males decreased 10 percent and 4 percent, respectively.

Sixty-five percent of all motor vehicle theft arrestees were adults. However, the number of adults arrested in 1999 declined 6 percent from the 1998 figure.

Total motor vehicle theft arrests in 1999 were down 6 percent from the previous year's total. Long-term trends indicate the 1999 arrest total was 24 percent below the 1995 level and 38 percent lower than the 1990 figure.

Glossary

Abet: To encourage another to commit a crime.

Accessory: One who harbors, assists, or protects another person, although he or she knows that person has committed or will commit a crime.

Accomplice: One who knowingly and voluntarily aids another in committing a criminal offense.

Acquit: To free a person legally from an accusation of criminal guilt.

Adjudicatory hearing: The fact-finding process wherein the court determines whether or not there is sufficient evidence to sustain the allegations in a petition.

Admissible: Capable of being admitted; in a trial, such evidence as the judge allows to be introduced into the proceeding.

Affirmance: A pronouncement by a higher court that the case in question was rightly decided by the lower court from which the case was appealed.

Affirmation: Positive declaration or assertion that the witness will tell the truth; not made under oath.

Alias: Any name by which one is known other than his or her true name.

Alibi: A type of defense in a criminal prosecution that proves the accused could not have committed the crime with which he or she is charged, since evidence offered shows the accused was in another place at the time the crime was committed.

Allegation: An assertion of what a party to an action expects to prove.

American Bar Association (ABA): A professional association, comprising attorneys who have been admitted to the bar in any of the 50 states, and a registered lobby.

American Civil Liberties Union (ACLU): Founded in 1920 with the purpose of defending the individual's rights as guaranteed by the U.S. Constitution.

Amnesty: A class or group pardon.

Annulment: The act, by competent authority, of canceling, making void, or depriving of all force.

Appeal: A case carried to a higher court to ask that the decision of the lower court, in which the case originated, be altered or overruled completely.

Appellate court: A court that has jurisdiction to hear cases on appeal; not a trial court.

Arbitrator: The person chosen by parties in a controversy to settle their differences; private judges.

Arraignment: The appearance before the court of a person charged with a crime. He or she is advised of the charges, bail is set, and a plea of "guilty" or "not guilty" is entered.

Arrest: The legal detainment of a person to answer for criminal charges or civil demands.

Autopsy: A postmortem examination of a human body to determine the cause of death.

Bail: Property (usually money) deposited with a court in exchange for the release of a person in custody to ensure later appearance.

Bail bond: An obligation signed by the accused and his or her sureties that ensures his or her presence in court.

Bailiff: An officer of the court who is responsible for keeping order in the court and protecting the security of jury deliberations and court property.

Bench warrant: An order by the court for the apprehension and arrest of a defendant or other person who has failed to appear when so ordered.

Bill of Rights: The first 10 amendments to the U.S. Constitution that state certain fundamental rights and privileges that are guaranteed to the people against infringement by the government.

Biocriminology: A relatively new branch of criminology that attempts to explain criminal behavior by referring to biological factors which predispose some individuals to commit criminal acts. *See also* Criminal biology.

Blue laws: Laws in some jurisdictions prohibiting sales of merchandise, athletic contests, and the sale of alcoholic beverages on Sundays.

Booking: A law-enforcement or correctional process officially recording an entry-into-detention after arrest and identifying the person, place, time, reason for the arrest, and the arresting authority.

Breathalizer: A commercial device to test the breath of a suspected drinker and to determine that person's blood-alcohol content.

Brief: A summary of the law relating to a case, prepared by the attorneys for both parties and given to the judge.

Bug: To plant a sound sensor or to tap a communication line for the purpose of surreptitious listening or audio monitoring.

Burden of proof: Duty of establishing the existence of fact in a trial.

Calendar: A list of cases to be heard in a trial court, on a specific day, and containing the title of the case, the lawyers involved, and the index number.

Capital crime: Any crime that may be punishable by death or imprisonment for life.

Career criminal: A person having a past record of multiple arrests or convictions for crimes of varying degrees of seriousness. Such criminals are often described as chronic, habitual, repeat, serious, high-rate, or professional offenders.

Case: At the level of police or prosecutorial investigation, a set of circumstances under investigation involving one or more persons.

Case law: Judicial precedent generated as a by-product of the decisions that courts have made to resolve unique disputes. Case law concerns concrete facts, as distinguished from statutes and constitutions, which are written in the abstract.

Change of venue: The removal of a trial from one jurisdiction to another in order to avoid local prejudice.

Charge: In criminal law, the accusation made against a person. It also refers to the judge's instruction to the jury on legal points.

Circumstantial evidence: Indirect evidence; evidence from which a fact can be reasonably inferred, although not directly proven.

Clemency: The doctrine under which executive or legislative action reduces the severity of or waives legal punishment of one or more individuals, or an individual exempted from prosecution for certain actions.

Code: A compilation, compendium, or revision of laws, arranged into chapters, having a table of contents and index, and promulgated by legislative authority. *See also* Penal code.

Coercion: The use of force to compel performance of an action; the application of sanctions or the use of force by government to compel observance of law or public policy.

Common law: Judge-made law to assist courts through decision making with traditions, customs, and usage of previous court decisions.

Commutation: A reduction of a sentence originally prescribed by a court.

Complainant: The victim of a crime who brings the facts to the attention of the authorities.

Complaint: Any accusation that a person committed a crime that has originated or been received by a law enforcement agency or court.

Confession: A statement by a person who admits violation of the law.

Confiscation: Government seizure of private property without compensation to the owner.

Conspiracy: An agreement between two or more persons to plan for the purpose of committing a crime or any unlawful act or a lawful act by unlawful or criminal means.

Contempt of court: Intentionally obstructing a court in the administration of justice, acting in a way calculated to lessen its authority or dignity, or failing to obey its lawful order.

Continuance: Postponement or adjournment of a trial granted by the judge, either to a later date or indefinitely.

Contraband: Goods, the possession of which is illegal.

Conviction: A finding by the jury (or by the trial judge in cases tried without a jury) that the accused is guilty of a crime.

Corporal punishment: Physical punishment.

***Corpus delicti* (Lat.):** The objective proof that a crime has been committed as distinguished from an accidental death, injury, or loss.

Corrections: Area of criminal justice dealing with convicted offenders in jails, prisons, on probation, or parole.

Corroborating evidence: Supplementary evidence that tends to strengthen or confirm other evidence given previously.

Crime: An act injurious to the public, which is prohibited and punishable by law.

Crime Index: A set of numbers indicating the volume, fluctuation, and distribution of crimes reported to local law enforcement agencies for the United States as a whole.

Crime of passion: An unpremeditated murder or assault committed under circumstances of great anger, jealousy, or other emotional stress.

Criminal biology: The scientific study of the relation of hereditary physical traits to criminal character, that is, to innate tendencies to commit crime in general or crimes of any particular type. *See also* Biocriminology.

Criminal insanity: Lack of mental capacity to do or refrain from doing a criminal act; inability to distinguish right from wrong.

Criminal intent: The intent to commit an act, the results of which are a crime or violation of the law.

Criminalistics: Crime laboratory procedures.

Criminology: The scientific study of crime, criminals, corrections, and the operation of the system of criminal justice.

Cross examination: The questioning of a witness by the party who did not produce the witness.

Culpable: At fault or responsible, but not necessarily criminal.

Defamation: Intentional causing, or attempting to cause, damage to the reputation of another by communicating false or distorted information about his or her actions, motives, or character.

Defendant: The person who is being prosecuted.

Deliberation: The action of a jury to determine the guilt or innocence, or the sentence, of a defendant.

Demurrer: Plea for dismissal of a suit on the grounds that, even if true, the statements of the opposition are insufficient to sustain the claim.

Deposition: Sworn testimony obtained outside, rather than in, court.

Deterrence: A theory that swift and sure punishment will discourage others from similar illegal acts.

Dilatory: Law term that describes activity for the purpose of causing a delay or to gain time or postpone a decision.

Direct evidence: Testimony or other proof that expressly or straightforwardly proves the existence of fact.

Direct examination: The first questioning of witnesses by the party who calls them.

Directed verdict: An order or verdict pronounced by a judge during the trial of a criminal case in which the evidence presented by the prosecution clearly fails to show the guilt of the accused.

District attorney: A locally elected state official who represents the state in bringing indictments and prosecuting criminal cases.

Docket: The formal record of court proceedings.

Double jeopardy: To be prosecuted twice for the same offense.

Due process model: A philosophy of criminal justice based on the assumption that an individual is presumed innocent until proven guilty.

Due process of law: A clause in the Fifth and Fourteenth Amendments ensuring that laws are reasonable and that they are applied in a fair and equal manner.

Embracery: An attempt to influence a jury, or a member thereof, in their verdict by any improper means.

Entrapment: Inducing an individual to commit a crime he or she did not contemplate, for the sole purpose of instituting a criminal prosecution against the offender.

Evidence: All the means used to prove or disprove the fact at issue. *See also* Corpus delicti.

Ex post facto (Lat.): After the fact. An *ex post facto* law is a criminal law that makes an act unlawful although it was committed prior to the passage of that law. *See also* Grandfather clause.

Exception: A formal objection to the action of the court during a trial. The indication is that the excepting party will seek to reverse the court's actions at some future proceeding.

Exclusionary rule: Legal prohibitions against government prosecution using evidence illegally obtained.

Expert evidence: Testimony by one qualified to speak authoritatively on technical matters because of her or his special training or skill.

Extradition: The surrender by one state to another of an individual accused of a crime.

False arrest: Any unlawful physical restraint of another's freedom of movement; unlawful arrest.

Felony: A criminal offense punishable by death or imprisonment in a penitentiary.

Forensic: Relating to the court. Forensic medicine would refer to legal medicine that applies anatomy, pathology, toxicology, chemistry, and other fields of science in expert testimony in court cases or hearings.

Grand jury: A group of 12 to 23 citizens of a county who examine evidence against the person suspected of a crime and hand down an indictment if there is sufficient evidence. *See also* Petit jury.

Grandfather clause: A clause attempting to preserve the rights of firms in operation before enactment of a law by exempting these firms from certain provisions of that law. *See also Ex post facto.*

***Habeas corpus* (Lat.):** A legal device to challenge the detention of a person taken into custody. An individual in custody may demand an evidentiary hearing before a judge to examine the legality of the detention.

Hearsay: Evidence that a witness has learned through others.

Homicide: The killing of a human being; may be murder, negligent or nonnegligent manslaughter, or excusable or justifiable homicide.

Hung jury: A jury which, after long deliberation, is so irreconcilably divided in opinion that it is unable to reach a unanimous verdict.

Impanel: The process of selecting the jury that is to try a case.

Imprisonment: A sentence imposed upon the conviction of a crime; the deprivation of liberty in a penal institution; incarceration.

***In camera* (Lat.):** A case heard when the doors of the court are closed and only persons concerned in the case are admitted.

Indemnification: Compensation for loss or damage sustained because of improper or illegal action by a public authority.

Indictment: The document prepared by a prosecutor and approved by the grand jury that charges a certain person with a specific crime or crimes for which that person is later to be tried in court.

Injunction: An order by a court prohibiting a defendant from committing an act, or commanding an act be done.

Inquest: A legal inquiry to establish some question of fact; specifically, an inquiry by a coroner and jury into a person's death where accident, foul play, or violence is suspected as the cause.

Instanter: A subpoena issued for the appearance of a hostile witness or person who has failed to appear in answer to a previous subpoena and authorizing a law enforcement officer to bring that person to the court.

Interpol (International Criminal Police Commission): A clearing house for international exchanges of information, consisting of a consortium of 126 countries.

Jeopardy: The danger of conviction and punishment that a defendant faces in a criminal trial.

Judge: An officer who presides over and administers the law in a court of justice.

Judicial notice: The rule that a court will accept certain things as common knowledge without proof.

Judicial process: The procedures taken by a court in deciding cases or resolving legal controversies.

Jurisdiction: The territory, subject matter, or persons over which lawful authority may be exercised by a court or other justice agency, as determined by statute or constitution.

Jury: A certain number of persons who are sworn to examine the evidence and determine the truth on the basis of that evidence. *See also* Hung jury.

Justice of the peace: A subordinate magistrate, usually without formal legal training, empowered to try petty civil and criminal cases and, in some states, to conduct preliminary hearings for persons accused of a crime, and to fix bail for appearance in court.

Juvenile delinquent: A boy or girl who has not reached the age of criminal liability (varies from state to state) and who commits an act that would be a misdemeanor or felony if he or she were an adult. Delinquents are tried in Juvenile Court and confined to separate facilities.

Law Enforcement Agency: A federal, state, or local criminal justice agency or identifiable subunit whose principal functions are the prevention, detection, and investigation of crime and the apprehension of alleged offenders.

Libel and slander: Printed and spoken defamation of character, respectively, of a person or an institution. In a slander action, it is usually necessary to prove specific damages caused by spoken words, but in a case of libel, the damage is assumed to have occurred by publication.

Lie detector: An instrument that measures certain physiological reactions of the human body from which a trained operator may determine whether the subject is telling the truth or lying; polygraph; psychological stress evaluator.

Litigation: A judicial controversy; a contest in a court of justice for the purpose of enforcing a right; any controversy that must be decided upon evidence.

Mala fides (Lat.): Bad faith, as opposed to *bona fides,* or good faith.

Mala in se (Lat.): Evil in itself. Acts that are made crimes because they are, by their nature, evil and morally wrong.

Mala prohibita (Lat.): Evil because they are prohibited. Acts that are not wrong in themselves but which, to protect the general welfare, are made crimes by statute.

Malfeasance: The act of a public officer in committing a crime relating to his official duties or powers, such as accepting or demanding a bribe.

Malice: An evil intent to vex, annoy, or injure another; intentional evil.

Mandatory sentences: A statutory requirement that a certain penalty shall be set and carried out in all cases upon conviction for a specified offense or series of offenses.

Martial law: Refers to control of civilian populations by a military commander.

Mediation: Nonbinding third-party intervention in the collective bargaining process.

Mens rea (Lat.): Criminal intent.

Miranda rights: Set of rights that a person accused or suspected of having committed a specific offense has during interrogation and of which he or she must be informed prior to questioning, as stated by the Supreme Court in deciding *Miranda v. Arizona* in 1966 and related cases.

Misdemeanor: Any crime not a felony. Usually, a crime punishable by a fine or imprisonment in the county or other local jail.

Misprison: Failing to reveal a crime.

Mistrial: A trial discontinued before reaching a verdict because of some procedural defect or impediment.

Modus operandi: A characteristic pattern of behavior repeated in a series of offenses that coincides with the pattern evidenced by a particular person or group of persons.

Motion: An oral or written request made to a court at any time before, during, or after court proceedings, asking the court to make a specified finding, decision, or order.

Motive: The reason for committing a crime.

Municipal court: A minor court authorized by municipal charter or state law to enforce local ordinances and exercise the criminal and civil jurisdiction of the peace.

Narc: A widely used slang term for any local or federal law enforcement officer whose duties are focused on preventing or controlling traffic in and the use of illegal drugs.

Negligent: Culpably careless; acting without the due care required by the circumstances.

Neolombrosians: Criminologists who emphasize psychopathological states as causes of crime.

No bill: A phrase used by a grand jury when it fails to indict.

Nolle prosequi (Lat.): A prosecutor's decision not to initiate or continue prosecution.

Nolo contendre (Lat., lit.): A pleading, usually used by a defendant in a criminal case, that literally means "I will not contest."

Notary public: A public officer authorized to authenticate and certify documents such as deeds, contracts, and affidavits with his or her signature and seal.

Null: Of no legal or binding force.

Obiter dictum (Lat.): A belief or opinion included by a judge in his or her decision in a case.

Objection: The act of taking exception to some statement or procedure in a trial. Used to call the court's attention to some improper evidence or procedure.

Opinion evidence: A witness's belief or opinion about a fact in dispute, as distinguished from personal knowledge of the fact.

Ordinance: A law enacted by the city or municipal government.

Organized crime: An organized, continuing criminal conspiracy that engages in crime as a business (e.g., loan sharking, illegal gambling, prostitution, extortion, etc.).

Original jurisdiction: The authority of a court to hear and determine a lawsuit when it is initiated.

Overt act: An open or physical act done to further a plan, conspiracy, or intent, as opposed to a thought or mere intention.

Paralegals: Employees, also known as legal assistants, of law firms, who assist attorneys in the delivery of legal services.

Pardon: There are two kinds of pardons of offenses: (1) the absolute pardon, which fully restores to the individual all rights and privileges of a citizen, setting aside a conviction and penalty, and (2) the conditional pardon, which requires a condition to be met before the pardon is officially granted.

Parole: A conditional, supervised release from prison prior to expiration of sentence.

Penal code: Criminal codes, the purpose of which is to define what acts shall be punished as crimes.

Penology: The study of punishment and corrections.

Peremptory challenge: In the selection of jurors, challenges made by either side to certain jurors without assigning any reason, and which the court must allow.

Perjury: The legal offense of deliberately testifying falsely under oath about a material fact.

Perpetrator: The chief actor in the commission of a crime, that is, the person who directly commits the criminal act.

Petit jury: The ordinary jury composed of 12 persons who hear criminal cases and determines guilt or innocence of the accused. *See also* Grand jury.

Plaintiff: A person who initiates a court action.

Plea bargaining: A negotiation between the defense attorney and the prosecutor in which the defendant receives a reduced penalty in return for a plea of "guilty."

Police power: The authority to legislate for the protection of the health, morals, safety, and welfare of the people.

Postmortem: After death. Commonly applied to an examination of a dead body. *See also* Autopsy.

Precedent: Decision by a court that may serve as an example or authority for similar cases in the future.

Preliminary hearing: The proceeding in front of a lower court to determine if there is sufficient evidence for submitting a felony case to the grand jury.

Premeditation: A design to commit a crime or commit some other act before it is done.

Presumption of fact: An inference as to the truth or falsity of any proposition or fact, made in the absence of actual certainty of its truth or falsity or until such certainty can be attained.

Presumption of innocence: The defendant is presumed to be innocent and the burden is on the state to prove his or her guilt beyond a reasonable doubt.

Presumption of law: A rule of law that courts and judges must draw a particular inference from a particular fact or evidence, unless the inference can be disproved.

Probable cause: A set of facts and circumstances that would induce a reasonably intelligent and prudent person to believe that a particular person had committed a specific crime; reasonable grounds to make or believe an accusation.

Probation: A penalty placing a convicted person under the supervision of a probation officer for a stated time, instead of being confined.

Prosecutor: One who initiates a criminal prosecution against an accused; one who acts as a trial attorney for the government as the representative of the people.

Public defender: An attorney appointed by a court to represent individuals in criminal proceedings who do not have the resources to hire their own defense council.

Rap sheet: Popularized acronym for record of arrest and prosecution.

Reasonable doubt: That state of mind of jurors when they do not feel a moral certainty about the truth of the charge and when the evidence does not exclude every other reasonable hypothesis except that the defendant is guilty as charged.

Rebutting evidence: When the defense has produced new evidence that the prosecution has not dealt with, the court, at its discretion, may allow the prosecution to give evidence in reply to rebut or contradict it.

Recidivism: The repetition of criminal behavior.

Repeal: The abrogation of a law by the enacting body, either by express declaration or implication by the passage of a later act whose provisions contradict those of the earlier law.

Reprieve: The temporary postponement of the execution of a sentence.

Restitution: A court requirement that an alleged or convicted offender must pay money or provide services to the victim of the crime or provide services to the community.

Restraining order: An order, issued by a court of competent jurisdiction, forbidding a named person, or a class of persons, from doing specified acts.

Retribution: A concept that implies that payment of a debt to society and thus the expiation of one's offense. It was codified in the biblical injunction, "an eye for an eye, a tooth for a tooth."

Sanction: A legal penalty assessed for the violation of law. The term also includes social methods of obtaining compliance, such as peer pressure and public opinion.

Search warrant: A written order, issued by judicial authority in the name of the state, directing a law enforcement officer to search for personal property and, if found, to bring it before the court.

Selective enforcement: The deploying of police personnel in ways to cope most effectively with existing or anticipated problems.

Self-incrimination: In constitutional terms, the process of becoming involved in or charged with a crime by one's own testimony.

Sentence: The penalty imposed by a court on a person convicted of a crime, the court judgment specifying the penalty, and any disposition of a defendant resulting from a conviction, including the court decision to suspend execution of a sentence.

Small claims court: A special court that provides expeditious, informal, and inexpensive adjudication of small contractual claims. In most jurisdictions, attorneys are not permitted for cases, and claims are limited to a specific amount.

Stare decisis (Lat.): To abide by decided cases. The doctrine that once a court has laid down a principle of laws as applicable to certain facts, it will apply it to all future cases when the facts are substantially the same.

State's attorney: An officer, usually locally elected within a county, who represents the state in securing indictments and in prosecuting criminal cases.

State's evidence: Testimony by a participant in the commission of a crime that incriminates others involved, given under the promise of immunity.

Status offense: An act that is declared by statute to be an offense, but only when committed or engaged in by a juvenile, and that can be adjudicated only by a juvenile court.

Statute: A law enacted by, or with the authority of, a legislature.

Statute of limitations: A term applied to numerous statutes that set limits on the length of time after which rights cannot be enforced in a legal action or offenses cannot be punished.

Stay: A halting of a judicial proceeding by a court order.

Sting operation: The typical sting involves using various undercover methods to control crime.

Subpoena: A court order requiring a witness to attend and testify as a witness in a court proceeding.

Subpoena *duces tecum:* A court order requiring a witness to bring all books, documents, and papers that might affect the outcome of the proceedings.

Summons: A written order issued by a judicial officer requiring a person accused of a criminal offense to appear in a designated court at a specified time to answer the charge(s).

Superior court: A court of record or general trial court, superior to a justice of the peace or magistrate's court. In some states, an intermediate court between the general trial court and the highest appellate court.

Supreme court, state: Usually the highest court in the state judicial system.

Supreme Court, U.S.: Heads the judicial branch of the American government and is the nation's highest law court.

Suspect: An adult or juvenile considered by a criminal agency to be one who may have committed a specific criminal offense but who has not yet been arrested or charged.

Testimony: Evidence given by a competent witness, under oath, as distinguished from evidence from writings and other sources.

Tort: A breach of a duty to an individual that results in damage to him or her, for which one may be sued in civil court for damages. Crime, in contrast, may be called a breach of duty to the public. Some actions may constitute both torts and crimes.

Uniform Crime Reports (U.C.R.): Annual statistical tabulation of "crimes known to the police" and "crimes cleared by arrest," published by the Federal Bureau of Investigation.

United States Claims Court: Established in 1982, it serves as the court of original and exclusive jurisdiction over claims brought against the federal government, except for tort claims, which are heard by district courts.

United States district courts: Trial courts with original jurisdiction over diversity-of-citizenship cases and cases arising under U.S. criminal, bankruptcy, admiralty, patent, copyright, and postal laws.

Venue: The locality in which a suit may be tried.

Verdict: The decision of a court.

Vice squad: A special detail of police agents, charged with raiding and closing houses of prostitution and gambling resorts.

Victim and Witness Protection Act of 1984: The federal VWP Act and state laws protect crime victims and witnesses against physical and verbal intimidation where such intimidation is designed to discourage reporting of crimes and participation in criminal trials.

Victimology: The study of the psychological and dynamic interrelationships between victims and offenders, with a view toward crime prevention.

Vigilante: An individual or member of a group who undertakes to enforce the law and/or maintain morals without legal authority.

Voir dire (Fr.): The examination or questioning of prospective jurors in order to determine his or her qualifications to serve as a juror.

Warrant: A court order directing a police officer to arrest a named person or search a specific premise.

White-collar crime: Nonviolent crime for financial gain committed by means of deception by persons who use their special occupational skills and opportunities.

Witness: Anyone called to testify by either side in a trial. More broadly, a witness is anyone who has observed an event.

Work release (furlough programs): Change in prisoners' status to minimum custody with permission to work outside prison.

World Court: Formally known as the International Court of Justice, it deals with disputes involving international law.

SOURCES

The Dictionary of Criminal Justice, Fourth Edition, © 1994 by George E. Rush. Published by McGraw-Hill/Duchkin, Guilford, CT 06437.

Index

Test Your Knowledge Form

We encourage you to photocopy and use this page as a tool to assess how the articles in **Annual Editions** expand on the information in your textbook. By reflecting on the articles you will gain enhanced text information. You can also access this useful form on a product's book support Web site at ***http://www.dushkin.com/online/.***

NAME: DATE:

_____

TITLE AND NUMBER OF ARTICLE:

_____

BRIEFLY STATE THE MAIN IDEA OF THIS ARTICLE:

_____

LIST THREE IMPORTANT FACTS THAT THE AUTHOR USES TO SUPPORT THE MAIN IDEA:

_____

WHAT INFORMATION OR IDEAS DISCUSSED IN THIS ARTICLE ARE ALSO DISCUSSED IN YOUR TEXTBOOK OR OTHER READINGS THAT YOU HAVE DONE? LIST THE TEXTBOOK CHAPTERS AND PAGE NUMBERS:

_____

LIST ANY EXAMPLES OF BIAS OR FAULTY REASONING THAT YOU FOUND IN THE ARTICLE:

_____

LIST ANY NEW TERMS/CONCEPTS THAT WERE DISCUSSED IN THE ARTICLE, AND WRITE A SHORT DEFINITION:

_____

ANNUAL EDITIONS revisions depend on two major opinion sources: one is our Advisory Board, listed in the front of this volume, which works with us in scanning the thousands of articles published in the public press each year; the other is you—the person actually using the book. Please help us and the users of the next edition by completing the prepaid article rating form on this page and returning it to us. Thank you for your help!

ANNUAL EDITIONS: Criminal Justice 01/02

ARTICLE RATING FORM

Here is an opportunity for you to have direct input into the next revision of this volume. We would like you to rate each of the 32 articles listed below, using the following scale:

1. **Excellent: should definitely be retained**
2. **Above average: should probably be retained**
3. **Below average: should probably be deleted**
4. **Poor: should definitely be deleted**

Your ratings will play a vital part in the next revision.
So please mail this prepaid form to us just as soon as you complete it.
Thanks for your help!

We Want Your Advice

RATING

ARTICLE

1. Crunching Numbers: Crime and Incarceration at the End of the Millennium
2. The Crime Bust
3. Land of the Stupid: When You Need a Used Russian Submarine, Call Tarzan
4. The Well-Marked Roads to Homicidal Rage
5. A Healing Approach to Crime
6. Childhood Victimization: Early Adversity, Later Psychopathology
7. Man and His Son's Slayer Unite to Ask Why
8. Every Day I Have to Forgive Again
9. Sweden's Response to Domestic Violence
10. Ethics and Criminal Justice: Some Observations on Police Misconduct
11. On-the-Job Stress in Policing—Reducing It, Preventing It
12. Policing the Police
13. Why Harlem Drug Cops Don't Discuss Race
14. How to Improve the Jury System
15. Q: Should Juries Nullify Laws They Consider Unjust or Excessively Punitive?
16. A Get-Tough Policy That Failed

RATING

ARTICLE

17. Looking Askance at Eyewitness Testimony
18. DNA: Fingerprint of the Future?
19. The Creeping Expansion of DNA Data Banking
20. Why the Young Kill
21. Young Women in the Juvenile Justice System
22. Racial Disparities Seen as Pervasive in Juvenile Justice
23. Youth Court of True Peers Judges Firmly
24. Juvenile Justice: A Century of Experience
25. The Maximum Security Adolescent
26. Juvenile Probation on the Eve of the Next Millennium
27. Reading, Writing, and Rehabilitation: Rikers Helps Inmates Whose Schooling Was Once Ignored
28. The Death Penalty on Trial
29. Ex-Cons on the Street
30. The Past and Future of U.S. Prison Policy: Twenty-Five Years After the Stanford Prison Experiment
31. Parole and Prisoner Reentry in the United States, Part I
32. Parole and Prisoner Reentry in the United States, Part II

(Continued on next page)

BUSINESS REPLY MAIL
FIRST-CLASS MAIL PERMIT NO. 84 GUILFORD CT

POSTAGE WILL BE PAID BY ADDRESSEE

McGraw-Hill/Dushkin
530 Old Whitfield Street
Guilford, CT 06437-9989

ABOUT YOU

Name _____ Date _____

Are you a teacher? ☐ A student? ☐
Your school's name _____

Department _____

Address _____ City _____ State ____ Zip ____

School telephone # _____

YOUR COMMENTS ARE IMPORTANT TO US !

Please fill in the following information:
For which course did you use this book?
_____

Did you use a text with this *ANNUAL EDITION*? ☐ yes ☐ no
What was the title of the text?
_____

What are your general reactions to the *Annual Editions* concept?
_____

Have you read any particular articles recently that you think should be included in the next edition?
_____

Are there any articles you feel should be replaced in the next edition? Why?
_____

Are there any World Wide Web sites you feel should be included in the next edition? Please annotate.
_____

May we contact you for editorial input? ☐ yes ☐ no
May we quote your comments? ☐ yes ☐ no